AF763803

Instruments of Public Law

The COVID-19 pandemic has revealed the need to verify the existing principles of functioning of public authorities, in relation to various decision-making processes, both at the conceptual and at law implementation levels. The action of the legislator and public administration towards the society and the economy is conducted using peculiar instruments to control the public administration system. These instruments are likely to be of a public or private law nature. This book takes a comparative approach to examine the issues related to digital transformation in the times of a pandemic regarding the use of public law instruments in Poland and the wider European context. In particular, the research aims to identify what stage the development of digital solutions in the state's organisation and its authorities has reached, including the organisation of public administration; what the pandemic has changed. Exploring the concepts of digital transformation, pandemic and public law instruments, it provides an analysis of European and national public law instruments using digital solutions, security and cyber security during a pandemic, and concrete issues such as public administration, health protection and social security, economic activity and the system of public finances, and how education during the pandemic is performed. Establishing whether particular solutions are durable and to what extent they create a certain standard of response to a threat, it makes recommendations for determining which of the existing solutions are useful for the functioning of the state and its organs and facilitating the performance of their tasks.

Irena Lipowicz is Full Professor in Law at Cardinal Stefan Wyszyński University in Warsaw, Poland. Ombudsman in Poland in 2010–2015, Honorary Doctor of the Osnabrück University. Member of the Board of the Association of the European Public Law SIPE. Member of the United Nations University Council (UNU) 2016–2018 and Ombudsman in 2010–2015, Polish ambassador in Austria in 2000–2004.

Grażyna Szpor is Full Professor in Law at Cardinal Stefan Wyszyński University in Warsaw, Poland. Vice-president of the Sectoral Council for Telecommunications and Cybersecurity Competencies. Scientific editor of the 12-volume monograph "Openness and its limitations" (C.H. Beck Warsaw, 2013–2016) and 11 volumes of the "Internet" series (C.H. Beck, Warsaw 2011–2021).

Aleksandra Syryt is Assistant Professor in Law at Cardinal Stefan Wyszyński University in Warsaw, Poland. Member of Croatian-Polish Scientific Network and Central European Professors' Network. Plenipotentiary of the Rector of the Cardinal Stefan Wyszyński University in Warsaw for legislative and legal matters. Lecturer at the National School of Public Administration in Poland.

Routledge Research in EU Law

Available titles in this series include:

The EU and the Proliferation of Integration Principles under the Lisbon Treaty
Francesca. Ippolito, Maria Eugenia Bartoloni, Massimo Condinanzi

Migration Law and the Externalization of Border Controls
European State Responsibility
Anna Liguori

Member States Interests and European Union Law
Revisiting the Foundations of Member State Obligations
Marton Varju

EU Law Enforcement
The Evolution of Sanctioning Powers
Stefano Montaldo, Francesco Costamagna, and Alberto Miglio

Constitutional Law and the EU Balanced Budget Principle
Elena-Simina Tănăsescu and Eric Oliva

Delegation of Powers in the EU Legal System
Annalisa Volpato

The Tangled Complexity of the EU Constitutional Process
The Frustrating Knot of Europe
Giuseppe Martinico

Instruments of Public Law
Digital Transformation during the Pandemic
Irena Lipowicz, Grażyna Szpor and Aleksandra Syryt

https://www.routledge.com/Routledge-Research-in-EU-Law/book-series/ROUTEULAW

Instruments of Public Law

Digital Transformation during the Pandemic

Edited by Irena Lipowicz, Grażyna Szpor and Aleksandra Syryt

Routledge
Taylor & Francis Group
LONDON AND NEW YORK

First published 2023
by Routledge
4 Park Square, Milton Park, Abingdon, Oxon OX14 4RN

and by Routledge
605 Third Avenue, New York, NY 10158

Routledge is an imprint of the Taylor & Francis Group, an informa business

British Library Cataloguing-in-Publication Data
A catalogue record for this book is available from the British Library

ISBN: 978-1-032-20515-1 (hbk)
ISBN: 978-1-032-20516-8 (pbk)
ISBN: 978-1-003-26396-8 (ebk)

DOI: 10.4324/9781003263968

Typeset in Times New Roman
by Deanta Global Publishing Services, Chennai, India

Contents

Figures

Contributors

Mateusz Badowski is Research Assistant at the Department of Informatics Law at the Faculty of Law and Administration of the Cardinal Stefan Wyszyński University in Warsaw. He was a member of expert bodies and a participant in research projects of the European Commission and the Council of Europe. He is an employee of the Polish Data Protection Authority. He conducts research in personal data protection and legal regulation of cyberspace.

Elena Buoso, PhD, is Associate Professor of Administrative Law at the School of Law of the University of Padua. Her research interests focus on constitutional and administrative law as well as environmental, urban and digital law.

Gherardo Carullo, PhD, is Associate Professor of Administrative Law at the University of Milan (Università degli Studi di Milano) and member of the Steering Committee of CERIDAP (https://ceridap.eu). His research interests focus on the impact of digital technologies on public administrations and their activities.

Ziemowit Cieślik, PhD, is Assistant Professor at the Department of Administrative Law and Territorial Self-Government at the Faculty of Law and Administration of the Cardinal Stefan Wyszyński University in Warsaw, author of publications in the field of administrative law and European Union law, attorney-at-law, long-time employee of the Parliamentary Bureau of Research (BAS), member of Societas Iuris Publici Europaei (SIPE) and the Law & Informatics Academic Center (NCPI).

Kamil Czaplicki, PhD, is Assistant Professor at the Department of Informatics Law at the Faculty of Law and Administration of the Cardinal Stefan Wyszyński University in Warsaw. He is a Member of the Board of the Law & Informatics Scientific Center (NCPI). He conducts research in e-government, verification of identity and cybersecurity.

Piotr Drobek, PhD, is Research Assistant at the Department of Informatics Law at the Faculty of Law and Administration of the Cardinal Stefan Wyszyński University in Warsaw. He was a member of expert bodies and a participant in research projects of the European Commission and the Council of Europe.

He is an employee of the Polish Data Protection Authority. He conducts research in personal data protection and legal regulation of cyberspace.

Cristina Fraenkel-Haeberle is Coordinator of the research programme "European Administrative Space" at the German Research Institute for Public Administration Speyer, where she is also Professor for Public law at the German University of Administrative Sciences Speyer, Germany. Her main research interests are in European and national administrative law, university and environmental law as well as democracy studies.

Diana-Urania Galetta is Full Professor of Administrative Law and EU Administrative Law at the Law Faculty of the University of Milan (Università degli Studi di Milano), Director of the PhD Programme in Public, International and EU Law and of CERIDAP (https://ceridap.eu). Her Research interests focus on Comparative and EU Administrative law, recently with a special focus also on the impact of ICT on Public Administrations and their activities.

Agnieszka Gryszczyńska, PhD in Law and IT Engineer, is Associate Professor at the Department of Informatics Law at the Faculty of Law and Administration of the Cardinal Stefan Wyszyński University in Warsaw. She researches the legal aspects of computerisation, openness and interoperability of public registers, cybercrime and cybersecurity, personal data protection and legally protected confidentiality. She is a public prosecutor – a coordinator of cybercrime proceedings.

Beata Konieczna-Drzewiecka, PhD, is Assistant Professor at the Department of Informatics Law at the Faculty of Law and Administration of the Cardinal Stefan Wyszyński University in Warsaw. Deputy Head of the 16th edition of the Data Protection and Classified Information Postgraduate Programme. She conducts research in the field of personal data and cybersecurity.

Irena Lipowicz is Full Professor in Law at the Faculty of Law and Administration of the Cardinal Stefan Wyszyński University in Warsaw. Ombudsman in Poland in 2010–2015, Honorary Doctor of the Osnabrück University. Member of the Board of the Association of the European Public Law SIPE. Member of the United Nations University Council (UNU) 2016–2018 and Ombudsman in 2010–2015, Polish ambassador in Austria in 2000–2004. Main academic interests: theory of administrative law, local government, innovations in public administration.

Ewa Marzec is ISMS lead auditor acc. to ISO/IEC 27001:2017. She has professional experience as a university lecturer, EU-funded project manager and data protection officer. She researches the use of information technologies in the education of visually impaired people.

Radosław Mędrzycki, PhD, is Assistant Professor at the Department of Administrative Law and Territorial Self-Government at the Faculty of Law and Administration of the Cardinal Stefan Wyszyński University in Warsaw, author of publications in the field of administrative law particularly concerning local government law and the rights of excluded people.

Marek Michalski is Full Professor at the Faculty of Law and Administration of the Cardinal Stefan Wyszyński University in Warsaw. He is a specialist in economic and commercial law as well as securities and capital market law, as well as new technologies law. He was or is a member of many supervisory boards, including the Warsaw Stock Exchange, Alior Bank S.A. and Supervisory Board of Metro Warszawskie sp. z o.o.

Agnieszka Piskorz-Ryń, PhD *habilitatus*, is Professor at the Faculty of Law and Administration of the Cardinal Stefan Wyszyński University in Warsaw; employee of the Department of Administrative Law and Territorial Self-Government at the Faculty of Law and Administration of the UKSW. She conducts research in the field of information, including public information, and the re-use of public sector information.

Konrad Stefan Radomiński is Research Assistant at the Department of Informatics Law at the Faculty of Law and Administration of the Cardinal Stefan Wyszyński University in Warsaw. He is a co-author of the project "Cybersecurity in Administration" Educational game awarded by the Minister of Digitization and NASK. He researches the legal regulation of computer games and their use for education.

Sebastian Sikorski, PhD, is Assistant Professor at the Faculty of Law and Administration of the Cardinal Stefan Wyszyński University in Warsaw. Lawyer at the District Bar Council in Warsaw, specialising in medical law. He conducts research in the field of health protection law, administrative law, including the role of public administration in health care and the impact of technological changes and digital progress on the provision of health services.

Wawrzyniec Święcicki is research assistant at the Department of Informatics Law at the Faculty of Law and Administration of the Cardinal Stefan Wyszyński University in Warsaw. He conducts courses as part of the subject of information technologies and legal search systems, and information techniques in international relations. Expert in the field of press release infographics.

Krzysztof Świtała, PhD, is Assistant Professor at the Department of Informatics Law at the Faculty of Law and Administration of the Cardinal Stefan Wyszyński University in Warsaw. He was the head of the R&D project: "Patients' rights to confidentiality of information and protection of their personal data in the context of implementing modern e-Health solutions and electronic medical documentation." He deals with the information security and administrative and legal aspects of computerisation processes in public administration and health care.

Aleksandra Syryt, PhD *habilitatus*, is Assistant Professor at the Faculty of Law and Administration of the Cardinal Stefan Wyszyński University in Warsaw.

Her research focuses on the field of constitutional law, including the principles of the system and the protection of human rights, the systemic foundations of local government, as well as legislation, the knowledge-based economy and the impact of technological changes and digital progress on law.

Grażyna Szpor is Full Professor. She is a head of the Department of Informatics Law and Centre for Leaders in Digital Transformation at the Cardinal Stefan Wyszyński University in Warsaw. She is Vice President of the Sector Council for Competence: Telecommunications and Cyber Security. She was the head of the R&D project: "The Model of regulation of openness and its limitation in the democratic state ruled by law." Her research interests are public law regulation of information systems, e-government and cyber security.

Aneta Szymczak, PhD, is Assistant Professor at the Faculty of Law and Administration of the University of Łódź. Conducts research in the field of public finance law, including constitutional principles of establishing and levying public levies, the financial system of local government and the state budget. She has twice taken part in Academic Days on Open Government & Digital Issues, organised by University Paris 1 Panthéon-Sorbonne.

Mariusz Szyrski, PhD *habilitatus*, is Professor at the Faculty of Law and Administration of the Cardinal Stefan Wyszyński University in Warsaw. He conducts research in the field of administrative law, including local government law and energy law. He also deals with the legal environment for startups. He has experience in managing and participating in research programmes, including interdisciplinary projects.

Ivan Uroda is Assistant Professor at the Department of Information Science and Business Informatics at the University of Rijeka, Faculty of Economics and Business. He has participated in scientific research projects, among other things: "FUTURE 4.0 Manufacturing education and training governance model for Industry 4.0 in the Adriatic-Ionian area" and "The Human Factor in Information and Communication Technologies." His research is on business informatics.

Beata Zbarachewicz, PhD, is Lecturer at the Department of Informatics Law at the Faculty of Law and Administration of the Cardinal Stefan Wyszyński University in Warsaw. She is a Member of the Board of the Law & Informatics Scientific Center (NCPI). She researches digitisation and electronic communication in higher education institutions.

Abbreviations

A.I.D. – The Act of 5 December 2008 on preventing and combating infections and infectious diseases in humans (Journal of Laws 2021, item 2069).

Access Act – Act of 6 September 2001 on access to public information 2001 (JoL 2020 item 2176).

CFREU – Charter of Fundamental Rights of the European Union [2012]OJ C 326/391.

CJEU – Court of Justice of the European Union.

Constitution – Constitution of the Republic of Poland [1997] Journal of Laws No 78 item 483 with amendments.

CT – Constitutional Tribunal.

COVID-19 Act – the Act of 2 March 2020 on special solutions related to the prevention, counteraction and combating of COVID-19, other infectious diseases and crises caused by them (Journal of Laws 2021, item 2095).

CRPD – Convention on the Rights of Persons with Disabilities New York, 13 December 2006 (open for signature 30 March 2007, entered into force 3 May 2008).

Digital Green Certificate – Regulation of the European Parliament and of The Council on a framework for the issuance, verification and acceptance of interoperable certificates on vaccination, testing and recovery to facilitate free movement during the COVID-19 pandemic (Digital Green Certificate).

EC – European Commission.

ECHR – European Convention of Human Rights.

ePUAP – Electronic Platform of Public Administration Services.

EU – Digital COVID-19 Certificate (COVID-19 Certificate).

EU – European Union.
FCC – Federal Constitutional Court.
GDPR – Regulation (EU) 2016/679 of the European Parliament and of the Council of 27 April 2016 on the protection of natural persons with regard to the processing of personal data and on the free movement of such data and repealing Directive 95/46/EC (General Data Protection Regulation) (OJ L 119, 4.5.2016, p. 1).
Gryszczyńska, Szpor, Cyberpandemic 2020 (eds.) – A. Gryszczyńska, G. Szpor (eds.), Internet. Cyberpandemia. Cyberpandemic. Warszawa 2020.
JoL – Journal of Laws.
MoH – Minister of Health.
SAO – Supreme Audit Office.
Shield 2 – The Act of 16 April 2020 on special support instruments in connection with the spread of the SARS-CoV-2 virus (Journal of Laws, item 695).
Skróty do publikacji – .
SAC – Supreme Administrative Court.
TFEU – Treaty on the Functioning of the European Union (JoL No 90, item 864).
The eIDAS – Regulation (EU) No 910/2014 of the European Parliament and of the Council of 23 July 2014 on electronic identification and trust services for electronic transactions in the internal market and repealing Directive 1999/93/EC.
WHO – World Health Organization.
WolKluw – Wolters Kluwer.

Digital Transformation during the Pandemic

Instruments of Public Law

Introduction

The time of the pandemic has revealed the need to verify the existing principles of functioning of public authorities, in relation to various decision-making processes, at the conceptual level and at law implementation. The action of the legislator and public administration towards the society and the economy is conducted using peculiar instruments, among others, to control the public administration system. These instruments are likely to be of a public or private law nature. The concept of "public law instruments" is crossed by the concept of "legal forms of the administration's activity," as they occur as public law and private law activities – e.g., an administrative contract or a civil law contract.

The pandemic has highlighted drawing attention to the fact that a phenomenon that will be of importance in the functioning of public law instruments is achievements linked to the digital transformation. In the absence of comprehensive coverage on the relationship between digital transformation and public law instruments during the pandemic, it is appropriate to begin a discourse in that regard and present the results of preliminary investigations an academic monograph. The sudden nature of the pandemic made it necessary to change many legal rules for the functioning of public administration. It also led to the transformation of many rights and obligations of citizens. A complex legal standard for digital transformation has already been developed and enacted in EU countries. Did the pandemic become a kind of catalyst for change since the physical distance of administration, so desirable in pandemic conditions, is part of digital transformation? What was the dynamism of change in the first phase of the pandemic regarding different legal systems – those that were more reserved and rigid, and those that were more flexible and open to new legal instruments?

The analyses are designed to address the research question, which serves as the basis for explaining the public law instruments in the context of digital transformation in the extraordinary circumstances of the pandemic. The aim of the authors is to indicate and explain (1) what is the current state of the law on digital transformation; (2) to what extent does the present regulatory framework for digital transformation allow the state to fulfil its tasks during the pandemic; (3) to what extent is the pandemic accelerating legislation and policy-making in the area

DOI: 10.4324/9781003263968-1

of digital transformation, and to what extent has it revised the already existing legal solutions in this regard; (4) to what extent is the response to the pandemic only crisis management, and to what extent is it a permanent alteration of the regulatory framework; (5) to what extent the actions of the state carried out during the pandemic fall within the limits of the rule of law; (6) why states of emergency were not declared in individual states; (7) to what extent the introduced legal instruments for digital transformation are a social innovation, and to what extent are they to serve the temporary improvement of the functioning of public authorities.

The above should identify how well-advanced are the legal instruments of the digital transformation in the functioning of the state and its authorities, including the organisation of public administration; and what the pandemic has changed. It clearly defines the method of the research conducted. It achieves results through the analysis of legal texts, case law and jurisprudence. The research focuses on the dogmatic analysis of legal developments that have reshaped the legal landscape of digital transformation in response to the pandemic. It will make a diagnosis if the solutions are durable, and if they carry a strategic advantage, and to what extent they create a certain standard of response to the threat. The considerations will be based on the example of Polish solutions. As an alternative, a public law solution related to the digital transformation in Germany, Italy and Croatia will be presented. The selection of these states for comparison is caused because in view of the substantial damage induced by the pandemic, they have taken specific measures with the use of digital instruments, which is an essential reference point for Polish solutions. The Polish example is also significant for another reason. Polish public law is static by nature. Its basic features are defined by a strictly closed catalogue of sources of a universally binding laws and a systemic aversion towards all consensual instruments. As a result, situation – created originally to strengthen the protection of the individual against interference by public authorities – makes it difficult for the public administration to respond flexibly to crisis situations and increases the risk of administrative action over the law. For this reason, Polish solutions may also interest external observers. They make up a stress test for traditional, unilateral administrative action in times of crisis; and form a reservoir of inspiring or, on the contrary, unsuccessful regulatory practices. The other countries included in the study take a very different approach in this respect – and interestingly complement the Polish perspective. The showed comparative legal perspective will allow for a provisional assessment of the extent to which Polish solutions resulting from digital transformation may play a useful role for the functioning of the EU and its members.

The monograph aims at bringing closer the issue related to digital transformation in the times of a pandemic regarding the use of public law instruments in Poland, but also recognising the comparative legal and European context. In particular, the research aims to identify what stage the development of digital solutions in the state's organisation and its authorities has reached, including the organisation of public administration; what the has pandemic changed. The starting point for considerations is to define the term "digital transformation," "pandemic" and "public law instruments." Based on these concepts, an analysis of EU and national public law instruments using digital solutions, security and cyber security during a pandemic, and concrete issues such as public administration, health protection and social security, economic activity and the system of public finances, and education during the pandemic is performed.

I

General Subjects

1 The Notion of Digital Transformation

Grażyna Szpor

1.1 Introduction

The benefits of digital transformation were made abundantly clear by the pandemic, during which the use of computers, mobile phones and other Internet-connected devices increased dramatically. These tools help reduce chaos and uncertainty in times of crisis. However, it can also be noted that without them, people would receive much less disturbing news about the types and scale of threats, among which it is not easy to distinguish data of informative value from disinformation.[1]

The purpose of this chapter is to establish the meaning of the term "digital transformation" and its usefulness as a legal term in public law research in the second decade of the 21st century.

The scope of research includes EU law and Polish law as an example of national law of the Member States. First, through a structural analysis of "juridisation", incorporation into law, the legitimacy of using the phrase "digital transformation" in research is verified, and through a contextual analysis of its occurrence in normative acts, a potential research area is delineated. Explanations of "digital transformation" and its technical aspects in publications from different scientific fields are then considered. The diversity of approaches in law and literature is an encouragement to formulate the definition. It should facilitate interdisciplinary arrangements in considering and regulating in public law the issues of digital transformation and the challenges of the pandemic, as well as formulating *de lege lata* comments and *de lege ferenda* postulates relating to the model of public law regulation of the digital transformation.

1.2 Structural analysis of juridisation

Verifying the validity of using the term "digital transformation" in legal research requires its structural analysis against alternative terms.

1 Gryszczyńska, Szpor, Cyberpandemic 2020 (eds.).

DOI: 10.4324/9781003263968-3

The phrase "digital transformation" appeared [until 28.11.2021] in 1,525 legal Acts and documents published in EUR-Lex.eng. It first appeared in the Communication from the Commission to the European Parliament, the Council, the European Economic and Social Committee and the Committee of the Regions. The Digital Agenda for Europe – Driving European growth digitally.[2] Since 2020, the frequency of the phrase in question has seen a sharp increase.[3] Hence, already the majority, over 900, are pandemic Acts, of which 10 are EU Parliament and Council regulations directly binding on Member States.

The phrase "digital transformation" is "transformacja cyfrowa" in Polish. In EUR-Lex.pl a search for "transformacja cyfrowa" yields 597 results, i.e., about 40% of searches for "digital transformation" in EUR-Lex.eng, which indicates a language barrier to full access to information on law, resulting from the lack of translations of some documents. A search for the phrase "transformacja cyfrowa" in LEX.pl shows that it occurred in 445 legal Acts published in official journals, of which as many as 425 are in the Official Journal of the EU, and only 8 are in the Polish Journal of Laws (*Dz. U*) and 5 in departmental journals.[4]

The occasional occurrence of the Polish-language equivalent of "digital transformation" in national legal Acts encourages us to determine whether a related, more common collective term such as digitalisation/digitisation ("cyfryzacja"), computerisation or informatisation could better designate the related research area of public law in times of pandemic.

A search for the word "cyfryzacja" [digitisation and/or digitalisation] in the LEX.pl system gave 10,424 results in total, including 3,523 legal Acts[5] and 5,196 judgments and official letters. The word "komputeryzacja" [computerisation] yielded 1,598 results, including 747 legal Acts[6] and 253 judgments and official letters. The most frequent was the word "informatyzacja" [informatisation and informatization]: a total of 20,579 results, of which 11,520 were legal Acts,[7] as well as 5,699 judgments and official letters.

2 COM/2012/0784 final.

3 2019 – 138, 2020 – 420, I–XI 2021 – 502.

4 The first Polish law containing the term "digital transformation" is the Act of 17.01.2019 on the Future Industry Platform Foundation [JoL 2019 item 229]. Pursuant to the Act of 23.01.2020 amending the Act on Departments of Government Administration and certain other acts [JoL 2020 item 284], in its current wording the Act of 4.09.1997 on Departments of Government Administration [JoL item 1220] states that the minister responsible for the economy includes the matters listed in para 2 in 14 points, including according to pt. 5 "digital transformation of the economy."

5 JoL (*Dz. U.*) and the Official Gazette of the Republic of Poland (*M.P.*) – 586, EU journals – 1,080, departmental journals – 954, provincial journals – 692, corporate acts – 53.

6 *Dz. U.* and *M.P.* – 81; EU journals – 123; departmental journals 68, provincial journals 458; corporate acts – 4.

7 *Dz. U.* and *M.P.* – 1,365, EU journals – 80, departmental journals – 1,321, provincial journals – 7,327, corporate acts – 233.

However, in EUR-Lex.eng, each of the three terms studied as alternatives appears in two forms: English American and English British.[8]

A structural analysis of the occurrence of the phrase "digital transformation" in the EUR-Lex and LEX.pl systems shows that it appears only occasionally in Polish domestic law, while for the last decade it has been introduced into EU law, and since 2020 intensively, which may support its use in the analyses of national legal orders covering national and EU Acts.

From the perspective of the Polish legal language, "informatyzacja" (informatisation) or "cyfryzacja" (digitisation, digitalisation) may be analysed as an umbrella term, but in the translation into English "informatyzacja" is both "informatisation" and "computerisation," and "cyfryzacja" may mean either "digitisation" or "digitalisation" or both these terms together.

Intensification of the occurrence of the term "digital transformation" in the Polish legal system in the years 2020–2021 is a derivative of its reception in the EU law, with a small share of national Acts. Yet, it is unambiguous in the comprehensive studies of multi-level regulation, which supports its treatment as a concept tool.

1.3 Contextual analysis of occurrence in normative Acts

The areas of juridisation of "digital transformation" are determined by the subject matter of directives and regulations of the European Parliament and of the Council in which this phrase appears. The contexts of its occurrence in individual acts also allow us to recognise the object and subject scope of the regulation. The potential response to the pandemic can be traced back to a compilation of five regulations (EU) of the European Parliament and of the Council issued before March 2020 and nine issued afterwards.

A contextual analysis reveals that digital transformation as a legal term in EU directives and regulations as occurred since 2016, but until 2020 it referred to the government, public administration and services. It referred to the accessibility of the websites and mobile applications of public sector bodies,[9] as well as to the open data and the re-use of public sector information.[10] It was mentioned as an area for investment, alongside investments in the areas of energy, environment

8 A search for the word "informatization" and "informatisation" yielded only 46 results (19 + 27), including 8 in 2021, and "computerization" and "computerisation" – 748 (517 + 731), of which in 2021– 28. The words "digitization" and "digitisation" – 2,137 (227 + 1,910) in 2021 – 298, "digitalization" – 4,130 (327 + 3,803) in 2021 – 888. "Digital transformation" –1,525 of which in 2020 – 420 and in 2021 – 502 [verified on 28.11.2021].

9 Directive (EU) 2016/2102 of the European Parliament and of the Council of 26.10.2016 on the accessibility of the websites and mobile applications of public sector bodies [OJ L 327, 2.12.2016, p. 1–15].

10 Regulation (EU) 2018/1724 of the European Parliament and of the Council of 2.10.2018 establishing a single digital gateway to provide access to information, to procedures and to assistance and problem-solving services and amending Regulation (EU) No 1024/2012 [OJ L 295, 21.11.2018, p. 1–38]; Directive (EU) 2019/1024 of the European Parliament and of the Council of 20.06.2019 on open data and the re-use of public sector information [OJ L 172, 26.6.2019, p. 56–83].

and climate action, social and human capital and related infrastructure, healthcare, research and innovation, cross-border and sustainable transport – but separately.[11] This term was hardly ever encountered.

This changed during the pandemic. In 2020, the Communication from the Commission Amendment to the Temporary Framework for State aid measures to support the economy in the current COVID-19 outbreak[12] stated that digital transformation together with green transformation will play a central and priority role in the successful recovery of the economy, and in the case of aid under this Communication, large enterprises will be required to report how the aid received supports their activities in line with EU objectives and national commitments related to green and digital transformation.

In 2021, "digital transformation" appeared in the 9 EU Regulations of the European Parliament and of the Council. The following phrases could be found in these regulations: "the digital transformation of health services and increase the interoperability of such services" and "the digital transformation of healthcare products and platforms for monitoring and collecting information on medicinal products,"[13] "the digital transformation of the Union economy,"[14] "the digital transformation of public procurement" and "the digital transformation of SMEs,"[15] "the digital transformation of the European economy, industry and society,"[16] "the green and digital transformation across industrial ecosystems" and "important driver for achieving the climate-neutrality objective,"[17] "the digital transformation of education and training, youth and sport,"[18] "the digital transformation of

11 Regulation (EU) 2017/2396 of the European Parliament and of the Council of 13.12.2017 amending Regulations (EU) No 1316/2013 and (EU) 2015/1017 as regards the extension of the duration of the European Fund for Strategic Investments as well as the introduction of technical enhancements for that Fund and the European Investment Advisory Hub [OJ L 345, 27.12.2017, p. 34–52].

12 2020/C 112 I/01.

13 Regulation (EU) 2021/522 of the European Parliament and of the Council of 24.03.2021 establishing a Programme for the Union's action in the field of health and repealing Regulation (EU) No 282/2014 [OJ L 107, 26.3.2021, p. 1–29].

14 Regulation (EU) 2021/523 of the European Parliament and of the Council of 24.03.2021 establishing the InvestEU Programme and amending Regulation (EU) 2015/1017 [OJ L 107, 26.3.2021, p. 30–89]; Regulation (EU) 2021/691 of the European Parliament and of the Council of 28.04.2021 on the European Globalisation Adjustment Fund for Displaced Workers (EGF) and repealing Regulation (EU) No 1309/2013 [OJ L 153, 3.5.2021, p. 48–70].

15 Regulation (EU) 2021/690 of the European Parliament and of the Council of 28.04.2021 establishing a programme for the internal market competitiveness of enterprises, including small and medium-sized enterprises, the area of plants, animals, food and feed, and European statistics (Single Market Programme) and repealing Regulations (EU) No 99/2013, (EU) No 1287/2013, (EU) No 254/2014 and (EU) No 652/2014 [OJ L 153, 3.5.2021, p. 1–47].

16 [OJ L 166, 11.5.2021, p. 1–34].

17 Regulation (EU) 2021/1119 of the European Parliament and of the Council of 30.06.2021 establishing the framework for achieving climate neutrality and amending Regulations (EC) No 401/2009 and (EU) 2018/1999 ('European Climate Law') [OJ L 243, 9.7.2021, p. 1–17].

18 Regulation (EU) 2021/817 of the European Parliament and of the Council of 20.05.2021 establishing Erasmus+: the Union Programme for education and training, youth and sport and repealing Regulation (EU) No 1288/2013 [OJ L 189, 28.5.2021, p. 1–33].

the economy and society."[19] Regulation (EU) 2021/241 indicated in the preamble that: "(10) Recovery should be achieved, and the resilience of the Union and its Member States enhanced, through the support for measures that refer to the policy areas of European relevance structured in six pillars, of which the second pillar is digital transformation" and further that "(21) Guaranteeing a high level of cybersecurity and trust in technologies is a pre-requisite for a successful digital transformation in the Union."[20]

The broadest explanation of the analysed phrase in subject and object terms is contained in Regulation (EU) 2021/694 of the European Parliament and of the Council of 29.04.2021 establishing the Digital Europe Programme and repealing Decision (EU) 2015/2240.[21] The phrase digital transformation appears repeatedly in Regulation on Digital Europe Programme [rec. 5, 9, 12, 14, 16, 31, 47–49, 51, 71 of the preamble and Art. 3 and 16]. In light of Art. 3 Objectives of the Programme:

> The general objectives of the Programme shall be to support and accelerate the digital transformation of the European economy, industry and society, to bring its benefits to citizens, public administrations and businesses across the Union, and to improve the competitiveness of Europe in the global digital economy while contributing to bridging the digital divide across the Union and reinforcing the Union's strategic autonomy, through holistic, cross-sectoral and cross-border support and a stronger Union contribution. The Programme shall be implemented in close coordination with other Union programmes as applicable and shall aim: (a) to strengthen and promote Europe's capacities in key digital technology areas through large-scale deployment; (b) in the private sector and in areas of public interest, to widen the diffusion and uptake of Europe's key digital technologies, promoting the digital transformation and access to digital technologies.

The preamble explains the origin of this approach, referencing the Tallinn Declaration on eGovernment at the ministerial meeting during Estonian Presidency of the Council of the EU on 6.10.2017 and elaborating on its findings (rec. 50–55). Article 3.2 indicates five interrelated specific objectives: 1 – High Performance Computing; 2 – Artificial Intelligence; 3 – Cybersecurity and Trust; 4 – Advanced Digital Skills; 5 – Deployment and Best Use of Digital Capacity and Interoperability.

The analysis shows that the legal basis for "digital transformation" is set by a dozen or so (EU) regulations, but as a legal term it is not unambiguous:

19 Regulation (EU) 2021/1153 of the European Parliament and of the Council of 7.07.2021 establishing the Connecting Europe Facility and repealing Regulations (EU) No 1316/2013 and (EU) No 283/2014 [OJ L 249, 14.7.2021, p. 38–81].

20 Regulation (EU) 2021/241 of the European Parliament and of the Council of 12.02.2021 establishing the Recovery and Resilience Facility [OJ L 57, 18.2.2021, p. 17–75].

21 OJ L 166, 11.5.2021, p. 1–34.

- it is sometimes referred to as a goal, objective, direction or process;
- it is essential for the cohesion, independence and competitiveness of the States and their associations (EU), either as a specific public task or an objective in itself;
- with a broad scope covering the economy, society and political-organisational systems, or a narrower scope limited to one of these elements, or a very narrow one, externalising the elements of the scope *sensu largo*;
- providing benefits to citizens, public administrations and businesses [business processes, products and models] – with the occasional caveat of requirements for new people skills and qualifications and cybersecurity;
- it is associated with digitisation, computerisation, cloud computing and big data, smart virtual-physical systems, application of large-scale computing and artificial intelligence but without a complete compilation of these elements.

The legal term "digital transformation" is therefore unclear, and the need for it to be considered in the application of law and further legislative processes justifies the need to agree on the meaning and possibly to formulate a general definition in EU law.

1.4 Explanations of the term "digital transformation" in the literature

The term "digital transformation" has only recently appeared in law and legal publications, but in scientific literature from other fields it could be encountered already in the 20th century.[22] The evolution of its understanding in the U.S. is manifested by publications from the MIT and Capgemini team's research, which focused on technical aspects firstly, then exposed strategies, their integration and absorption,[23] and more recently the need for changes in skills and qualifications.[24]

In the "Journal of Business Research," digital transformation has appeared in 520 publications since 1989, including as many as 333 in 2020–2021. New research in this area assumes that digital transformation and the resulting innovations in business models have fundamentally altered consumer expectations and behaviours, putting immense pressure on traditional enterprises, and disrupting

22 K. Patel, M. Mc Carthy. Digital Transformation: The Essentials of E-Business Leadership April 2000. McGraw-Hill Professional.

23 G. Westerman, Didier Bonnet and Andrew McAfee. "The Nine Elements of Digital Transformation," MIT Sloan Management Review, January 2014. G. Westerman, A. McAfee, D. Bonnet. "Leading digital. Turning technology into business transformation" Harvard Business Review Press, Boston, Massachusetts 2014.

24 D. Bonnet and P. Michelman. What Digital Transformation Means in 2018 and Beyond. 22.08.2018 https://sloanreview.mit.edu/video/what-digital-transformation-means-in-2018-and-beyond/business transformation; D. Bonnet and G. Westerman. The New Elements of Digital Transformation. MIT Sloan Management Review, Magazine Winter 2021 Issue. https://sloanreview.mit.edu/article/the-new-elements-of-digital-transformation/.

numerous markets. The following are described: growth strategies for digital companies and the assets and capabilities required for successful digital transformation. Three major external factors are identified driving the need for digital transformation:

> First, since the advent of the World Wide Web WWW and its worldwide adoption, an increasing number of accompanying technologies [...] have contributed to the growth of e-commerce. Second: the ubiquity of big data and third, the emergence of new digital technologies, such as artificial intelligence (AI), blockchain, internet of things (IoT) and robotics will have a far-reaching impact on business. In available literature, three stages of digital transformation are distinguished: digitisation, digitalisation and digital transformation.[25]

It can be noted that the same term is articulated to refer to this three-stage process as well as the third stage of the process. There are differentiated views in the literature on the relationship of digital transformation towards digitisation and digitalisation. In the first approach – i.e., according to Sharifullah Khan – digital transformation is their effect; in the second – there are three phases of transformation with an increasing level of "maturity," generating new sources of value.[26]

The scope of the phenomenon is also looked at in different ways. French management experts point out that the term "transformation digital" or "numérique" aims to conceptualise the impact on the organisation of the changes associated with the development of digital technology and the Internet, replacing the earlier "e-transformation," metaphorically called by Michel Germain "the energy of change initiated by the dynamics of the Internet, the potential of information and communication technologies, and the will of people in a business world marked by digital convergence"; it encompasses the technical, cultural and behavioural determinants of faster action on a larger scale.[27] In the *German Encyclopedia of Business Information Science*, the term "digital transformation" refers to significant active changes in everyday life, the economy and society using digital technologies and techniques and their effects, assuming that one dimension of digital transformation is the value creation model.[28] As essential components of

25 P. C. Verhoef, Thijs Broekhuizen, Y. Bart, A. Bhattacharya, J. Qi Dong, Nicolai Fabian, Michael Haenlein. Digital transformation: A multidisciplinary reflection and research agenda. Journal of Business Research Volume 122, January 2021, 889–901.

26 G. Szpor, Jawność i jej ograniczenia, t.1. Idee i pojęcia. Warsaw 2016; Z. Korachi and B. Bounabat. General Approach for Formulating a Digital Transformation Strategy. Journal of Computer Science 2020, 16 (4).

27 C. Malaison. C'est quoi la transformation numérique? 10 experts répondent – 4.06. 2020. https://exob2b.com/cest-quoi-la-transformation-numerique-10-experts-repondent/.

28 K. Pousttchi. Wissenschaftliche Definition "Digitale Transformation"im Lexikon der Wirtschaftsinformatik (online abrufbar). GITO Verlag, Berlin 2017. https://www.enzyklopaedie-der-wirtschaftsinformatik.de.

the digital transformation process, the following are listed: ubiquitous data, connectivity and decision-making.[29]

Differences in the approaches towards digital transformation adopted by different fields of science should be the subject of interdisciplinary agreements concerning its scope, elements, and time caesuras.

In legal publications the term "digital transformation" has been appearing only recently, occasionally and incidentally, while many representatives of legal sciences in the past half-century were interested in various elements now included in the scope of digital transformation.[30] The findings of the legal doctrine, especially the European one, are elaborated on, among others, in the collective monographs of the "Internet" series published by C.H. Beck, concerning such issues as protection of freedom, property and security [2011], problems of net, portals and e-services [2012], data processing in the clouds [2013], public databases and big data [2014], Internet of things and safety in the smart city [2015], security strategies [2017], spatial information [2018], processing of personal data [2019], data analytics [2019], cyberpandemic [2020] and global games [2021].[31] The results of these studies of legal and non-legal aspects of transformation, confronted within an interdisciplinary, international team, endorse a holistic view of digital transformation.

From the legal perspective in Europe, the time caesuras relate to EU strategies, whose importance in the transformation results from considering both axiological aspects and technological trends and guiding legislative work and priorities of development funding. On this basis, the following phases can be distinguished: the phase up to 2000, the decade of the Lisbon Strategy implementation, the decade of the Europe 2020 strategy and a new phase of implementation of the Digital Europe strategy initiated in 2021.

The following can be indicated as important legal issues of the transformation undertaken in the doctrine of law:

- balancing freedom of information and data protection, considering the global diversity of political and organisational systems;
- weakening of traditional legal instruments of the influence of public authorities on economic operators and possibilities to enforce compliance with the law by the consumers of e-services;
- shaping relations between institutions of continental European law based on analogous axiological foundations and American law, which – due to the dominant position of the USA in the operation of the Internet, including search engines and social networking sites – has a global "regulatory power";

29 A. Young and P. Rogers. A Review of Digital Transformation in Mining. Mining, Metallurgy & Exploration 36, 683–699 (2019).

30 G. Szpor, Jawność i jej ograniczenia, t.1. Idee i pojęcia, op. cit.

31 A. Gryszczyńska, G. Szpor, W. Wiewiórowski (eds.), Internet. Globalne gry. Global games. Warsaw 2021.

- increasing digital accessibility and social inclusion through miniaturisation and reduction of prices of devices and software as an offshoot of cloud computing;
- the pathologies of using big data for profiling and "datafication"[32]-related regulatory dilemmas for public databases;
- the fusion of the virtual and the real in the Internet of Things (IoT), billions of microscopic devices with low power, low bandwidth and high reliability, embedded in various "smart" objects and communicating with each other without human intervention;
- expanding the space available to humans and shrinking of the space under human control, enabling them to satisfy their basic needs independently and the role of GIS systems in these processes;
- the development of AI and the responsibility for AI training, and implications of applications of self-learning algorithms and "thinking things" – the devices into which they are embedded;
- reconciling partly contradictory postulates of the legal sciences responding to current challenges and maintaining distance from them, which determines objectivity, by using game theory and gamification in research on digital transformation;
- overcoming the devastating impact of the global and rapid spread of pandemics and cyberattacks on humans and the economy.

This last issue, called "cyberpandemic," induces us to trigger off the need to review the adequacy of many existing legal instruments for digital transformation to meet new needs.

The widespread threats to life and health, and the restriction of privacy in overcoming these threats have drawn attention to the collision of interests and to the new aspects of finding the right scope of their protection, among others, as part of "digital solidarity." Distinguishing the public interest from the private interest of individuals and legal persons is much more complicated than it used to be 20 years ago when restrictions on human rights and freedoms were justified by increasing the effectiveness of the fight against terrorism. The specific nature of activities in the cyberspace results in their global reach.[33] They are also more likely to cause extensive damage with the use of limited resources available to perpetrators, at the same time maintaining their anonymity.[34] Recently, an extensive, multi-level legal regulation, necessary to counter (mainly cross-border) cyberattacks, has

32 V. Mayer-Schönberger and K. Cukier, Big Data: A Revolution That Will Transform How We Live, Work, and Think. Mariner Books. Boston, 2014; K. Cukier and V. Mayer-Schoenberger. "The Rise of Big Data: How It's Changing the Way We Think About the World." *Foreign Affairs*, vol. 92, no. 3, Council on Foreign Relations, 2013, pp. 28–40.

33 Sh. Zuboff. The Age of Surveillance Capitalism: The Fight for a Human Future at the New Frontier of Power Hardcover – Publisher: PublicAffairs 2019.

34 B. Corcoran, "A Comparative Study of Domestic Laws Constraining Private Sector Active Defense Measures in Cyberspace," Harvard National Security Journal 11, no. 1 (2020).

been developed (NIS Directive, ENISA Regulation, Polish law on the national cyber security system), but 2021 has seen intensive work on its fundamental strengthening, including the support from EU funds for cybersecurity activities. The 2020 cyberattack targeting the European Medicines Agency and the scale of disinformation related to the pandemic manifest that cyberoperations are a great threat, and, due to the rules of attribution of actions in cyberspace to a specific state, it is difficult to subject them to international legal accountability.

Studies focusing on various problems of legal effectiveness also indicate the need to examine them separately in relation to the public sector and to the private sector, although universal technical and technological considerations are noticeable. On the other hand, healthcare (healthcare informatics) is an area of very specific solutions in which it is sometimes difficult to distinguish between public and private aspects.

Another issue is that isolation forced by the pandemic has verified the existing potential of remote education. Due to new regulatory administrative and legal instruments, the previously auxiliary IT tools have become the principal or the only ones available, changing the conditions for the effectiveness of their use as well. Gaps in the knowledge and skills emerged, resulting in severe consequences, to which the response was multiple amendments to numerous regulations as well as attempts to develop good remote working and education practices, useful not only in times of pandemic.[35]

A review of the literature confirms the importance and complexity of the issues of digital transformation, but also the shortcomings of the conceptual grid and the need to clarify the basic terms. More clearly than legal acts, it reveals the negative aspects of the transformation, undermining the rationality of looking at it as a goal. It also provides arguments for interdisciplinary reconciliation of definitions.

A proposal is made to take as a basis for further research that digital transformation is a process initiated by the transcription of data into digital form (digitisation) and their automatic processing (digitalisation), in which the reduction of time and space barriers to communication and the development of network structures influence business models, political-organisational systems, social relations and value systems, facilitating the steering of uncertainty (entropy) reduction, qualified positively or negatively with respect to the goal.[36]

1.5 Digital transformation in public administration

During the pandemic, public and national authorities – within the shields and EU – in their fund distribution plans, construct incentives to use digital transformation solutions in mitigating its impact. However, to make these findings more specific, references are required to legal regulations and literature on particular phenomena

35 A. Gryszczyńska, G. Szpor, Cyberpandemic 2020 (eds.).

36 G. Szpor, L. Grochowski (eds.) Wielka Encyklopedia Prawa. Tom XXII Prawo Informatyczne. Warsaw 2021, p. 445.

with which this transformation is coupled, such as: Cloud computing (processing of data on servers in places unknown to end users), big data (processing of rapidly changing large data sets, often from anonymous sources), Internet of Things (billions of small, low-cost, low-bit-rate sensors connected to the Internet and embedded in physical objects) or artificial intelligence (self-learning algorithms that find dependencies, relationships between data provided to them and search for similar patterns in unstructured resources).

Digital transformation makes it possible to shift the satisfaction of various needs from real space to cyberspace. E-commerce, e-banking, e-culture, e-sports and their regulation – mainly in private law – are developing. Also, in the public sphere there appear new forms of activity of the administration: interfering, providing and distributing, which induces the validation of the adequacy of public-legal instruments.

In Poland, with the use of public e-registers, ePUAP, electronic signatures, including the trusted signature in official matters, as well as e-deliveries, it is possible to run personal and specific errands decided in administrative proceedings without the physical presence of the interested parties in offices or other administration entities: within the scope of interfering administration (e.g. tax or customs matters), providing administration (e.g. payment of pensions, allowances or e-prescriptions) and regulating administration (e.g. registration of entities or obtaining permits on the pharmaceutical market, confirmation of entitlement to free-of-charge medical services or allocation to individual recipients in the form of an administrative decision of what is insufficient for all, using the patient's e-account and e-prescriptions).[37] In all administrative offices audited by the Supreme Audit Office in the initial period of the COVID-19 epidemic in Poland, there was a significant, sometimes more than doubled, increase in interest in e-services.[38]

The public digital information infrastructure also changes the implementation of tasks not directly related to individual cases, e.g., within the framework of development initiatives for smart cities and smart villages.[39]

According to the EC, the future prosperity will rely on investment in strategic digital infrastructure, but above all, strategic digital skills and raising qualifications as well as "modernising" the relationship between authorities and citizens.[40] This means new challenges for administration staff to increase data processing efficiency by using IT tools where it is positive and blocking the power when threats outweigh opportunities, e.g., in the event of cybercrime or cyberoperations. Reports of the Supreme Audit Office show that in most Polish offices a sat-

37 I. Lipowicz, G. Szpor, M. Świerczyński. Telemedycyna i e-Zdrowie. Prawo i informatyka. WolKluw., Warsaw 2019.

38 Informacja o wynikach kontroli Realizacja usług publicznych dla obywateli z wykorzystaniem platformy ePUAP. SAO nr ewid. 200/2020/P/20/004/KAP, pp. 56–58.

39 Z. Duniewska, R. Lewicka, M. Lewicki (eds.), Władza w przestrzeni administracji publicznej. Warsaw 2020.

40 Proposal for a Regulation of the European Parliament and of the Council establishing the Digital Europe programme for the period 2021–2027. COM/2018/434 final.

isfactory level of public e-services has not been achieved, i.e., due to the shortage of skills related to digital transformation among employees of the administration. However, for instance, the shortage of public data resource analysts, broadly referred to in the media as epidemiological data, is a shortage in many public services, whereas in business the analyst lands a much higher paying job. The same is true for the recruitment of cybersecurity specialists, who are required to be hired by new statutory regulations.

1.6 Conclusions

The massive and sudden shift from the reality affected by the pandemic to cyberspace has heightened the awareness of the opportunities associated with digital transformation, not only in healthcare. It has also revealed inadequate preparation for using cyberspace. It has made it a priority for public authorities, citizens and businesses alike to make greater use of remote communication tools and to strengthen cybersecurity.

The law should respond to the new valorisation of deficits and become, as W. Pańko indicated, a platform for compromise between the need for stabilisation and the necessity of development. These postulates relate to the regulation of digital transformation.

This legal term, with its broad scope adopted in the EU in 2021, is a convenient concept tool for modelling multi-level regulation. The content of legal acts predominantly exposes the benefits of digital transformation, but scientific publications are more likely to point to numerous drawbacks of using technical innovations. Therefore, digital transformation should not be included in legal acts as a goal but verified and qualified positively if the benefits outweigh the risks, or negatively if this is not the case.

From the vantage point of multidisciplinary research, digital transformation can be defined as a process initiated by the transcription of data into digital form (digitisation) and their automatic processing (digitalisation), in which increasing information resources, the reduction of time and space barriers to communication and the development of network structures, influence business models, political-organisational systems, social relations and value systems.

From a legal perspective, in the EU, efficient information processing using algorithms, programs and devices in which the programs are implemented should be considered in the context of steering (managing) the reduction of uncertainty (entropy), qualified positively or negatively, considering the criterion of compliance with the fundamental values set out in conventions, treaties and constitutions.

Works cited

Bonnet, D., and Westerman, G., 'The New Elements of Digital Transformation' *MIT Sloan Management Review* (Winter 2021).

Corcoran, B., 'A Comparative Study of Domestic Laws Constraining Private Sector Active Defense Measures in Cyberspace' (2020) 11(1) Harvard National Security Journal

1–53. https://harvardnsj.org/wp-content/uploads/sites/13/2020/01/CORCORAN_Vol.-11.1.pdf

Cukier, K., and Mayer-Schoenberger, V., 'The Rise of Big Data: How It's Changing the Way We Think about the World' (2013) 92(3) Foreign Affairs 28–40.

Duniewska, Z., Lewicka, R., and Lewicki, M. (eds), *Władza w przestrzeni administracji publicznej* (Wolters Kluwer, Warsaw 2020).

Gryszczyńska, A., Szpor, G., and Wiewiórowski, W. (eds.), *Internet. Globalne Gry. Global Games* (C.H. Beck, Warsaw 2021).

Korachi, Z., and Bounabat, B., 'General Approach for Formulating a Digital Transformation Strategy' (2020) 16(4) Journal of Computer Science 493–507.

Lipowicz, I., Szpor, G., and Świerczyński, M., *Telemedycyna i e-Zdrowie. Prawo i informatyka* (Wolters Kluwer, Warsaw 2019).

Mayer-Schönberger, M., and Cukier, K., *Big Data: A Revolution that Will Transform How We Live, Work, and Think* (Mariner Books, Boston 2014).

Malaison, C., 'C'est quoi la transformation numérique? 10 experts répondent' <https://exob2b.com/cest-quoi-la-transformation-numerique-10-experts-repondent/> (4 juin 2020).

Patel, K., and Pat McCarthy, M., *Digital Transformation: The Essentials of E-Business Leadership* (McGraw-Hill Professional 2000).

Pousttchi, K., *Wissenschaftliche Definition "Digitale Transformation"im Lexikon der Wirtschaftsinformatik (online abrufbar)* (GITO Verlag, Berlin 2017). <https://www.enzyklopaedie-der-wirtschaftsinformatik.de>.

Szpor, G., *Jawność i jej ograniczenia, t.1. Idee i pojęcia* (C.H. Beck, Warsaw 2016).

Szpor, G., and Grochowski, L. (eds.), *Wielka Encyklopedia Prawa. Tom XXII Prawo Informatyczne* (Fundacja "Ubi societas, ibi ius", Warsaw 2021).

Westerman, G., Bonnet, D., and McAfee, A., 'The Nine Elements of Digital Transformation' *MIT Sloan Management Review* (January 2014).

Zuboff, Sh., *The Age of Surveillance Capitalism: The Fight for a Human Future at the New Frontier of Power* (PublicAffairs 2019). https://onlinelibrary.wiley.com/doi/10.1111/jacc.13051

2 The Pandemic Phenomenon

A Few General Remarks

Marek Michalski

2.1 Introduction

The pandemic has affected social, economic and political life. It has led to widespread supply shortages exacerbated by panic. Numerous educational institutions and public areas have been partially or fully closed, and many events have been cancelled or postponed. Misinformation has circulated through social and mass media, and political tensions have been exacerbated. The pandemic revisited the analysis of discrimination, health care and the balance between public health imperatives and individual rights.

Studying COVID-19 issues requires explaining what the term "pandemic" means. It is important to understand what contexts it occurs in and how it influences the shaping of public law instruments.

A pandemic is defined as an epidemic that is particularly large and affects a large area. The study's main objective is to define this concept, taking account of the reconstructed legal and social context. The definition will be reconstructed via references to legal acts and through the analysis of the relevant literature.

2.2 The term "pandemic"

Despite the variety of approaches, the common understanding of a pandemic comes down to a reference to the Greek root pan, meaning "all," and demos, meaning "people," – as epidemics of particularly large proportions, involving countries or even continents.[1] The *Cambridge Dictionary* (cf. pandemic) already refers to an epidemic covering most of a given territory or a specific group: people, animals or plants.[2]

The definition of a pandemic appears in the *Dictionary of Epidemiology*. According to this definition, "an epidemic occurring worldwide, or over a very wide area, crossing international boundaries and usually affecting a large number

1 Encyklopedia PWN (on – line), 28.11. 2021.
2 Cambridge Dictionary (on – line), 28.11. 2021.

DOI: 10.4324/9781003263968-4

of people."[3] The classical definition includes nothing about population immunity, virology or disease severity. Pandemics can be said to occur annually in each of the temperate southern and northern hemispheres, given that the definition of the term is so wide. Seasonal epidemics are not considered pandemics. Modern definitions include "extensive epidemic," "epidemic [...] over a very wide area and usually affecting a large proportion of the population" and "distributed or occurring widely throughout a region, country, continent or globally," among others.[4]

In the case of influenza, biologists also require that pandemic strains undergo key genomic mutations, known as antigenic shifts. For WHO to pronounce a level six pandemic alert, there must be sustained transmission in at least two regions simultaneously. WHO's standard definition of pandemic influenza refers to a situation in which a new and highly pathogenic viral subtype, one to which no one in the human population has immunological resistance and is easily transmissible between humans, establishes a foothold in the human population. At this point, it rapidly spreads worldwide.[5]

In modern times, until 2019, the phenomenon of virus spread – in global terms – was linked to influenza epidemics. In May 2009, because of the virus's reach, WHO: A/H1N1 (swine flu) included a description of an influenza pandemic as a global epidemic. Adding that an influenza pandemic can occur when a new influenza virus emerges to which people are not immune, which can be mild or severe, leading to illness and death.[6]

The word "pandemic" is used extensively, and it appears in phrases such as "pandemic preparedness," "pandemic influenza" and "pandemic potential". A Google Scholar search returns 25,800 results using the term "pandemic" for 2019.[7]

Therefore, in the case of a pandemic, one can speak of a state of spreading disease over a large territory, with the infection spreading to new environments.[8] In this context, an epidemic undoubtedly has a local, and therefore territorially limited, dimension. In contrast, a pandemic causes these boundaries to be crossed, which is also linked to economies of scale, i.e., a significant – and from a certain point onwards growing geometrically – increase in infections. In one other case, i.e., epidemic and pandemic, we deal with a phenomenon of considerable spread and high incidence of a disease caused by a pathogen. Still, the starting point must be the epidemic state.

3 J.M. Last, R.A. Spasoff and S. Harris, (eds.), A Dictionary of Epidemiology, Fourth Edition (Oxford University Press, New York 2000).

4 D.M. Morens, G.K. Folkers and A.S. Fauci, 'What is a pandemic?', *Journal of Infectious Diseases* 2009, 200 (7), 1018-1021.

5 W. Qiu et al, The Pandemic and its Impacts. Health, Culture and Society Vol 9–10 (2016–2017).

6 https://www.who.int/csr/resources/publications/plague/WHO_CDS_CSR_EDC_99_2_EN/en/.

7 B.J. Singer et al., The effect of the definition of 'pandemic' on quantitative assessments of infectious disease outbreak risk. Sci Rep 11, 2547, 2021.

8 M. Michalski, Pandemia – między zdrowiem, gospodarką a codziennością [in]: Gryszczyńska, Szpor, Cyberpandemic 2020 (eds.).

2.3 A short story about pandemic COVID-19

The story of the – ongoing since 2019 – pandemic caused by the spread of the SARS-CoV-2 causing the disease defined as COVID-19 – although short, is not only instructive, due to the speed of its spread and the scale of the measures taken to counteract it, but also confirms observations made since antiquity and establishing the mechanisms and scenarios of the course of events. It is, therefore, worth briefly presenting the course of events.

Well, on 30 December 2019, an ophthalmologist from a hospital in the 11-million-year-old city of Wuhan, Dr Li Wenliang informed the authorities about the mysterious plague, which, however, did not meet with a reaction from the authorities, apart from the accusation of "sowing social confusion" against the informant.[9] It was only on 23 January 2021 that the first remedial steps were taken, which took place on the eve of the Chinese New Year holidays.[10] The first hard lockdown was then applied, covering the city of Wuhan and the entire 60 million-strong Hubei province. As B. Góralczyk, an outstanding expert on contemporary China, emphasises, the passivity and silence of the central authorities in the first days of the epidemic can only be speculated. One can only imagine the passivity and silence of the central authorities in the first days of the still spreading epidemic.[11]

On 11 March 2020, the head of the WHO announced the spread of the SARS-CoV-2 virus, causing the disease defined as COVID-19 to be called a pandemic state. Since then, we have been dealing with a situation that until now was known only from historical accounts, very distant in time, but also not very recent, as in the case of the influenza pandemic caused by the H1N1 virus, commonly known as "Spanish flu," which decimated the world's population between 1918 and 1920. However, the dynamics of the spread of the SARS-CoV-2 virus seem to significantly exceed all previous pandemics because this was taking place at a time of another – extremely advanced – stage of globalisation. Of course, one can try to draw different boundaries and ranges of this phenomenon, which is, after all, an uninterrupted process that has been going on with varying intensity since around the turn of the 16th century.[12] And it will always be a conventional approach.

Nevertheless – guided by breakthrough moments – four basic stages of globalisation can be identified, i.e., the first – the time of the great geographical discoveries (15th/16th centuries); the second – the time of the first and second industrial revolution (19th century); the third – the period of the industrial and technological revolution (second half of the 20th century), and the fourth – the time of the so-called 4.0 revolution (beginning of 21st century). At the same time – as S.

9 B. Góralczyk, *Nowy Długi Marsz. Chiny ery XI Jinpinga*, 2021.

10 Ibid.

11 Ibid.

12 The Globalisation and Development Reader. Perspectives on Development and Global Change. (eds.) J. Timmons Roberts, A. Bellone Hite, N. Chorev, Wiley Blackwell, 2021.

P. Huntington notes – creating the so-called universal civilisation intensifies.[13] The EU is also experiencing increased ease and speed of movement, removing, or reducing administrative barriers that have slowed down people's mobility. Undoubtedly, this circumstance will significantly contribute to the speed with which the SARS-CoV-2 virus has spread across the globe, which seems to be suggested by the already cited B. Góralczyk in his political science analysis.

2.4 Pandemic and epidemic issues in Polish law and practice

The lack of terminological uniformity concerning the concept of a pandemic, and the additional occurrence of the idea of the epidemic in national acts, makes it worthwhile to look at these two expressions. The comments will refer to the Polish legal system.

The law does not define a pandemic, but the term pandemic is used to describe an epidemic of an infectious disease in various environments, over a large area – different continents at the same time. The disease is usually easy to spread, most often by droplets.

The legal definition of an "epidemic" can be found in the A.I.D. According to Art. 2 p. 9, an "epidemic" is an "occurrence in a given area of infections or outbreaks of an infectious disease in a significantly higher number than in the preceding period or occurrence of infections or infectious diseases not occurring before." What is important for the present considerations, by "state of epidemics" and "state of epidemic threat," the indicated act means not a factual state. Still, a legal situation was introduced in each area. On the other hand, a pandemic is an epidemic of global character; it is declared by the WHO.

The A.I.D. introduces the institution of the state of the epidemic. Its meaning results from Art. 2 pt. 22 A.I.D. According to this provision, the state of an epidemic is a legal situation introduced in each area in connection with an epidemic to undertake the anti-epidemic and preventive measures specified in the Act to minimise the epidemic's effects.

The announcement of an epidemic in Poland may be issued under Art. 46(2) and (4) of the A.I.D. According to the rules mentioned above, if an epidemic occurs in more than one voivodeship, the state of the epidemic is announced and cancelled, using a regulation, by the minister for health matters in consultation with the minister competent for public administration, at the request of the Chief Sanitary Inspector. If the epidemic occurs in an area limited to a voivodeship or part thereof, the state of the epidemic is announced and recalled by the voivode. The state of an epidemic is introduced when the actual occurrence of an epidemic has already been confirmed, and not simply at the risk of its occurrence.

The epidemic area may cover a selected area of the territory of Poland or the entire country. If the area covers a specific voivodeship, the voivode announces and recalls the epidemic. If the area extends beyond one voivodeship, the MoH

13 S.P. Huntington, Zderzenie cywilizacji i nowy kształt ładu światowego (Warsaw2018).

is responsible for announcing and recalling the epidemic. If an epidemic is announced in each area, healthy persons may be required to undergo preventive vaccinations.

Persons staying in the territory covered by the epidemic are obliged to undergo sanitary procedures, preventive vaccinations, post-exposure prophylactic use of drugs, sanitary and epidemiological tests, including procedures aimed at collecting or submitting material for these tests, epidemiological supervision, quarantine, treatment, hospitalisation and isolation.

Additionally, sick people will be obliged to refrain from performing any work where there is a possibility of transmitting infection or an infectious disease to others (see the A.I.D.).

The legislator has not yet decided to introduce the concept of a pandemic into the legal system. Public authorities derive their legitimacy from acting in connection with COVID-19 primarily from the general competencies relating to responding to threats and ensuring the security of the state and citizens, and from the A.I.D. The activities related to combating the pandemic occur in the above-mentioned state of the epidemic, introduced based on the A.I.D.

On 14 March 2020, the government introduced an epidemic emergency in Poland. With it, the first strict restrictions began to apply. Foreigners could not come to Poland except for work, but they had to undergo a 14-day quarantine. The same procedure was used for Poles returning to the country. The work of shopping malls was reduced, and international air traffic was suspended. All bars, restaurants and pubs were closed. Assemblies of more than 50 people were forbidden.

From 16 March 2020, Poland's universities, schools and kindergartens were closed for two weeks. As it turned out later, pupils and students did not return to the traditional form of education by the end of the school year. On 25 March 2020, it was replaced by online learning.

By regulation of the MoH of 20 March 2020, in the period from 20 March 2020, until further notice, an epidemic was announced in the territory of the Republic of Poland in connection with SARS-CoV-2 virus infections.

On 24 March 2020, the Polish government introduced further restrictions. It was forbidden to gather in parks and boulevards, no more than five people were allowed to attend masses. They were allowed to go out to work, the store and help others. The rules entered into force on 25 March 2020.

On 2 March 2020, the COVID-19 Act was passed. It entered into force on 8 March 2020. This Act amends many acts, including the A.I.D., and allows administrative, budgetary and epidemiological measures in the fight against COVID-19 and its consequences.

2.5 Conclusions

Although epidemics, or even pandemics, have plagued humankind since ancient times, as we are convinced by Tukidides in Book II of the Peloponnesian War, describing the plague in Athens with horror and by Procopius of Caesarea reporting on the plague in Constantinople in the 6th century A.D. For example, Pride haunted European countries regularly, between 1346 and 1352[14] and then, among others, in the years 1359–1361, 1369–1372, 1380–1380, 1449, 1460, 1473, 1482–1483, 1521–1527, 1575–1582 or 1596–1602, so that the period from 1400 to 1800. F. Braudel calls the long-lasting ancient regime biological,[15] from 1400 to 1800. F. Braudel calls the long-lasting ancient regime biological. Nevertheless, the current situation seems to confirm the previously observed scenarios, on the one hand. On the other hand, it presents a decidedly different picture, e.g., due to countermeasures taken by the state authorities (including the use of, e.g., AI), but also due to the efforts of science and the pharmaceutical industry aimed at developing and producing effective preventive as well as curative measures.

It should be said that the COVID-19 pandemic has had a great impact on the world. It cost millions of lives, and it has disrupted economies and education systems and taken away livelihoods.

States, governments, businesses and individuals have had to adapt in many cases leaning on an existing digital transformation that was already underway. The technological workarounds adopted during the pandemic have changed lives forever.

As said at the World Economic Forum, the long-term impacts of the pandemic on the economy and society will be varied, and there are other social and economic transitions looming. Many of the trends spurred by digital acceleration are anchored in the developed world and may not apply to developing economies in the same way. The World Economic Forum's report Accelerating Digital Inclusion in the New Normal has pointed out important gaps in infrastructure, connectivity, access and affordability to technologies in emerging markets. The challenges to digital transformation are addressed comprehensively for the world.[16]

Works cited

Benedictow, J., *The Black Death 1346–1353. The Complete History* (The Boydell Press, Woodbridge 2004).

Braudel, F., S*truktury codzienności. Kultura materialna, gospodarka I kapitalizm XV – XVIII wiek, vol. 1* (Państwowy Instytut Wydawniczy, Warsaw 2019).

Cambridge Dictionary (on – line), 28.11.2021.

Encyklopedia PWN (on – line), 28.11.2021.

Góralczyk, B., *Nowy Długi Marsz. Chiny ery XI Jinpinga* (Wydawnictwo Akademickie Dialog, Warsaw 2021).

Last, J.M., Spasoff, R.A. and Harris, S. (eds.), *A Dictionary of Epidemiology* (Oxford University Press, New York 2000).

Huntington, S.P., *Zderzenie cywilizacji i nowy kształt ładu światowego* (Warsaw 2018, wyd. Zysk i S-ka).

14 J. Benedictow, The Black Death 1346–1353. The Complete History (The Boydell Press, Woodbridge 2004).

15 F. Braudel, 'Struktury codzienności. Kultura materialna, gospodarka I kapitalizm XV – XVIII wiek', vol. 1 (Warsaw2019).

16 World Economic Forum: https://www.weforum.org/agenda/2021/08/covid19-long-term-effects-society-digital/.

Konieczny, J., *Bezpieczeństwo zdrowia publicznego w zagrożeniach epidemiologicznych. Teoria- Praktyka – Metodologia – Etyka. Poznanie naukowe. Studia i Materiały* (Nowiny Nauki o Bezpieczeństwie, Poznań. E – Biuletyn no 1/2020). https://wnpid.amu.edu.pl/__data/assets/pdf_file/0025/117196/Jerzy-Konieczny.pdf

Michalski, M., *Pandemia – między zdrowiem, gospodarką a codziennością: Internet. Cyberpandemia,* (eds.) A. Gryszczyńska and G. Szpor (C.H. Beck, Warsaw 2020).

Morens, D.M., Folkers, G.K., and Fauci, A.S., 'What is a Pandemic?' (2009) 200(7) Journal of Infectious Diseases 1018–1021.

'Plague Manual: Epidemiology, Distribution, Surveillance and Control' <https://www.who.int/csr/resources/publications/plague/WHO_CDS_CSR_EDC_99_2_EN/en/>.

Qiu, W., Rutherford, S., Mao, A., and Chu, C., 'The Pandemic and its Impacts' (2016–2017) 9–10 Health, Culture and Society 3–11.

Singer, B.J., Thompson, R.N., and Bonsall, M.B., 'The Effect of the Definition of 'Pandemic' on Quantitative Assessments of Infectious Disease Outbreak Risk' (2021) 11 Sci Rep 2547.

Benedictow, O.J., *The Black Death 1346–1353. The Complete History* (The Boydell Press, Woodbridge 2004).

Timmons Roberts, J., Bellone Hite, A., and Chorev, N., *The Globalisation and Development Reader. Perspectives on Development and Global Change* (Wiley Blackwell, Malden-Oxford 2021).

3 Public Law Instruments

Irena Lipowicz

3.1 Introduction

An area of this research is the current emergency – a pandemic – which poses new challenges to all three authorities: legislative, executive and judicial. The aim of this study is, among other things, to find out how public law instruments were used in each country: legal forms of action, instruments and other means of the influence of what kind they were and what challenges to the rule of law the pandemic posed to parliament, public administration and the judiciary. This chapter plays the role of the opening remarks in the book.

The response of public authorities to the COVID-19 epidemic in diverse areas of substantive law is interesting. Public authorities can implement their constitutional and statutory tasks and competencies in diverse forms.[1] As emphasised by P. Kirchhof in legal science, unlike in systems theory, the possibilities of control by law are appreciated.[2] At the same time, the primary means of state influence are law-making, financial means, the use of personnel resources of the administration and authoritative means of force flowing from executive power. Out of these four elements, state authorities' three legal forms of action serve to carry out tasks in a future-oriented manner. Therefore, these enact universally binding laws, individual acts acting in the present and post-factum control applied according to legal criteria.[3] Within the tripartite division of powers system, the legislative power is of fundamental importance for the legal determination of the action of subjects – natural and legal persons. The primary instrument of its activity is the normative act.

Acting through law-making, issuing universally binding norms in the external sphere by the parliament in an appropriate, strictly defined procedure ensures control over the entire system in a democratic state under the rule of law. However, a

1 E. Schmidt-Aßmann, Verwaltungsrechtliche Dogmatik: Eine Zwischenbilanz zu Entwicklung, Reform und künftigen Aufgaben: Eine Zwischenbilanz Zu Entwicklung, Reform Und Kunftigen Aufgaben (J.C.B. Mohr) 2013.

2 P. Kirchhof, 'Mittel staatlichen Handelns' in Josef Isensee, Paul Kirchhof (eds.), *Handbuch des Staatsrechts, Band V: Rechtsquellen, Organisation, Finanzen* (3rd edn, C.F. Müller 2007) 7.

3 Ibid., 18–19.

DOI: 10.4324/9781003263968-5

normative act issued in the external sphere is also one of the essential elements of public administration's orderly shaping of social relations. As a rule, legislative activity is immanent to the legislature, which, unlike the executive and judicial authorities, creates the legal basis for its activity on its own, limited only by the constitution. Consequently, the public law instruments of action affecting social relations are concentrated at different times with different intensities. It is interesting to what extent there has been a shift towards the executive under pandemic conditions. It is a question whether it was justified or just a pretext for expanding the already growing role of the executive in many countries.

A normative act is an efficient instrument of public law, allowing for regulation of the legal situation of the addressee in a general and abstract way. The studies presented in this volume discuss the framework and constitutional grounds for the actions of public authority. However, in the case of Poland, because it did not make use of the formula of the constitutional state of emergency due to a natural disaster, the focus was on the numerous laws passed in connection with COVID-19 and the public law instruments and forms of administrative action. The concept of the statute matter is familiar to Polish, Italian and German doctrine. Therefore, it does not require further exposition; in each case, it refers to a general, abstract normative act passed by parliament in an appropriate procedure and constituting a source of universally binding law. The negative evaluation of episodic laws is also typical, with rare exceptions.

Although commonly accepted in the conceptual grid of our countries, the concept of legal forms and instruments of administrative action has more varied approaches.

3.2 Polish doctrine

It must be stated that the theory of legal forms of administrative action belongs – at least in Poland – to those areas where the difference of views is the greatest. In the Polish doctrine of administrative law, many authors presented proposals for approaching this issue. Adam Błaś even wrote about a "terminological tumulus" fuelled by the indecision of the legislator.[4] Krystian Ziemski stated that "by the legal form of administrative action we shall understand a separate or distinguishable, legally determined, with fixed features conventional or factual action, or a set of such actions of a specific entity (or a group of entities) appointed to perform public administration tasks to fulfil public administration tasks."[5]

These views have been gradually shaped. Kazimierz Kumaniecki divided all acts of administrative authority into fundamental creative acts (including public

4 A. Błaś, 'Formy prawne w sferze działań zewnętrznych administracji publicznej' in R. Hauser, Z. Niewiadomski and A. Wróbel (eds.), System prawa administracyjnego, t. V, Prawne formy działania administracji (C.H. Beck 2013) 277.

5 K. Ziemski, *Indywidualny akt administracyjny jako forma prawna działania administracji* (Wydawnictwo Naukowe UAM 2005) 138.

care acts, regulatory-supervisory acts) and auxiliary acts — supplementing the fundamental act.[6] Stanisław Kasznica emphasised later, that legal acts of public law may be undertaken only by entities performing public administration (public services) and only in the public interest.[7]

A significant influence on the development in Poland was exerted by Jerzy Starościak; in System Prawa Administracyjnego, by legal form of action of administration. He understood how administrative organs realised tasks based on law, distinguished also between legal forms of administration action and the policy of applying means, instruments, forms, dividing into two spheres of administration, external and internal.[8]

Jerzy Starościak presented a whole catalogue of legal forms of administrative activity: making generally binding regulations, issuing administrative acts in the narrow sense, concluding administrative agreements and contracts, conducting a social and organisational activity and performing material and technical activities.[9] He wrote about concluding administrative agreements in the first versions of his monograph, which only changed in 1977 when he recognised that the administrative agreement "belonged" to the capitalist state and had no raison d'être in a communist system. After so many years, it is astonishing that this unconscious ideological caesura persists. The Code of Administrative Procedure still does not distinguish it as a principal, separate category of administrative agreement. However, such agreements already exist in substantive law. Polish doctrine has long been unanimous about the necessity of enriching the catalogue of legal forms of administrative action in this way.[10] It is perhaps the most severe difference to German and Italian doctrine; gradual, cautious recognition of new forms of action is evident.

It should be considered whether the legal forms of administrative action are identical with the concept of instruments of administrative action. The new treatment of legal instruments within the German New Administrative Law reform framework significantly broadens the research perspective. Although, against the background of Polish doctrine, it should be recognised that these concepts are often used interchangeably, "instrument of action" rather appears in the context of systems theory and management. In this study, we clearly distinguish between public-legal instruments and forms and private-legal ones, in which the administration also acts. In analysing how the proportions of the forms used to change and how the forms of action themselves evolve under the influence of the exterior, the spheres of administration activity as a basis for distinguishing forms taken, respectively, in the external and internal spheres of administration activity.

6 K.W. Kumaniecki, *Akt administracyjny* (Towarzystwo Biblioteki Słuchaczów Prawa Uniwersytetu Jagiellońskiego 1936) 29–30.

7 S. Kasznica, *Polskie prawo administracyjne* (Księgarnia Akademicka 1946) 8.

8 J. Starościak, 'Prawne formy i metody działania administracji' in T. Rabska and J. Łętowski (eds.), *System prawa administracyjnego, t. III* (Ossolineum 1978) 39–129.

9 J. Starościak, *Prawo administracyjne* (Państwowe Wydawnictwo Naukowe 1977) 230–231.

10 Z. Cieślik, Umowa administracyjna w państwie prawa (Zakamycze 2004) 113.

Only the third criterion is the nature of legal norms constituting the legal basis of administration activities – as a basis for distinguishing public-legal and private-legal forms.[11]

The distinction between public and private law activities in Polish administrative law literature was already present in the works of Władysław Leopold Jaworski and Stanisław Kasznica.[12] In the interwar period, this criterion was primary, Stanisław Kasznica wrote about so-called "administrative notification activities," e.g., buying or renting, which had a private law character. Marian Zimmermann consolidated in Polish doctrine the conviction that civil or administrative law norms can regulate acts of administration. Also, Janusz Borkowski considered an essential criterion for distinguishing administrative act consolidated in the Polish doctrine, as Krystian Ziemski points out, by both Marek Wierzbowski and Aleksandra Wiktorowska, as well as by Zygmunt Niewiadomski.[13] Janusz Borkowski continued the research and adopted as an ordering criterion the issue of producing direct legal, considering as legal actions those actions which aim at producing such direct effects. He defined such actions as general and individual decisive actions. External individual acts could be one- or two-sided. He also allowed for authoritative bilateral acts.[14] Thus, if one can speak of a prevailing consensus in Polish doctrine concerning the legal forms of action of the administration, one can mention this same criterion, except for the slightly different approach of W. Chróścielewski.[15] Only the connection of this criterion with wielding power is disputable. However, it should be noted, that the presence of the feature of wielding power determines the public-legal character of certain forms.[16] Still, the lack of this feature does not allow them to be automatically assigned to the category of public- or private-legal activities. The importance of the measure of public and private law has been preserved.

At the same time, the doctrinal prediction that, with time, the instruments of power would diminish in favour of those who are powerless did not come true. The situation of the epidemic brought it into sharp focus, encouraging further research. In the subsequent studies in this volume, it is possible to see how public authority under pressure, but sometimes under the pretext of circumstances,

11 K. Ziemski, 'Podstawy problematyki' in R. Hauser, Z. Niewiadomski and A. Wróbel (eds.), *System prawa administracyjnego, t. V, Prawne formy działania administracji*, 47, 51–52.

12 W.L. Jaworski, *Nauka prawa administracyjnego: zagadnienia ogólne* (Instytut Wydawniczy Bibljoteka Polska 1924) 78 et seq; S. Kasznica, op. cit., 112.

13 J. Borkowski, Decyzja administracyjna (Wydawnictwo Naukowe PWN 1970); M. Wierzbowski and A. Wiktorowska, in M. Wierzbowski (ed) *Prawo administracyjne* (7th edn, Wydawnictwo Prawnicze LexisNexis 2007) 302; Z. Niewiadomski, 'Prawne formy działania administracji i ich sądowa kontrola' in Zygmunt Niewiadomski (ed), *Prawo administracyjne* (Wydawnictwo Prawnicze LexisNexis 2013) 126.

14 J. Borkowski, op. cit., 56–71.

15 W. Chróścielewski, Akt administracyjny generalny (Wydawnictwo Uniwersytetu Łódzkiego 1994) 62–65.

16 K. Ziemski, 'Podstawy problematyki' in R. Hauser, Z. Niewiadomski and A. Wróbel (eds.), *System prawa administracyjnego, t. V, Prawne formy działania administracji*, 52.

reverts to the crudest forms of authority. The normative act and the administrative act remain the main form of reaction. Therefore, attention must be paid to those forms of material-technical and social-organisational activities that are already on the borderline with factual acts, and which in German doctrine, for example, Hartmut Maurer classifies as factual administrative acts (Realakten).[17]

The certificates and public warnings and the processing of personal data as a material and technical act, are very important in a pandemic.[18] Certificates were qualified to the group (of administrative acts), and in the post-war period as factual actions (M. Wierzbowski) or actions of administration other than current actions (E. Ochendowski). The literature often points out the difference between certificates and administrative decisions: an administrative act, unlike a certificate, enjoys a presumption of validity; the effectiveness of a certificate depends on its truthfulness, it also does not bind the authority that issued it; in the Code of Administrative Procedure a certificate is an official confirmation of specific facts or a legal state. Certificates are acts of knowledge and not of will.[19]

In the specific situation of a pandemic, certificates, e.g., of a negative virus infection test, of having received a vaccination, gain significant importance. A certificate may be a condition to go abroad, take up a particular job or leave a given territory. Although a certificate does not have any legal effect on the legal situation of a party, it can nevertheless be important. Certificates in Starościak's "classical catalogue" are counted among legal forms of administrative action. As Marek Wierzbowski points out, a certificate may be issued at the request of a person having a legal interest in obtaining it. The authority's knowledge is the limitation for issuing certificates. The NSA in its judgment of 9 January2009: "an authority may not certify the existence of circumstances of which it does not know."[20]

The pandemic period bore the brunt of the need for public participation. The high level of fear, the unquestionable necessity to use administrative acts and normative acts did not reduce the importance of using non-authoritative forms and unilateral forms: public promises, warnings and incentives, calls. One may think that these forms will remain with us to a large extent for longer.[21] Classical forms of participation, significantly developed in the last 30 years, are missing (Dolnicki, Marchaj, Szlachetko).

The material-technical activities, external and internal, constitute a kind of reservoir of new forms of administration activity. Most authors include both material-technical and social-organisational actions to the so-called other forms

17 H. Maurer, Ogólne prawo administracyjne (Kolonia Limited 2003) 399 et seq.

18 L. Klat-Wertelecka, *Zaświadczenie w prawie administracyjnym* (Difin 2001) 33 et seq.

19 M. Wierzbowski and J. Jagielski (eds.), *Prawo administracyjne* (WolKluw. 2019) 48; C. Banasiński, D. Szafrański and A. Wiktorowska, 'Zaświadczenie jako warunek złożenia wniosku o podjęcie działalności koncesjonowanej' (1996) 7 Monitor Prawniczy 241; A. Adamczyk, Publicznoprawne formy działania administracji. Teoria i praktyka (Difin 2013) 241–245.

20 II FSK 1382/07.

21 A. Adamczyk, op. cit., 259–260.

of action.[22] They indicate that material and technical actions based on a clear legal basis are undertaken based on a normative or administrative act. Małgorzata Stahl emphasises that they are undertaken based on and to implement binding legal norms, but are not aimed directly at the creation, change or abolition of legal relations; they may produce specific legal effects through facts.[23]

The development of information technologies caused, as Jerzy Supernat points out, a reduction of direct and personal participation of a citizen in many administration processes. This author analyses actions of administrative bodies mainly in terms of instruments, not forms of action. He distinguishes information instruments: individualised as to the addressee, general and of atypical character.[24] Translating the informative activities of the bodies into the more common category of legal forms of action of the legislator and the public administration, most authors consider the provision of information as a material-technical action. Among these activities, we find, for example, official warnings called public notices. Although actual administrative acts may concern especially the threat of sanitary safety, they are issued based on statutory authorisations and within the statutory limitations allowed by the legislator. Both in Poland and Germany, acts of this category are subject to the control of administrative courts.

According to the Polish authors,[25] the general principles of public authorities' actions should be respected to a greater extent than the provided statutory limitations. The growing importance of the processing of personal data leads to the assumption that there will be a gradual development of this form as a new one.

The complicating activity of public administration leads to proposals enriching the systematics of legal forms of administration activity. However, as M. Stahl rightly notes, these efforts have not yet led to establishing a new, entire catalogue of forms of action. These new forms proposed in the literature include acts of supervision, of control, of planning, acts of cooperation, coordination and acts of knowledge. There are also mixed forms of "established" forms in doctrine.

Knowledge acts are expressions of knowledge possessed by the administration. The distinction of them is attributed to the European integration and the Europeanisation of administrative law; the most stable category here is certificates. They are characterised by the fact that, given their unilateral character, they are not statements of will but statements of knowledge. The object of these acts is an official confirmation of a factual or legal state known to the authority. The separation of knowledge acts from the material-technical activities of

22 E. Ura and E. Ura, *Prawo administracyjne* (8th edn, Wydawnictwo Prawnicze LexisNexis 2009) 111.

23 M. Stahl, 'Czynności materialno-techniczne' in Małgorzata Stahl (ed) *Prawo administracyjne. Pojęcia, instytucje, zasady w teorii i orzecznictwie* (5th edn, WolKluw. 2016) 504–508; vide A. Błaś, op. cit., 302–303.

24 J. Supernat, 'Informacyjne instrumenty działania administracji publicznej' in Jan Łukasiewicz (ed), *Nauka administracji wobec wyzwań współczesnego państwa prawa: międzynarodowa konferencja naukowa* (Towarzystwo Naukowe Organizacji i Kierownictwa 2002) 147.

25 A. Błaś, op. cit., 111.

the administration is not generally recognised yet. Acts of knowledge (approvals, opinions, announcements and notices) go beyond certificates. To finally distinguish these categories, it would be necessary to accept a cross between the existing categories of concepts. Vaccination certificates, for example, may be issued in the form of administrative acts; quality certificates, service certificates or foreign language certificates appear in many substantive laws. Gradually, a new form of knowledge act is being distinguished. In pandemic conditions, this category is expanding, official certificates of health, communications and health certificates play an increasingly important role.[26]

Thus, a characteristic feature of recent years is the gradual separation of new legal forms of administrative action – the act of supervision and other specific consensual forms. No widespread acceptance yet exists for the act of coordination and organisation.[27] However, doubts are formulated about their stability as a separate legal form.[28]

A due place among the legal forms of administrative action is gradually being occupied by the administrative promise,[29] which – as an act of a particular kind – seems to be gaining distinctness from the administrative act.[30] Małgorzata Stahl emphasises that a promise is essential from the predictability of public administration and stabilisation of a citizen's legal situation – important for fulfilling the principle of good administration.[31]

3.3 German doctrine

It is necessary to briefly present the approach of German public law doctrine to the means of state action, with a rich doctrinal background.

German doctrine regards the statutory act as the most important democratic instrument of public steering. It is reinforced by the principle of statutory substance, which is also generally accepted in other countries. At the same time, it

26 Z. Kmieciak, *Instytucja zaświadczenia w prawie administracyjnym* (Wydawnictwo Uniwersytetu Marii Curie-Skłodowskiej 2002) 13; J. Lang, 'Akty potwierdzające w administracji państwowej' (1990) 18 Studia Iuridica 125 et seq.

27 M. Stahl, 'Szczególne prawne formy działania administracji' in R. Hauser, Z. Niewiadomski and A. Wróbel (eds.), *System prawa administracyjnego, t. V, Prawne formy działania administracji*, 373, 357–358.

28 Z. Duniewska et. al, 'Plany, strategie, programy i inne zbliżone formy prawne działania administracji' in Podmioty administracji publicznej i prawne formy ich działania. Studia i materiały z Konferencji Naukowej Poświęconej Jubileuszowi 80-tych urodzin Profesora Eugeniusza Ochendowskiego (Dom Organizatora w Toruniu 2005); H. Maurer, op. cit., 222.

29 M. Stahl, 'Szczególne prawne formy działania administracji', 394–396.

30 M. Chlipala, 'Przyrzeczenie administracyjne w unormowaniach materialnoprawnych' in J. Jagielski, M. Wierzbowski (eds.), Prawo administracyjne dziś i jutro (WolKluw. 2018) 257; J. Łukaszewicz and K. Kłosowska, 'Słowo o przyrzeczeniu administracyjnym' in Jan Boć, Ludmiła Dziewięcka-Bokun (eds.), Umowy w administracji (Kolonia Limited 2008); W. Taras, 'Przyrzeczenie administracyjne' in Marek Mozgawa (ed), Polska lat dziewięćdziesiątych. Przemiany państwa i prawa. Materiały z konferencji, Lublin-Kazimierz 28–30 kwietnia 1997 r. (Wydawnictwo UMCS 1997).

31 M. Stahl, 'Szczególne prawne formy działania administracji', 397.

is emphasised that every statutory empowerment of the administration is at the same time a delegation of competence, authorising decisions. It is considered that the administration is called upon to fill with its legislation and decisions the space falling within the statutory authorisation.[32]

The recognised public-law instrument is the budget adopted by parliament in the form of a budget law. All reforms of the Budget Law have subjected it to major changes (decentralisation, controlling, agreements on budgetary objectives). Parliamentary scrutiny, not only in the form of a motion of no-confidence, parliamentary interpellations and questions, or committees of inquiry, remains an important instrument to ensure the link between parliament and administration. As in the other legal orders discussed here, a phenomenon of recent years is the inclusion of forms of direct democracy in the existing catalogue of parliamentary and administrative activities to revive democratic legitimacy. There is no doubt about the increasing role of consultation, participation in information measures, petitions and new activities such as citizens' panels.[33]

What is the evolution of systematics? Ernst Forsthoff, in presenting a typology of legal forms of administrative action, distinguished unilateral forms and bilateral forms, though not yet named so explicitly. He was the first to distinguish between the enactment of legal norms, an administrative act, enforcement actions and declarations of will occurring in forms like private law but with several administrative-law restrictions. Among the bilateral forms, the author distinguished contracts, agreements and settlements, and other acts that require consensual declarations of will by the participants.[34]

H.G. König, writing about administrative action (das Verwaltungshandeln), distinguished between actions with external effect, directed at independent subjects and those directed at subordinate issues, between a normative act and an administrative act, emphasising the typical administrative act called a general ordinance, i.e., one in which the addressee is a circle of specific subjects, or establishes the public law nature of a thing or how it is used. As a stabilised form, the author presented an administrative contract. He included both special-purpose associations of communes and those which would be referred to as settlements. The author also clearly distinguished forms constituting expressions of public authorities in the external sphere, which do not contain binding regulations – also declarations of knowledge.[35]

The well-known book of Hartmut Maurer divides the legal forms of administrative action into public law and private law forms. In each of these spheres, there are general and abstract and concrete actions. The author distinguishes regulations and statutes and an administrative contract in bilateral actions among external,

32 P. Kirchhof, op. cit.; W. Kahl, 'Verwaltungsrechts in Europa: Grundzüge' in A. von Bogdandy, S. Cassese and P.M. Huber (eds.), *Handbuch Ius Publicum Europaeum, Band V* (C.F. Müller 2014) 127.

33 W. Kahl, op. cit., 132.

34 E. Forsthoff, *Lehrbuch des Verwaltungsrechts*, t. 1 (10th edn, C.H. Beck 1973) 273–284.

35 H.G. König, *System des Verwaltungsrechts* (Carl Heymanns Verlag König 1983) 89–96, 116–118.

abstract-general acts. Unilateral actions include administrative acts and legally significant declarations of will.[36]

As Wolfgang Kahl points out, the concept of legal forms of administrative action is a "central collective concept." According to Mayer's classic formula, legal forms of action are a gateway through which the diverse, amorphous administration activities are passed into the ordered world of law. It is believed that the doctrine of legal forms of administrative action combines the idea of form and the system as typical of continental legal thinking. In legal instruments of administrative action, the doctrine sees an increasing diversification – new forms and new instruments are constantly being formed. On the other hand, despite the diversification, there is a constant assignment of multiple forms to certain basic categories; instruments and mixed forms are multiplying.[37] As Wolfgang Hoffmann-Riem points out, legal forms have an ordering function, serving orientation, and a matrix function for concrete solutions. Gradually, forms were extended to Realakte and ordinary factual actions, the increasing multipolarity of legal relations was considered. A distinction is made between forms of action (Handlungsformen), which are already stylised practices of administrative action, legally defined but not yet "concentrated" in legal form.[38] There has long been a shift from focusing on the normative and administrative act to concentrating on administrative action. The science of legal forms has become more future-oriented and flexible. New areas of administrative activity are theoretically "joined."

Even the administrative act, that most classical, "model" legal form of administrative action, is gradually enriched with new subcategories. The act fully integrated into the categories of the other forms is the administrative contract, described as the form of consensual administrative action. The form, which still seemed unthinkable to Otto Mayer, is now a fully recognised category. It is precisely in the field of the administrative contract that German doctrine has played a pioneering role, paving the way for a kind of international offensive of consensual forms of administrative action. W. Hoffmann-Riem emphasises the still-existing need for better theoretical treatment of consensual and cooperative forms.[39]

The importance of administrative legislation is increasing; statutes play a significant role. They are also more internally differentiated, guaranteeing a proper, although supervision-limited, freedom of action for the self-government administration.[40] In the internal sphere of public administration, administrative regulations of an abstract and general nature occupy a central place. As internal law, they

36 H. Maurer and Ch. Waldhoff, *Allgemeines Verwaltungsrecht* (20th edn, C. H. Beck 2020).

37 W.Kahl, op. cit., 118–119.

38 W. Hoffmann-Riem, 'Rechtsformen, Handlungsformen, Bewirkungsformen' in W. Hoffmann-Riem, E. Schmidt-Aßmann and A. Voßkuhle (eds.), *Grundlagen des Verwaltungsrechts, Band II* (C.H. Beck 2012) 952.

39 Ibid., 1004–1006.

40 F. Ossenbühl, 'Autonome Rechtsetzung der Verwaltung' in J. Isensee, P. Kirchhof (eds.), *Handbuch des Staatsrechts, Band V: Rechtsquellen, Organisation, Finanzen* (3rd edn, C.F. Müller 2007) 306 et seq.

cannot directly regulate the rights and obligations of citizens; however, the externalisation of internal regulations on the one hand and their documented internal operation as flexible instruments of action on the other has long been recognised.

As pointed out in the German theory, the importance of the plan as an instrument of action has increased considerably under the influence of Europeanisation. It appears, as Kahl emphasises, "in the garments of all classical forms of action,"[41] so it can be an Act, a Regulation, a Statute, but also an administrative act or an administrative rule (the coexistence of analytical, predictive and design elements).

The other instruments already recognised are factual administrative actions. Informal administrative actions had their heyday in doctrine when they were seen as a hope to de-bureaucratisation. Still, gradually disappointment came due to their lack of transparency and threat to stability for the party to the proceedings. Krystian Ziemski, comparing the systematics of Polish and German legal forms of administrative action, emphasises the greater pragmatism and flexibility of the German doctrine.[42] With the broadly accepted new science of administrative law, forms of action and influence are more precisely distinguished from established legal forms.[43]

3.4 Italian doctrine

As pointed out by S. Cassese,[44] the administration activity can be considered in dynamic terms, examining how this activity is carried out. Cassese stressed that administrative functions are carried out by issuing legal norms, authorisation, contracting and providing pensions or medical care. The specific content of administrative functions can, according to the author, take various legal forms. We find here declarations of will, knowledge, judgments as well as material acts. Cassese emphasises the importance of the silence of public administration. The central place among the legal forms of unilateral character is still occupied by administrative acts using which the administration executes the powers granted to it to realise the public interest, which produces legal effects for other subjects. An administrative act should be distinguished from other acts which have an auxiliary function, such as opinions, proposals, requests for information.

In more recent Italian doctrine,[45] administrative acts are defined by statutory law and subject to a specific legal regime. They are universally binding and unilateral acts and may be binding or based on administrative discretion. The exercise of public authority may imply determining a specific legal position in a single case or universally binding on indefinite entities. Italian law fully recognises administrative action in private law forms, including through a civil law contract.

41 W. Kahl, op. cit., 122.
42 K. Ziemski, *Indywidualny akt…*, 93.
43 W. Hoffmann-Riem, op. cit., 949.
44 S. Cassese, Istituzioni di diritto amministrativo (5th edn, Giuffre Editiore 2015) 283–285.
45 D. de Pretis, 'Grundzüge des Verwaltungsrechts in gemeineuropäischer Perspektive: Italien' in A. von Bogdandy, S. Cassese and P.M. Huber (eds.), *Handbuch Ius Publicum Europaeum, Band V* (C.F. Müller 2014) 397.

Crucial among public law instruments is the concept of an administrative act (atto amministrativo). The idea of an administrative act has been developed, particularly in case law. Administrative acts also include a town planning act, while consent or taking a position belongs to the different category of ordinary, simple acts (mero atto).[46]

Italian law fully recognises administrative action in private law forms, including a civil law contract.[47]

The basic principles and the nature of an administrative act are described similarly to Polish and German administrative law doctrines. The category of administrative discretion, the control of the limits of administrative discretion and its abuse also play a similarly important role in this context.

Another important concept among the legal forms of administrative action is the public law contract. It has been discussed and was finally formalised in the Code of Administrative Procedure in 1990.[48] It should also be mentioned that the Italian doctrine devotes much attention to regulatory acts of a general and abstract character, which, being normative acts, are issued by the public administration. It is emphasised that, unlike in administrative acts, there is no need to formulate a statement of reasons, even though it is an instrument of public administration.

As Paolo Tanda writes,

> It should emphasize that this consensual activity of the public administration can never lead to a free activity as to its purpose or cause (basis), in the sense that it can never be freed from its institutional function of realizing the collective interest.[49]

An important part of the legal forms of action of the administration are contracts related to public procurement; due to their legal nature, the administration's action in concluding a contract is treated as an act of public authority.

Among the new forms of administrative action, legal institutions for public consultation and other forms of participation should be mentioned.[50] Legal forms of access to public information have developed with a similar delay as in Poland. The problems of moving away from confidentiality of administrative actions are also similar.

Important for the activities that link parliament and public administration are the instruments that enable the parliaments to exercise control over the administration even during the pandemic.[51] On the other hand, a special feature of Italian

46 Ibid., 398.

47 P. Tanda, *Manuale di Diritto Amministrativo I* (Edicusano 2019) 13–15.

48 G. Falcon, Le convenzioni pubblicistiche. Ammissibilità e caratteri (Giuffrè Editore 1984).

49 P. Tanda, op. cit., 14–15.

50 D. de Pretis, op. cit., 412–413.

51 F. Longchamps de Bérier, *Współczesne kierunki w nauce prawa administracyjnego na Zachodzie Europy* (Kolonia Limited 2001) 178; V. Boehme-Neßler, 'Das Parlament in der Pandemie – Zum Demokratiegrundsatz am Beispiel von § 28a InfSchG' (2021) 6 DÖV 243 et seq.

administrative law is the numerous laws stipulating that the administration report regularly to parliament; there are already hundreds of such laws.

In the Italian case, the steady growth of the role of the public administration is diagnosed, freeing itself from the political influence of the parliament and the political direction of the government. There is a loosening of the relationship between the administration seen separately from government and parliament. The parliament's new information and inquiry instruments do not change this situation. However, the parliament is trying to compensate for the diminution of its role by influencing the appointment of the heads of independent administrative units (the data protection commissioner but also the telecommunications, gas and electricity authorities). On the one hand, the independent regulators report to the parliament, while on the other, they can make proposals, information and recommendations to both chambers. The concern to preserve the parliament's position, especially in times of crisis, is expressed in both the German and Italian doctrines and enriched by proposals for solutions.[52]

3.5 Conclusions

The public administration is constantly enriching its forms of action. Sometimes those forms with which high hopes were placed have not lived up to expectations regarding their diffusion into substantive law. Others, such as information activities, have developed in a way that bursts the framework of the traditional catalogue of legal forms of administrative action. As Lothar Michael[53] points out, the answer to the increasing difficulty of adapting complex administrative action to the performance of tasks under conditions of uncertainty is the use of mixed forms (Verwaltungs-mix) of legal administrative action and even factual actions (Realakte), which go beyond the known forms of combining instruments of administrative action and allow for an effective reduction of complexity of action. While the law, as Jan Boć points out, determines the main paths and basic divisions, the role of doctrine in the field of research on legal forms of action is a constant theoretical search, fulfilling an ordering function. Despite all the differences between the three legal orders, the basic notions are similar in meaning. The studies show public law instruments remaining under pressure from the convergence of two powerful factors: the digital transformation of the state and the economy and a deep crisis related to the COVID-19 pandemic, which challenges the entire public administration with modernising its forms of action and instruments of classical regulation, increasing flexibility of action and switching not only the administration providing services to digital tracks.

52 H. Dreier, 'Rechtsstaat, Föderalismus und Demokratie in der Corona-Pandemie' (2021) 6 DÖV 229 et seq.; Ch. Gusy, op. cit., DÖV 764 et seq.

53 L. Michael, 'Formen- und Instrumentenmix' in W. Hoffmann-Riem, E. Schmidt-Aßmann and A. Voßkuhle (eds.), *Grundlagen des Verwaltungsrechts, Band II*, 1648 et seq.

Works cited

Adamczyk, A., *Publicznoprawne formy działania administracji. Teoria i praktyka* (Difin, Warsaw 2013).

Banasiński, C., Szafrański, D., and Wiktorowska, A., 'Zaświadczenie jako warunek złożenia wniosku o podjęcie działalności koncesjonowanej' (1996) 7 Monitor Prawniczy.

Boć, J., and Dziewięcka-Bokun, L. (eds.), *Umowy w administracji* (Kolonia Limited 2008).

Boehme-Neßler, V., 'Das Parlament in der Pandemie – Zum Demokratiegrundsatz am Beispiel von § 28a InfSchG' (2021) 6 DÖV 243–251.

Bogdandy, A von, Cassese, S., and Huber Peter, M. (eds.), *Handbuch Ius Publicum Europaeum, Band V* (C.F. Müller 2014).

Borkowski, J., *Decyzja administracyjna* (Wydawnictwo Naukowe PWN 1970).

Cassese, S., *Istituzioni di diritto amministrativo* (5th edn, Giuffre Editiore 2015).

Chróścielewski, W., *Akt administracyjny generalny* (Wydawnictwo Uniwersytetu Łódzkiego, Lódź 1994).

Cieślik, Z., *Umowa administracyjna w państwie prawa* (Zakamycze, Kraków 2004).

Dreier, H., 'Rechtsstaat, Föderalismus und Demokratie in der Corona-Pandemie' (2021) 6 DÖV 229–243.

Falcon, G., *Le convenzioni pubblicistiche. Ammissibilità e caratteri* (Giuffrè Editore 1984).

Forsthoff, E., *Lehrbuch des Verwaltungsrechts, t. 1* (10th edn, C.H. Beck 1973).

Hauser, R., Niewiadomski, Z., and Wróbel, A. (eds.), *System prawa administracyjnego, t. V, Prawne formy działania administracji* (C.H. Beck, Warsaw 2013).

Hoffmann-Riem, W., Schmidt-Aßmann, E., and Voßkuhle, A. (eds.), *Grundlagen des Verwaltungsrechts, Band II* (C.H. Beck 2012).

Isensee, J., and Kirchhof, P. (eds.), *Handbuch des Staatsrechts, Band V: Rechtsquellen, Organisation, Finanzen* (3rd edn, C.F. Müller 2007).

Jagielski, J., and Wierzbowski, M. (eds.), *Prawo administracyjne dziś i jutro* (WolKluw. Polska 2018).

Jaworski Leopold, W., *Nauka prawa administracyjnego: zagadnienia ogólne* (Instytut Wydawniczy Bibljoteka Polska 1924).

Kasznica, S., *Polskie prawo administracyjne* (Księgarnia Akademicka 1946).

Klat-Wertelecka, L., *Zaświadczenie w prawie administracyjnym* (Difin 2001).

Kmieciak, Z., *Instytucja zaświadczenia w prawie administracyjnym* (Wydawnictwo Uniwersytetu Marii Curie-Skłodowskiej 2002).

König, H.-G., *System des Verwaltungsrechts* (Carl Heymanns Verlag König 1983).

Kumaniecki Władysław, K., *Akt administracyjny* (Towarzystwo Biblioteki Słuchaczów Prawa Uniwersytetu Jagiellońskiego 1936).

Lang, J., 'Akty potwierdzające w administracji państwowej' (1990) 18 Studia Iuridica.

Longchamps de Bérier, F., *Współczesne kierunki w nauce prawa administracyjnego na Zachodzie Europy* (Kolonia Limited 2001).

Łukasiewicz, J. (ed.), *Nauka administracji wobec wyzwań współczesnego państwa prawa: międzynarodowa konferencja naukowa* (Towarzystwo Naukowe Organizacji i Kierownictwa 2002).

Maurer, H., and Waldhoff, Ch, *Allgemeines Verwaltungsrecht* (20th edn, C. H. Beck 2020).

Maurer, H., *Ogólne prawo administracyjne* (Kolonia Limited 2003).

Mozgawa, M. (ed.), *Polska lat dziewięćdziesiątych. Przemiany państwa i prawa. Materiały z konferencji, Lublin-Kazimierz 28–30 kwietnia 1997 r.* (Wydawnictwo UMCS 1997).

Niewiadomski, Z. (ed.), *Prawo administracyjne* (Wydawnictwo Prawnicze LexisNexis 2013).

Podmioty administracji publicznej i prawne formy ich działania. Studia i materiały z Konferencji Naukowej Poświęconej Jubileuszowi 80-tych urodzin Profesora Eugeniusza Ochendowskiego (Dom Organizatora w Toruniu, Toruń 2005).

Rabska, T., and Łętowski, J. (eds.), *System prawa administracyjnego, t. III* (Ossolineum 1978).

Schmidt-Aßmann, E., *Verwaltungsrechtliche Dogmatik: Eine Zwischenbilanz zu Entwicklung, Reform und künftigen Aufgaben: Eine Zwischenbilanz Zu Entwicklung, Reform Und Kunftigen Aufgaben* (J.C.B. Mohr 2013).

Stahl, M. (ed.), *Prawo administracyjne. Pojęcia, instytucje, zasady w teorii i orzecznictwie* (5th edn, WolKluw. 2016).

Starościak, J., *Prawo administracyjne* (Państwowe Wydawnictwo Naukowe 1977).

Tanda, P., *Manuale di Diritto Amministrativo I* (Edicusano 2019).

Ura, E., and Ura, E., *Prawo administracyjne* (8th edn, Wydawnictwo Prawnicze LexisNexis, Warsaw 2009).

Wierzbowski, M. (ed.), *Prawo administracyjne* (7th edn, Wydawnictwo Prawnicze LexisNexis, Warsaw 2007).

Wierzbowski, M., and Jagielski, J. (eds.), *Prawo administracyjne* (WolKluw., Warsaw 2019).

Ziemski, K., *Indywidualny akt administracyjny jako forma prawna działania administracji* (Wydawnictwo Naukowe UAM, Poznań 2005).

II

European and National Public Law Instruments and Public Instruments of Digital Transformation

1 The Digital Transformation of the European Union in Times of Pandemic

Selected Issues of Public Law

Ziemowit Cieślik

1.1 Introduction

The COVID-19 pandemic represents an unprecedented challenge in the history of the EU. In mid-March 2020 the WHO identified Europe as one of the epicentres of the spread of the disease.[1] Although the threat is inherently transboundary, the main burden of fighting the disease lies with Member States. The EU is committed to fighting the pandemic only within the limits of its Treaty competences, and the measures of the EC, which are implemented as part of the common European response to the pandemic, i.e., a series of legal Acts and non-binding regulatory documents that cover a number of areas of EU activity, including the labour market and the economy, public health, travel and transport, research and crisis management and solidarity, are currently of fundamental importance. The present study is devoted to anti-crisis measures taken by the EU in a particular area of its activity – digital technologies. The EU response to the pandemic, which is primarily determined by the objectives of human health protection, clashes in this respect with the assumptions of the EU Digital Strategy, i.e., a series of EU actions that respond to the rapidly progressing digital transition of the internal market. The current EU regulatory policy on digital technologies must take both perspectives into account.

1.2 EU Digital Strategy

The regulatory and administrative actions of the EU relating to the digital transition are undertaken as part of the EU's Digital Strategy, which was formally launched by the EC on 19 February 2020.[2] This strategy includes the Commission's key

1 <https://www.euro.who.int/en/health-topics/health-emergencies/coronavirus-covid-19/novel-coronavirus-2019-ncov> (1.01.2022).

2 Shaping Europe`s Digital Future <https://ec.europa.eu/info/sites/info/files/communication-shaping-europes-digital-future-feb2020_en_4.pdf> (1.01.2022); K. Dumancic, 'The EU Regulatory Activities in the Area of Digital Platforms and Services Provision' [2021] 5 (1) EU and Comparative Law Issues and Challenges 689–690.

DOI: 10.4324/9781003263968-7

plans to respond to the ever-increasing impact of digital technologies on society. These plans involve the use of the EU's diverse competences, which are scattered across a number of EU policies, and the use of regulatory measures of different legal nature.[3] The adoption of the EU Digital Strategy was announced by Ursula von der Leyen in her political guidelines for the next Commission's term of office (2019–2024) (priority: A Europe fit for the digital age),[4] and its programme builds on the political principles of the institution's previous agenda under the leadership of Jean-Claude Juncker, which were enshrined in binding EU legislation on, inter alia, the free flow of non-personal data,[5] cyber security[6] and open data and the re-use of public sector information,[7] and, in parallel to this legislation, in the Artificial Intelligence Strategy of 25 April 2018.[8] The Commission will also consider the coordinated plan, agreed with Member States on 7 December 2018,[9] as well as the ethical guidelines on trustworthy artificial intelligence presented by the High-Level Expert Group on Artificial Intelligence in April 2019.[10] In line with the declarations of its creators, the EU's Digital Strategy builds on the principles on which the previous Commission policy was based.[11] As it stands at present, it finds its basic formulation in the Communications "Shaping Europe's digital future," "A European Data Strategy"[12] and "Digital Compass for 2030: the European way in the digital decade."[13] In addition, on the same day as the first two Communications, the Commission published a White Paper on Artificial Intelligence.[14] In its most general form, the EU's Digital Strategy is included in Work Programme 2020–2021: Data, information, and knowledge management at the EC,[15] and in Work Programme 2022: Making Europe stronger together.[16]

The current approach of the EU to the digital transition is based on three main pillars, which set out the main objectives of the planned actions: "Technology that works for people," "A fair and competitive digital economy" and "Open, democratic and sustainable society." Within each of these strategic objectives,

3 D. Zetzche, D. Arner, R. Buckley and R.H. Weber, 'The Evolution and Future of Data-Driven Finance in the EU' [2020] 57 (2) Common Market Law Review 340–344.

4 EC, 'A Union that strives for more. My agenda for Europe. By candidate for President of the European Commission Ursula von der Leyen, Political Guidelines for the Next European Commission 2019-2024' 13–14.

5 Regulation (EU) 2018/1807.

6 Directive (EU) 2016/1148.

7 Directive 2019/1024.

8 COM(2018) 237 final.

9 COM(2018) 795 final.

10 EC, Independent High-Level Expert Group on Artificial Intelligence set up by the European Commission <https://european-union.europa.eu/priorities-and-actions/common-eu-response-covid-19_en> (1.01.2022).

11 <https://ec.europa.eu/info/strategy/priorities-2019-2024/europe-fit-digital-age_en> (1.01.2022).

12 COM(2020) 66 final.

13 COM(2021) 118 final.

14 COM(2020) 65 final.

15 <https://ec.europa.eu/info/sites/info/files/imsb_factsheet_wp_2020-21_8-web.pdf> (1.01.2022).

16 COM(2021) 645 final.

individual sub-actions have been grouped together and planned in a timetable covering the next five years, as reflected in the plans for the adoption of specific (and legally distinct) Acts by the EU institutions. The overall objective of the strategy is to ensure that the digital solutions currently and future generations of EU society are rooted in common European values.[17] The strategy also states that, in view of the challenges of digital transition today, it is necessary to guarantee European technological sovereignty to protect Europe's digital infrastructure and communication networks and to reduce dependence on other parts of the world in this respect. These general principles are an expression of the EC's political ambition to make the EU a strong, independent player in the field of digital transition and to have a real influence on the directions of the transition on a global scale.[18] The outlined approach is further developed and reinforced in – already referring explicitly to pandemic challenges at many points – the "Digital Compass for 2030." In the light of this Communication, EU digital transformation policy is to focus on four directions: educating the public and digital professionals, developing secure, efficient and sustainable digital infrastructures, digital transformation of businesses and digitisation of public services.[19] According to the EU strategy, the objectives are to be implemented primarily by means of legislative, binding measures. Similarly, the digital policy agenda outlined in the "Digital Compass" is intended to be binding.[20]

1.3 Digital technologies: the EU response to a pandemic

The EU Digital Strategy was formulated on the eve of a pandemic outbreak. The first two EC documents cited above, which set out the objectives of this policy agenda, do not contain any specific reference to the challenges involved in combatting and preventing the spread of COVID-19. A common European response to the pandemic, the first major chord of which was the "Coronavirus Response Investment Initiative,"[21] followed immediately after the announcement of the EU Digital Strategy and included measures that fall within its scope.[22] According to the Commission's declarations, "in the face of the coronavirus crisis, this strategy gains renewed importance."[23] Responding to the pandemic threat, the Commission has taken several actions in different areas of its digital activities. These actions, as well as the EU Digital Strategy itself, are supported by the different competences

17 H-W. Micklitz, 'The COVID-19 Thread: An Opportunity to Rethink the European Economic Constitution and European Private Law' [2020] 11 European Journal of Risk Regulation 254.

18 EC (n 4) 3.

19 COM(2021) 118 final.

20 COM(2021) 118 final 17; Cf. COM(2021) 574 final.

21 COM(2020) 143; Regulation (EU) 2020/460.

22 A.M. Pacces and M. Weimer, 'From Diversity to Coordination: A European Approach to COVID-19' [2020] 11 European Journal of Risk Regulation 283–287.

23 <https://ec.europa.eu/info/live-work-travel-eu/health/coronavirus-response/digital_en> (1.01.2022).

of the EU and have a different legal nature. They focus on areas identified by the Commission: "Innovative solutions," "National contact tracing and warning apps," "Artificial intelligence," "European supercomputers fighting the coronavirus," "Coronavirus response – data from space," "Networks and connectivity," "Online platforms fighting disinformation," "Staying safe online," "Upskilling for life after a pandemic" and "Online learning."[24]

The most advanced measures, also in legislative terms, were taken in the areas of "Innovative solutions" and "National contact tracing and warning apps." Already by the first phase of the pandemic, in mid-2020, application solutions were introduced for contact tracing and warning against contact with COVID-19 positive persons. Such applications are installed on phones by many users and process sensitive data about their health. The EU has not opted for centralised solutions to this extent (although it encourages Member States to work on them), its regulatory effort has been focused on ensuring that the use of any such applications is carried out in compliance with data security and EU fundamental rights, including the right to privacy and personal data protection.[25] As the originally very strict restrictions on freedom of movement within the EU are now gradually being lifted, the problem of interoperability of applications running in different EU Member States and security of data exchange between these applications also arises.[26] The EC has taken up these challenges by adopting numerous regulatory Acts.

The Commission Recommendation (EU) 2020/518 of 8 April 2020 on a common Union toolbox for the use of technology and data to combat and exit from the COVID-19 crisis, in particular concerning mobile applications and the use of anonymised mobility data, was the first to be issued.[27] This Recommendation has formed the basis for the development by Member States, through a voluntary network with the support of the Commission (eHealth Network),[28] of an EU set of guidelines on the use of mobile applications for contact tracing and alert generation.[29] A little later, on 13 May 2020, guidelines on the interoperability of contact tracing applications and other specific documents and instructions were adopted, which also involved arrangements between the Commission and Member States.[30] In addition, acting alone this time, the Commission adopted on 17 April 2020 the

24 Ibid.

25 C. Cattuto and A. Spina, 'The Institutionalisation of Digital Public Health: Lessons Learned from the COVID-19 App.' [2020] 11 European Journal of Risk Regulation 231; Cf. H. van Kolfschooten and A. de Ruijter, 'COVID-19 and privacy in the European Union: A legal perspective on contact tracing' [2020] 41 Contemporary Security Policy 478–491.

26 Ch. Etteldorf, 'EU Member State Data Protection Authorities Deal with Covid-19: An Overview' [2020] 6 (2) European Data Protection Law Review 266.

27 C(2020) 2296 final 7.

28 Art. 14 of Directive 2011/24/EU.

29 Mobile applications to support contact tracing in the EU's fight against COVID-19. Common EU Toolbox for Member States, Brussels, 15.04.2020.

30 Interoperability guidelines for approved contact tracing mobile applications in the EU, Brussels, 13.05.2020; Guidelines to the EU Member States and the European Commission on Interoperabil-

Guidelines for applications supporting the fight against the COVID-19 pandemic with regard to data protection[31] and Implementing Decision (EU) 2020/1023 of 15 July 2020 as regards the cross-border exchange of data between national contact tracing and warning mobile applications with regard to combatting the COVID-19 pandemic.

In the context of the Commission's activities on data processing in a pandemic,[32] it is also worth mentioning the Declaration of 19 March 2020 on the processing of personal data[33] and the Guidelines of 21 April 2020 on the use of location data and contact tracing tools in the context of the COVID-19 pandemic,[34] which were presented by the European Data Protection Board, an independent body of the EU composed of representatives of national data protection authorities and the European Data Protection Supervisor.[35]

The eHealth Network became the forum where – in another year of the pandemic – solutions were developed to facilitate the exercise of the Treaty freedom of movement under pandemic conditions by enabling the confirmation of COVID-19 status, accepted throughout the EU. This solution, the EU digital COVID-19 certificate, was implemented on 1 July 2021 and is recognised by the EC itself as an essential element of the EU pandemic response and, in terms of policy success, an "international benchmark and global standard."[36] The operation of the COVID-19 certificate is based on two EU legislative Acts: the Regulations of the European Parliament and of the Council of 14 June 2021, the first of which sets out a common framework for the issuance, verification and recognition of interoperable certificates of vaccination, test result or recovery in relation to COVID-19 to facilitate the free movement of Union citizens and their family members during a pandemic[37] and the second extends the framework of the COVID-19 Certificate to third-country nationals legally residing or living in the EU.[38] The implementation of these regulations crowned a number of earlier regulatory actions taken in the EU since the beginning of the pandemic, which aimed to coordinate Member States' approaches to restrictions on movement within the EU.[39] In addition to their primary purpose of providing a framework for the issuance, verification and recognition of COVID-19 certificates, they are also intended to facilitate the

ity specifications for cross-border transmission chains between approved apps Detailed interoperability elements between COVID+ Keys driven solutions, eHealth Network, Brussels, 16.06.2020.

31 C(2020) 2523 final.

32 Etteldorf (n 29) 268–269.

33 Statement on the processing of personal data in the context of the COVID-19 outbreak, adopted on 19.03.2020.

34 Guidelines 04/2020 on the use of location data and contact tracing tools in the context of the COVID-19 outbreak, Adopted on 21.04.2020.

35 Articles 68 et seq. of Regulation (EU) 2016/679.

36 COM(2021) 649; Cf. Oskar Gstrein, 'The EU Digital COVID Certificate: A Preliminary Data Protection Impact Assessment' [2021] 12 EJRR 370–373.

37 Regulation (EU) 2021/953.

38 Regulation (EU) 2021/954.

39 COM(2021) 130, p. 1; Cf. Gstrein (n 36) 373.

gradual lifting of free movement restrictions imposed by Member States in a coordinated manner and to provide a legal basis for the processing of personal data necessary for the issuance of such certificates in full compliance with EU law. The COVID-19 certificates referred to in these regulations are issued by EU Member States in paper or digital form or in both forms.

The regulatory measures that the EC and other EU bodies are taking as part of the EU's Digital Strategy in response to the pandemic are accompanied by several factual actions. In the other areas of activity identified by the Commission, apart from "Data, supercomputers and artificial intelligence," such activities even dominate. In particular, the Commission declares that, to combat the pandemic, it will use, in cooperation with the European Space Agency, the EU space programme, with the Galileo positioning[40] and earth observation systems developed under the Copernicus programme ("Data from space").[41] Moreover, the Commission calls also for the management of online film services, telecommunication operators and users to take action to reduce the network load and enable everyone to use the Internet ("Networks and connectivity")[42] as well as pursuing an active policy of promoting reliable sources and verifying false or misleading content that is available on the network ("Online platforms fighting disinformation").[43] Ensuring network security is another major challenge. Specific measures are taken to address the risks that affect children and Internet fraud ("Staying safe online").[44] Action to facilitate the use of online resources is a separate thread. To this end, the Commission has published guidelines on digital competence ("Upskilling for life after a pandemic") and copious educational material that can be used during a pandemic ("Online learning").[45] These publications are addressed to teachers and pupils, as well as to those in education, research and training.

1.4 Implementation of the EU regulatory programme in Poland

The basic means of regulatory counteraction to the effects of the COVID-19 pandemic in Poland were legal Acts included in successive regulatory packages, the so-called anti-crisis shields.[46] For the most part, these packages consist of numerous amendments to laws regulating various areas of social life and the economy.

40 <https://www.gsa.europa.eu/GNSS4Crisis#Tracking> (1.01.2022).

41 <https://race.esa.int> (1.01.2022).

42 Joint Statement from the Commission and the Body of European Regulators for Electronic Communications (BEREC) on coping with the increased demand for network connectivity due to the Covid-19 pandemic. See Regulation (EU) 2018/1971.

43 JOIN(2020) 8 final; COM(2018) 236 final.

44 <https://www.europol.europa.eu/activities-services/staying-safe-during-covid-19-what-you-need-to-know> (1.01.2022); Cf. Flavia Durach, Alina Bargaoanu and Cătălina Nastasiu, 'Tackling Disinformation: EU Regulation of the Digital Space' [2020] 20 Romanian Journal of European Affairs 14-15; Cf. Editorial comments, [2020] 57 (2) Common Market Law Review 328–329.

45 EC, 'DigComp at Work Implementation Guide (Luxembourg 2020).

46 <https://www.gov.pl/web/tarczaantykryzysowa> (1.01.2022).

A specific regulation concerning counteracting the COVID-19 pandemic is contained in the COVID-19 Act. Digital solutions are devoted to some provisions of the second edition of the shield. The Act of 3 April 2020[47] provides, in particular, for the abolition of fees for the use by the subscriber of telecommunications services from public websites containing information on the pandemic (Art. 35), the upgrading of the rank of a government official who may become a plenipotentiary of the Council of Ministers for the provision of cyber security (Art. 61), faster than originally assumed launching of the Broadband Fund in order to co-finance and develop the telecommunications network and extend access to a high speed connection (Art. 83), providing schools with equipment necessary to teach remotely (Art. 58) and simplification of some administrative activities and postal services through the introduction of IT solutions (Arts. 37–39, 63, 73, point 48). Procedural facilitation by replacing the requirement of written form for legal actions taken by means of digital solutions is provided for in the COVID-19 Act (e.g., Art. 11f, Art. 31zy,[15] Art. 31 zze). In the other laws that make up the successive editions of the anti-crisis package, issues concerning technology hardly appear. In general, based on these laws, the EU regulatory programme in the field of digitisation does not play a major role, giving way decisively to instruments of financial support for victims of the pandemic and organisational transformations, especially in the health care sector, which are intended to help limit its negative consequences.[48] Also, those statutory provisions that refer to digital technologies are not so much a response to a programme that has been formulated by the EU as an expression of national regulatory approaches. In the most general sense, the national measures that the EU is encouraging as part of its digital agenda only include Internet access facilities and support mechanisms for remote learning. From a formal point of view, the laws defining the anti-crisis framework do not constitute laws implementing EU law (see Art. 95a para. 1 and para. 2 of the Resolution of the Sejm of 30 July 1992).[49]

In contrast to the regulatory activities, the organisational and factual actions undertaken by the Polish public administration are much more relevant to the objectives of the EU Digital Strategy. Poland was one of the first EU Member States to make a mobile application for tracking infections available to all interested parties free of charge. The Polish application is called ProtGO Safe (STOP COVID)[50] and in its first version was made public on 20 April 2020.[51] In accordance with the statement of the Ministry of Digitization, this application was

47 JoL 2020 item 569.

48 K. Renaud, C. Orgeron, M. Warkentin and P. E. French, 'Cyber Security Responsibilization: An Evaluation of the Intervention Approaches Adopted by the Five Eyes Countries and China' [2020] 80 Public Administration Review 577–589.

49 M.P. of 2020, item 476 with amendments.

50 <https://www.gov.pl/web/protegosafe> (1.01.2022).

51 <https://www.gov.pl/web/cyfryzacja/pokonajmy-razem-koronawirusa--poznaj-protego-safe> (1.01.2022).

developed taking into account the EU data processing security requirements.[52] Moreover, Poland is an active participant in the work of the eHealth network, which is to enable the interoperability of applications of this type throughout the EU.[53] The EU digital certificate COVID-19 has been integrated into the public mobile application mObywatel (mCitizen).[54] The public administration is also actively involved in activities aimed at limiting data or money fraud under the guise of fighting a pandemic[55] and supporting the process of remote learning.[56] Finally, it is worth noting that within the structure of government administration there is a government plenipotentiary for cyber security and this function is currently performed by a member of the Council of Ministers – the minister in charge of informatisation (Art. 61 of the Act of 5 July 2018).[57] The EU Digital Strategy is a permanent – and clear – context for the activities of the Polish public administration, which are undertaken in the era of a pandemic.

1.5 Form of measures taken by the EU: legal nature and legal basis

The EU actions that are taken in relation to digital technologies in a pandemic are predominantly factual or informal in nature. The binding Acts in this regard are Regulations (EU) 2021/953 and 2021/954, concerning EU COVID-19 digital certificates, and Commission Implementing Decision (EU) 2020/1023, issued in July 2020. Commission Recommendation (EU) 2020/518 is a non-binding Act within the meaning of the fifth para. of Art. 288 TEU. The Commission guidelines and communications, both issued alone and in collaboration with Member States' representatives on the eHealth Network, are of a similar nature. Due to the dispositive nature of some of their provisions, such Acts are classified by doctrine as EU soft law.[58]

The basic criterion for assessing the legality of the EC's actions is determined by their legal basis, resulting from binding EU law. The EU COVID-19 Digital Certificate Regulations are based on Art. 21(2) TFEU and Art. 77(2)(c) TFEU respectively. The first of these provisions concerns EU citizens and allows for the issuance of rules facilitating the exercise by such citizens of the Treaty freedom to move and reside freely within the EU. The second provision concerns EU border control policy and provides the basis for adopting measures concerning the

52 <https://www.gov.pl/web/cyfryzacja/protego-safe-juz-dla-wszystkich> (1.01.2022).

53 <https://www.gov.pl/web/cyfryzacja/z-protego-safe-bezpiecznie-po-unii-europejskiej> (1.01.2022).

54 <https://www.gov.pl/web/mobywatel> (1.01.2022).

55 <https://www.gov.pl/web/cyfryzacja/koronawirus--oszusci-do-blokady> (1.01.2022).

56 <https://www.gov.pl/web/zdalnelekcje> (1.01.2022).

57 JoL item 1560 with amendments.

58 L. Senden, 'Soft Law in European Community Law' (Bloomsbury Publishing 2004) 123–138; M. Ruffert in Ch. Calliess and M. Ruffert (eds.), 'EUV/AEUV Das Verfassungsrecht der Europäischen Union mit Europäischer Grundrechtecharta' (Beck 2011) 2479.

conditions of free movement of third-country nationals, in the short term, within the EU. Both involve the adoption of EU legislative Acts by the Council and the European Parliament. The basis for the Commission Implementing Decision (EU) 2020/1023 is set out in Art. 14(3) of Directive 2011/24/EU. This Decision amends (based on the same provision) Commission Implementing Decision (EU) 2019/1765, which lays down rules for the establishment, management and functioning of a network of national authorities responsible for eHealth. The EU competence on which all these Acts are based falls within the field of European activities for the protection and improvement of human health. In this area, the EU has limited[59] competence to support, coordinate and supplement the actions of the Member States (Art. 6(a) TFEU).[60] It is worth noting that Directive 2011/24/EU is based on Arts. 114 and 168 TFEU. The former empowers EU legislation that establishes measures for the approximation of the laws, regulations and administrative provisions of the Member States for the establishment and functioning of the internal market, the latter including incentive measures to protect and improve human health, to combat cross-border health threats, and measures for monitoring, early warning of and combatting serious cross-border threats to health. Non-binding Acts, including recommendations, guidelines and communications from the Commission, are issued within the limits of EU competence, which are exercised by its bodies.[61]

The specific legal basis and modalities of the law-making procedure refer to the guidelines which are issued with the participation of the EC in the framework of the eHealth Network. They are laid down in Directive 2011/24/EU and Commission Implementing Decision (EU) 2019/1765. The Implementing Decision, in its current version, establishes, inter alia, the detailed basis for activities that may be undertaken by this network. The Network's activities are intended to serve the objectives set out in Art. 14(2) in conjunction with para 1 of this Article. The Network, in particular, provides guidance to Member States and facilitates the exchange of good practice in areas such as the development of various digital health services, including telemedicine or new technologies in the area of large data collections and artificial intelligence, supports for health promotion, disease

59 A. Alemanno, 'The European Response to COVID-19: From Regulatory Emulation to Regulatory Coordination?' [2020] 11 European Journal of Risk Regulation 307; Pacces & Weimer (n 22) 286; K. Kowalik-Bańczyk, 'Kompetencje Unii Europejskiej wobec epidemii COVID-19' [2020] 5 Europejski Przegląd Sądowy 4–11; M. Kożuch, 'Stosowanie środków doraźnych związanych ze zwalczaniem koronawirusa SARS-nCoV-2 przez Unię Europejską' [2020] 5 Europejski Przegląd Sądowy 12–19.

60 D. Townend, R. van de Pas, L. Bongers et al., 'What is the role of the European Union in the COVID-19 Pandemic?' [2020] 39 Med Law 252–253; K.P. Purnhagen, A. de Ruijter, M.L. Flear, T. K. Hervey, A. Herwig, 'More Competences than You Knew? The Web of Health Competence for European Union Action in Response to the COVID-19 Outbreak' [2020] 11 European Journal of Risk Regulation 297–306; M.Malczewska, 'Unia Europejska wobec pandemii SARS-CoV-2. Inicjatywy związane z ochroną zdrowia publicznego' [2020] 6 Europejski Przegląd Sądowy 4–19.

61 H.C.H. Hofmann, G.C. Rowe and A.H. Türk, 'Administrative Law and Policy of the European Union' (OUP 2011) 569.

prevention and improvement of healthcare services through better use of health data and improvement of the digital skills of patients and health professionals, as well as the exchange of health data between Member States and enabling citizens to access and exchange their own health data (Art. 4(1)(b)–(d) of Commission Implementing Decision (EU) 2019/1765).

Member State authorities are responsible for eHealth and have been designated by the participating Member States take part in the work of the network as members. Pursuant to Art. 14(1) of Directive 2011/24/EU participation in the network is not compulsory: Member States inform the Commission of decisions to participate and withdraw from the network (Art. 3 of Commission Implementing Decision (EU) 2019/1765). The Commission participates in the work of the network and publishes the results thereof. The legal basis and the law-making procedure applicable for the guidelines issued in the framework of the eHealth Network are also provided for in Commission Recommendation (EU) 2020/518. This Act sets out non-binding instructions which are addressed to the participating Member States. According to its provisions, the eHealth Network should, in view of its constituent entities and its competences, be the main forum for debate on the data needs of public health authorities and research institutions, including officials from national regulatory authorities for electronic communications, ministries in charge for digital matters and data protection authorities. In addition, the eHealth Network and the Commission should cooperate closely with other authorities and networks that can provide the information necessary to implement the Recommendation, including, inter alia, the European Data Protection Board (Recitals 28 and 29 of the preamble to C(2020) 2296, cf. also points 5–7 and 14 of C(2020) 2296). In the context of the findings, it is worth noting that the obligation of the Commission to cooperate with this Board also stems from Commission Implementing Decision (EU) 2019/1765. According to its Art. 4(2), when developing guidelines on effective methods to enable the use of medical information for public health and research purposes, the eHealth Network shall take account of the guidelines adopted by the European Data Protection Board and shall consult it where appropriate. The Council shall in turn act based on Art. 70(1)(e) of Regulation (EU) 2016/679 (General Data Protection Regulation), according to which, on its own initiative or at the request of one of its members or the Commission, it shall examine any question concerning the application of that Regulation and issue guidelines, recommendations and identify best practices to encourage its consistent application.

An analysis of the EC's response to the pandemic as part of the EU's digital agenda in the light of the legal basis laid down in EU law leads to the conclusion that these measures do not go beyond its powers. It can even be concluded that, contrary to the much more ambitious objectives of the EU's Digital Strategy, the Commission uses its powers very cautiously in fighting the pandemic, relying primarily on factual, informal and non-binding measures and, if at all (as in the case of interoperability of mobile applications), reaching for binding measures only at an advanced stage of its policy implementation.

1.6 The scope of measures taken by the EU: general characteristics

The analysis of the content of the digital solutions adopted by the EC and other EU bodies in response to the pandemic leads to some general conclusions. The observations concern the scope of changes in relation to the initial regulatory standard, addressees of provisions that are included in the adopted measures, the temporal scope of rules and the type of implementation activities that their provisions assume.

EU anti-crisis measures do not so much transform but rather consolidate the initial regulatory standard that is enshrined in existing EU law. The regulatory objective of the Commission's and other EU bodies' Acts mainly boils down to clearing the pre-existing normative criterion for assessing digital crisis solutions introduced by Member States. The Commission's statements focus on the threats that such solutions pose to the integrity of the single market and to the fundamental rights and freedoms of the EU, with particular emphasis on the protection of personal data and the right to privacy.[62] EU legislation complements the protective actions of Member States, which take them autonomously, within the framework of national constitutional systems.[63] In particular, this safeguard objective refers, in Commission Recommendation (EU) 2020/518, to the legal basis for Member States to lay down rules enabling them to process personal data concerning health for reasons of public interest. This basis is derived from the General Data Protection Regulation (Art. 6(1)(c) or (e) and Art. 9(2)(i) of Regulation (EU) 2016/679).[64] As the Commission points out, in the light of existing EU law, processing of data is allowed, also with regard to sensitive data, provided that, in any event, the purposes and means of processing, as well as the data to be processed and by whom, are clear and specific. The basis invoked refers to digital crisis solutions that Member States are taking.[65]

In addition, notwithstanding the interpretative guidance on the application of binding EU law, coordination mechanisms are established in the regulatory documents of the Commission and other EU bodies to better exploit the protective potential of different national solutions.[66] With the exception of the regulations on the EU COVID-19 digital certificate, these mechanisms are essentially expressed in non-binding material standards that define common boundary conditions for the operation of digital solutions, and in voluntary interoperability procedures that form the basis for the exchange of information and good practices relevant to the fight against pandemics. Again, it is proposed to use the regulatory options avail-

62 Cf. Cattuto & Spina (n 28) 233–35. Cf. Gstrein (n 36) 374–381.

63 F.Hase, 'Corona-Krise und Verfassungsdiskurs' [2020] 14 Juristen Zeitung 697–756.

64 Cf. Townend et al. (n 61) 260.

65 See points 10, 15–16 of C(2020) 2296 and recitals 7, 8, 10, 13, 17 of the preamble to C(2020) 2296; Cf. J. Błachut, S. Dudzik and D. Olczyk, 'Ochrona danych osobowych pracownika w warunkach epidemii (wybrane zagadnienia)' [2020] 5 Europejski Przegląd Sądowy 43–46.

66 Cf. Malczewska (n 61) 18.

able to Member States under existing EU law and established before the outbreak of the pandemic. As in the case of actions to better protect rights and freedoms, the Commission therefore issues regulatory acts to draw Member States' attention to the means available to them under existing EU law and proposes a (non-binding) specific way of using them. Coordination mechanisms that may be established by Member States are referred to, for example, in Commission Recommendation (EU) 2020/518. This Act identifies actions that may be taken on the basis of Decision No 1082/2013/EU of the European Parliament and of the Council[67] whereby the Commission, in consultation with the Member States, ensures coordination and exchange of information between the mechanisms and structures established by the Decision and similar mechanisms and structures established at Union level or under the Euratom Treaty, whose actions are relevant for preparedness and response planning, monitoring, early warning of and combatting serious cross-border threats to health (Art. 2(5) of Decision 1082/2013/EU read in conjunction with point (a) of the Annex).[68] This basis allows, in particular, for the development and adoption by Member States and the Commission of a set of practical measures, including a European approach for mobile applications for COVID-19 and for the use of mobility data for modelling and predicting changes in the spread of the virus, as requested by the Commission (Point 4 of C(2020) 2296).[69] The solutions adopted by Member States in cooperation with the Commission in the framework of the eHealth Network are in turn an example of non-binding standards that relate to digital technologies. Unilateral binding measures – such as Regulations (EU) 2021/953 and (EU) 2021/94 and Commission Implementing Decision (EU) 2020/1023 – complement, on a point basis, the arrangements that Member States adopt voluntarily in the framework of cooperation which they have established under existing EU legislation (Art. 1(5) and recitals 5–6 of the preamble to Commission Implementing Decision (EU) 2020/1023).

Regulatory Acts, which define the digital crisis solutions for the EU, are primarily addressed to Member States (Point 2 of C(2020) 2296, Art. 10 of Commission Implementing Decision (EU) 2019/1765). In addition to the Member States, these regulatory Acts are sometimes also addressed to national and EU authorities directly involved in the fight against a pandemic, or other actors (e.g., mobile application developers).[70] All the Acts under consideration were issued in direct response to the outbreak of a pandemic and for the urgency of responding to the threats caused by it. The fight against a pandemic is a fundamental regulatory objective of these Acts, which is highlighted in their preambles. In any event, these instruments do not contain provisions which would limit their scope to the period of pandemic risk alone. Their regulatory effect will therefore remain valid

67 Cf. Pacces & Weimer (n 22) 291–295.
68 Cf. Alemanno (n 60) 305.
69 Cf. Durach, Bargaoanu and Nastasiu (n 44) 14.
70 Point 1, para 6, of C(2020) 2523; EDPB, Statement on the processing of personal data in the context of the COVID-19 outbreak, Adopted on 19.03.2020 1.

even after the threat has ceased and may (through voluntary action by the Member States) strengthen and harmonise the general standard of protection in the EU. Again, an important exception to this is the EU Digital Certificate COVID-19 Regulations, which are in force for a limited period (Art. 17 of Regulation (EU) 2021/953, Art. 3 of Regulation (EU) 2021/954).

Acts adopted by the Commission and other EU bodies indicate their typical implementation measures. Member States are encouraged to take coordinated regulatory action, leading to the results advocated in those Acts, and to implement or promote certain technical solutions relating to the digital technology used on their territory. The Acts also assume that Member States' actions will be agreed within existing cooperation structures (e.g., eHealth Network) and will also consider the positions presented by EU bodies. Numerous reporting and information requirements are an additional regulatory element (Para. 21-24 of C(2020) 2296). EU crisis regulation does not create new types of institutional or procedural arrangements in this respect.[71]

1.7 Conclusions

The EU response to the COVID-19 pandemic in digital technologies does not go beyond the established regulatory standard. The specific situation faced by the EU has not led it to develop innovative legal solutions, either in form or content. Despite the scale and diversity of the threats posed by the pandemic, the EU is very reticent in using its competences to counter the crisis. Contrary to the ambition of the EU's Digital Strategy, the common European response to a pandemic is mainly supported by non-binding instruments: recommendations, guidelines and incentives. Strictly legislative activity is undertaken relatively rarely in this area. As a result, the EU response to the pandemic is mainly of an administrative nature and is limited to detailed and technical issues. It does not usually take the form of horizontal anti-crisis solutions that are valid throughout the EU. Against this backdrop, the EU's COVID-19 digital certificate appears to be a glaring exception. In essence, the EU is not so much leading the fight against a pandemic as it is supporting and coordinating the dispersed – and essentially autonomous – anti-crisis responses of the Member States.

The formula for action adopted by the Union reflects the narrow scope of the Treaty's powers in the field of human health protection, but leaves open the question, particularly in the field of digital regulation, as to whether the Union can make use of the "harder" powers it has under other policies. This question is particularly relevant in the light of the experience of a Member State whose anti-crisis regulation addresses the protection issues which are at the heart of EU policy, only on the margins of its solutions.

71 Alberto Alemanno, 'Taming COVID-19 by Regulation: An Opportunity for Self-Reflection' [2020] 11 European Journal of Risk Regulation 192.

Works cited

Alemanno, A., 'Taming COVID-19 by Regulation: An Opportunity for Self-Reflection' (2020a) 11 European Journal of Risk Regulation 187–194.

Alemanno, A., 'The European Response to COVID-19: From Regulatory Emulation to Regulatory Coordination?' (2020b) 11 European Journal of Risk Regulation 307–316.

Błachut, J., Dudzik, S., and Olczyk, D., 'Ochrona danych osobowych pracownika w warunkach epidemii (wybrane zagadnienia)' (2020) 5 Europejski Przegląd Sądowy 5.

Cattuto, C., and Spina, A., 'The Institutionalisation of Digital Public Health: Lessons Learned from the COVID-19 App.' (2020) 11 European Journal of Risk Regulation 228–235.

O'Keeffe, W. (ed.), *DigComp at Work Implementation Guide* (Publications Office of the European Union, Luxembourg 2020).

Dumancic, K., 'The EU Regulatory Activities in the Area of Digital Platforms and Services Provision' (2021) 5(1) EU and Comparative Law Issues and Challenges 688–705.

Durach, F., Bargaoanu, A., and Nastasiu, C., 'Tackling Disinformation: EU Regulation of the Digital Space' (2020) 20 Romanian Journal of European Affairs 4–20.

Editorial comments, (2020) 57(2) Common Market Law Review.

Etteldorf, C., 'EU Member State Data Protection Authorities Deal with Covid-19: An Overview' (2020) 6 European Data Protection Law Review 265–280.

Gstrein, O., 'The EU Digital COVID Certificate: A Preliminary Data Protection Impact Assessment' (2021) 12 European Journal of Risk Regulation 370–381.

Hase, F., 'Corona-Krise und Verfassungsdiskurs' (2020) 14 Juristen Zeitung 697–704.

Hofmann, H.C.H., Rowe, G.C., and Türk, A.H., *Administrative Law and Policy of the European Union* (Oxford University Press, Oxford 2011).

Kolfschooten, H. van, and Ruijter, A. de, 'COVID-19 and Privacy in the European Union: A Legal Perspective on Contact Tracing' (2020) 41 Contemporary Security Policy478–491.

Kowalik-Bańczyk, K., 'Kompetencje Unii Europejskiej wobec epidemii COVID-19' (2020) 5 Europejski Przegląd Sądowy 4–11.

Kożuch, M., 'Stosowanie środków doraźnych związanych ze zwalczaniem koronawirusa SARS-nCoV-2 przez Unię Europejską' (2020) 5 Europejski Przegląd Sądowy 11–19.

Malczewska, M., 'Unia Europejska wobec pandemii SARS-CoV-2. Inicjatywy związane z ochroną zdrowia publicznego' (2020) 6 Europejski Przegląd Sądowy4–19.

Micklitz, H.-W., 'The COVID-19 Thread: An Opportunity to Rethink the European Economic Constitution and European Private Law' (2020) 11 European Journal of Risk Regulation249–255.

Pacces, A.M., and Weimer, M., 'From Diversity to Coordination: A European Approach to COVID-19' (2020) 11 European Journal of Risk Regulation283–296.

Purnhagen, K.P., Ruijter, A. de, Flear, M.L., Hervey, T.K., and Herwig, A., 'More Competences than You Knew? The Web of Health Competence for European Union Action in Response to the COVID-19 Outbreak' (2020) 11 European Journal of Risk Regulation297–306.

Renaud, K., Orgeron, C., Warkentin, M., and French, P.E., 'Cyber Security Responsibilization: An Evaluation of the Intervention Approaches Adopted by the Five Eyes Countries and China' (2020) 80 Public Administration Review577–589.

Calliess, C., and Ruffert, M., *EUV/AEUV Das Verfassungsrecht der Europäischen Union mit Europäischer Grundrechtecharta* (C.H. Beck, München 2011).

Senden, L., *Soft Law in European Community Law* (Bloomsbury Publishing, London 2004).

Townend, D., Pas, R. van de, Bongers, L., et al. 'What is the role of the European Union in the COVID-19 Pandemic?' (2020) 39 Medicine and Law 249–268.

Zetzche, D., Arner, D., Buckley, R., and Weber, R., 'The Evolution and Future of Data-Driven Finance in the EU' (2020) 57(2) Common Market Law Review 331–360.

2 Polish Constitutional Institutions in a Pandemic

Aleksandra Syryt

2.1 Introduction

The term "pandemic" is usually associated with an epidemic of infectious diseases of particularly large proportions across an entire country or one or more continents simultaneously.[1] In the Polish legal system, the concept of an epidemic has its legal definition contained in Art. 2.9 of A.I.D. An epidemic is occurrence in each area of infections or outbreaks of infectious diseases in a significantly higher number than in the previous period or occurrence of infections or infectious diseases not occurring before. Because the pandemic phenomenon is not indifferent to the state system and the functioning of its organs, constitutional institutions have specific tasks and duties related to responding to the spread of infectious disease on the territory of a given country.

This chapter aims to review the provisions of the Constitution and to identify whether there are specific legal solutions in the Polish constitutional system that should or could be applied in the context of a pandemic. In addition, an attempt will be made to assess to what extent digital transformation relates to constitutional institutions and to what extent digital instruments can be applied in legislating and applying the law in an infectious disease emergency.

2.2 Constitutional tasks and obligations of the state regarding the response to a pandemic

Article 1 of the Constitution says the Republic of Poland shall be the common good of all its citizens. The common good is the total of the conditions of social life which, either to associations or to individual members of society, make it possible to achieve more fully and more easily their own perfection.[2] The Constitution's commentators explain that the principle of the common good in Art. 1 of the Constitution expresses the general obligation of the state authorities to ensure

1 M. Honigsbaum, Pandemic. The Lancet. 2009, 373: 1939.

2 Pastoral Constitution Gaudium et Spes, 1965, "Znak Miesięcznik. Social Teaching of the Church" 1982: 332–334 (7–9); 890.

DOI: 10.4324/9781003263968-8

such a shape of the political community that will provide the proper development of each individual and guarantee the observance of inherent rights and freedoms.[3] This obligation is realised using specific public-legal instruments and remains valid in the pandemic state. Its concretisation is the objective of the state included in Art. 5 of the Constitution.

From the pandemic perspective, those tasks that concern ensuring human and civil liberties and rights and the security of citizens seem to be particularly important. The concept of security should be understood as a state that gives a sense of certainty and stability and guarantees its protection.[4] It refers to a state free from any threats, including to life and health.

Ensuring human and civil rights and freedoms relates to the implementation by the state and its organs of obligations of both a negative nature (the responsibility to respect rights and freedoms and not to infringe them) and of a positive nature (the duty to protect rights and liberties from infringements). This task means that the state is to create a legal system in which a person will exercise freedoms and rights to the extent to which they are entitled.[5]

The concretisation of the objectives of the state is to respect and protect human dignity[6] and the order to legally safeguard life.[7] They are complemented by the constitutional right to health protection, which is a derivative of dignity and the right to the protection of life.[8] In this context, attention should be drawn to the programme norm set out in Art. 68(4) of the Constitution, according to which public authorities are obliged to combat epidemic diseases and prevent the negative health effects of environmental degradation. The obligation concerns preventive measures, prevention, hygiene care, control of infections and immediate treatment of these diseases through medical care. The manner of its implementation must be concretised through legislation developing the constitutional provisions. It can be considered that the primary source of law in this regard, directly concerning the pandemic, is the A.I.D.

The tasks, principles and human rights that may directly relate to pandemics should be complemented by one more constitutional solution, namely the principle of proportionality derived from Art. 31(3) of the Constitution. This principle allows for limiting the use of constitutional freedoms and rights. Any limitation upon the exercise of constitutional freedoms and rights may be imposed only by statute, and only, when necessary, in a democratic state for the protection of its security or public order, or to protect the natural environment, health or public

3 E. Zwierzchowski E., 'Dobro wspólne,' in ed. W. Skrzydło, S. Grabowska, R. Grabowski, *Konstytucja Rzeczypospolitej Polskiej. Komentarz encyklopedyczny* (Warsaw 2009), 142.

4 M. Florczak-Wątor, 'Art. 5 Konstytucji RP,' in: ed. M. Safjan, L. Bosek, Konstytucja RP. Tom I. Komentarz do art. 1–86 (Warsaw 2016), Nb 34; B. Banaszak, *Konstytucja Rzeczypospolitej Polskiej. Komentarz* (Warsaw 2012), Nb 6.

5 M. Florczak-Wątor, op. cit., Nb 30; B. Banaszak, op. cit. Nb 3–5.

6 Art. 30 Constitution.

7 Art. 38 Constitution.

8 Art. 68 Constitution.

morals, or the freedoms and rights of other persons. Such limitations shall not violate the essence of freedoms and rights.

The principle in Art. 31(3) of the Constitution can be applied during a pandemic to various legislative actions of the state directed at preventing or removing threats. Firstly, it can serve to justify interference with human freedoms and rights to ensure the protection of health and life.[9] Secondly, it may justify the state's failure to take certain normative actions due to the impassable constitutional framework of permissible interference. According to Art. 31(3) a person will expect from the state that their freedoms and rights will be duly protected. It is also an expression of the implementation of the principle of trust in the state and the law created by it, which is derived from Art. 2 of the Constitution.[10] This principle is closely related to the legal security of the individual. A way of making and applying the law cannot become a trap for a citizen. On the basis on this principle, the people should arrange their affairs in the confidence that they will not be exposed to legal consequences that they could not foresee when taking decisions and actions.[11]

The above confirms that in the Constitution, there are provisions concerning general principles and requirements defining the standards of protection of human rights, which must be the point of reference for the creation of legal solutions that would be a response to a pandemic. These legal solutions constitute an impassable framework for the legislative activity of public authorities relating to the shaping of the status of an individual in connection with preventing and combating a pandemic and its consequences.

In this context, the above-mentioned constitutional models will be relevant to such issues as the principles and ways of introducing restrictions concerning the sphere of personal and private life, freedom of movement, information autonomy, the right to decide about one's own life. When the state is functioning normally, they will be the determinant of legislative activities and the criteria that must be considered in legal application. However, this is not the only constitutional sphere that is related to the pandemic.

2.3 The institution of constitutional extraordinary measures and pandemics

2.3.1 Extraordinary constitutional measures are an institutionalised reaction to specific threats to the state and its inhabitants. It is assumed in the literature that the term "state of emergency" in a democratic state means a legal regime introduced in the event of a particular threat, the removal of which is possible only through measures of exceptional character. This regime is primarily characterised

9 See, e.g., the judgment of the CT of 10.12.2013, U 5/13, OTK ZU No 9/A/2013, item 136.

10 See, e.g., judgment of the CT of 20.12.1999, K 4/99, OTK No 7/1999, item 165.

11 See the judgment of the CT of 7.02.2001, K 27/00, OTK No 2/2001, item 29; judgment of the CT of 2.04.2007, SK 19/06, OTK ZU No 4/A/2007, item 37.

by restriction (suspension) of certain rights and freedoms of the individual. There may also be a shift of competencies between public authorities or granting them special powers to remove the threat that has arisen.[12]

The Polish legislature also established the threat response regime. In the light of Art. 228(1) of the Constitution, in situations of special threats, if ordinary constitutional measures are insufficient, an appropriate state of emergency may be introduced: a martial law, a state of emergency or a state of natural disaster. In subsequent editorial units of Art. 228 of the Constitution, it is stipulated that the introduction of a state of emergency must have a specific statutory legal basis and that it is subject to additional public information (s. 2). Actions taken because of the introduction of a state of emergency must correspond to the degree of danger and should aim to restore the normal functioning of the state as soon as possible.

During a period of introduction of extraordinary measures, as well as within 90 days following its termination, the term of office of the Sejm may not be shortened, nor may a nationwide referendum, nor elections to the Sejm, Senate, organs of local government nor elections for the Presidency be held. The term of office of such organs shall be appropriately prolonged. Elections to organs of local government shall be possible only in those places where the extraordinary measures have not been introduced. In practice, the discussion about introducing any constitutional states of emergency in Poland due to the pandemic coincided with the calendar of presidential elections in the summer of 2020. In the end, none of the states of constitutional extraordinary measures was introduced, which meant that there was no change in the length of the term of office of the President of the Republic of Poland, and no postponement of the elections after the end of a given state.[13]

2.3.2 The Constitution provides for three constitutional extraordinary measures corresponding to different threats. These are:

1) martial law, which may be imposed in the event of an external threat to the state, an armed attack on the territory of the Republic of Poland or when an international agreement results in the obligation of joint defence against aggression;[14]
2) a state of emergency introduced in the event of a threat to the constitutional system of the state, security of citizens or public order;[15]

12 Prokop 2005; 9.

13 See on this problem. A. Rakowska-Trela, M. Rakowski, Stan nadzwyczajny komplikuje wybory prezydenckie, https://www.prawo.pl/samorzad/stan-nadzwyczajny-pociaga-za-soba-powtorzenie-czynnosci,498846.html, (06.06.2020; R. Piotrowski, Trzeba ogłosić stan klęski żywiołowej i przesunąć wybory, https://www.prawo.pl/samorzad/zmiana-terminu-wyborow-wg-prof-piotrowskiego-trzeba-wprowadzic,498718.html, (06.06.2020); P. Uziębło, (2020). Is it possible to hold elections during a state of epidemics? https://www.batory.org.pl/2020/03/26/czy-mozliwe-jest-przeprowadzenie- election-podczas-epidemii-opinia-prawna/ (20.06.2020).

14 Art. 229 Constitution.

15 Art. 230 Constitution.

3) a state of natural disaster. Its purpose is to prevent the effects of natural disasters or technical failures bearing the hallmarks of a natural disaster and to remove them.[16]

The extraordinary constitutional measures mentioned above, as well as the rules of restricting the exercise of freedoms and human rights and the scope of obligations during the duration of a given state, are specified by relevant Acts.[17]

The general nature of the premises in the case of both a state of emergency and a state of natural disaster makes it possible to consider their application to a state of the pandemic without the need to refer to statutory solutions, which do not apply to states of emergency.

2.3.3 Considering the general characteristics of individual constitutional extraordinary measures, it should be considered that it would be inappropriate to impose martial law in response to a pandemic. The rationale for such a state is not appropriate to the threat posed by a pandemic. The situation is different with a state of emergency and a state of natural disaster.

2.3.3.1 In the case of a state of emergency, there must be a threat to the state's constitutional system, security of citizens or public order. The indicated prerequisites are so undefined that they leave a great deal of freedom of interpretation to the bodies authorised to request and introduce this state and a considerable margin of decision-making.[18]

Commentators on Art. 230 of the Constitution analysing the issue of a threat to the security of citizens or public order point out that the safety of citizens is one of the values which, by Art. 5 Constitution, are subject to protection by the Republic of Poland. They affirm that the premise of the state of emergency refers to a threat to the life and health of citizens and their property, which cannot be countered by ordinary constitutional means.[19]

The law on the state of emergency in Art. 2(1) provides that in a situation of a particular threat to the constitutional system of the state, security of citizens or public order, including acts of a terrorist nature or acts in cyberspace, which the use of ordinary constitutional means cannot remove, the Council of Ministers may adopt a resolution to send a request to the President of the Republic of Poland to impose a state of emergency. Interestingly, the legislator defined cyberspace in Art. 2(1a). It means the space for processing and exchange of information created by ICT systems, as expressed in Art. 3(3) of the Act of 17 February 2005 on

16 Art. 232 Constitution.

17 That is, the Act of 29.08.2002 on martial law and on the competences of the Commander-in-Chief of the Armed Forces and the principles of his subordination to the constitutional bodies of the Republic of Poland, JoL 2017, item 1932; the Act of 21.06.2002 on the state of emergency, JoL 2017, item 1928; and the Act of 18.04.2002 on the state of natural disaster, JoL 2017, item 1897.

18 K. Prokop, *Stany nadzwyczajne w Konstytucji Rzeczypospolitej Polskiej* (Białystok 2005), 75–76.

19 K. Wojtyczek, *Granice ingerencji ustawodawczej w sferę praw człowieka w Konstytucji RP*, (Kraków 1999), 253.

Informatisation of the Activities of Entities Performing Public Tasks,[20] together with the links between them and relations with users.

The context in which the state of emergency is discussed makes it associated with threats originating from humans or resulting from processes that humans can influence. However, it is possible to apply such an interpretation in which a virus will connect a threat to the security of citizens, and this will be a sufficient circumstance for the President of the Republic to introduce a state of emergency. This interpretation is supported by the notion that "security of citizens" in Art. 230 of the Constitution should be interpreted in the same way as in Art. 5 of the Constitution.[21] Thus, since Art. 5 determines the shape of legislation on the prevention and control of the coronavirus, the same meaning may be ascribed to the introduction of the state of emergency.

The consequence of this will be to outline the permissible framework of interference in human freedoms and rights. As it is indicated by Art. 233(1) and (2) of the Constitution:

First, a law defining the scope of restrictions on human and civil liberties and rights during a state of emergency may not restrict the freedoms and rights set out in Arts. 30 (human dignity), 34 and 36 (citizenship), 38 (protection of life), Art. 39, 40 and 41(4) (humane treatment), 42 (criminal responsibility), 45 (access to court), 47 (personal rights), 53 (conscience and religion), 63 (petitions) and 48 and 72 (family and child).

Second, it is also unacceptable to restrict human and civil liberties and rights solely based on race, sex, language, religion, or lack thereof, social origin, birth and property.

It is of additional importance in enforcing minimum protection guarantees for citizens (individuals) in a state of already existing danger. The rationale for such a solution is to maintain the requirement of building loyalty (trust) of the state towards its citizens enshrined in the principle of a democratic state of law.

The wording used in the Constitution is not entirely clear.

2.3.3.2 In the case of a state of natural disaster, the legislator provides for the prevention of the effects of natural disasters or technical failures bearing the hallmarks of a natural disaster and their elimination. Unlike martial law and a state of emergency, in the case of a state of natural disaster, the source of the threat is not so much deliberate human activity as forces of nature. And although the threatened good is still the security of citizens or public order, the reason for this threat is different.[22]

It should be added that the literature notes that it is irrelevant "whether a particular disaster or emergency has already occurred or is yet to occur. It is because it follows from the purpose of the introduction that the application of the state

20 JoL 2017, item 570
21 B. Banaszak, op. cit., Nb 2.
22 K. Prokop, op. cit., 101.

of natural disaster may take place both before and after a natural disaster and a technical failure."[23]

The institution of the state of natural disaster is further specified in the Act on the state of natural disaster. Article 2 of the Act, repeating to some extent the Constitution, states that the state of natural disaster may be imposed to prevent the effects of natural disasters or technical failures bearing the hallmarks of a natural disaster and to remove them. More interesting is the definition of concepts constituting the above-mentioned institution. Thus, the legislator explained that whenever the Act refers to:

1) natural disaster – shall be understood as a natural catastrophe or technical failure, the effects of which endanger the life or health of many people, property in large quantities or the environment in large areas, and the assistance and protection can be effectively undertaken only with the use of extraordinary measures, in cooperation of various bodies and institutions and specialist services and formations acting under unified direction.
2) natural disaster – shall be understood as an event connected with the operation of natural forces, in particular lightning, seismic shocks, strong winds, intense precipitation, the prolonged occurrence of extreme temperatures, landslides, fires, droughts, floods, ice phenomena on rivers and the sea, lakes and reservoirs, mass occurrence of pests, plant or animal diseases or human infectious diseases, or the action of another element.
3) technical failure – shall be understood as sudden, unforeseen damage or destruction of a building, technological device or a system of technological devices causing an interruption in their use or a loss of their properties.
4) cyberspace - means the space for processing and exchange of information created by ICT systems, as defined in Art. 3.3 of the Act of 17.02.2005 on Informatisation of the Activities of Entities Executing Public Tasks, together with links between them and relations with users (Art. 3.1 of the Disaster Act).

The legislator confirmed that a natural disaster or technical failure may also be caused by events in cyberspace and acts of a terrorist nature (Art. 3(2) of the Disaster Act).

Looking at the definitions indicated above, especially at the concept of natural disaster, with which the mass occurrence of infectious diseases of humans has been linked, it can be concluded that the constitutional institution of the state of natural disaster includes such a state of emergency which is caused by a coronavirus pandemic. Such a state could therefore be introduced as a reaction to a given threat, which would make it possible to intervene more broadly in human freedoms and rights. Indeed, by Art. 233(3) of the Constitution, the law specifying the scope of restrictions on human and civil liberties and rights in a state of

23 M. Brzeziński, *Stany nadzwyczajne w polskich konstytucjach* (Warsaw 2007), 216.

disaster may restrict the freedoms and rights such as freedom of economic activity, personal freedom, inviolability of the dwelling, freedom of movement and residence in the territory of Poland, right to strike, right to property, freedom of work, right to safe and hygienic working conditions and right to rest. The scope of regulation would thus be simpler to determine than if the legislator relied only on the proportionality test.

Although the principle of proportionality may limit the exercise of individual freedoms and human rights according to the general rules, the direct constitutional authority to interfere with specific rights and liberties during the state of disaster allows for a quicker reaction, which is important because of the dynamics of changes related to threats, including threats caused by a pandemic.

2.3.4 Considering the general and fundamental considerations indicated above. It can be concluded that the current constitutional state allows for the introduction of a state of emergency in connection with a coronavirus pandemic. Among the possible solutions, it could be a state of emergency or a state of natural disaster. A possible decision in this regard should consider the purpose of introducing a given state and the assumed scope of interference in constitutional freedoms and rights.

Meanwhile, the activities of the state and its bodies related to responding to threats posed by a pandemic are based on the A.I.D. and the COVID-19 Act.

Because of this, one should consider how rational and right it is to combat a pandemic through special laws and executive acts issued on their basis if there are legal solutions in constitutional provisions that could be used by public authorities to fulfil the tasks of Art. 5 of the Constitution. For the coherence of the legal system, to ensure transparency of the state's activities and to build its confidence in citizens, it would be more correct to operate within the framework of the existing legal solutions and possibly modify them as a response to a new threat.

The introduction of a dualism of solutions for responding to threats and the available constitutional instruments may hinder the implementation of protecting the freedoms and rights of citizens and ensuring their security.

2.4 The use of digital solutions in a pandemic – constitutional institutions

In constitutional law, the coronavirus pandemic has not only become a reason to consider the guarantees of protection of freedoms and human rights with actions taken by public authorities in connection with the existing threat. Nor was it merely a pretext for resuming the discussion on the shape of the institution of states of emergency in the Constitution.

As in many other areas, the pandemic also forced certain actions to be taken so that constitutional bodies of public authority could function and make decisions in conditions of social distance and isolation.

In the case of working meetings, direct communication tools, with the possibility of teleconferencing, became a permanent feature of functioning. It made it necessary to review internal Acts on the organisation of work in individual institutions. The aim was to create conditions for the secure flow of information. The indicated measures were present in the constitutional bodies of the states before, but rather as additional exotic support in communication, rather than as a working tool, determining that the body can operate without disruption.

From the perspective of the analysed topic, i.e., the use of technology in the decision-making processes of the constitutional organs of the state, it should be noticed that several changes had been introduced by the resolution of the Sejm of 26 March 2020 on amending the Regulations of the Sejm.[24] This Act introduced the possibility to hold sessions of the Sejm, committees and subcommittees with the use of electronic means of communication allowing remote communication.

The new legal solutions assume that in the event of (1) the introduction of a state of emergency, a state of natural disaster or a state of war, or (2) a state of epidemic within the meaning of the A.I.D. – a meeting of the Sejm may be conducted using means of electronic communication enabling remote communication. The Speaker of the Sejm shall decide to hold a sitting of the Sejm using electronic means of remote communications after consulting the Convention of Seniors. Following the decision to hold the session of the Sejm using electronic means of remote communications, the Chancellery of the Sejm shall ensure that all Members who so request have access to the technical means of participation in the session (Art. 198a of the Regulations of the Sejm).

The requirements for electronic means of remote communication, the procedure for applying for access to such standards and the manner of providing such means to Members and other entitled persons shall be specified by the Speaker of the Sejm by way of an ordinance in such a way that such standards ensure the identification of the person using them, real-time communication, in particular taking the floor, participating in voting, submitting formal motions and at the same time provide a guarantee of the security of the data communications system.

An MP's participation in a session of the Sejm using electronic means of remote communications shall be on equal footing with other forms of participation in the session of the Sejm. It may not cause any exclusion or restriction of the MP's rights outlined in the law provisions. A Member using electronic means of remote communications shall confirm their presence at a sitting of the Sejm by logging in to the voting system and submitting printouts of their voter participation.

During a sitting of the Sejm conducted using electronic means of remote communications, whenever the provisions of the Sejm provide for the submission of documents in writing, such documents may be submitted in electronic form. Suppose a meeting of the Sejm is conducted using means of electronic communication allowing for remote communications. In that case, the openness of the session of the Sejm shall be ensured, particularly using transmission of the meeting via a data communications network.

Speeches made during the consideration of an item on the agenda of a sitting of the Diet shall not exceed 5 minutes in duration. The Speaker of the Sejm may grant permission for a speech to be longer. No Member's speech in a debate may

24 (M.P. item 327).

last longer than 3 minutes, except speeches made by members of a club, which may not exceed 15 minutes. A Member may speak only once during a debate on a given matter. During a sitting of the Sejm conducted under Rule 198a(1), voting may be performed using electronic means of remote communications. Casting a vote using electronic means of remote communications complying with the requirements outlined in the regulations issued based on Art. 198b of the Rules of the Sejm shall be tantamount to casting a vote under the procedure. The official record of the proceedings of a sitting of the Sejm held using electronic means of remote communications shall be audiovisual. Similar solutions were provided for meetings of the Sejm's bodies, committees and subcommittees.

It transpired from the justification of the draft resolution that the directives dictated the proposed amendments to the law to guarantee the ability of the Sejm to perform its legislative function, reduce the risk of infections and ensure citizen representation in the law-making process. Therefore, amendments to the Regulations of the Sejm were proposed, which would allow MPs to participate in a session of the Sejm, a committee or a subcommittee using electronic means of remote communication. The extraordinary nature of the proposed procedures was highlighted. They could be used only in enumerative indicated cases – the introduction of one of the states of emergency or the introduction of a state of epidemiological emergency or a state of epidemic within the meaning of the A.I.D.

Justifying the amendments, the proponent referred to the principle of the autonomy of the Sejm's rules of procedure expressed in Art. 112 of the Constitution, which means that the Sejm defines its internal organisation and the order of its work, the process of appointment and activities of its bodies in a specific resolution, i.e., the rules of procedure of the Sejm. However, it was emphasised that the by-laws must remain consistent with the provisions of the Constitution. It has also been pointed out that during the work on the Constitution in the first half of the 1990s, no provisions were included in it that would allow participation in the work of the Sejm using electronic communication enabling remote communication. However, the requirements of the Constitution do not prohibit the use of such solutions. That is to say, the provisions of the Constitution do not preclude the introduction in the Regulations of the Sejm of requirements making it possible to participate in the proceedings of the Sejm using electronic communication enabling remote communication. It has been explained that the principle expressed in Art. 109 of the Constitution that the Sejm shall hold sessions does not mean that these sessions must be held in a specific location (a specific hall). Sittings of the Sejm in sessions are the opposite of the session mode of work of the Sejm applied before 1989. In turn, the requirement expressed in Art. 120 of the Constitution that half of the statutory deputies must be "present" means that at least 230 deputies must take part in voting on a Bill. Therefore, the provision above expresses the requirement that there be a quorum when voting, not that Members deliberate in one room. The condition does not require Members to be present during the sitting but rather during the vote on the Bill, and it is a requirement that at least half of the legal number of Members participate in the voting procedure. It was emphasised that the proposed provisions also realise other constitutional values, e.g., the requirement expressed in Art. 113 of the Constitution for the openness of Sejm proceedings. The possibility for MPs to use electronic means of remote communication does not mean that the openness of the session is excluded.[25]

Similar solutions for remote proceedings have been introduced in the Rules of Procedure of the Senate. Section VIa, "Participation in meetings of the Senate and Senate committees by remote means," was added under the resolution of the Senate of the Republic of Poland on 4 June 2020 on amending the Senate Rules (M.P. pos. 500).

The legal solutions discussed above made it possible for the organs of the legislative power to exercise their constitutional competencies, not only in the scope of enacting laws but also in the scope of making other decisions, including those that relate to the implementation of the creative and controlling functions of the Sejm.

The above confirms that the coronavirus pandemic has drawn attention to the importance of digital technologies in the functioning of public authorities and their performance of constitutional tasks. Although the solutions in question – as their proposers stipulated – are extraordinary, in time, they may become ordinary forms of operation of the bodies if their functionality proves effective in crisis situations.

The introduction of specific solutions concerning remote meetings of state bodies and the possibility of taking decisions using distance communication opens a discussion on the extent to which it is justified to discuss the significance of digitisation for the constitutional system of the state and whether the given issues should not become the subject of constitutional matter.

2.5 Conclusions

The issues presented above have shown that the issue of constitutional institutions during a pandemic can be analysed in many aspects. The chapter presents only those that have demonstrated the pandemic's impact on constitutional matters in the author's opinion.

Therefore, it has been established that the Constitution must be a point of reference for the actions of the state taken in connection with the response to threats caused by the pandemic. As the Act with the highest legal force in the state, it sets the benchmarks for law-making (both at the statutory and sub-statutory level) and its application.

The norms concerning general principles related to ensuring the security of the state and its residents and those constituting the status of an individual in the state, confirming human dignity and the right to the protection of life and health are therefore the point of reference for shaping the content of legal norms, especially in times of pandemics. They can also be a benchmark for controlling the legality or constitutionality of issued and binding normative acts and acts of legal

25 Print no. 289 of 24.03.2020, Sejm of the 9th term, pp. 5–9.

application. The constitutional principle of building trust in the state is realised by prohibiting the creation of legal traps for the citizen. In this way, the guarantees of human rights protection are strengthened.

In addition, it has been stressed that the Constitution also contains solutions relating to the reaction of the state and its bodies to various types of threats. These are norms shaping some general principles associated with the state's security and its citizens. In particular, it is helpful in the process of shaping the content of legal norms, as well as systemic and procedural regulations, giving the possibility to respond to the state of emergency, e.g., related to the danger to the life and health of citizens, or those who are at a given time under the authority of the Republic. It was confirmed that extraordinary constitutional measures: a state of emergency or a state of natural disaster could be used to combat threats caused by a pandemic and reverse its effects. The creation of special laws next to the solutions having a direct basis in the Constitution makes the legal system incoherent and non-transparent, which translates into reservations raised in the public debate, as well as in court proceedings, as to the legality of given legal solutions, especially those that concern interference in constitutional freedoms and rights.

Finally, the review of legal solutions concerning systemic issues related to the pandemic led to an important regulation, which enabled the organs of legislative power to function in conditions of social distance and isolation. The introduction of the possibility to hold remote sittings and votes in the Sejm and Senate, in states of emergency in the state of the epidemic, made it possible to maintain the continuity of the activities of these bodies. At the same time, the new legal solutions, currently defined only at the level of the rules of procedure of both chambers of parliament, may contribute to the debate on the use of technology to a broader extent as a principle in the decision-making processes of constitutional state bodies.

Although prima facie the pandemic did not significantly affect the systemic digitisation of the constitutional organs of the state, the implementation of digital solutions into the legislative process was a breakthrough. It is not only because a given answer was introduced through amendments to the rules of procedure of the Sejm and Senate and not through amendment of the Constitution, but also because a certain mental barrier concerning the use of technology in matters of constitutional character was broken.

Works cited

Steinborn, S. '230 Konstytucji RP' in (eds.) M. Safjan and L. Bosek, *Konstytucja RP. Tom II.* Komentarz do art. 87–243 (C.H. Beck, Warsaw 2016).

Banaszak, B., *Konstytucja Rzeczypospolitej Polskiej. Komentarz* (C.H. Beck, Warsaw 2012).

Brzeziński, M., *Stany nadzwyczajne w polskich konstytucjach* (Wydawnictwo Sejmowe, Warsaw 2007).

Dobrzeniecki, K., *Prawo wobec sytuacji nadzwyczajnych. Między legalizmem a koniecznością* (Dom Organizatora, Toruń 2018).

Eckhardt, K., *Stany nadzwyczajne jako instytucja polskiego prawa konstytucyjnego* (Przemyśl–Rzeszów 2012).

Florczak-Wątor, M., 'Art. 5 Konstytucji RP' in (eds.) M. Safjan and L. Bosek, *Konstytucja RP*. Tom I. Komentarz do art. 1–86 (C.H. Beck, Warsaw 2016).

Honigsbaum, M., 'Pandemic' (2009) 373 The Lancet 1939.

Konstytucja duszpasterska Gaudium et spes, 1965, „Znak Miesięcznik. Społeczne nauczanie Kościoła" 1982, 332–334(7–9).

Piotrowski, R., 'Trzeba ogłosić stan klęski żywiołowej i przesunąć wybory' (2020) <https://www.prawo.pl/samorzad/zmiana-terminu-wyborow-wg-prof-piotrowskiego-trzeba-wprowadzic,498718.html> (06.06.2020).

Prokop, K., *Stany nadzwyczajne w Konstytucji Rzeczypospolitej Polskiej* (Białystok 2005).

Rakowska-Trela, A., and Rakowski, M., 'Stan nadzwyczajny skomplikowałby wybory prezydenckie' (2020) <https://www.prawo.pl/samorzad/stan-nadzwyczajny-pociaga-za-soba-powtorzenie-czynnosci,498846.html> (06.06.2020).

Uziębło, P., 'Czy możliwe jest przeprowadzenie wyborów podczas stanu epidemii?' (2020) <https://www.batory.org.pl/2020/03/26/czy-mozliwe-jest-przeprowadzenie-wyborow-podczas-epidemii-opinia-prawna/> (20.06.2020).

Wojtyczek, K., *Granice ingerencji ustawodawczej w sferę praw człowieka w Konstytucji RP* (Zakamycze, Kraków 1999).

Zwierzchowski, E., 'Dobro wspólne' in (eds.) W. Skrzydło, S. Grabowska, and R. Grabowski, *Konstytucja Rzeczypospolitej Polskiej. Komentarz encyklopedyczny* (WolKluw., Warsaw 2009).

3 Using Technology to Support Administrations in Controlling the Sars-Cov-2 Pandemic[1]

Diana-Urania Galetta and Gherardo Carullo

3.1 Introduction

The spread of the SARS-CoV-2 virus, also known as COVID-19 (acronym of COronaVIrus Disease 19), has led most countries' authorities to adopt stringent quarantine measures. Italy was one of the first nations to be severely hit by COVID-19 after China. The Government thus adopted a series of Acts that rapidly intensified controls and restrictions.[2] With the decree of 23 February 2020,[3] n. 6, all activities not expressly allowed were quickly suspended and/or prohibited.[4]

Thanks to the development of different vaccines, which have proved effective in reducing the impact of the virus, the pandemic situation has slowly improved. However, new cases are still recorded in all countries every day. The effectiveness of vaccines in avoiding the spread of the pandemic is linked to the percentage of the population vaccinated. The higher the number of subjects covered by the vaccine, the more the spread of the virus can be slowed down.

For various reasons, however, a part of the population, at least in almost all European countries, has strongly opposed the vaccine. Consequently, to verify who is vaccinated and persuade people to get the vaccine, the authorities have introduced the so-called Green Pass, i.e., a certification of the vaccination status of each subject.

This measure was strongly opposed by the population. Some see it as an undue and excessive intrusion into the sphere of personal freedom.[5] Nonetheless, the adoption of the Green Pass has been somewhat an inevitable consequence of the inability, on the part of the public authorities in charge, to understand the potential of IC technologies to help contain the spread of the pandemic. We want to focus

1 Paragraphs 3.1–3.5 are by Gherardo Carullo, paragraph 3.6–3.7 are by Diana-Urania Galetta, and paragraph 3.8 is by both authors.
2 The list of regulatory acts adopted at the state level: https://www.gazzettaufficiale.it/attiAssociati/1/;jsessionid=Zwqrd4FZQjDKkdj7CVr8nw__.ntc-as5-guri2b?areaNode=13. A list of a selection of the relevant official materials, both of a state, regional and local character: http://ceridap.unimi.it/speciale-covid-19/.
3 "Urgent measures for the containment and management of the epidemiological emergency from COVID-19."
4 See Art. 1, c. 1, lett. a), dpcm of 22.03.2020.
5 See *infra*, para. 7.

DOI: 10.4324/9781003263968-9

on here, in fact, how public authorities failed to intervene in the initial phase of the pandemic with appropriate technological tools to limit the spread of the pandemic. In our view, from the initial stages of the pandemic, more could have been done to improve contact tracing. It could have avoided reaching the much more restrictive measures currently arranged with the so-called Green Pass.

In the following paragraphs, we will therefore analyse in what terms technology could have been used to limit the spread of the virus from the very beginning.

3.2 The response of the technology

To understand whether, and to what extent, technology could have supported public administrations in the difficult mission of monitoring and controlling the development of the pandemic, and therefore also the effectiveness of the containment measures, we can take into consideration two technological solutions that Italian Regional and National public administrations introduced at the beginning of the pandemic.

In the Lombardy Region, the one most severely hit by COVID-19 from the very beginning, the app *AllertaLOM* was updated to include new features related to the pandemic. *AllertaLOM* is an app of the Civil Protection of thc Lombardy Rcgion available on the Apple Store[6] and Google Play Store[7] and which is designed to disseminate alerts issued by the Natural Risk Monitoring Functional Center in anticipation of events that may cause damage on the regional territory.

With the coronavirus emergency, the app has been equipped with new features to allow citizens to actively participate in the acquisition of useful data for monitoring the virus and disseminating useful information on relevant regional measures. As explained in the app's description, active participation takes place in this case by completing a survey that allows the Lombardy Region to quantify the level of spread of the infection and the territorial distribution of people testing positive, based on the symptoms reported by users. The data collected are used for statistical and epidemiological analysis, which are essential to help health authorities define models and strategies to fight against coronavirus.[8]

Data useful for the administration to inform its decisions are collected in this way directly by the population concerned, thus creating a form of co-creation of the public information assets. It, therefore, allows the collection of data that public administrations would not have the resources to acquire on their own, but which, when entered directly by private individuals, may still play a crucial role in the perspective of public authorities' decisions and, more in general, for the community to fight more effectively against coronavirus (Carullo 2019, 699).

6 https://apps.apple.com/it/app/allertalom/id1455220682.

7 https://play.google.com/store/apps/details?id=it.lispa.sire.app.mobile.allertalom.

8 Extract of the description of the app found on the stores referred to in the links in the previous notes, relating to version 1.5.0 of the app.

A positive and worthy of mention aspect of the *AllertaLOM* questionnaire is that everything takes place completely anonymously. It is not necessary to register for data entry, nor is it required to provide any personal data. Likewise, the app does not even require authorisation to detect the user's geolocation. In this way, most psychological and technical barriers to completing the questionnaire are reduced or overcome because the user is assured that participation by sending the information cannot have any negative individual effect. Even when a user declares having all the symptoms of COVID-19, the administration cannot directly identify the patient.

As a matter of fact, those choices appear entirely consistent with the purpose of the app. Since *AllertaLOM* is aimed at large-scale data collection, minimising any obstacle that could have reduced participation percentage turns out to be consistent and reasonable.

Another tool that can count on a very large user base is the *COVID-19 Community Mobility Reports* made available by Google.[9] The aim is to provide useful data to combat the COVID-19 virus to all public authorities in as many countries as possible.[10] It is a portal that anonymously aggregates data on people's movements as recorded by the Google Maps app, especially from mobile devices. This application, where the functionality is activated, essentially monitors all movements in the *background* even when the user has not requested directions.

As in the case of *AllertaLOM*, the Google service *COVID-19 Community Mobility Reports* also has the advantage of reusing an infrastructure already available to put it at the service of the fight against the virus. As far as is known, Google, to create this new service, has reused the travel data it already collected before the pandemic, aggregating them, and making them accessible online. This has thus made it possible to collect data on a large scale, reusing the technological solutions already widely used among users, such as Google Maps. The advantage, in this case, is the diffusion of the technologies used by Google, which allows for the collection of many data globally immediately. Except, in this case, the availability of such data, and therefore the concrete uses that can be made of them, and therefore their usefulness is left solely to Google's decision. For example, to download or use the data and reports, it is necessary to agree to the Google Terms of Service.

Regarding monitoring population movements, it may be useful to also report on the app called *Safepaths*, created by the Massachusetts Institute of Technology.[11] In this case, the app aims to track all the movements of the last 28 days of any individual, still testing negative who uses the app. Location data are not shared with third parties if the user is COVID-free. Vice versa, only if the result of the

9 Available at https://www.google.com/covid19/mobility/.

10 The reports are currently available separately for 131 countries. Last consultation date: 03.04.2020.

11 Also available for iOS and Android devices, for the time being in beta on the project website. At the date of publication of this contribution, the app can be downloaded from the website: https://safepaths.mit.edu/download-safe-paths.

COVID-19 test is positive, then the position data, duly anonymised, are published. In this way, all those who have been to places where the positive testing has also been to can have immediate news about it and act accordingly.

Therefore, this example again demonstrates how data to contain the epidemic can be collected directly from the population by using Information and Communication Technologies (ICT). In this case, there is even a form of passive interaction since the collection of data on the movements of people is carried out by the software, without the need for any interaction by the user itself.

The examples dealt with show how ICT can be used to collect information on the progress of the epidemic, verify its flows and alert people of potential contacts with infected individuals. All this can be of great use to public administrations.

3.3 The Italian *Immuni* app

The three functions outlined in the paragraph above had been effectively incorporated by a private company into a single application called the *Immuni*, donated to the Italian public administration and made available to download.[12]

The app *Immuni*, which translates to "*Immunes*," was created to help fight the COVID-19 pandemic. As explained on the official website, "users who the app has notified of a possible infection can isolate themselves to avoid infecting other people. By doing so, they help contain the epidemic and speed up the return to normal life."[13] The app uses technology to warn users that they have been exposed to the virus, even if they are so far asymptomatic. The aim is to interrupt the chain of infections by informing individuals who have been potentially exposed to the virus. In this case, the Italian Government aims to achieve this result not by tracking their displacements but by resorting to the sensors normally found in mobile devices. It is explained that

> the app sends a notification to people who were in close contact with a user who tested positive for the COVID-19 virus, alerting them of the risk of infection. Thanks to Bluetooth Low Energy technology, this takes place without the app gathering any data on the identity or the location of its users.[14]

The objective is to guarantee users' privacy, minimising or even completely excluding the collection of personal data.

It is stressed that

> Immuni has been designed and developed while taking great care to safeguard user privacy. Any data collected and managed by the Ministry of Health and

12 On the App Store (https://apps.apple.com/it/app/immuni/id1513940977) and on the Google Play Store (https://play.google.com/store/apps/details?id=it.ministerodellasalute.immuni&hl=it).

13 See https://www.immuni.italia.it/.

14 Ibid.

by public bodies is stored on servers located in Italy. All the data and app connections with the server are protected.

According to the official website, *Immuni* does not gather the first name, last name, date of birth of any person, or telephone number, email address, the identity of the people met by the user or the location or location movements of users.

In practice, according to the official website, the app works as follows:[15] each smartphone on which *Immuni* is installed sends continuously a Bluetooth Low Energy signal that contains a public code. When two smartphones on which *Immuni* is installed are in proximity, they mutually store each other's public code, taking note of that event. The two smartphones also note how long the event lasted and the approximate distance between the two devices.

The codes are generated based on one or more private keys stored on the user's device through a cryptographic algorithm, and they do not contain any information about the user or their device. They also change several times each hour, protecting users' privacy even more.

If the smartphone owner on which *Immuni* is installed later tests positive for SARS-CoV-2, thanks to a healthcare operator's help, the user can transfer his/her cryptographic private key(s) to a server. It is possible to derive the user's public codes from these keys.

For each user, the app regularly downloads all the new cryptographic keys sent to the server by those users who tested positive for the virus. The app uses these keys to derive the public codes and checks if any correspond to those stored in the device memory from previous days. As such, the app installed on a device of a person that has previously entered contact with a person later found positive will find the random code of the infected person, it will check the length and the distance of the contact to evaluate the risk of infection, and, if necessary, it will notify the user.

The code of the app is entirely available in open source on GitHub.[16] It has two advantages. First, those with the technical skills can analyse the source code and verify its functioning. In this way, it is possible to verify in practice whether the application really works as stated and, therefore, if it really does not collect personal data.

Second, the fact that the *Immuni* app is available in open source makes it easy to reuse its code and deploy it in other countries. Other administrations, from any nation in the world, could easily adopt it too, which would make monitoring the virus far more effective.

This last issue, which is the diffusion of the app, leads us to a further problem that needs to be analysed, namely that of fragmentation of technological solutions.

15 The following description is inferred from the FAQ available at: https://www.immuni.italia.it/faq.html.

16 See https://github.com/immuni-app.

3.4 The problem of fragmentation in the urgency of the pandemic

The examples analysed here – to which undoubtedly others could be added[17] – clearly show us the existence of a widespread sentiment to positively contribute to overcoming the pandemic. On the other hand, these new ICT tools must have a very wide diffusion to be truly effective. The fact that a critical mass of people uses a certain service or platform for that service or platform to be useful is indeed a very well-known issue. This problem can be seen, for example, in any *social network*. A service such as *Facebook* is of any utility to users only if enough people use it. The same also applies to messaging services: however quick and efficient. They are completely useless if there is no person to send messages to. It is because an essential element of these systems is that they are meant to connect people. In the same way, an app like *Immuni* is of no use if a large audience of users does not employ it.

Under normal market conditions, we know that technology, for various reasons that cannot be analysed here, tends towards standardisation, both as regards the technologies used for the realisation of the IT systems themselves (Lemley 1996, 1041; Montagnani 2007, 623), and as regards the applications used by users. An important phenomenon is known as the *tipping point* (Gladwell 2006). If a service manages to acquire a certain threshold of users, the number of which varies according to various factors, there is a tendency for market convergence towards this solution.

For this to happen, however, a certain time is normally necessary, in which the market, according to the different dynamics that regulate it, is oriented towards one or the other option.

However, the Italian public authorities have chosen not to make the use of *Immuni* mandatory. For various reasons – among which the most relevant ones put forward by the authorities were related to the protection of personal data – it was decided to leave the use of the app to the free choice of citizens. It resulted in a complete failure of the initiative. These reasons for personal data protection appear unsubstantiated though, considering that the *Immuni* app does not collect any personal data.

3.5 The need for centralised coordination and privacy concerns

To facilitate the dissemination of technological solutions that can best assist the competent authorities in carrying out their functions aimed at protecting public health and overcoming the pandemic crisis, it seems necessary that there is centralised coordination. In other words, it appears essential that, based on their

17 For reasons of space, as well as for the continuous evolution of software that aims to contribute to the fight against coronavirus, it is not possible here to analyse all the solutions currently available on the market.

respective competences, each authority indicates which technological tools can or should be adopted by citizens to support their activities.

This could even lead to the forced use of a specific app, or of a specific device, within the limits and conditions strictly necessary for the achievement of the aim pursued. For example, it has been seen that the collection of data on the progress of the epidemic and the movement of people does not necessarily postulate the acquisition of personal data.

The fact that an app such as *Immuni* for tracking the pandemic does not collect personal data could root out any privacy-related concerns under EU law. Pursuant to Art. 2, para. 1 GDPR, the "Regulation applies to the processing of personal data wholly or partly by automated means and to the processing other than by automated means of personal data which form part of a filing system or are intended to form part of a filing system." It follows that, where personal data are not processed, the Regulation does not apply.

However, it should be remembered that the *Immuni* app, on closer inspection, in case of contagion, might allow health officials to link the private key of the user to a natural person. As far as is known, this private key is not associated to the natural person and therefore does not allow the rest of the users to identify the infected person. However, from a technical point of view, whoever can associate the private key with the identity of the infected person can always identify the natural person behind the private key. Therefore, for those who can make this association (private key-natural person), the key must be qualified as personal data and all public codes obtained from this key that have been sent to other users.

On this point, it is possible to recall the provisions of recital 30 of the regulation, pursuant to which

> natural persons may be associated with online identifiers provided by their devices, applications, tools and protocols, such as internet protocol addresses, cookie identifiers or other identifiers such as radio frequency identification tags. This may leave traces which, in particular when combined with unique identifiers and other information received by the servers, may be used to create profiles of the natural persons and identify them.

In this regard, by analogy, it is also possible to recall that the CJEU held

> that a dynamic IP address registered by an online media services provider when a person accesses a website that the provider makes accessible to the public constitutes personal data within the meaning of that provision, in relation to that provider, where the latter has the legal means which enable it to identify the data subject with additional data which the internet service provider has about that person.
>
> (CJEU, judgment of 19.10.2016, C-582/14, *Breyer*, ECLI:EU:C:2016:779, p. 49)

It cannot be excluded that the association between the private key and the identity of the infected person might be carried out by the public authority once a patient is diagnosed with the virus and, therefore, his/her status in the app is qualified as an infected person.

This being the case, the GDPR would apply, as there would be processing of personal data.

However, even if that is the case, it must be held that it would still be possible to require citizens to install the app. The data subject's consent is not necessarily required for processing personal data, where other conditions of lawfulness exist. In the specific case, the processing of personal data could well be based on the condition of lawfulness referred to in Art. 6(1)(e), GDPR. Pursuant to this rule, the processing is lawful when it is "necessary for the performance of a task carried out in the public interest or in the exercise of official authority vested in the controller." In such cases, the EU Regulation requires that the basis for the processing is laid down by either EU law or Member State law to which the controller is subject and that such processing meets an objective of public interest and is proportionate to the legitimate aim pursued.

3.6 Should the use of an app like *Immuni* have been mandatory? A question of proportionality

The SARS-CoV-2 pandemic situation corresponds to the characteristic scenario where society's interests and human rights need to become part of a unified legal structure that, at the same time, determines the scope of human rights and allows for their limitation. A context in which the principle of proportionality typically comes into play (Barak 2010).

As a matter of fact, when deciding if or not to render the use of an app like *Immuni* mandatory, a complex balance needed to be struck. On the one side, there was the public interest to contain the spread of the virus, which was essential to protecting public health and the lives of people. On the other side, there was the need to protect a fundamental right such as privacy, which is in turn essential to autonomy and the protection of human dignity.

This is precisely the context for applying the principle of proportionality, which is a tool for balancing that sets criteria for deciding between the marginal benefit to the public good and the marginal limit to human rights.[18]

Stemming from German law and widely used in the EU law context, the principle of proportionality has been used from the very beginning exactly for such complex balancing purposes (Galetta 1998).

18 See: "A difference of treatment in the exercise of a right laid down by the Convention must not only pursue a legitimate aim: Art. 14 will also be violated when it is clearly established that there is no reasonable relationship of proportionality between the means employed and the aim sought to be realised." ECHR: *Glor v. Switzerland*, 13444/04 30/04/2009. The same reasoning on "such a justification must be assessed in relation to the aim and the effects of the measure concerned and the principles which normally prevail in democratic societies" is applied to all other rights protected by the ECHR, v. https://hudoc.echr.coe.int/fre#{%22itemid%22:[%22003-2724329-2974120%22]}, (30.08.2020).

With its structured three steps test, it has the advantage of restricting too wide a discretion in balancing while making the act of balancing "more transparent, more structured, and more foreseeable" (Barak 2010).

The first step of the proportionality assessment is the suitability test, which implies a prediction to be made on the basis of an *ex-ante* judgment. In this case, a judgment which needs to be made as quickly as possible, though!

The basic assumption, as for this first step of the proportionality test, is that Legislator and Public Administration possess specific expertise allowing them to make complex evaluations and assessments that, at least as a matter of principle, need to be respected in the context of the *ex post* evaluation made by a judge (Galetta 2022).

This is certainly even more true in the present case.

The second step is the necessity test, which is the most important part of the structured proportionality assessment. The expression well describes the underlying idea: "imposition of the milder means." Suppose there is a choice among various means, all abstractly suitable for achieving the set objective. In that case, the one that involves the least negative consequences for the freedom/right/opposing interest at stake must be chosen.

There is no doubt, here, that the effectiveness of such an app like *Immuni* is directly proportional to the number of people who use it, so that mandatory use of *Immuni* would basically have had no alternative from an effectiveness-of-the-means-used perspective.

As for the proportionality *stricto sensu* part of the test, this consists of a further comparison: in the present case, a comparison between the means used (the supposedly mandatory use of the app) and its impact on the users' privacy.

Once put on the two different sides of the scale, the problem is normally how to "assign a weight," which allows for comparing both elements put on the scale. This problem becomes much easier to solve in cases such as the one we are dealing with here, as the goal is to effectively track infections to avoid a further widespread of the SARS-CoV-2 virus (and the probable death of many people) and is certainly invaluable. So that, in such a situation, the third part of the proportionality test did not even apply, in my opinion. Once made clear that the obligation to use the *Immuni* app would have passed the suitability and necessity test, no judge could have, in my opinion, legitimately discussed *ex post* its proportionality *stricto sensu*. Because doing that would have been tantamount to slipping into control on the merits of the (very much) political decision (Galetta 2022) that its compulsory use would have involved.

As the CJEU put it again recently,

> in order to satisfy the requirement of proportionality according to which derogations from and limitations on the protection of personal data must apply only in so far as is strictly necessary, the legislation in question which entails the interference must lay down clear and precise rules governing the scope and application of the measure in question and imposing minimum safeguards [...]. It must, in particular, indicate in what circumstances and

> under which conditions a measure providing for the processing of such data may be adopted, thereby ensuring that the interference is limited to what is strictly necessary.[19]

The problem here was rather to identify the appropriate level of government, which needed to make this decision to render it really valuable in terms of effectiveness.

A problem that was neither identified as such nor addressed at the time has been dealt with when adopting the so-called "Green Pass" Regulation, which we now need to explain.

3.7 The 2021 Regulation introducing an "interoperable EU Digital COVID Certificate": from a subsidiarity and proportionality perspective

In October 2020, the Council adopted a Recommendation[20] seeking a coordinated approach to the restriction of free movement on grounds of public health and in response to the pandemic and because citizenship of the Union confers on every citizen of the Union the right of free movement.

This was only the first preparatory step as in March 2021, the EU Commission adopted a proposal for the adoption of a Regulation on a framework for the issuance, verification and acceptance of interoperable certificates on vaccination, testing and recovery to facilitate free movement during the COVID-19 pandemic (Digital Green Certificate).[21]

From the very first lines, a clear emphasis was put on the importance of this instrument (the Digital Green Certificate) to facilitate – during the COVID-19 pandemic – free movement of persons within the EU, which is described in the first part of its explanatory Memorandum as "one of the EU's most cherished achievements."[22] The Regulation was finally adopted in June 2021 (Digital Green Certificate). From a subsidiarity principle point of view, it clearly stated that its objectives (namely: "to facilitate the free movement within the EU during the COVID-19 pandemic"[23] by establishing secure and interoperable certificates on the holder's vaccination, testing and recovery status) could not have been sufficiently achieved by the Member States independently. Because of the action's scale and effects, the objectives could certainly have been better achieved at the EU level.[24]

19 CJEU, 16.07.2020, C311/18, ECLI:EU:C:2020:559, para. 176.

20 Council Recommendation (EU) 2020/1475 on a coordinated approach to the restriction of free movement in response to the COVID-19 pandemic, ELI: http://data.europa.eu/eli/reco/2020/1475/oj.

21 Brussels, 17.3.2021, Doc. COM(2021) 130 final (Document 52021PC0130).

22 See Para 1 of the Explanatory Memorandum, devoted to "Reasons for and objectives of the proposal."

23 Ibid.

24 See Recital no. 61 of the EU Digital COVID Certificate Regulation.

In fact, if ICT had to be used to help in the fight against the pandemic – and to make sure that free movement was "given back to citizens" (Banks 2021) – a common approach for the issuance, verification and acceptance of COVID-19 certificates, based on mutual trust, had certainly to be put in place.

Action at the EU level was thus considered necessary from the subsidiarity principle's perspective.

As for proportionality, Recital no. 14 Digital Green Certificate underlines how "This Regulation is intended to facilitate the application of the principles of proportionality and non-discrimination with regard to restrictions to free movement during the COVID-19 pandemic, while pursuing a high level of public health protection." But it also specifies that "It should not be understood as facilitating or encouraging the adoption of restrictions to free movement, or restrictions to other fundamental rights, in response to the COVID-19 pandemic, given their detrimental effects on Union citizens and businesses." So that "Any verification of the certificates making up the EU Digital COVID Certificate should not lead to further restrictions to the freedom of movement within the Union or to restrictions on travel within the Schengen area."

It is important to recall this here as, paradoxically enough, in public as well as in some expert's opinion, the COVID-19 Certificate has been wrongly perceived as a tool to further restrict free movement and other fundamental freedoms and rights of citizens, rather than the contrary (Gentilucci 2021).

We do not wish to enter here the details of this complex debate (Poggi 2021), which is obviously related also to how the COVID-19 Certificate has been implemented in the national legal orders of the Member States.[25] It is nonetheless necessary to draw attention to a fact that is too often forgotten: the legal base for the adoption of the EU Regulation providing for the COVID-19 Certificate was Art. 21 para 2 TFUE. The EU Regulation was thus adopted "for the purpose of facilitating the holders' exercise of their right to free movement during the COVID-19 pandemic." [26]

In fact, already in Art. 1, para 1, of the Regulation, it is highlighted that "This Regulation shall also contribute to facilitating the gradual lifting of restrictions to free movement put in place by the Member States, in accordance with Union law, to limit the spread of SARS-CoV-2, in a coordinated manner." This is the "Subject matter" of the EU Regulation, clearly stated in its Art. 1!

Therefore, the specific point about proportionality here is that if "Member States may, in accordance with Union law, limit the fundamental right of free movement on grounds of public health," such limitations should nonetheless be compatible with such principle. Therefore, they should not only be suitable to reach the goal of protecting public health (by restricting the free movement of persons within the Union to limit the spread of SARS-CoV-2). They should also "be strictly limited in scope and time, in line with the efforts to restore free movement

25 As for Italy, there still is a huge public and experts' debate on the topic!

26 Art. 1, para. 1, *alinea* 1 of the Digital Green Certificate Regulation quoted above.

within the Union, and should not extend beyond what is strictly necessary to safeguard public health."[27]

From this point of view, the COVID-19 Certificate is certainly a tool compatible with the *necessity* test of the proportionality principle. According to the evidence available when the decision was taken, it certainly was the "solution," which one could assume would have had the least negative consequences for other rights/interests involved (Art. 11 of the Digital Green Certificate Regulation).

As for its proportionality in the strict sense, it has already been highlighted that the COVID digital certificate "can effectively help prevent the spread of the infection and promote free movement, while upholding the right to health as much as possible."[28]

We agree with that. From the principle of proportionality point of view, there is not much more one can ask the decision-maker in a time of uncertainty and unpredictability as possible future evolutions! This is, in fact, the situation where, from a proportionality perspective, complex assessments and evaluations and a delicate balance are required from the decision-makers (Zilioli 2019). With the consequence that the final decision can be questioned only if it should turn out that there was a manifest error of appreciation by the decision-maker (Galetta 2022).

3.8 Conclusions

The first conclusive remarks concern the subsidiarity issue. The COVID-19 pandemic has made even clearer to us that, in a multilevel-government context like the present one, competences are often shared (from the municipal level up to the EU level) and it may not always be easy to identify the competent administration. It must be done from time to time based on the concrete measures to be taken, however taking into due consideration that the virus, like any natural element, ignores the legal boundaries that our societies have set themselves. Therefore, in geographically interlinked or in any case related areas, at least a shared action is necessary. It is true both nationally and supranationally, starting with the EU (Ziller 2020).

The extreme "compartmentalisation of the world into states," which has been complained about during the two years of the COVID-19 pandemic (Kochenov/Veraldi 2021, 405), has been largely overcome, within Europe, with a broad and successful vaccination campaign. The COVID-19 Certificate – digital proof that a person has been vaccinated against COVID-19, has recovered from COVID-19 or has a test result – has facilitated the re-establishing of free movement within the EU. At the same time, though the pandemic continues, it has thus allowed the EU citizens to regain, at least partially, their freedom of movement at least within the EU borders.

27 Recital no. 6 of the Digital Green Certificate Regulation.
28 G. Montanari/Vergallo/Zaami/Negro/Brunetti/Del Rio/Marinelli 2021.

From this point of view, the interoperability of the COVID-19 Certificate is certainly essential. From the point of view of the principle of subsidiarity, the adoption by the EU of a common standard is a fundamental aspect. If each Member State had independently chosen its technical standard, the risk would have been the impossibility of mutual recognition of the certificates. It would have prevented people from circulating freely in Europe, thus to the detriment of the fundamental freedoms protected by the Union. For this reason, the intervention of the EU, aimed at identifying a single technical standard, appears more than appropriate.

The second point we want to stress here, and which is related to the first one, is how the experience of the SARS-CoV-2 pandemic and the resulting emergency situation ultimately serve as an acknowledgement of the need to resort to innovative technological solutions.

We have already dismissed all criticism concerning the proportionality of the COVID-19 Certificate as such. Nonetheless, one problem remains, and it concerns the use of technology precisely to support the coordinated efforts to fight against the virus. As it was already underlined, the point is that until now, the technological and the organisational implementation concerning the COVID-19 Certificate have essentially been left to the Member States, which have therefore developed "tracing and identification systems" of their own (Gstrein 2021). With all the associated problems.

That's one of the reasons why, most recently, the EC has proposed to update the rules on coordination of safe and free movement in the EU, which are related to the COVID-19 Certificate, and move to a "person-based approach" in order to "avoid diverging measures throughout the EU."[29]

Nonetheless, while doing that, two important elements need to be kept in mind and which emerged clearly from the examples shown here.

Firstly, to introduce innovative solutions, it is not necessary to revolutionise or redesign existing systems. As the example of the Lombardy Region shows (*AllertaLOM*), it may be sufficient to adapt and implement tools already in place, thus maximising the usefulness of the existing technological infrastructures.

Secondly, it is important to emphasise that the use of technologies like the app *Immuni* can constitute important support for administrative activities without further affecting the rights of citizens, as the examples above have shown in relation to the protection of *privacy*.

More intruding technological solutions, such as implementing the COVID-19 Certificate, should be confined as much as possible and as a last resort measure. Indeed, in hindsight, the use of technologies that can allow a higher degree of users' privacy should have been preferred by Governments at the earliest possible moment. In this way, it would have also been possible to ensure greater

29 See EU Commission, Press release of 25 November 2021, Commission proposes to strengthen coordination of safe travel in the EU, at https://ec.europa.eu/commission/presscorner/detail/en/ip_21_6186.

compliance with the provision of Art. 2 of Protocol No. 4 to the European Convention on Human Rights on the Freedom of movement.

From this point of view, an important difference must be stressed between the underlying interests justifying the policies adopted at the European level and those adopted at the national level. As mentioned, at the European level, the objective pursued by the legislator is to coordinate the technologies used to guarantee the mutual recognition of COVID-19 Certificate and so the fundamental freedoms set out in the EU Treaties. This is made clear by the EU legislator itself, at the very first Recital of Regulation 2021/953/EU, where it is stated that "every citizen of the Union has the fundamental right to move and reside freely within the territory of the Member States, subject to the limitations and conditions laid down in the Treaties and by the measures adopted to give effect to them." For this reason, we argue that the proportionality test can be deemed fulfilled by EU provisions.

Conversely, at the national level, the interests to be protected change considerably. It is not the protection of the EU fundamental freedoms that motivates the national legislator. That falls well outside the competences of national authorities. At the national level, the proportionality assessment must consider a much more complex set of rights and obligations, ultimately aimed at guaranteeing the coexistence of the administered population.

Unfortunately, national Governments have favoured policies that seem to not have always been fully consistent with this objective. First, they have not deemed it necessary to impose apps like *Immuni* to safeguard citizens' privacy, even if such apps did not raise any concrete privacy concern. Later, due to the seriousness of the situation, they abruptly changed course and imposed much more intrusive technologies beyond what the EU was concerned with.

This contradictory and inconsistent behaviour is particularly disappointing both because it has failed to protect the health of citizens and because it led to strong discontent, which has resulted in lively disputes across Europe. The hope for the upcoming months is that a more coherent attitude is adopted at all levels of government to protect public health and to ensure the harmonious coexistence of all social actors.

Works cited

Banks, M., 'New EU Digital COVID Certificate Paves Way for Europeans to Get Freedom Back, Says MEP' *The Parliament Magazine* (2021) <https://www.proquest.com/magazines/new-eu-digital-covid-certificate-paves-way/docview/2538373651/se-2?accountid=12459> (08.06.2021).

Barak, A., 'Proportionality and Principled Balancing' (2010) 1 Law & Ethics of Human Rights 1–18.

Carullo, G., 'Open Data e partecipazione democratica' (2019) 3 Istituzioni del federalismo 685–700.

Gentilucci, P., 'Green pass e profili di legittimità costituzionale' *Diritto & Diritti* (2021) <https://www.diritto.it/green-pass-e-profili-di-legittimita-costituzionale/> (9.08.2021).

Galetta, D.U., *Principio di proporzionalità e sindacato giurisdizionale nel diritto amministrativo* (Giuffrè, Milano 1998).

Galetta, D.U., 'The EU Law Principle of Proportionality and Judicial Review: Its Origin, Development, Dissemination and the Lessons to Be Learnt from the EU Court of Justice' in Continuity and Change - How the Challenges of Today Prepare the Ground for Tomorrow: ECB Legal Conference 2021 (Publications Office of the European Union, Lussemburgo 2022) 55–76.

Gladwell, M., *The Tipping Point: How Little Things Can Make a Big Difference* (Little, Brown, New York 2006).

Gstrein, O.J., 'The EU Digital COVID Certificate: A Preliminary Data Protection Impact Assessment' (2021) 12 European Journal of Risk Regulation 370.

Kochenov, D.V., and Veraldi, J.D., 'The Commission against the Internal Market and European Union Citizens' Rights: Trying to Shoot Down Sputnik with the 'Digital Green Certificate'?' (2021) 12 European Journal of Risk Regulation 404.

Lemley, M.A., 'Antitrust and the Internet Standardization Problem' (1996) 28 Connecticut Law Review 1041.

Montagnani, M.L., 'Remedies to Exclusionary Innovation in the High-Tech Sector: Is There a Lesson from the Microsoft Saga?' (2007) 4 World Competition 623.

Montanari, V., Zaami, S., Negro, F., Brunetti, P., Del Rio, A., and Marinelli, E., 'Does the EU COVID Digital Certificate Strike a Reasonable Balance between Mobility Needs and Public Health?' (2021) 57 Medicina 1077.

Poggi, A., 'Green Pass, obbligo vaccinale e le scelte del Governo' (2021) 21 Federalismi. it iv-x.

Zilioli, Ch., 'Proportionality as the Organising Principle of the European Banking Regulation' in ed. Th. Baums, H. Remsperger, M. Sachs, V.W. Wieland, *Zentralbanken, Währungsunion und stabiles Finanzsystem. Festschrift für Helmut Siekmann* (Duncker & Humblot GmbH, Berlin 2019), 257.

Ziller, J., 'Unione europea e Coronavirus' (2020) 1 *CERIDAP* 1–6.

4 The Pandemic as a Chance for Administrative Modernisation

Some Notes from Germany[1]

Cristina Fraenkel-Haeberle and Elena Buoso

4.1 Introduction

The pandemic crisis has driven developments in digitisation already underway in Germany. It has been an opportunity to proceed with more determination with reforms induced by technological progress and internal and external needs. Some innovations and simplifications are specific to the COVID-19 emergency and will cease once normal life resumes. However, others have initiated new developments that will promote a major "update"[2] of public administration.

4.2 The current state of digitisation in Germany

In relation to e-government, Germany still has much to do, as its digitalisation index is relatively low by European standards.[3] Structural problems, such as gaps in mobile telephone network coverage (so-called *Funklöcher*), need to be overcome,[4] and in some regions, delays have for years affected the laying of optical fibres, indispensable for fast data exchange. As part of an incentive programme, the Federal Government has therefore set the objective of creating a broadband network that even covers areas where it is not convenient from an entrepreneurial perspective.[5]

1 This paper is the result of common reflections; however, sections 4.1–4.3 and 4.6 can be attributed to Cristina Fraenkel-Haeberle and sections 4.4–4.5 to Elena Buoso. The publication was prepared with status as of 15.10.2021.

2 M. Seckelmann, and M. Brunzel. 2021. Das Onlinezugangsgesetz im Kontext einer digital vernetzten Gesellschaft und datengetriebenen Wirtschaft: Zur Einleitung. In *Handbuch Onlinezugangsgesetz*, ed. M. Seckelmann, and M. Brunzel 1-13. Berlin: Springer.

3 See the 2017 annual report of the *Nationaler Normenkontrollrat* (National Regulations Control Council), 35 ff.

4 In this regard, in November 2019 the Federal Network Agency (*Bundesnetzagentur*) published a map showing in detail the quality of radio links in Germany and identifying the areas not covered by the networks. See on this point https://www.pcwelt.de/news/Bundesnetzagentur-veroeffentlicht-Funkloch-Karte-fuer-Deutschland-10698252.html (12.09. 2021).

5 Compare: www.bmvi.de/DE/Themen/Digitales/Breitbandausbau/Breitbandfoerderung/breitband-foerderung.html (12.09.2021).

DOI: 10.4324/9781003263968-10

However, apart from infrastructure problems, it should generally be acknowledged that classic administrative activity is "analogue,"[6] namely that of a public administration acting under the old paradigm of paper documents without self-certification, which in other legal systems has been a first essential form of administrative simplification.[7] Proof of this is the fact that the country currently ranks 12th in the Digital Economy and Society Index (DESI), created by the EU.[8] This is why an analysis of the "digital compatibility" of existing legislation was already required before the pandemic. The federal e-government law of 2013 envisaged examination of all federal administrative law for the purpose of promoting digitisation.[9] The law triggered a far-reaching process and led to promulgation of various laws by the *Länder* (as in Bavaria)[10] to increase the digitisation of administrative procedures.[11]

The e-government law obliges administrations to store documents electronically.[12] Since January 2020, electronic archives have become mandatory, provided electronic format is not uneconomical for the administration in a long-term perspective.[13] The law envisages the conversion of paper documents into electronic format.[14]

As a further step towards digitisation, a law was enacted in 2017 with the aim of systematically pruning German administrative law of the written-form

6 L. Prell. 2018. E-Government: Paradigmenwechsel in der Verwaltung und Verwaltungsrecht. *Neue Zeitschrift für Verwaltungsrecht* 17:1255–1259.

7 See, e.g., in Italy, Decreto del Presidente della Repubblica (DPR) no. 445 of 28.12.2000 (G.U. 20.2.2001, no. 42), which lists the certifications and documents that can be replaced by a simple self-declaration. See also Law no. 183 of 12.11.2011 (G.U. 14.11.2011, no. 265), which requires public administrations to accept such self-produced documents, prohibiting the request for official certificates.

8 See The Digital Economy and Society Index (DESI) (europa.eu) and also F. 36von Harbou, 2020. Abschied vom Einzelfall? Perspektiven der Digitalisierung von Verwaltungsverfahren, *Juristen-Zeitung* 7:340-348. In its annual "European Digital Progress Report", the European Commission places Germany well below the European average in the "Digital Public Services" column. Germany also ranks 18th on a European scale in "digital administrative supply" (M. Martini. 2017. Transformation der Verwaltung durch Digitalisierung. *Die Öffentliche Verwaltung* 11:443–455).

9 *Gesetz zur Förderung der elektronischen Verwaltung* (*E-Government-Gesetz* – *EGovG*) of 25.07.2013 (*BGBl.* I, 2749).

10 *Gesetz über die elektronische Verwaltung in Bayern* (*Bayerisches E-Government-Gesetz* – *BayE-GovG*) of 22.12.2015 (*GVBl.* 458). In the meantime, also the *Länder* Baden-Württemberg, Berlin, Bremen, Mecklenburg-Vorpommern, Nordrhein-Westfalen, Saarland, Sachsen, Schleswig-Holstein and Thüringen have issued their own e-government laws (A. Guckelberger. 2019. E-Government: Ein Paradigmenwechsel in Verwaltung und Verwaltungsrecht? *VVDStRL* 78:235–288).

11 T. Siegel. 2019. Der Europäische Portalverbund – Frischer Digitalisierungswind durch das einheitliche digitale Zugangstor ('Single Digital Gateway'). *Neue Zeitschrift für Verwaltungsrecht* 13:905–909.

12 EGovG § 6, par. 1.

13 EGovG § 6, par. 2.

14 EGovG § 7.

requirement.[15] Accordingly, as proposed by the coordinating body of the Federation and the *Länder* in the field of digital technologies (*IT Planungsrat*),[16] on 14 October 2016, the Joint Conference of Prime Ministers of the Federation and the *Länder* decided to set up an "integrated website" (*Portalverbund*), a sort of digital one-stop-shop to access public services on a national basis.[17]

This reform required a constitutional amendment attributing legislative competence in this field to the Federation. The constitutional law of 13 September 2017 (on the reform of financial federalism)[18] amending the *Grundgesetz* (*GG*, the German Constitution), introduced a new art. 91(5) *GG*, by which the Federation has exclusive legislative competence and the task of regulating institution of the website, from which all public services at federal and *Länder* level are accessed. This laid the foundations for the great federal e-government project, whereby administrations are required to publish the range of services available on their homepage. The strategy pursued is twofold and goes by the names "digital first" (priority to the digital process) and "once only" (entering data once and making it accessible by all administrations at national level).[19]

The constitutional amendment allowed promulgation of the Online Access Act (*Onlinezugangsgesetz – OZG*)[20] on 14 August 2017, with the aim of allowing access to public services without temporal or spatial constraints.[21] According to the multichannel principle, § 1 OZG provides that the Federation and the *Länder* must offer their respective services "also" in electronic form through the integrated website by 12 December 2022 and connect their respective homepages (§ 1 para. 1 and 2 OZG).[22] In the framework of the digitisation programme, 575 service packages were identified and assigned to 14 subject areas. Particularly important public concerns, such as subsidies for university students (*BaföG*), building permits, housing allowances and so forth, are discussed in so-called digitisation laboratories to support the planning phase. At least one digitisation laboratory is assigned to each topic.[23] Exemptions from digitisation are only made for services

15 *Gesetz zum Abbau verzichtbarer Anordnungen der Schriftform im Verwaltungsrecht des Bundes vom 29.3.2017* (*BGBl.* I 2017, 626).

16 https://www.it-planungsrat.de/DE/Home/home_node.html (12.09.2021). See more extensively A. Guckelberger. 2019. E-Government: Ein Paradigmenwechsel in Verwaltung und Verwaltungsrecht? (no. 10) 257.

17 See more extensively C. Fraenkel-Haeberle. 2020. Fully digitalised administrative procedures in the German legal system. *Erdal* 1:105-111.

18 *BGBl.* I 2347.

19 F. von Harbou. 2020. Abschied vom Einzelfall? Perspektiven der Digitalisierung von Verwaltungsverfahren (no. 8) 341.

20 *BGBl.* I 3122, 3138; see T. Siegel. 2018. Auf dem Weg zum Portalverbund – Das neue Onlinezugangsgesetz (OZG). *Die Öffentliche Verwaltung* 5:185–191.

21 Compare art. 9 of the *Gesetz zur Neuregelung des bundesstaatlichen Finanzausgleichs ab dem Jahr 2020 und zur Änderung haushaltsrechtlicher Vorschriften* of 14.08.2017 (*BGBl.* I, 2787).

22 T. Siegel. Auf dem Weg zum Portalverbund – Das neue Onlinezugangsgesetz (no. 20) 188.

23 C. Voss. Die Implementation der Europäischen Dienstleistungsrichtlinie – lessons learned im Hinblick auf das Wirksamwerden der Single Digital Gateway-Verordnung und des Onlinezugangsge-

unsuitable for offer online.[24] An essential requirement for the functioning of the integrated website is the standardisation of IT components, which must be jointly defined by a regulation.[25]

The integrated website is a link between the federal, *Länder* and local homepages. It is not a separate platform on which administrative services are offered. A link also has to be established to the EU single digital gateway, which is being set up on the basis of Regulation (EU) 2018/1724.[26] There is considerable overlap between the Single Digital Gateway Regulation and the Online Access Act. Since the Online Access Act is wide in scope, it encompasses the administrative services regulated by European Law.[27] This creates a network of municipal and *Länder* portals, national portals and the European portal (*metaportal network*). From an e-government perspective, mandatory online access is essential.[28]

This virtual interface is a tool with which Germany aims to overcome its digital shortcomings through technical integration of the websites of the multi-level system. It is a "front-office" portal, which like the provisions of the Bolkestein Directive 123/2006,[29] does not change the structure of the "back office," namely the administrations of the three levels of government (federal, *Länder* and municipal). It should also be borne in mind that since transposition of the services directive, the so-called *Behördenportale*[30] have become increasingly widespread in Germany.[31]

Comprehensive digitisation of the public administration is now carried out under the economic recovery plan elaborated to offset the aftermath of COVID-19

---

setzes. In *Handbuch Onlinezugangsgesetz*, ed. M. Seckelmann, and M. Brunzel, 199–225. Berlin: Springer.

24 OZG § 1 (1) second sentence.

25 See § 4 OZG on IT components; § 5 OZG on safety standards; § 6 OZG on communication standards.

26 In October 2018, the European legislator had the idea of a single website of its own with Regulation (EU) 2018/1724 on the single digital gateway as a prominent element of the digital strategy of the EU. This "metaportal" was set up by the Commission (art. 2) with the function of front office, and therefore without affecting back-office tasks of member states, in line with their procedural autonomy, as can be seen from recitals 24–26. EU regulation 2018/1724 envisages establishment of this portal for accessing information, procedures, and support services in the case of difficulties (art. 7). It refers to information and procedures relevant for the internal market. It came into force on 12.12.2020 (art. 39, para. 2). In legal science, the goal of one-stop government without changing the spheres of competence of the single administrations has long been pursued. See T. 29Siegel. 2019. Der Europäische Portalverbund – Frischer Digitalisierungswind durch das einheitliche digitale Zugangstor ("Single Digitale Gateway"). *Neue Zeitschrift für Verwaltungsrecht* 9:905-909; C. Voss. 2021. Die Implementation der Europäischen Dienstleistungsrichtlinie – lessons learned im Hinblick auf das Wirksamwerden der Single Digital Gateway-Verordnung und des Onlinezugangsgesetzes (no. 23) 214.

27 Ibid. 213.

28 Ibid. 212.

29 Directive 2006/123/CE of the European Parliament and of the Council of 12.12.2006 on services in the internal market, L 376/36 2006.

30 Also called *Verwaltungsportale* or *Bürgerportale*.

31 T. Siegel. 2018. Auf dem Weg zum Portalverbund – Das neue Onlinezugangsgesetz (no. 20) 192.

with an endowment of three billion euros.[32] This recovery plan envisages a "one for all" model, consisting in a procedure based on a division of labour. A digital process developed in a *Land* is then made available to the other *Länder* and at the municipal level, thus saving resources.[33] The digital transformation of the public administration can only be successfully implemented by well-qualified public administration employees. This requires appropriate professional training of the personnel assigned to digitisation in the framework of specific training programmes, now underway.[34] In the wake of the pandemic, a new form of cooperative federalism "2.0" is gaining momentum.[35]

4.3 The pandemic as driver of the digital workplace and electronic public procurement?

The digital workplace, or "*mobiles Arbeiten*," has become a preferred way of working, has became a preferred way of working during the lockdown period. However, this model was intensely practised in Germany, compared to other countries, even before the pandemic. According to a survey conducted at the end of March 2020, 43% of respondents already worked at home at least one day a week before COVID-19, and particularly appreciated being able to use travelling time productively, especially in the case of long commutes on congested roads or overcrowded trains. By comparison, the incidence of smart working before the pandemic is estimated at around 22% in Italy and France.[36]

The same survey showed that 71% of respondents believed working from home will continue to increase in frequency after the pandemic. In this regard, on 1 April 2020, the *Fraunhofer-Institut für Angewandte Informationstechnik* (FIT) also launched an Internet inquiry on the home office, the results of which are now available.[37] They show that most respondents (over 80%) are satisfied with digital

32 See Bundesfinanzministerium - Das Konjunkturprogramm› (12.09.2021).

33 M. Richter. 2021. Geleitwort. In *Handbuch Onlinezugangsgesetz*, ed. M. Seckelmann, and M. Brunzel (no. 2) V–VI.

34 The IT planning council (*IT-Planungsrat*) and the *Land* Hessen support the "eGovCampus" project to promote digital skills. This initiative is supplemented by the "Qualifica Digitalis" project, also initiated by the IT planning council and the *Land* Bremen, as well as the "KommunalCampus" project started by the Rhine-Neckar metropolitan region and the Bergstraße district; see M. Seckelmann, M. Brunzel, M. 2021. Das Onlinezugangsgesetz im Kontext einer digital vernetzten Gesellschaft und datengetriebenen Wirtschaft: Zur Einleitung (no. 2) 10.

35 M. Seckelmann, and M. Brunzel. 2021. Das Onlinezugangsgesetz im Kontext einer digital vernetzten Gesellschaft und datengetriebenen Wirtschaft: Zur Einleitung (no. 2) 4.

36 https://ap-verlag.de/home-office-ist-mehr-als-eine-voruebergehende-krisenmassnahme/59444/ (12.09.2021). The survey also shows that in an international comparison, German workers are well equipped for mobile work, as 57% of them have a room or area of the house dedicated to the purpose. They also report that 49% spend the same amount of time in the home office as in the workplace. 74% also stated that productivity at home is the same if not higher than in the office, while the remaining 26% complained of a loss of productivity due to the distance from colleagues and consequent communication difficulties.

37 https://www.fit.fraunhofer.de/de/fb/cscw/homeoffice-studie.html (12.09.2021).

work, noting an increase in productivity, which in their eyes is more important than physical proximity to colleagues and informal communication, certainly not favoured by electronic communication.[38]

However, introduction of the home office has brought out several data security and privacy issues. The employer remains responsible for the processing of personal data, even if this occurs in the home environment. He is therefore required to establish remote access that is virtually like the business context, in which company communication and data saving technically takes place. At the same time, the worker must be able to guarantee that third parties (family members or cohabitants) do not have access to company data. The situation of the pandemic has led to the development of solutions that allow an adequate balance of the various interests, for example, using modern cryptographic techniques. A particular problem is the processing of sensitive data (for example patient records), in relation to which the home office may not be allowed.[39]

Even in procurement law, the German legal system has reacted very cautiously, while in other legal systems – such as the Italian one – it triggered intense discussion on the need for simplification and ad hoc procedures, some of which have been introduced.[40] The German Ministry for the Economy and Energy first issued an interpretative circular (19 March 2020),[41] which called for normal simplified procedures among the negotiated procedures already contemplated (for example § 14, IV, no. 3 VgV and § 3a, III, no. 4 EU VOB/A) in line with the EU's subsequent recommendations for contracts above the EU-threshold (1 April 2020).[42] It was not until July 2020 that the Ministry intervened with binding directives and various measures to make procurement procedures simpler and faster, raising the thresholds for direct awards, with provisions in force until 31 December 2021.[43]

On the other hand, there has been no acceleration of digitisation of above-threshold contracts, regulation of which is a federal competence and is largely derived from EU rules. This ongoing process followed the previously decided roadmap, especially in relation to the existing electronic register of procedures and online access to procurement documents.[44] However, some interventions of

38 For more details, see E. Buoso. 2021. Main issues raised by Covid-19 response in selected topics. *GPN Journal* 1-2: 109–114. https://www.aracneeditrice.eu/it/pubblicazioni/legal-policy-pandemics-first-volume-9791259944351.html.

39 M. Wuschelbaum. 2020. COVID-19: Pandemiebewältigung und Datenschutz – Kollektivevereinbarungen als krisentaugliches DS-GVO-Instrument? *Neue Zeitschrift für Arbeitsrecht* 10:612-616 (614).

40 Law Decree no. 18 of 17.3.2020, as amended by Law no. 27 of 24.4.2020 (G.U. 29.04.2020, no. 110).

41 https://www.bmwi.de/Redaktion/DE/Downloads/P-R/rundschreiben-anwendung-vergaberecht.pdf?__blob=publicationFile&v=6 (12.09.2021).

42 https://eur-lex.europa.eu/legal-content/DE/TXT/?uri=CELEX:52020XC0401(05), (12.09.2021).

43 https://www.bmwi.de/Redaktion/DE/Downloads/H/handlungsleitlinien-vergr-corona.pdf?__blob=publicationFile&v=4 (12.09.2021).

44 https://www.bundesregierung.de/breg-de/themen/digital-made-in-de/digitalisierung-der-oeffentlichen-beschaffung-1547012; https://www.bmwi.de/Redaktion/DE/Dossier/oeffentliche-auftraege

the *Länder* for procurements below the EU-threshold are noteworthy, as they have introduced the possibility of submitting bids by email[45] or have extended the possibility of using the simplified electronic procedure by raising the thresholds.[46]

4.4 Digital strategy to manage the pandemic crisis in Germany

Tracing-apps have been an important element of digital management strategy related to the pandemic crisis. The first was developed in April 2020 by the Robert Koch Institute to process smartwatch and fitness device data "donated" by users. Since the German approach to data sharing is usually very cautious, it came as a surprise that more than half a million users downloaded and are using the app, even though the shared data is not anonymous and includes sensitive data on personal health.[47]

The "Corona-warn-app"[48] has also been available since June 2020. It was developed as an open-source system and operates according to the Pan-European Privacy-Preserving Proximity Tracing Protocol.[49] The app is produced and distributed by the Robert Koch Institute and offers a voluntary double-approval system: for its use and for the transfer of anonymous epidemiologically-relevant data, limited to the last two weeks.[50] Its digital contact tracing system differs from those of other countries, because it aims at "tracking."[51] The extra letter *k* indicates something different from "tracing," i.e. that no data is collected on GPS position or the repeater (as in the case of a traditional tracing-app) and only Bluetooth technology is used. The German Corona-App only registers devices that come within

-und-vergabe.html; https://www.evergabe-online.de/start.html (12.09.2021); compare I. Reichling, N. Scheumann, N. K., Lampe, O. 2020. "eVergabe" – Ist das Vergaberecht im Zeitalter der Digitalisierung angekommen? (Teil I). *Gewerbearchiv* 7-8:248–251.

45 Bayern, *Verwaltungsvorschrift* of 24.03.2020 (Az. B II 2 - G17/17 – 2).

46 Hamburg, 20.03.2020, http://www.forum-vergabe.de/fileadmin/user_upload/Downloads/2020.03.20_HHVergaberecht_FB_42_Corona-Rundschreiben_Vergaberecht.pdf (12.09.2021).

47 A detailed description of the project and analysis of the collected data, elaborated by the Robert Koch Institute, are accessible at: https://corona-datenspende.de/science/ (29.09.2021).

48 See www.bundesregierung.de/breg-de/themen/corona-warn-app (20.09.2021). On the legal issues raised by this app see T. Köllmann. 2020. Die Corona-Warn-App. Schnittstellen zwischen Datenschutz und Arbeitsrecht. *Neue Zeitschrift für Arbeitsrecht*, 13:831-836; M. Wünschelbaum. 2020. COVID-19: Pandemiebewältigung und Datenschutz. Kollektivvereinbarungen als krisentaugliches DS-GVO-Instrument? *Neue Zeitschrift für Arbeitsrecht*, 10: 612–616.

49 See also F. Buccafurri, V. De Angelis. and C. Labrini. 2020. A privacy-preserving solution for proximity tracing avoiding identifier exchanging. Paper presented at the 2020 International Conference on Cyberworlds (CW), https://ieeexplore.ieee.org/ielx7/9240475/9240501/09240513.pdf (2.10.2021).

50 The Corona-warn-app was commissioned by the federal government to Deutsche Telekom and SAP group. The Fraunhofer, Helmholtz and Robert Koch Institutes participated in the project as well. Federal Privacy Supervisor, Ulrich Kelber, followed the procedure.

51 See more extensively E. Buoso and C. Fraenkel-Haeberle. 2020. La Germania alla prova del coronavirus tra Stato di diritto e misure emergenziali. *Federalismi*, 20:75-104. www.federalismi.it. https://www.federalismi.it/nv14/articolo-documento.cfm?Artid=43704.

two metres of each other for at least 15 minutes. Smartphones scan their surroundings at regular intervals and the app communicates once a day with a central server, sending an alert if a COVID-positive individual, who uses the app and has uploaded a positive test, is approached. The user is than invited by a push message to be tested for SARS-CoV-2. Use of the warn-app is voluntary and privacy-safe, because it is based on randomly generated identification numbers, which change at regular intervals so that the developers and managers do not know the identity, or the position of a given ID.

The Corona-warn-app has two more functions: it can be used to obtain and store the QR-code of the COVID-19 Certificate, which can otherwise be requested from medical doctors and authorised pharmacies,[52] and to register (by scanning a cluster-specific QR-code) with the digital guest list of restaurants and cultural events, for contact-tracing purposes. The latter function is also provided by a commercial app (Luca-app), available since the beginning of 2021, however in this case some security issues have been reported.[53] The number of downloads is relatively high (45 million for the Corona-warn-app[54] and 35 million for the Luca-app),[55] but these apps have not proven to be effective for pandemic containment[56] unless associated with the so-called 3G-rule introduced by the Federal Government and the *Länder*.[57]

It is not unlikely that these and many other strategies to enable daily activities while preventing contagion have affected society and people's habits and could effectively be irreversible, regardless of whether they are imposed by regulation: for example, electronic payment of even small sums and the endless possibilities of online work and education platforms.[58]

52 The system is well explained on the website of the Ministry for Health www.bundesgesundheitsministerium.de/coronavirus/faq-covid-19-impfung/faq-digitaler-impfnachweis.html (3.10. 2021).

53 T. Stadler, W. Lueks, K. Kohls, C. Troncoso. 2021. Preliminary analysis of potential harms in the Luca tracing system. arXiv [preprint].

54 Details are available on the website of the RKI: www.rki.de/DE/Content/InfAZ/N/Neuartiges_Coronavirus/WarnApp/Archiv_Kennzahlen/WarnApp_KennzahlenTab.html (1.10.2021).

55 J. Breithut. 2021. Von Smudo bis Blockchain – so frickelt Deutschland an digitalen Helfern. Der Spiegel (11.04.2021). https://www.spiegel.de/netzwelt/apps/corona-warn-app-luca-und-impfnachweis-so-geht-es-weiter-mit-den-digitalen-helfern-a-5f7d5400-7425-468e-8b85-cac1c8208283 (3.10.2021).

56 A. Dix. 2021. Mit Apps gegen Corona – Was bringen Luca und Corona-Warn-App? *ZD-Aktuell*, 04441; J-P Stroscher and P. Schomberg. 2021. Digitale Kontaktnachverfolgung per App – ist ein Ende der Zettelwirtschaft in Sicht. *ZD-Aktuell*, 05138.

57 Geimpft, Genesen oder Gestestet (vaccinated, healed or tested). The rule is in force since 23.08.2021, and the *Länder* may derogate in areas with a low incidence of infection.

58 More about home working and home schooling in E. Buoso. 2021. Main issues raised by Covid-19 response in selected topics (no. 38).

4.5 The German style of pandemic management: federalism and the rule of law

From a systematic and regulatory point of view, the rules introduced since March 2020, i.e., measures to reduce contagion, to deal with the economic consequences of contagion or to enable political bodies to function, are all expressly defined as emergency law and ceased in December 2021. Other examples concern the provisions amending the Parliament's Rules of Procedure,[59] the functioning of corporate bodies in *Bürgerliches Gesetzbuch* (BGB),[60] tax benefits,[61] the construction of COVID-19-related health care facilities and some special rules of the *Infektionsschutzgesetz* (*InfSchG*).[62] In the latter Act, the *Bundestag* was given new powers to declare a pandemic emergency of national importance (§ 5), which then empowers the Ministry of Health to issue national regulations in areas of competence previously attributed to the *Länder*; however, the duration of these regulations is limited by the Act itself to the duration of the pandemic (§ 5, par. 4). While in the initial phase of the pandemic, the Federal Government managed not to restrict the sphere of autonomy of the *Länder*,[63] the enduring emergency led Parliament to enact the so-called "emergency brake" (*Bundesnotbremse*), which sets automatically restrictive measures when certain levels of incidence are exceeded.[64]

In other words, it seems that the pandemic has not been an attempt to introduce permanent changes in the balance of power between the Federation and the *Länder*, nor between the three powers of the state, nor has it been used for substantial innovations that will remain in the system, having only, at most,

59 Bekanntmachung of 25.03.2020 (*BGBl.* I, 764). See M. Friehe. 2020. Was heißt hier immun? Quarantäne, Bundestagsabgeordnete und die Funktionsfähigkeit des Parlaments. VerfBlog (11.03.2020). https://verfassungsblog.de/was-heisst-hier-immun (3.10.2021). Id. 2020. Freiheit in höchsten Nöten: Warum die Corona-Krise nicht zum Verfassungsnotstand stilisiert werden darf. VerfBlog (28.03.2020). https://verfassungsblog.de/freiheit-in-hoechsten-noeten/ (3.10. 2021).

60 *Gesetz zur Abmilderung der Folgender COVID-19-Pandemie im Zivil-, Insolvenz- und Strafverfahrensrecht* of 27.3.2020, *BGBl.* I, 569. See C.Wolf, R. Eckert, Denz, et al. 2020. Die zivilrechtlichen Auswirkungen des COVID-19-Gesetzes. *Juristische Arbeitsblätter* 52:401, 403.

61 *Zweites Gesetz zur Umsetzung steuerlicher Hilfsmaßnahmen zur Bewältigung der Corona-Krise* of 30.06.2020 (*BGBl.* I, 1512).

62 *Epidemieschutzgesetz* (*Gesetz zum Schutz der Bevölkerung bei einer epidemischer Lage von nationaler Tragweite*) of 27.03.2020 (*BGBl.* I, 587), which amended the *Infektionsschutzgesetz* of 20.07.2000 (*BGBl.* I, 1045) and the Urban Planning Code (*Baugesetzbuch*). See also *Gesetz zum Ausgleich COVID-19 bedingter finanzieller Belastungen der Krankenhäuser und weiterer Gesundheitseinrichtungen* (*COVID-19-Krankenhausentlastungsgesetz*) of 27.03.2020 (*BGBl.* I, 580), which amended the law about hospital financing *Krankenhausfinanzierungsgesetz* of 10.04.1991 (*BGBl.* I, 886).

63 On the role of the federal State and of the federal Parliament in the pandemic, see H. Dreier. 2021. Rechtsstaat, Föderalismus und Demokratie in der Corona-Pandemie. *Die Öffentliche Verwaltung* 6:229–243; V. Boehme-Neßler. 2021. Das Parlament in der Pandemie. *Die Öffentliche Verwaltung* 6:243–251.

64 *Vierten Gesetz zum Schutz der Bevölkerung bei einer epidemischen Lage von nationaler Tragweite* of 22.04.2021 (BGBl. I, 802).

accelerated the processes already underway. On one hand, this has guaranteed the stability of the balance of powers and fundamental rights; on the other, in some cases it slowed down some reactions to the pandemic: digitisation is a clear example of this.

It can be noted that the *Bund* and *Länder* have both paid particular attention to managing the pandemic within normal parliamentary procedures and emergency management tools. This extends to all state powers:

1) at legislative level, the *Bundestag* reacted swiftly by emending its Rules of Internal Procedure so as to be able to function even with a small number of Members of Parliament, while guaranteeing representation, and by intervening with a strong and wide-ranging package of laws;
2) at administrative level, the Federal and *Länder* ministries have coordinated through political consultation that has mostly proved effective, adapting existing pandemic plans to COVID-19 and following the recommendations of the *Robert Koch Institut*;[65]
3) at judicial level, the mechanisms for review of legislative and administrative decisions, and a check of the constitutional legitimacy of laws, immediately came into effect, ensuring fundamental rights. In 2020, more than 10,000 summary proceedings and lawsuits against anti-COVID measures were decided by the administrative and constitutional courts.[66] Also direct appeal to the FCC (Bundesverfassungsgericht) and the *Länder* Constitutional Courts (*Verfassungsbeschwerde*) played an important role.[67] Most legal actions have been declared inadmissible or rejected, such as appeals against the *Bundesnotbremse*,[68] nonetheless there are some significant decisions based on:
   - the principle of proportionality in the compression of a fundamental right: e.g. freedom of movement,[69] the right to protest[70] and freedom of religion.[71] It is interesting that the uncertainty under which containment

65 The national *Pandemieplan* issued by the Robert Koch Institute in 2005 and now in force in the version of 2.03.2017 contains two parts (the first dedicated to organisational and antipandemic measures; the second on the scientific basis of the different measures) and an addendum about COVID-19 22.09.2021: https://www.rki.de/DE/Content/InfAZ/N/Neuartiges_Coronavirus/ZS/Pandemieplan_Strategien.html. Every *Land* has its updated pandemic plan.

66 See the statement of the German Judges Association (DRB), Richterbund: Mehr als 10.000 Eilverfahren und Klagen gegen Corona-Auflagen. Neue Osnabrücker Zeitung (8.03.2021). www.presseportal.de/pm/58964/4857338 (19.09.2021).

67 See the official statistic of the FCC available at www.bundesverfassungsgericht.de/DE/Verfahren/Jahresstatistiken/2020/gb2020/vorwort.html (19.09.2021).

68 FCC (Bundesverfassungsgericht - BVerfG) 1.06.2021, 1 BvR 927/21 www.bverfg.de/e/rk20210601_1bvr092721.html (28.08.2021; BVerfG 31.05.2021, 1 BvR 794/21 www.bverfg.de/e/rk20210531_1bvr079421.html (28.08.2021).

69 High Constitutional Court of Baden-Württemberg (VGH Baden-Württemberg), decision 5.02.2021, http://lrbw.juris.de/cgi-bin/laender_rechtsprechung/document.py?Gericht=bw&nr=33772 (29.09.2021).

70 BVerfG, 15.04.2020, 1 BvR 828/20 www.bverfg.de/e/rk20200415_1bvr082820.html (29.09.2021).

71 BVerfG, 29.04.2020, 1 BvQ 44/20 www.bverfg.de/e/qk20200429_1bvq004420.html (29.09.2021).

measures were taken and certain judgments were passed led to a change in the structure of the judgment of proportionality: the first step, relating to the suitability of the choices made by the public administration, has acquired new relevance;

- the incompleteness of the preliminary investigation or scientific basis;[72]
- the use of an administrative legal instrument to impose general measures that require a formal regulation.[73]

With the *Bundesnotbremse*, the Federal State has centralised the decision about containment measures if the pandemic crisis exceeds a certain threshold. The federal enactment also centralised judicial protection, conferring jurisdiction on the FCC instead of the administrative or constitutional courts of the *Länder*. This outcome has been harshly criticised, because it favours legal certainty and stability but could possibly lower protection of fundamental rights.

The emergency has been a huge stress test for the polycentric democratic structure of the German system, revealing strengths and weaknesses of the multi-level *Bund-Länder* consultations for deciding the measures to take. Such a political solution requires very transparent communication of decision-making processes. The *Bund* immediately moved in this direction, coordinating measures very different from those of the various *Länder*, which based on *InfSchG* rules are normally responsible for administrative implementation and concrete choices about contagion containment measures. This allowed uniform management of the lockdown, differentiated according to local needs but without creating excessive disparities, even in the economic situations of the *Länder*.[74] This approach changed, however, in 2021 as the pandemic worsened and the federal brake was introduced. The consequence was an undoubted centralisation of power, albeit limited exclusively to the COVID-19 emergency.

Although art. 35(3) *Grundgesetz* provides that in the event of a natural disaster or disaster involving several *Länder*, the *Bund* may use its so-called emergency competence, this rule (which had never hitherto been applied) presupposes that the *Länder* are unable to deal with the situation.[75] In any case, the constitution does not provide for federal substitutive power, but only legitimises the power to require local governments to make their police forces available and authorises the

72 Constitutional Court of Saarland (VerfGH Saarland) 28.03.2020 - Lv 7/20 eA https://verfassungsgerichtshof-saarland.de/frames/index.html. (29.09.2021); Administrative Court Berlin (VG Berlin), 31.05.2021, VG 3 L 180/21 https://openjur.de/u/2341796.html (29.09.2021).

73 Administrative Court Munich (VG München) 24.03.2020, M 26 S 20.1255 www.vgh.bayern.de/media/muenchen/presse/pm_2020-03-24_b1.pdf (29.09.2021).

74 See for example the deliberation of the *Bund-Länder* joint table of 22.03.2020, www.bundesregierung.de/breg-de/themen/coronavirus/besprechung-der-bundeskanzlerin-mit-den-regierungschefinnen-und-regierungschefs-der-laender-1733248. 26.09.2020. Further resolutions and minutes of the meetings are available on the same website.

75 H-G. Dederer. 2020. Art. 35 GG. In *Grundgesetz Kommentar*, (eds.) T. Maunz, G. Dürig. 89th ed. München: Beck.

Bund to use the army to support the public security authorities; these measures must be revoked immediately if the *Bundesrat* (the house of representatives of the *Länder*) so requests. The choice was therefore not to apply this provision, which would have required application by analogy, increasing the powers of the central government, but instead to give the national Parliament the power to declare the pandemic emergency, which bestows extraordinary regulatory powers. At the level of the *Länder*, no atypical acts were adopted, and the procedures laid down in the *InfSchG* and pandemic plans were followed.

On the whole, it can therefore be said that the German emergency response was managed according to the principles of the rule of law and the requirements of federalism.[76] Regarding the first point, compliance with the rule of law emerges in the formal sense, i.e. as respect for the procedures and form of the Acts, and in the substantive sense, through close judicial review of the authority's decisions in order to guarantee respect for fundamental rights, also ensured by the vigilant eye of the doctrine.[77] With regard to the second point, the Federal Government played a role of political coordination through issuing joint recommendations of *Bund-Länder* consultations, and the acts of the central ministries did not take over the administration of the *Länder*. Furthermore, the strict measures of the federal emergency brake were adopted by the Parliament and are subject to specific prerequisites.

4.6 Conclusions

The solutions introduced for the pandemic are part of a digitisation process already underway, albeit not yet particularly well rooted in the German legal system. They were implemented by the laws on e-government, digital access

76 On the compatibility of the federal system with effective pandemic response, see F. Palermo. 2020. Is there a space for federalism in times of emergency? VerfBlog (13.05.2020). https://verfassungsblog.de/is-there-a-space-forfederalism-in-times-of-emergency/ (14.08.2021); and the papers published by Forum of Federations at the link: www.forumfed.org/collection/federalism-and-covid-country-perspectives/ (14.08.2021).

77 See T. Kingreen. 2020. Whatever it Takes? Der demokratische Rechtsstaat in Zeiten von Corona. VerfBlog, (20.03.2020). https://verfassungsblog.de/whatever-it-takes/ (18.08.2021); U. Volkmann. 2020. Der Ausnahmezustand. VerfBlog 30.03.2020). https://verfassungsblog.de/der-ausnahmezustand/ (18.08.2021); O. Lepsius. 2020. Vom Niedergang grundrechtlicher Denkkategorien in der Corona-Pandemie. VerfBlog (16.04.2020). https://verfassungsblog.de/vom-niedergang-grundrechtlicher-denkkategorien-in-der-corona-pandemie/ (18.08.2021); R. Mehring. 2020. Carl Schmitt und die Pandemie. Teil I. VerfBlog (11.05.2020). https://verfassungsblog.de/carl-schmitt-und-die-pandemie-teil-i/ (18.08.2021); Id. 2020. Carl Schmitt und die Pandemie. Teil II, VerfBlog, (12.05.2020). https://verfassungsblog.de/carl-schmitt-und-die-pandemie-teil-ii/ (18.08.2021); K.A. Schwarz. 2020. Das Infektionsschutzgesetz und die Grundrechte – ein Lehrstück zum verfassungsrechtlichen Freiheitsverständnis bei drohenden Gefahren. *Juristische Arbeitsblätter* 5:321-326. See also the opinion published by the National Academy of Sciences, Leopoldina, on 13.04.2020: www.leopoldina.org/publikationen/detailansicht/publication/coronavirus-pandemie-die-krise-nachhaltig-ueberwinden-13-april-2020/ (18.08.2021).

to public services and fully digitised administrative Acts, introduced in 2017.[78] These reforms also fit into a broader context, moving in directions suggested by EU law. Many of these choices have strategic value and are likely to be maintained even after the end of the pandemic, as COVID-19 only accelerated an inevitable process.

Although the pandemic required emergency measures and imposed digitisation of communications, in principle, the German legal system followed traditional paths. It did not abandon democratic mechanisms but adopted solutions deliberated *in presence* by the Parliament. In addition, the pandemic showed that despite the federal structure of the German legal system, it was possible to obtain wide agreement on the fundamental decisions for tackling the pandemic, at least in the initial phase of the lockdown. This allowed consistency in the solutions adopted, also in the field of digital administration.

Works cited

Boehme-Neßler, V., Das Parlament in der Pandemie. (2021) 6 *Die Öffentliche Verwaltung* 243–251.

Breithut, J., 'Von Smudo bis Blockchain – so frickelt Deutschland an digitalen Helfern' *Der Spiegel* (2021).

Buccafurri, F., De Angelis, V., and Labrini, C., 'A Privacy-Preserving Solution for Proximity Tracing Avoiding Identifier Exchanging' in Paper presented at the *2020 International Conference on Cyberworlds (CW)* (2020) <https://ieeexplore.ieee.org/ielx7/9240475/9240501/09240513.pdf> (2.10.2021).

Buoso, E., 'Main Issues Raised by Covid-19 Response in Selected Topics' (2021) 1 GPN Journal.

Buoso, E., and Fraenkel-Haeberle, C. 'La Germania alla prova del coronavirus tra Stato di diritto e misure emergenziali' (2020) 20 Federalismi 75–104.

Buoso, E. 'Fully Automated Administrative Acts in the German Legal System' (2020) 1 Erdal 113–122.

Carl Schmitt und die Pandemie, 'Teil II' *VerfBlog* (2020) <https://verfassungsblog.de/carl-schmitt-und-die-pandemie-teil-ii/> (18.08.2021).

Dederer, H.-G., 'Art. 35 GG' in (eds.) T. Maunz and G. Dürig, *Grundgesetz Kommentar*, (Beck, München 2020).

Dix, A., *Mit Apps gegen Corona – Was bringen Luca und Corona-Warn-App?* (ZD-Aktuell 2021).

Dreier, H., 'Rechtsstaat, Föderalismus und Demokratie in der Corona-Pandemie' (2021) 6 Die Öffentliche Verwaltung 229–243.

Fraenkel-Haeberle, C., 'Fully Digitalized Administrative Procedures in the German Legal System' (2020) 1 Erdal 105–111.

Friehe, M., 'Was heißt hier immun? Quarantäne, Bundestagsabgeordnete und die Funktionsfähigkeit des Parlaments' *VerfBlog* (2020) (11.03.2020). https://verfassungsblog

78 See art. 20 of the *Gesetz zur Modernisierung des Besteuerungsverfahrens* (*StVfModG*) of 18.07.2016, *BGBl.* I, 1679, that came into force on 1.01.2017. Compare E. Buoso. 2020. Fully Automated Administrative Acts in the German Legal System. *Erdal* 1:113-122.

.de/was-heisst-hier-immun (3.10. 2021). Id. 2020. Freiheit in höchsten Nöten: Warum die Corona-Krise nicht zum Verfassungsnotstand stilisiert werden darf. *VerfBlog* (28.03.2020) <https://verfassungsblog.de/freiheit-in-hoechsten-noeten/> (3.10.2021).

Guckelberger, A., 'E-Government: Ein Paradigmenwechsel in Verwaltung und Verwaltungsrecht?' (2019) 78 VVDStRL 235–288.

Kingreen, T., 'Whatever it Takes? Der demokratische Rechtsstaat in Zeiten von Corona' *VerfBlog* (2020) <https://verfassungsblog.de/whatever-it-takes/> (18.08.2021).

Köllmann, T., 'Die Corona-Warn-App. Schnittstellen zwischen Datenschutz und Arbeitsrecht' (2020) 13 Neue Zeitschrift für Arbeitsrecht 831–836.

Lepsius, O., 'Vom Niedergang grundrechtlicher Denkkategorien in der Corona-Pandemie' *VerfBlog* (2020) <https://verfassungsblog.de/vom-niedergang-grundrechtlicher-denkkategorien-in-der-corona-pandemie/> (18.08.2021).

Martini, M., 'Transformation der Verwaltung durch Digitalisierung' (2017) 11 Die Öffentliche Verwaltung 443–455.

Mehring, R., 'Carl Schmitt und die Pandemie. Teil I' *VerfBlog* (2020) <https://verfassungsblog.de/carl-schmitt-und-die-pandemie-teil-i/> (18.08.2021).

Nationaler Normenkontrollrat, 'The 2017 Annual Report of the Nationaler Normenkontrollrat (National Regulations Control Council)' (2017) 35 ff.

Palermo, F., 'Is There a Space for Federalism in Times of Emergency?' *VerfBlog* (2020) <https://verfassungsblog.de/is-there-a-space-forfederalism-in-times-of-emergency/> (14.08.2021).

Prell, L., 'E-Government: Paradigmenwechsel in der Verwaltung und Verwaltungsrecht' (2018) 17 Neue Zeitschrift für Verwaltungsrecht 1255–1259.

Reichling, I., Scheumann, N. K., and Lampe, O., 'eVergabe' – Ist das Vergaberecht im Zeitalter der Digitalisierung angekommen? (Teil I)' (2020) 7–8 Gewerbearchiv 248–251.

Richter, M., 'Geleitwort' in (eds.) M. Seckelmann and M. Brunzel, *Handbuch Onlinezugangsgesetz* (no. 2) (Springer 2021) V–VI.

Schwarz, K.A., 'Das Infektionsschutzgesetz und die Grundrechte – ein Lehrstück zum verfassungsrechtlichen Freiheitsverständnis bei drohenden Gefahren' (2020) 5 Juristische Arbeitsblätter 321–326.

Seckelmann, M., and Brunzel, M., 'Das Onlinezugangsgesetz im Kontext einer digital vernetzten Gesellschaft und datengetriebenen Wirtschaft: Zur Einleitung' in (eds.) M. Seckelmann, and M. Brunzel, *Handbuch Onlinezugangsgesetz* (Springer, Berlin 2021), 1–13.

Siegel, T., 'Auf dem Weg zum Portalverbund – Das neue Onlinezugangsgesetz (OZG)' (2018) 5 Die Öffentliche Verwaltung 185–191.

Siegel, T., 'Der Europäische Portalverbund – Frischer Digitalisierungswind durch das einheitliche digitale Zugangstor ('Single Digitale Gateway')' (2019) 13 Neue Zeitschrift für Verwaltungsrecht 905–909.

Stadler, T., Lueks, W., Kohls, K., and Troncoso, C. 'Preliminary Analysis of Potential Harms in the Luca Tracing System' (2021) arXiv [preprint].

Stroscher, J.-P., and Schomberg, P., *Digitale Kontaktnachverfolgung per App – ist ein Ende der Zettelwirtschaft in Sicht* (2021) *ZD-Aktuell*.

Volkmann, U., 'Der Ausnahmezustand' *VerfBlog* (2020) <https://verfassungsblog.de/der-ausnahmezustand/> (18.08 2021).

von Harbou, F., 'Abschied vom Einzelfall? Perspektiven der Digitalisierung von Verwaltungsverfahren (no. 8)' (2020) 341.

Voss, C., 'Die Implementation der Europäischen Dienstleistungsrichtlinie – lessons learned im Hinblick auf das Wirksamwerden der Single Digital Gateway-Verordnung und des Onlinezugangsgesetzes' in (eds.) M. Seckelmann and M. Brunzel, *Handbuch Onlinezugangsgesetz* (Springer, Berlin 2021) 199–225.

Wuschelbaum, M., 'COVID-19: Pandemiebewältigung und Datenschutz – Kollektivevereinbarungen als krisentaugliches DS-GVO-Instrument?' (2020) 10 Neue Zeitschrift für Arbeitsrecht 612–616 (614).

5 Public Instruments of Digital Transformation during Times of Pandemic in the Republic of Croatia

Ivan Uroda

5.1 Introduction

The recent widespread COVID-19 pandemic (henceforth, pandemic) caught the Republic of Croatia (henceforth, Croatia) in late February 2020 (almost) by surprise, i.e., without a pandemic preparedness plan for this pandemic, comparable to the one that all EU countries and many other countries have for influenza pandemics.[1] Since this pandemic was, at least reportedly, spreading from Asia, i.e., from geographically east of Croatia, in early 2020 there was just enough time to adequately prepare for the incoming pandemic.

Expectedly, during preparations and in the first months this pandemic, Croatian public bodies played an important and constructive role. Such role of Croatian public bodies was, at least in the initial period, defined by the social obligation to communicate the important messages and by the vital necessity to introduce appropriate prevention and protection measures, to the people. In addition, they had to come up with various public instruments of digital transformation with the unified aims of maintaining the sufficiently stable state of Croatian economy and avoiding the weakening of the Croatian economy as much as possible.

Conveniently, since then, a number of those Croatian public instruments of digital transformation were devised and presented to the public. What is more, each of those Croatian public instruments of digital transformation was devised for a specific purpose and they have rather specialised functionalities, thus providing more than enough data to consider them in this chapter.

Along these lines, it is possible to define a purpose of study in this chapter that revolves around the research on the specifics of Croatian public instruments of digital transformation that Croatian public bodies have devised until now, from the first signs of this pandemic in late February 2020, to the most recent developments regarding this pandemic at the time when the author was adding the final touches to this chapter in mid-October 2020.

1 European Centre for Disease Prevention and Control, 'Influenza Pandemic Preparedness Plans' (2018) <https://www.ecdc.europa.eu/en/seasonal-influenza/preparedness/influenza-pandemic-preparedness-plans> (05.07.2020).

DOI: 10.4324/9781003263968-11

The subjects of research in this chapter are the Croatian public instruments of digital transformation, with the focus on the ones that have been devised during times of pandemic. To get the full picture of this matter, public instruments of digital transformation devised by various Croatian public bodies (i.e., bodies governed by public law, that, in Croatia include: public administration bodies, other public bodies, bodies of local and regional self-government units as well as legal entities that have public authority) were clearly presented.[2]

By taking everything previously mentioned into account, it is possible to address and examine, a total of four research questions in this chapter:

1) What was the chronology of the pandemic in the Croatia?
2) How to define, describe, systematise, contextualise and compare digital transformation and its components in the Croatia and in the EU?
3) How to properly summarise all Croatian public instruments of digital transformation that were devised during times of pandemic?
4) What is the future outlook of Croatian public instruments of digital transformation?

To sum up, since a relatively short time period, i.e., from late February 2020 to mid-October 2020, is covered in this chapter, the whole research was based on a total of four assumptions of research, which have helped the author to define what to expect from his research findings:

1) It is possible to identify the distinct periods i.e., months and distinct numbers i.e., people (in Croatia reported as diagnosed with pandemic-related disease), when it comes to the chronology of the pandemic in the Croatia.
2) There are components of digital transformation in the Croatia that can be compared with those in the EU.
3) It is possible to make a comprehensive and concise synopsis of Croatian public instruments of digital transformation during times of pandemic.
4) Based on everything previously researched, it is possible to define the adequate outlook of Croatian public instruments of digital transformation.

5.2 Short chronology of the pandemic in the Republic of Croatia

This subchapter contains a short chronology of the pandemic in Croatia, that was still ongoing in mid-October 2020, i.e., at the time when the author was adding the final touches to this chapter. Hence, the author has decided to present herein only the most relevant numerical data and factual data, to put this subchapter

2 Ministry of Public Administration of the Republic of Croatia, 'Koja su javnopravna tijela' (n.d.) <https://uprava.gov.hr/drzavni-strucni-ispit-789/primjeri-pitanja-i-odgovora-za-provjeru-znanja/primjeri-pitanja-i-odgovora-za-srednju-strucnu-spremu/upravni-postupak-i-upravni-sporovi/koja-su-javnopravna-tijela/12263> (11.07.2020).

primarily in the Croatian context and to lay the foundation for all subsequent subchapters.

Apropos the population-related numerical data that is linked to the pandemic and other matters, it is worth mentioning that according to the most recent population estimate of Croatia for the year 2019, i.e. in mid-2019 it had just over 4 million inhabitants, or to be more exact 4,065,253 inhabitants.[3] This number of inhabitants, according to the official estimates of all EU member countries, makes Croatia the 20th (21st if the United Kingdom is taken into account) EU member country, out of 27 (28 if the United Kingdom is taken into account) EU member countries, by number of inhabitants.[4] Accordingly, all numerical data in this subchapter were presented as numbers.

On 25 February 2020, the first person in Croatia was reported as diagnosed with, what was later to be called pandemic-related disease. Only 15 days later, i.e., on 11 March 2020, for the very first time, the WHO carried out its assessment that this disease and its spreading may well be regarded as the pandemic.[5]

In the coming days and months, the number of people in Croatia reported as diagnosed with pandemic-related disease has, expectedly, increased. To display this data in the most concise, yet representative form, the author has created Table II.5.1 containing data about average, maximum and minimum number of people in Croatia reported as newly diagnosed with pandemic-related disease at a monthly level, logically in the year 2020.

As it can be seen from the Table II.5.1, so far and as empirically expected, the largest average was 465.41, the largest maximum was 1,131 and the largest minimum was 138, whereat all those numbers were related to October 2020. As for other numbers, monthly averages and monthly maximums are more representative observing from April 2020 onwards, while monthly minimums eventually became representative starting from July 2020 onwards.

Moreover, these numbers were smaller from (late) February (especially in May) to late June because of the Croatian lockdown and rather strict Croatian prevention and protection measures. Yet, there were also some coordinated temporary restrictions at the level of the entire EU that helped to keep those Croatian numbers smaller. Firstly, on 17 March 2020, EU leaders agreed to restrict all non-essential travel to the EU (from the third countries) until 30 June 2020 (after several prolongations).[6] Secondly, on 11 June 2020, the EC recommended the lift of internal controls at EU borders, both to member countries of the Schengen area

3 Croatian Bureau of Statistics, 'Population Estimate of Republic of Croatia, 2019' (2020) <https://www.dzs.hr/Hrv_Eng/publication/2020/07-01-03_01_2020.htm> (11.09.2020).

4 Eurostat, 'Population on 1 January' (2020) <https://ec.europa.eu/eurostat/databrowser/view/TPS00001> (15.07.2020).

5 World Health Organization, 'Timeline of WHO's response to COVID-19' (2020) <https://www.who.int/emergencies/diseases/novel-coronavirus-2019/interactive-timeline> (22.07.2020).

6 Council of the European Union, 'Council agrees to start lifting travel restrictions for residents of some third countries' (2020) <https://www.consilium.europa.eu/en/press/press-releases/2020/06/30/council-agrees-to-start-lifting-travel-restrictions-for-residents-of-some-third-countries> (24.07.2020).

and to associated countries of the Schengen area (including Croatia), in the coming days, i.e., by 15 June 2020.[7]

However, after 30 June 2020, i.e., after permitting travels from the third countries to the EU and after lifting internal controls at borders, the numbers (more or less) gradually started to become larger. Empirically, this happened mainly due to the less strict Croatian prevention and protection measures at that time as well as due to the traditional arrival of large numbers of tourists in summer months (according to the currently available data) whereat there were 642,000 arrivals of foreign tourists in June 2020, 2,000,000 arrivals of foreign tourists in July 2020 and 2,100,000 arrivals of foreign tourists in August 2020.[8,9,10] Even though prevention and protection measures proposed at that time seemed sufficient and the numbers of tourist arrivals were smaller than in the previous years, yet the number of people in Croatia reported as newly diagnosed with pandemic-related disease, more than evidently, became larger with the passage of time, i.e., in the coming few months.

Table II.5.1 Data about average, maximum and minimum number of people in Croatia reported as newly diagnosed with pandemic-related disease at a monthly level[a]

Month and Year / Data	*(1)*	*(2)*	*(3)*
February 2020	1.25	2	1
March 2020	28.04	91	0
April 2020	42.40	96	7
May 2020	5.94	36	0
June 2020	15.97	95	0
July 2020	75.68	140	16
August 2020	162.97	358	22
September 2020	208.57	369	48
October* 2020	465.61	1131	138

[a]Data tabulated and calculated by the author based on Croatian Institute of Public Health, "KORONAVIRUS.HR", 18.10.2020, https://www.koronavirus.hr/en.
(1) Average number of newly diagnosed
(2) Maximum number of newly diagnosed
(3) Minimum number of newly diagnosed
* Until and including 18.10.2020

7 European Commission, 'Coronavirus: Commission recommends partial and gradual lifting of travel restrictions to the EU after 30 June, based on common coordinated approach' (2020) <https://ec.europa.eu/commission/presscorner/detail/en/ip_20_1035> (25.07.2020).

8 Croatian Bureau of Statistics, 'Tourism, June 2020' (2020) <https://www.dzs.hr/Hrv_Eng/publication/2020/04-03-01_06_2020.htm> (13.08.2020).

9 Croatian Bureau of Statistics, 'Tourism, July 2020' (2020) <https://www.dzs.hr/Hrv_Eng/publication/2020/04-03-01_07_2020.htm> (11.09.2020).

10 Croatian Bureau of Statistics, 'Tourism, August 2020' (2020) <https://www.dzs.hr/Hrv_Eng/publication/2020/04-03-01_08_2020.htm> (18.10.2020).

Lastly, numerical data presented in this subchapter ascertains that it was well worth it to timely and carefully devise and consider prevention and protection measures that would result in smaller or, at least, a somewhat stable number of people in Croatia reported as newly diagnosed with pandemic-related disease in the future. However, based on numerical data followed until 18 October 2020, an increased number of people in Croatia reported as newly diagnosed with pandemic-related disease may lead to the enforcement of some stricter prevention and protection measures that will, hopefully once again, lead to concrete results, i.e., smaller numbers of people in Croatia reported as newly diagnosed with pandemic-related disease, soon after their implementation.

5.3 Brief overview of digital transformation and its components in the Republic of Croatia in comparison to the EU

Like the preceding subchapter, this subchapter also represents the foundation for all subsequent subchapters. However, in this subchapter the focus is put on digital transformation and its components in Croatia, set side by side with their counterparts in EU.

However, before further elaboration on digital transformation and its components, it is essential to clearly define what digital transformation is. For that purpose, the author has specially and carefully selected five definitions of digital transformation.

Digital transformation is understood by the EC as a fusion of advanced technologies that integrates physical and digital systems and when combined with innovative business models and processes, leads to the creation of smart products, services and significant improvement of productivity.[11]

Digital transformation is the cultural, organisational and operational change of an organisation, industry or ecosystem through a smart integration of digital technologies, processes and competencies across all levels and functions in a staged and strategic way.[12]

Digital transformation is the process of using digital technologies to create new – or modify existing – business processes, culture and customer experiences to meet changing business and market requirements.[13]

Digital transformation is generally viewed as an aggregation of modern tools and processes leveraged to solve business problems and satisfy customers.[14]

11 EU4Digital, 'Digitising industry: best practices to promote the digital transformation of SMEs in traditional sectors of the economy' (2020) <https://eufordigital.eu/digitising-industry-best-practices-to-promote-the-digital-transformation-of-smes-in-traditional-sectors-of-the-economy> (26.07.2020).

12 i-SCOOP, 'Digital transformation: online guide to digital business transformation' (2014) <https://www.i-scoop.eu/digital-transformation> (26.07.2020).

13 Salesforce, 'What Is Digital Transformation?' (2018) <https://www.salesforce.com/products/platform/what-is-digital-transformation> (26.07.2020).

14 Boulton, C., 'What is digital transformation? A necessary disruption' (2020) <https://www.cio.com/article/3211428/what-is-digital-transformation-a-necessary-disruption.html> (19.09.2020).

Digital transformation is the integration of digital technology into all areas of a business, fundamentally changing how you operate and deliver value to customers.[15]

Furthermore, to portray both qualitative and quantitative aspects of digital transformation and its components, especially because both Croatia and the EU were taken into consideration to get a more realistic overview of the Croatian situation, the author has decided to analyse and synthesise selected data from the Digital Economy and Society Index (DESI). Beside DESI having Overall Composite values as shown in Table II.5.2, it also has five dimensions, i.e., Connectivity as shown in Table II.5.3, Human Capital as shown in Table II.5.4, Use of Internet Services as shown in Table II.5.5, Integration of Digital Technology as shown in Table II.5.6 and Digital Public Services as shown in Table II.5.7, with each of these dimensions having the corresponding numerical values.[16] What is more, these five dimensions of DESI actually represent various components of digital transformation, for an individual EU member country (in the case of this chapter: Croatia) and for the whole EU, that provide a more detailed overview of the matters under consideration.

In the context of this whole chapter, some of those five dimensions of DESI are less important and some are more important, yet the author has decided to portray all of them and in the same order as they are presented in official DESI-related publications. While DESI has been calculated yearly since 2015, the author has acquired data from its latest, i.e., DESI 2020 edition, that contains the newest data for DESI 2018 (data from the year 2017), DESI 2019 (data from the year 2018) and DESI 2020 (data from the year 2019), thus making the mentioned analysis and synthesis as contemporary as possible. At last, regarding ranks in all of the related tables, those are represented individual ranks of Croatia among all 28 EU countries (including the United Kingdom).

Regarding Overall Composite DESI, as shown in Table II.5.2, both the score for the EU and the score for Croatia were steadily increasing from DESI 2018 to DESI 2020. Encouraging is the fact that Croatia's rank has increased by 1, i.e., from 21 in DESI 2018 to 20 in DESI 2019 and DESI 2020. That shows that, all things considered, Croatia is clearly moving in the right direction when it comes to digital transformation.

Table II.5.2 Overall Composite DESI 2018–2020

Index / Year	*2018*	*2019*	*2020*
Overall Composite DESI score EU	46.5	49.4	52.6
Overall Composite DESI score Croatia	40.8	44.3	47.6
Overall Composite DESI rank Croatia	21	20	20

15 The Enterprisers Project, 'What is digital transformation?' (2020) <https://enterprisersproject.com/what-is-digital-transformation> (01.10.2020).

16 European Commission, 'Digital Economy and Society Index 2020, Croatia' (2020) <https://ec.europa.eu/newsroosmallm/dae/document.cfm?doc_id=66908> (29.07.2020).

Table II.5.3 First DESI Dimension (Connectivity) 2018–2020

Index / Year	*2018*	*2019*	*2020*
1st DESI Dimension score EU	39.9	44.7	50.1
1st DESI Dimension score Croatia	32.1	37.2	41.2
1st DESI Dimension rank Croatia	26	25	25

Table II.5.4 Second DESI Dimension (Human Capital) 2018–2020

Index / Year	*2018*	*2019*	*2020*
2nd DESI Dimension score EU	47.6	47.9	49.3
2nd DESI Dimension score Croatia	45.8	46.8	49.2
2nd DESI Dimension rank Croatia	13	14	13

Table II.5.5 Third DESI Dimension (Use of Internet Services) 2018–2020

Index / Year	*2018*	*2019*	*2020*
3rd DESI Dimension score EU	51.8	55.0	58.0
3rd DESI Dimension score Croatia	49.2	53.4	55.5
3rd DESI Dimension rank Croatia	17	14	15

Table II.5.6 Fourth DESI Dimension (Integration of Digital Technology) 2018–2020

Indicator / Year	*2018*	*2019*	*2020*
4th DESI Dimension score EU	37.8	39.8	41.4
4th DESI Dimension score Croatia	36.7	38.5	41.5
4th DESI Dimension rank Croatia	16	17	12

Table II.5.7 Fifth DESI Dimension (Digital Public Services) 2018–2020

Index/Year	*2018*	*2019*	*2020*
5th DESI Dimension score EU	61.8	67.0	72.0
5th DESI Dimension score Croatia	43.7	50.8	55.8
5th DESI Dimension rank Croatia	25	24	25

Apropos the first DESI Dimension (Connectivity), as shown in Table II.5.3, both the score for the EU and the score for Croatia were also steadily increasing from DESI 2018 to DESI 2020. Although Croatia's rank has increased by 1, i.e., from 26 in DESI 2018 to 25 in DESI 2019 and DESI 2020, it is worrying that

Croatia is the fourth worst EU member country in this regard. However, to find the reasons for this, considerably lower, rank it is necessary to take into consideration 8 sub-Dimensions of the first DESI Dimension (Connectivity), that were consciously excluded from Table II.5.3 to save space, i.e., Overall fixed broadband take-up, At least 100 Mbps fixed broadband take-up, Fast broadband (NGA) coverage, Fixed Very High Capacity Network (VHCN) coverage, 4G coverage, Mobile broadband take-up, 5G readiness and Broadband price index. Among those eight sub-Dimensions, each of which has corresponding numerical values, it is notable that (ranging from the sub-Dimension that requires the most Croatian effort to come near the EU's numerical values, to the sub-Dimension that requires the least Croatian effort to come near the EU's numerical values) Croatia still has to work on 5G readiness, At least 100 Mbps fixed broadband take-up and Mobile broadband take-up. Among those sub-Dimensions, the most contentious one is the 5G readiness sub-Dimension with EU value of 21%, whereat both pros and cons of 5G are still being researched, what makes some EU countries, including Croatia, more careful and, yet they are consequently valued as 0%, i.e., as not being 5G ready. As for At least 100 Mbps fixed broadband take-up, there are currently 20 percentage points (pp) of difference between the Croatian value of 6% and the EU value of 26%, but it is reasonable to expect that the Croatian valuc will increase in the coming years. At last, regarding Mobile broadband take-up, there are currently 11 subscriptions per 100 people of difference between Croatian 89 subscriptions per 100 people and EU 100 subscriptions per 100 people, yet it is more than reasonable to expect that this Croatian value will also increase in the coming years, because, at least empirically, more and more people in Croatia are using Mobile broadband to access the Internet. All in all, the first DESI Dimension (Connectivity) in Croatia is at a good level, yet much effort must be made in the future if Croatia wants to reach the level of the EU in this regard.

Concerning the second DESI Dimension (Human Capital), as shown in Table II.5.4, this is the first in line out of three DESI Dimensions in which, on the entirely positive note, the Croatian score is the closest to the EU score. Once again, both the score for the EU and the score for Croatia were also steadily increasing from DESI 2018 to DESI 2020. Also concerning this DESI Dimension, Croatia's rank has decreased by 1, i.e., from 13 in DESI 2018 to 14 in DESI 2019, yet it has increased also by 1, i.e., from 14 in DESI 2019 to 13 in DESI 2020. Noteworthy is the fact that in 2020 the Croatian score of 49.2 is just 0.1 lower than the EU score of 49.3 despite Croatia's relatively small number of inhabitants, whereat in the future that score should be pretty encouraging and motivating for Croatia when it comes to holding, or ideally attaining a bit higher, rank for this DESI Dimension. Reasons for such (moderately high) rank (as far as Croatia is concerned) and (also in this case) score, can be found within the six sub-Dimensions of the second DESI Dimension (Human Capital), that were consciously excluded from Table II.5.4 to save space, i.e., At least basic digital skills, Above basic digital skills, At least basic software skills, ICT specialists, Female ICT specialists and ICT graduates. Among those six sub-Dimensions, each of which has corresponding numerical values, it is possible to identify notable sub-Dimensions in which Croatia is better than the EU (both, what led to such (rather high) rank (as far as Croatia is concerned) and (also in this case) score) i.e., ICT graduates and Above basic digital skills. Considering ICT graduates, the Croatian value of 5.5% is 1.9 pp higher than the EU value of 3.6%, which is highly encouraging for Croatia in the future years, to the extent that this sub-Dimension should become a Croatian nationwide priority within the second DESI Dimension (Human Capital). Moreover, apropos the Above basic digital skills, the Croatian value of 35% is 2 pp higher than the EU value of 35%, which is also a considerable incentive for Croatia to keep this score high in the coming years. Overall, the second DESI Dimension (Human Capital) in Croatia is at an excellent level, but sustained effort must be made in the future if Croatia wants to keep up with the level of the EU in this respect.

Regarding the third DESI Dimension (Use of Internet Services), as shown in Table II.5.5, this is the second in line out of three DESI Dimensions in which, on the entirely positive note, the Croatian score is the closest to the EU score. Yet again, both the score for the EU and the score for Croatia were also steadily increasing from DESI 2018 to DESI 2020. Also, regarding this DESI Dimension, Croatia's rank had steeply increased by 3 i.e., from 17 in DESI 2018 to 14 in DESI 2019, yet it has decreased by 1 i.e., from 14 in DESI 2019 to 15 in DESI 2020. Therefore, in the case of this DESI Dimension, the 2020 Croatian score of 55.5 is high, yet 2.5 lower than the EU score of 58.0. The reasons for such (somewhat higher) rank and (also in this case) score, can be found within 11 sub-Dimensions of the third DESI Dimension (Use of Internet Services), that were consciously excluded from Table II.5.5 to save space, i.e., People who have never used the Internet, Internet users, News, Music and videos and games, Video on demand, Video calls, Social networks, Doing an online course, Banking, Shopping and Selling online. Among those 11 sub-Dimensions, each of which has corresponding numerical values, it is possible to find a rather broad range of values. Still, based on their values, there are three most notable sub-Dimensions in which Croatia is worse than the EU. Apropos of (Internet) Shopping, the Croatian value of 57% is 14 pp lower than the EU value of 71%. Concerning People who have never used the Internet, the Croatian value of 18% is, at least superficially, 9 pp higher than the EU value of 9%, yet with this sub-Dimension the reverse logic should be applied i.e., the portion of people in Croatia who have used the Internet is 9 pp lower than the corresponding portion of Internet users in the EU. Considering Internet users, the Croatian value of 77% is 8 pp lower than EU value of 85%. From those three sub-Dimensions it is possible to deduce that, for whatever reasons, a small, but evident portion of people in Croatia are still ignorant of the Internet per se and the benefits that the Internet provides, most notably deprived of the benefits of (Internet) Shopping, yet it reasonable to expect that in these regards things will turn out for the better in the coming years. In contrast, once again based on their values, there are also three most notable sub-Dimensions, but in this case ones in which Croatia is better than the EU. Apropos Music and Videos and the Internet, the Croatian value of 88% is 7 pp higher than the EU value of 81%. Concerning Social networks, the Croatian value of 73% is 8 pp higher than the EU value of 65%. Considering (Internet) News, the Croatian value of 91% is 19 pp higher than the EU value of 72%. What can be deduced from those three sub-Dimensions is the fact that people in Croatia can use the Internet, however, quite expectedly, for purposes that are interesting to them personally, which will probably continue in the coming years; thus it will be interesting to follow the movements of percentages in these three sub-Dimensions. All in all, the third DESI Dimension (Use of Internet Services) in Croatia is at a very good level, yet some effort must be made in the future if Croatia wants to keep up the level of the EU in this regard.

Apropos the fourth DESI Dimension (Integration of Digital Technology), as shown in Table II.5.6, this is the third in line out of three DESI Dimensions in which, on the entirely positive note, the Croatian score is the closest to the EU score. Once more, both the score for the EU and the score for Croatia were also steadily increasing from DESI 2018 to DESI 2020. Also, apropos this DESI Dimension, Croatia's rank had decreased by 1 i.e., from 16 in DESI 2018 to 17 in DESI 2019, yet it has steeply increased by 5 i.e. from 17 in DESI 2019 to 12 in DESI 2020. Therefore, in the case of this DESI Dimension, the 2020 Croatian score of 41.5 is a record high, i.e., exclusively for this DESI Dimension, it is 0.1 higher than the EU score of 41.4. The reasons for such (extremely high) rank (as far as Croatia is concerned) and (in this case, record high) score, can be found within seven sub-Dimensions of the fourth DESI Dimension (Integration of Digital Technology), that were consciously excluded from Table II.5.6 to save space, i.e., Electronic (Digital) information sharing, Social media, Big data, Cloud, SMEs selling online, e-Commerce turnover and Selling online cross-border. Among those seven sub-Dimensions, each of them also has corresponding numerical values. Hence, it is possible to, rather easily, identify a single sub-Dimension whose low value has dampened the extremely high rank (as far as Croatia is concerned). Namely, it is Electronic (Digital) information sharing, whose Croatian value of 26% is 8 pp lower than the EU value of 34%. Thankfully, with every passing day, as observable empirically, more and more enterprises in Croatia are sharing information electronically (digitally) among them, which should, hopefully, lead to the increase of this Croatian value in the coming years. In contrast, it is possible to, clearly, identify 3 sub-Dimensions whose high values have contributed the most to the extremely high rank (as far as Croatia is concerned). Apropos (SMEs) Selling online cross-border, the Croatian value of 10% is 2 pp higher than the EU value of 8%. Regarding SMEs selling online, the Croatian value of 21% is 3 pp higher than the EU value of 18%. Concerning (Enterprises that use solutions based on) Cloud, the Croatian value of 22% is 4 pp higher than the EU value of 18%. From three sub-Dimensions it is possible to conclude that when it comes to Croatian enterprises and the integration of digital technology within them, Croatia has built a solid basis that will, expectantly, enable its enterprises to achieve approximately equal or better values in the near future. On the whole, the fourth DESI Dimension (Integration of Digital Technology) in Croatia is at an excellent level, but continued effort must be made in the future if Croatia wants to keep up with the level of the EU in this respect.

Concerning the fifth DESI Dimension (Digital Public Services) i.e., the most important and relevant DESI Dimension in the context of this chapter, as shown in Table II.5.7, both the score for the EU and the score for Croatia were also steadily increasing from DESI 2018 to DESI 2020. Though Croatia's rank has increased by 1 i.e., from 25 in DESI 2018 to 24 in DESI 2019, it has decreased also by 1 i.e., from 24 in DESI 2019 to 25 in DESI 2020. Consequently, it is, once again, worrying that Croatia is also the fourth worst EU member country in this regard. However, to find the reasons for this, considerably lower, rank it is necessary to take into consideration five sub-Dimensions of the fifth DESI Dimension (Digital Public Services), that were consciously excluded from Table II.5.7 to save space, i.e., e-Government users, Pre-filled forms, Online service completion, Digital Public Services for businesses and Open data. Each of those five sub-Dimensions has corresponding numerical values. Accordingly, it is possible to, rather easily, identify three sub-Dimensions that Croatia must work on to, once again, increase its rank for the fifth DESI Dimension (Digital Public Services). Concerning Pre-filled forms (from public administration to user), the Croatian value of 33% is 26 pp lower than the EU value of 59%. In Digital Public Services for businesses, the Croatian value of 65% is 23 pp lower than EU value of 88%. Apropos (possibility of) Online service completion, the Croatian value of 73% is 17 pp lower than EU value of 90%. Therefore, all things considered, it is perfectly clear in which, more than obvious, ways Croatia should improve its ranking for the fifth DESI Dimension (Digital Public Services) in the coming years, since these ways are directly related to three previously listed sub-Dimensions. Counter to these, there is a single sub-Dimension i.e., Open data, whose Croatian value of 69% is 3 pp higher than the EU value of 69%. Even though the Croatian value related to this sub-Dimension is just a little bit larger than the EU value, it is very encouraging for Croatia in its, expected and probable, imminent striving to heighten its rank for the fifth DESI Dimension (Digital Public Services). All in all, the fifth DESI Dimension (Digital Public Services) in Croatia is at a sufficient level, yet a lot of effort must be made in the future if Croatia wants to reach the level of the EU in this regard.

To sum up, as it is shown and demonstrated in this subchapter, it is possible to critically analyse and systematically synthetise DESI-related data. That way, it is possible to timely recognise and to reasonably conclude what the country should do in the years to come, to try to hold and/or to heighten its rank related to DESI and/or the five DESI Dimensions.

5.4 Concise synopsis of Croatian public instruments of digital transformation during times of pandemic

From late February 2020 to mid-October 2020 Croatia as a country, the Croatian Government as well as numerous Croatian public bodies introduced a considerable number of specifically directed public instruments of digital transformation, mainly to cope with the necessity to maintain the sufficiently stable state of the Croatian economy and to avoid the weakening of the Croatian economy as such as possible, thus trying to avoid the pandemic-related economic crisis as the absolute imperative.

Therefore, in the subsequent paragraphs, 16 Croatian public instruments of digital transformation, introduced, so far, during the times of pandemic i.e., from late February 2020 to mid-October 2020, are listed chronologically, along with the dates of their introduction and their short descriptions composed in the context of this chapter. In accordance with the currently prevailing tendency, the word digital (and its derivatives) are used instead of words such as electronic, online and other previously more popular words.

On 11 March 2020, a digital agriculture identification card was announced by the Croatian Ministry of Agriculture.[17] It can replace all existing cards that Croatian farmers used thus far, i.e., the green agricultural card, the card for blue diesel fuel and the card used to obtain plant protection products. Moreover, it enables farmers to (complete digitally) submit their requests for agriculture support in the Croatian AGRONET system.

On 16 March 2020, according to the guidelines by the Croatian Ministry of Science and Education, all Croatian primary schools and secondary schools started with distance teaching and learning.[18] What also started simultaneously was the television-based teaching for first grade to fourth grade of primary schools on a regular weekly basis throughout the rest of school year 2019/2020, from Monday to Friday.

On 19 March 2020, the Croatian Health Insurance Fund and Croatian Chamber of Pharmacists announced that the Croatian Health Insurance Fund had enabled the integration of the Croatian database of persons in pandemic-related self-isolation with the Croatian Central Healthcare Information System, whereat related data were made available to pharmacists and doctors of family medicine.[19] Since then, it is very easy to check whether a person is, either voluntarily or involuntarily, in pandemic-related self-isolation, by entering his/her unique insured patient registration number in digital form within the Croatian Central Healthcare Information System and the related business information systems.

On 20 March 2020, according to the guidelines by Croatian Ministry of Science and Education, all Croatian higher learning institutions started with distance teaching and learning.[20] However, it was necessary to ensure that distance teaching and learning would be held continuously and without obstructions.

17 Ministry of Agriculture of the Republic of Croatia, 'Prvi korak u digitalizaciji poljoprivrede - zatražite svoju elektroničku poljoprivrednu iskaznicu' (2020) <https://poljoprivreda.gov.hr/vijesti/prvi-korak-u-digitalizaciji-poljoprivrede-zatrazite-svoju-elektronicku-poljoprivrednu-iskaznicu/3899> (29.07.2020).

18 Ministry of Science and Education of the Republic of Croatia, 'Uputa svim osnovnim i srednjim školama vezano uz nastavak organizacije nastave na daljinu' (2020) <https://mzo.gov.hr/vijesti/uputa-svim-osnovnim-i-srednjim-skolama-vezano-uz-nastavak-organizacije-nastave-na-daljinu/3592> (29.7.2020).

19 Croatian Chamber of Pharmacists, 'VAŽNO - Provjera kršenja samoizolacije_dodatni plakati' (2020) <http://www.hljk.hr/Vijesti/tabid/37/ctl/Details/mid/4861/ItemID/6364> (02.08.2020).

20 Ministry of Science and Education of the Republic of Croatia, 'Odluka o izmjeni Odluke o obustavi izvođenja nastave u visokim učilištima, srednjim i osnovnim školama te redovnog rada ustanova predškolskog odgoja i obrazovanja i uspostavi nastave na daljinu - uputa' (2020) <https://mzo.gov.hr/UserDocsImages/dokumenti/Vijesti/2020/Uputa%20-%20osnovne%20i%20srednje%20skole%20-%2019.%203.%202020..pdf> (02.08.2020).

On 27 March 2020, due to the pandemic-related situation, the Croatian Health Insurance Fund upgraded its business information system with functionalities that have provided employers with the insight into data about the sick leave of their employees in digital form, i.e., a digitalised report on an employee's temporary inability to work and a digital certificate on an employee's temporary inability to work.[21] Beside data related to the report and certificate mentioned above, employers can see a digital version of data necessary for the calculation and payment of salary compensation during temporary inability to work regardless of the reason for it and data related to rights to maternity benefits and parental benefits for employed and self-employed beneficiaries, i.e., employees.

On 1 April 2020 Croatian Ministry of Public Administration introduced the e-pass system, since, due to pandemic-related travel restrictions back then, digital e-passes were needed by all Croatian citizens who had to travel outside of their place of residence.[22] The mentioned e-pass system was devised in order to digitalise the complete process, i.e., from issuing e-passes via email (after them being digitally requested by either the person's employer or general practitioner or civil protection authority), across keeping a register of all issued e-passes, to simplifying and accelerating the control of issued e-passes.

On 7 April 2020 Croatian Ministry of Agriculture introduced and launched the Croatian national Internet (farmer's) market.[23] Essentially, it is the digital platform which enables buying and selling of homemade products made by Croatian farmers and family agricultural farms from the whole of Croatia. This way, Croatian farmers and family agricultural farms got the Internet place for free placement and quick sale of their products, while buyers got the Internet place to browse and buy a wide range of quality homemade food products.

On 21 May 2020, the Croatian Ministry of Public Administration announced that it is now possible to register the birth of a child digitally by utilising written registration by parents via the service called e-Newborn.[24] By using this service parents can be certain that the most important documents for their newborn baby (e.g., birth certificate, record of citizenship, certificate of residence, application for compulsory health insurance, certificate of approved one-time financial support for a newborn child, newborn child-related personal tax deduction percentages for tax administration) will be delivered to them digitally, i.e., in a digital form.

21 Croatian Health Insurance Fund, 'eDoznake - privremena nesposobnost za rad' (2020) <https://www.hzzo.hr/en/edoznake-privremena-nesposobnost-za-rad> (03.08.2020).

22 Ministry of Public Administration of the Republic of Croatia, 'Ministar Malenica predstavio digitalizirane propusnice' (2020) <https://uprava.gov.hr/vijesti/ministar-malenica-predstavio-digitalizirane-propusnice/16300> (03.08.2020).

23 Ministry of Agriculture of the Republic of Croatia, 'Tržnica.hr - hrvatska internet tržnica domaćih poljoprivrednih proizvoda' (2020) <https://trznica.mps.hr/o-trznici> (03.08.2020).

24 Central State Portal of the Republic of Croatia, 'Prijava rođenja djeteta' (2020) <https://gov.hr/moja-uprava/obitelj-i-zivot/roditeljstvo/prijava-rodjenja-djeteta/326> (09.08.2020).

On 2 June 2020, the Croatian Ministry of Construction and Physical Planning issued the official call to citizens of Zagreb, i.e. the capital of Croatia, as well as Zagreb County and Krapina-Zagorje County, i.e., neighbouring counties, that were all struck by a very strong earthquake measuring 5.5 on the Richter scale on 22 March 2020 for allocation of financial assistance for temporary and necessary protection as well as for repair of buildings damaged by the earthquake, ideally digitally, i.e. by using the service called e-Urgent repair of buildings damaged in the earthquake.[25] Citizens who apply for and receive this financial assistance can use it to cover the expenses of necessary works, installations and project documentation associated with their buildings.

On 25 June 2020, Croatian Ministry of Public Administration presented benefits of the service called e-Fees.[26] Essentially e-Fees represent administrative fees in digital form. So, instead of citizens buying revenue stamps to pay for administrative fees (until a few years ago exclusively with cash), citizens can now also pay for administrative fees either by credit card (in county offices and in registry offices) or, alternatively, digitally. This e-Fees service also enables citizens to pay (by credit card) for fees such as judicial, notarial, touristic and others that could have been previously paid, exclusively, via a bank.

On 1 July 2020, Croatian Ministry of Public Administration revealed that it is now possible to use the service called e-Application Wedding.[27] This service enables a bride and a groom, who are adults, i.e., Croatian citizens aged 18+, to submit their application, i.e., to announce their intention to enter into marriage in civil form, which can take place in any registry office in Croatia (or other Croatian official premises), which can be done 30–45 days ahead, completely digitally. This service supports digital payments of administrative fees, whereupon all related documents are sent digitally to a bride and to a groom.

On 3 July 2020, the Croatian Pension Insurance Institute announced their new service called e-Request for getting the right to child allowance.[28] As its name says, this service enables citizens to submit their application for getting the right to child allowance, but now it is possible to do it completely digitally.

25 Ministry of Construction and Physical Planning of the Republic of Croatia, 'Objavljen Javni poziv za dodjelu novčane pomoći' (2020) <https://mgipu.gov.hr/vijesti/objavljen-javni-poziv-za-dodjelu-novcane-pomoci/10829> (09.08.2020).

26 Ministry of Public Administration of the Republic of Croatia, 'e-Pristojbama omogućeno građanima online plaćanje pristojbi i naknada' (2020) <https://uprava.gov.hr/vijesti/e-pristojbama-omoguceno-gradjanima-online-placanje-pristojbi-i-naknada/16339> (09.08.2020).

27 Ministry of Public Administration of the Republic of Croatia, 'e-Prijava vjenčanja' (2020) <https://uprava.gov.hr/istaknute-teme/e-prijava-vjencanja/16347> (09.08.2020).

28 Croatian Pension Insurance Institute, 'Nova e-usluga Hrvatskog zavoda za mirovinsko osiguranje - od 3. srpnja omogućeno podnošenje e-Zahtjeva za ostvarivanje prava na doplatak za djecu' (2020) <https://www.mirovinsko.hr/hr/nova-e-usluga-hrvatskog-zavoda-za-mirovinsko-osiguranje-od-3-srpnja-omoguceno-podnosenje-e-zahtjeva-za-ostvarivanje-prava-na-doplatak-za-djecu/792> (09.08.2020).

On 3 July 2020 Croatian Ministry of Public Administration presented the service called e-Tachograph.[29] The mentioned service enables drivers (owning at least a Category B driving licence) to digitally submit their request for a smart tachograph, i.e., the device that stores data on the driver's activities and, in turn, receive associated identification cards for drivers from the distance and in digital form.

On 13 July 2020, the Croatian Ministry of Finance, Customs Administration announced the service named e-Application for calculation of special tax on motor vehicles.[30] This service enables taxpayers (both natural persons and legal entities) to digitally submit their tax application for this individual tax and, later, to pay for it digitally.

On 28 July 2020, the Croatian Ministry of Health introduced the mobile app named Stop COVID-19 that they have devised.[31] In short, it was devised to hold back the spread of the pandemic in the Croatian population by alerting its users if they were in contact with someone newly diagnosed with pandemic-related disease. Conveniently, this app is developed both for Android devices and for iOS devices, it guarantees maximum privacy, its installation and its utilisation are voluntary, it is possible to utilise it without registration, it utilises Bluetooth to interchange random digital keys (interchanged several times a day between users as randomly generated strings of characters).

On 15 October 2020, the Croatian Ministry of the Interior announced the service called e-Offences.[32] It, at least currently, has these digital functionalities: notice of traffic offence, overview of details for various road traffic offences, i.e. (as of now) speeding offences, delivery of payment confirmation related to a fine for traffic offence, delivery of various driver-related data (if the driver who caused the road traffic offence is a different person than the owner of the vehicle), delivery of appeal for a traffic offence, i.e., contract with new vehicle owner and status tracking for traffic offences. Conveniently, the owner of the vehicle involved in a traffic offence also receives a notice of traffic offence on paper to his/her home address, whereat it also contains an access code that can be used, by both Croatian citizens and citizens of other countries, to check the status of an individual road traffic offence.

Concisely, all of the above Croatian public instruments of digital transformation, introduced, so far, during the times of pandemic, i.e., from late February

29 Government of the Republic of Croatia, 'Servis e-Građani omogućio elektronički zahtjev za karticu vozača' (2020) <https://vlada.gov.hr/vijesti/servis-e-gradjani-omogucio-elektronicki-zahtjev-za-karticu-vozaca/29910> (13.08.2020).

30 Croatian Ministry of Finance, Customs Administration, 'e - Prijava za obračun posebnog poreza na motorna vozila - sustav elektroničkog podnošenja porezne prijave za obračun i plaćanje posebnog poreza na motorna vozila' (2020) <https://carina.gov.hr/e-carina/aplikacije-u-produkciji/e-prijava-za-obracun-posebnog-poreza-na-motorna-vozila-sustav-elektronickog-podnosenja-porezne-prijave-za-obracun-i-placanje-posebnog-poreza-na-motorna-vozila/4294> (13.08.2020).

31 Croatian Institute of Public Health, 'Stop COVID-19' (2020) <https://www.koronavirus.hr/stop-covid-19-723/723> (13.08.2020).

32 Croatian Ministry of the Interior, 'Ministarstvo unutarnjih poslova razvilo novu uslugu Obavijest o prekršaju u prometu' (2020) <https://mup.gov.hr/vijesti/ministarstvo-unutarnjih-poslova-razvilo-novu-uslugu-obavijest-o-prekrsaju-u-prometu/286610> (18.10.2020).

2020 to mid-October 2020, have demonstrated that Croatian public bodies can come up with some comprehensive instruments of digital transformation i.e., services when the compelling need, in this case a pandemic-related set of circumstances, arises. Most importantly, all of the herein presented Croatian instruments of digital transformation are, essentially, here to stay, whereat they will certainly serve as role models for new ones that can, presumably, be expected soon.

5.5 Future outlook of Croatian public instruments of digital transformation

Since Croatia has shown that it can devise working and useful public instruments of digital transformation during times of pandemic, it would now be an excellent time for Croatia to carefully consider future steps towards its forthcoming public instruments of digital transformation. Among those future steps, particularly important is the one related to future funding of Croatian public instruments of digital transformation.

On the one hand, there are a few Croatian public instruments of digital transformation (including some among those 16 Croatian public instruments of digital transformation described in the preceding subchapter, but also including some that are still in one of the pre-release phases) for which funding is already, partially, or fully, secured by Croatia and/or the EU. This fact is encouraging because, due to the funding schemes, these Croatian public instruments of digital transformation were already and will be (with reasonable certainty) completely devised.

On the other hand, there are some public instruments of digital transformation that will (inevitably) be devised in the coming months and years, but due to the foreseeable increase in overall Croatian public spending (mainly because of the pandemic along with the earthquake in Zagreb and its surroundings), one may suppose that Croatian public spending for funding public instruments of digital transformation will considerably reduce in the future. What also contributes to this supposition is the (pandemic-related) concern, according to the EC's institutional paper, i.e., the report named European Forecast that was published in July 2020, that in 2020 Croatian Gross Domestic Product (GDP) will experience −10.8%, i.e., a negative percentage change in comparison to 2019 (EU value is −8.3%), yet in 2021 Croatian GDP will experience +7.5%, i.e., positive percentage change in comparison to 2020 (EU value is +5.8%), which means that (forecasted) Croatian GDP in 2021 will (still) be lower than it was (for real) in 2019.[33]

Fortunately, in mid-July 2020 the EU via the EC approved the upcoming long-term budget that will help EU countries reach their long-term objectives from 2021 to 2027.[34] This budget, in the meantime named Recovery Plan for Europe,

33 European Commission, Directorate-General for Economic and Financial Affairs, 'European Economic Forecast, Summer 2020 (Interim)' (2020) <https://ec.europa.eu/info/sites/default/files/economy-finance/ip132_en.pdf> (13.08.2020).

34 European Council, 'Special meeting of the European Council (17, 18, 19, 20 and 21 July 2020) - Conclusions' (2020) <https://www.consilium.europa.eu/media/45109/210720-euco-final-conclusions-en.pdf> (13.08.2020).

is perceived by the public as a historical breakthrough since it includes both a recovery plan (activity-based approach) and a recovery package (funding-based approach) that promise solidarity and readiness to meet the needs of EU citizens both during times of pandemic and (probably) later. In that direction, the Recovery Plan for Europe has a total budget of 1,824.3 billion euros, that is divided into two distinct parts, i.e., 1,074.3 billion euros (58.89%) will be allocated for Multiannual Financial Framework (MFF) and 750 billion euros (41.11%) will be allocated for Next Generation EU (NGEU). In the context of this chapter, NGEU is comparatively more important, because EU countries plan to predominantly use it, i.e., those 750 billion euros for NGEU in their efforts to recover from the pandemic and its consequences, whereat its largest portion, i.e., 672.5 billion euros (89.67% of NGEU) will be allocated to Recovery and Resilience Facility (RRF), i.e., 312.5 billion euros (46.47% of RRF) will be allocated as RRF grants and 360 billion euros (53.53% of RRF) will be allocated as RRF loans.

When it comes to Croatia and RRF grants of 312.5 billion euros, Croatia can count on a total of 5.95 billion euros of RRF grants (1.904% of RRF grants).[35] However, out of 5.95 billion euros of RRF grants, Croatia (like every other EU country) will have to allocate at least 20% of its RRF grants, i.e., 1.19 billion euros, to further so called digital transition (in essence, step-by-step digital transformation).[36] Since the EU and EC strive, in turn, to provide concrete benefits for EU citizens (including Croats) and EU economies (including Croatia), i.e., to create jobs and to generate economic growth, they have actively encouraged EU member countries (including Croatia) to invest and/or to introduce reforms, in a number of areas. These areas are (in alphabetical order): connect – roll-out of rapid broadband services, modernise – digitalisation of public administration, reskill and upskill – education and training to support digital skills, scale-up – data cloud capacities. As it can be seen from the names of areas listed above, they represent good foundations that should help Croatia to devise future public instruments of digital transformation. On the one hand, it is quite irrational to expect that all 20% of its RRF grants, i.e., all 1.19 billion euros to further digital transition, will be allocated exclusively to future Croatian public instruments of digital transformation. On the other hand, that funding should be more than sufficient for the period from 2021 to 2027, if Croatia manages to efficiently allocate this funding to public instruments of digital transformation, according to the clearly defined order of priorities.

35 European Commission, 'The pillars of Next Generation EU' (2020) <https://ec.europa.eu/info/live-work-travel-eu/health/coronavirus-response/recovery-plan-europe/pillars-next-generation-eu_en> (21.08.2020).

36 European Commission, 'Recovery and Resilience Facility' (2020) <https://ec.europa.eu/info/business-economy-euro/recovery-coronavirus/recovery-and-resilience-facility_en> (21.08.2020).

5.6 Conclusions

As it can be seen from all the preceding subchapters, it is essential to address the question of public instruments of digital transformation from various angles, especially during times of pandemic, which requires both a realistic and a multi-faceted outline of various related matters. Such an integrated approach was necessary to simultaneously take into consideration these matters in the chronology of the pandemic in Croatia, the overview of digital transformation and its components in Croatia and the EU, the synopsis of Croatian public instruments of digital transformation during times of pandemic and the future outlook of Croatian public instruments of digital transformation.

Apropos the chronology of the pandemic in Croatia along with the related number of people that were newly diagnosed with pandemic-related disease, it is possible to conclude, based on calculated values (average value, maximum value and minimum value), instead of based on constantly changing daily values, that, at least in Croatia, numbers were smaller from late February 2020 (when the 1st person in Croatia was reported as diagnosed with what was later to be called pandemic-related disease) to late June 2020 and early July 2020, i.e., essentially, while Croatian lockdown and/or rather strict Croatian prevention and protection measures were still in place. Yet, a gradually increased number of people in Croatia, from August 2020 to mid-October 2020, reported as newly diagnosed with pandemic-related disease, may again point to the conclusion for this subchapter that stricter prevention and protection measures will be, probably, needed to, once again, achieve smaller, i.e., previously achieved numbers.

Concerning the overview of digital transformation and its components in Croatia and the EU, it can be concluded that, based on DESI and its five Dimensions (at least currently) since Croatia holds a rank of 20 (out of 28 EU countries) and since this rank is slowly increasing, when digital transformation is considered, Croatia is moving in the right direction. However, when individual DESI Dimensions are considered, as of Integration of Digital Technology and Human Capital – Croatia is (at least currently) at the excellent level, as of Use of Internet Services – Croatia is (at least currently) at the very good level, as of Connectivity – Croatia is (at least currently) at the good level and as of Digital Public Services – Croatia is (at least currently) at the sufficient level. The logical conclusion of this subchapter comes down to the fact that there is (at least currently) a great Croatian urgency to increase the levels of its various Digital Public Services in the future years. To rationally conclude, these Digital Public Services are especially important because they represent the individual DESI Dimension that is, probably, the most visible and criticised from the outside, i.e., by citizens of Croatia as well as other countries and because these services, usually, serve as a looking glass in the overall level of development of a country's digital transformation.

In connection to the synopsis of Croatian public instruments of digital transformation during times of pandemic, in Croatia, it is possible to conclude that there was a total of 16 Croatian public instruments of digital transformation that were introduced, so far, from late February 2020 to mid-October 2020, i.e., during the times of pandemic. Based on the descriptions of all 16 Croatian public instruments of digital transformation, it can be observed that all of them are devised as comprehensive, i.e., they were all complete and ready-to-use when they were presented to the public, which is especially important when such compelling need suddenly arises, like the pandemic did in February 2020. Hence, since all 16 described Croatian instruments of digital transformation are, expectedly, here to stay, it is reasonable to conclude that they will be role models for new ones in the immediate future that should, at least during times of pandemic, also be carefully devised before they are presented to the public.

Regarding the future outlook of Croatian public instruments of digital transformation, it can be concluded that, while the increase in overall Croatian public spending (mainly because of the pandemic along with the earthquake in Zagreb and its surroundings) is foreseeable, it is also possible to foresee that Croatia will allocate a considerable portion of 1.19 billion euros (that it will receive from long-term EU budget for the period from 2021 to 2027, i.e., from its RRF grants that are intended to help EU countries to reach their objectives from 2021 to 2027) to further digital transition, which is, in its essence, step-by-step digital transformation. In that regard, part of this funding will surely also be allocated to Croatian public instruments of digital transformation, whereat the most reasonable conclusion, in this regard, is that Croatia should allocate this funding to the clearly defined order of priorities, which can, in turn, result with such Croatian public instruments of digital transformation that will truly be the most effective and valuable during times of pandemic and (most probably) later.

Works cited

Boulton, C., 'What is Digital Transformation? A Necessary Disruption' (2020) <https://www.cio.com/article/3211428/what-is-digital-transformation-a-necessary-disruption.html> (19.09.2020).

Central State Portal of the Republic of Croatia, 'Prijava rođenja djeteta' (2020) <https://gov.hr/moja-uprava/obitelj-i-zivot/roditeljstvo/prijava-rodjenja-djeteta/326> (09.08.2020).

Council of the European Union, 'Council Agrees to Start Lifting Travel Restrictions for Residents of Some Third Countries' (2020) <https://www.consilium.europa.eu/en/press/press-releases/2020/06/30/council-agrees-to-start-lifting-travel-restrictions-for-residents-of-some-third-countries> (24.07.2020).

Croatian Bureau of Statistics, 'Population Estimate of Republic of Croatia, 2019' (2020) <https://www.dzs.hr/Hrv_Eng/publication/2020/07-01-03_01_2020.htm> (11.09.2020).

Croatian Bureau of Statistics, 'Tourism, August 2020' (2020) <https://www.dzs.hr/Hrv_Eng/publication/2020/04-03-01_08_2020.htm> (18.10.2020).

Croatian Bureau of Statistics, 'Tourism, July 2020' (2020) <https://www.dzs.hr/Hrv_Eng/publication/2020/04-03-01_07_2020.htm> (11.09.2020).

Croatian Bureau of Statistics, 'Tourism, June 2020' (2020) <https://www.dzs.hr/Hrv_Eng/publication/2020/04-03-01_06_2020.htm> (13.08.2020).

Croatian Chamber of Pharmacists, 'VAŽNO - Provjera kršenja samoizolacije_dodatni plakati' (2020) <http://www.hljk.hr/Vijesti/tabid/37/ctl/Details/mid/4861/ItemID/6364> (02.08.2020).

Croatian Health Insurance Fund, 'eDoznake - privremena nesposobnost za rad' (2020) <https://www.hzzo.hr/en/edoznake-privremena-nesposobnost-za-rad> (03.08.2020).

Croatian Institute of Public Health, 'Stop COVID-19' (2020) <https://www.koronavirus.hr/stop-covid-19-723/723> (13.08.2020).

Croatian Ministry of Finance, Customs Administration, 'e - Prijava za obračun posebnog poreza na motorna vozila - sustav elektroničkog podnošenja porezne prijave za obračun i plaćanje posebnog poreza na motorna vozila' (2020) <https://carina.gov.hr/e-carina/aplikacije-u-produkciji/e-prijava-za-obracun-posebnog-poreza-na-motorna-vozila-sustav-elektronickog-podnosenja-porezne-prijave-za-obracun-i-placanje-posebnog-poreza-na-motorna-vozila/4294> (13.08.2020).

Croatian Ministry of the Interior, 'Ministarstvo unutarnjih poslova razvilo novu uslugu Obavijest o prekršaju u prometu' (2020) <https://mup.gov.hr/vijesti/ministarstvo-unutarnjih-poslova-razvilo-novu-uslugu-obavijest-o-prekrsaju-u-prometu/286610> (18.10.2020).

Croatian Pension Insurance Institute, 'Nova e-usluga Hrvatskog zavoda za mirovinsko osiguranje - od 3. srpnja omogućeno podnošenje e-Zahtjeva za ostvarivanje prava na doplatak za djecu' (2020) <https://www.mirovinsko.hr/hr/nova-e-usluga-hrvatskog-zavoda-za-mirovinsko-osiguranje-od-3-srpnja-omoguceno-podnosenje-e-zahtjeva-za-ostvarivanje-prava-na-doplatak-za-djecu/792> (09.08.2020).

EU4Digital, 'Digitising Industry: Best Practices to Promote the Digital Transformation of SMEs in Traditional Sectors of the Economy' (2020) <https://eufordigital.eu/digitising-industry-best-practices-to-promote-the-digital-transformation-of-smes-in-traditional-sectors-of-the-economy> (26.07.2020).

European Centre for Disease Prevention and Control, 'Influenza Pandemic Preparedness Plans' (2018) <https://www.ecdc.europa.eu/en/seasonal-influenza/preparedness/influenza-pandemic-preparedness-plans> (05.07.2020).

European Commission, 'Coronavirus: Commission Recommends Partial and Gradual Lifting of Travel Restrictions to the EU after 30 June, Based on Common Coordinated Approach' (2020) <https://ec.europa.eu/commission/presscorner/detail/en/ip_20_1035> (25.07.2020).

European Commission, 'Digital Economy and Society Index 2020, Croatia' (2020) <https://ec.europa.eu/newsroosmallm/dae/document.cfm?doc_id=66908> (29.07.2020).

European Commission, 'Recovery and Resilience Facility' (2020) <https://ec.europa.eu/info/business-economy-euro/recovery-coronavirus/recovery-and-resilience-facility_en> (21.08.2020).

European Commission, 'The Pillars of Next Generation EU' (2020) <https://ec.europa.eu/info/live-work-travel-eu/health/coronavirus-response/recovery-plan-europe/pillars-next-generation-eu_en> (21.08.2020).

European Commission, Directorate-General for Economic and Financial Affairs, 'European Economic Forecast, Summer 2020 (Interim)' (2020) <https://ec.europa.eu/info/sites/default/files/economy-finance/ip132_en.pdf> (13.08.2020).

European Council, 'Special meeting of the European Council (17, 18, 19, 20 and 21 July 2020) – Conclusions' (2020) <https://www.consilium.europa.eu/media/45109/210720-euco-final-conclusions-en.pdf> (13.08.2020).

Eurostat, 'Population on 1 January' (2020) <https://ec.europa.eu/eurostat/databrowser/view/TPS00001> (15.07.2020).

Government of the Republic of Croatia, 'Servis e-Građani omogućio elektronički zahtjev za karticu vozača' (2020) <https://vlada.gov.hr/vijesti/servis-e-gradjani-omogucio-elektronicki-zahtjev-za-karticu-vozaca/29910> (13.08.2020).

i-SCOOP, 'Digital Transformation: Online Guide to Digital Business Transformation' (2014) <https://www.i-scoop.eu/digital-transformation> (26.07.2020).

Ministry of Agriculture of the Republic of Croatia, 'Prvi korak u digitalizaciji poljoprivrede – zatražite svoju elektroničku poljoprivrednu iskaznicu' (2020) <https://poljoprivreda.gov.hr/vijesti/prvi-korak-u-digitalizaciji-poljoprivrede-zatrazite-svoju-elektronicku-poljoprivrednu-iskaznicu/3899> (29.07.2020).

Ministry of Agriculture of the Republic of Croatia, 'Tržnica.hr - hrvatska internet tržnica domaćih poljoprivrednih proizvoda' (2020) <https://trznica.mps.hr/o-trznici> (03.08.2020).

Ministry of Construction and Physical Planning of the Republic of Croatia, 'Objavljen Javni poziv za dodjelu novčane pomoći' (2020) <https://mgipu.gov.hr/vijesti/objavljen-javni-poziv-za-dodjelu-novcane-pomoci/10829> (09.08.2020).

Ministry of Public Administration of the Republic of Croatia, 'e-Prijava vjenčanja' (2020) <https://uprava.gov.hr/istaknute-teme/e-prijava-vjencanja/16347> (09.08.2020).

Ministry of Public Administration of the Republic of Croatia, 'e-Pristojbama omogućeno građanima online plaćanje pristojbi i naknada' (2020) <https://uprava.gov.hr/vijesti/e-pristojbama-omoguceno-gradjanima-online-placanje-pristojbi-i-naknada/16339> (09.08.2020).

Ministry of Public Administration of the Republic of Croatia, 'Koja su javnopravna tijela' (n.d.) <https://uprava.gov.hr/drzavni-strucni-ispit-789/primjeri-pitanja-i-odgovora-za-provjeru-znanja/primjeri-pitanja-i-odgovora-za-srednju-strucnu-spremu/upravni-postupak-i-upravni-sporovi/koja-su-javnopravna-tijela/12263> (11.07.2020).

Ministry of Public Administration of the Republic of Croatia, 'Ministar Malenica predstavio digitalizirane propusnice' (2020) <https://uprava.gov.hr/vijesti/ministar-malenica-predstavio-digitalizirane-propusnice/16300> (03.08.2020).

Ministry of Science and Education of the Republic of Croatia, 'Odluka o izmjeni Odluke o obustavi izvođenja nastave u visokim učilištima, srednjim i osnovnim školama te redovnog rada ustanova predškolskog odgoja i obrazovanja i uspostavi nastave na daljinu - uputa' (2020) <https://mzo.gov.hr/UserDocsImages/dokumenti/Vijesti/2020/Uputa%20-%20osnovne%20i%20srednje%20skole%20-%2019.%203.%202020..pdf> (02.08.2020).

Ministry of Science and Education of the Republic of Croatia, 'Uputa svim osnovnim i srednjim školama vezano uz nastavak organizacije nastave na daljinu' (2020) <https://mzo.gov.hr/vijesti/uputa-svim-osnovnim-i-srednjim-skolama-vezano-uz-nastavak-organizacije-nastave-na-daljinu/3592> (29.7.2020).

Salesforce, 'What is Digital Transformation?' (2018) <https://www.salesforce.com/products/platform/what-is-digital-transformation> (26.07.2020).

The Enterprisers Project, 'What is Digital Transformation?' (2020) <https://enterprisersproject.com/what-is-digital-transformation> (01.10.2020).

World Health Organization, 'Timeline of WHO's Response to COVID-19' (2020) <https://www.who.int/emergencies/diseases/novel-coronavirus-2019/interactive-timeline> (22.07.2020).

III

Cyber Security

1 Information Security and Cybersecurity in a Pandemic

Krzysztof Świtała

1.1 Introduction

The aim of this chapter is to present legal issues related to information and cyber security in the context of the challenges posed by the global epidemic threat posed by the SARS-CoV2 virus. The right to information (including the right to obtain public information) will be analysed in the context of limitations related to it, arising from the protection of privacy and personal data, as well as ensuring cyber security. These issues will also be considered in relation to the strand on ensuring interoperability with due respect for these values.

The research hypothesis assumes that in epidemic emergency situations, the cohesion of regulations related to the interoperability of data sources and ensuring information security at the national and European level, as well as the complementarity of the adopted solutions with technical standards relating to this issue and guidelines of specialised institutions, such as ENISA, are of particular importance.

This chapter will discuss the issue of the right to information, as well as ways to protect its confidentiality, integrity and availability during an epidemic threat. No less important will be the presentation of privacy guarantees for individuals affected by such resources. This subject will be presented in the context of ensuring interoperability allowing effective data exchange between ICT systems while duly respecting the values of privacy and information security.

1.2 Information and related rights

Information is considered as a transferable intangible good that reduces uncertainty.[1] The freedom to provide such a resource is guaranteed in Poland by the Constitution (Art. 54), as well as by Acts of international law (Art. 10(1) of the ECHR, Art. 19 of the UDHR). Regarding the activities of public entities, we are dealing with the right of persons to obtain public information (Art. 61 of the

1 I. Lipowicz, Z. Niewiadomski, K. Strzyczkowski, G. Szpor, Prawo administracyjne. Część materialna (LexisNexis 2004) 9.

DOI: 10.4324/9781003263968-13

Constitution). Detailed issues related to its realisation are regulated in the Access Act, as well as the Act of 11 August 2021 on open data and re-use of public sector information implementing similar titled Directive 2019/1024 of the European Parliament and of the Council of 20 June 2019. As regards environmental information, the Act of 3 October 2008 on the provision of information on the environment and its protection, public participation in environmental protection and environmental impact assessments is in force, in turn implementing the Directive of 28 January 2003 on public access to environmental information and repealing Council Directive 90/313/EEC. The establishment of those Acts results also from obligations of Poland and other Member States resulting from ratification of the Convention on Access to Information, Public Participation in Decision-making, and Access to Justice in Environmental Matters, drawn up in Aarhus on 25 June 1998. An important document shaping the legal framework for openness of information in the public sector is also the Council of Europe Convention on Access to Official Documents, adopted in Tromso on 18 June 2009. Even though this Act has not been ratified by Poland so far, its content influences the current application of the law relating to the issues of access to public information (i.e., judgment of the SAC of 3 March 2017, I OSK 1163/15, LEX nr 2260512). Both the provisions of national law, EU regulations and Acts of international law ensure respect for the essence of the freedom to process information and the right of access to it.

The free flow of reliable information is essential in shaping mature civil societies. In times of pandemics, the exercise of this freedom allows people to access trusted and independent information on the current health situation, enabling them to make rational decisions in the social and economic spheres.[2] It is important that, at such a particular time, the information autonomy of the individual is not unduly restricted in connection with undertakings to counter epidemic threats. The justification for such actions may be to ensure the health security of the individual and his/her environment by collecting related data and their analysis and protecting the individual against false information that may lead to harm affecting him/her. However, it should be added that in pursuing these values, we should not violate the essence of rights such as privacy and informational autonomy.

1.3 Privacy protection and security of personal data

The right to privacy is guaranteed both in national legal regulations (Art. 47 of the Constitution) and in acts of international law (Art. 2 of the UDHR, Art. 17 of the International Covenant on Civil and Political Rights, Art. 8 of the ECHR) and the legal system of the EU (Art. 7 of the CFREU). However, a person's privacy is also protected under Art. 10 of the 1997 Council of Europe Convention on Human Rights and Biomedicine, which has not been ratified by Poland.

2 J.M. Ackerman, I.E. Sandoval-Ballesteros, 2006. 'The global explosion of freedom of information laws' (2006) 58(1) Administrative Law Review 92.

Privacy is a personal right belonging to a person, which, however, does not have its own uniform definition, either legally or doctrinally. Originally it was identified with the right to be left alone.[3] A. Kopff pointed out that it includes "everything which, because of the individual's legitimate seclusion from society at large, serves him to develop his physical and mental personality and to maintain the social position he has achieved."[4] In American literature, privacy is considered a conglomeration of elements such as solitude, anonymity or the secrecy of information concerning the person,[5] intimacy and the most subtle area related to the individual sphere of human personality.[6] According to H. Nissenbaum, privacy preservation provides individuals with the space for an adequate flow of information useful to them in accordance with contextual information norms defining the data subject, the sender, the recipient, the type of information and the transmission rules.[7] The conception of understanding of this value and its limits is undoubtedly influenced by socio-economic and technological development. New methods of automated information processing and the related risks have led to the emergence of a separate right to personal data protection from the right to privacy.

In the EU, the right to personal data protection is confirmed in Art. 8 of the CFREU. In turn, this issue is regulated in detail in the GDPR. In the Council of Europe system, the issues at stake are regulated by Convention No. 108 of the Council of Europe for the Protection of Individuals about Automatic Processing of Personal Data, drawn up in Strasbourg on 28 January 1981, which was updated in 2018. The extensive European regulations of international law relating to the protection of personal data confirm the leading role of countries on this continent in promoting legal standards in this area corresponding to the challenges of modern times.

Sensitive personal data, which include health data, are subject to special legal protection. This is confirmed by the wording of Art. 9 of the GDPR, as well as by specialised soft law instruments such as Recommendation CM/Rec (2019) 2 of the Committee of Ministers to Member States on the protection of health data. The processing of personal data during an epidemic emergency poses new challenges in terms of maintaining the lawfulness of such processes. The European Data Protection Board, in its Guidelines 03/2020 on the Processing of Health Data for Research Purposes in the Context of the COVID-19 Pandemic, adopted on 21 April 2020, stresses that existing legal regulations are flexible enough to effectively address population health concerns using health data in treatment and research processes. However, this should be done while respecting the principles

3 S.D. Warren, L.D. Brandeis, 'The Right to Privacy' (1890) 4(5) Harvard Law Review, 195.

4 A. Kopff, 'Ochrona sfery życia prywatnego jednostki w świetle doktryny i orzecznictwa' (1982) 10 Zeszyty Naukowe Uniwersytetu Jagiellońskiego. Prace Prawnicze 30.

5 R. Gavison, 'Privacy and the Limits of Law' (1980) 89(3) The Yale Law Journal 433.

6 A.F. Westin, 'Science, privacy, and freedom: issues and proposals for the 1970's' (1966) 66 (6) Columbia Law Review 1020–1029.

7 H.Nissenbaum, Privacy in Context: Technology, Policy, and the Integrity of Social Life (Stanford University Press 2009) 140–148.

of processing such resources and the rights of data subjects. Privacy by design should be considered and, where justified, data protection impact assessments should be carried out to take preventive measures to safeguard the information used.

1.4 Information security and cyber security

The issue of information security is closely related to the problems of personal data protection and cyber security. Effective protection of such resources requires a holistic approach, which is confirmed by the content of technical standards in management and information technology. ISO 27001 indicates that an information security management system cannot be considered to comply with the requirements of ISO 27001 if it does not ensure due observance of the country-specific regulations concerning the guarantee of privacy and the protection of personally identifiable information. Standard 27032 indicates that cyber security is defined as the information security of cyberspace, which is considered in ISO 27000 as the confidentiality, integrity and availability of information. In addition, other properties such as authenticity, accountability, non-repudiation and reliability may also be taken into account. Information security is a cross-cutting concept referring to the entire processing of these resources in a specific organisation.

Until 2016, the EU did not have an Act of common law that horizontally addressed the information security issues of the organisation and its Member States. Only soft law Acts, including communications and strategies relating to these issues, formed the basis for cyber security activities. For example, in 2013, the EU Cyber Security Strategy was adopted, a policy initiative of the Union responding to cyber threats and their associated risks in cyberspace. In 2016, Directive 2016/1148 of the European Parliament and of the Council (EU) of 6 July 2016 on measures for a high common level of security of networks and information systems within the Union was established. The wording of Art. 1(1) indicates that the primary objective of this Act is to achieve a level of security maturity of key ICT-based solutions in the EU to ensure the smooth functioning of the internal market. The provisions implementing this regulation in EU Member States refer to the imposition of obligations relating to cyber security on operators of key and digital services, as well as public administration, in terms of implementing strategies in this area and responding to identified incidents, along with the exchange of information on related circumstances. Mention should also be made of Regulation (EU) 2019/881 of the European Parliament and of the Council of 17 April 2019 on ENISA (European Union Agency for Cyber-security) and ICT cyber -security certification and repealing Regulation (EU) No 526/2013 (Cybersecurity Act). It strengthened the legal, organisational and financial position of this institution. These trends are manifested in the conferral of competencies on this Agency for the development and implementation of Union policy and law in cyber security, strengthening its role in operational cooperation at the Union level in this area, and standardisation and certification processes.

Since electronic services, new communication technologies, information systems and networks have become part of our daily lives, the occurrence of incidents disrupting IT services and critical infrastructure elements poses a serious threat to the functioning of the economy and the public sector in EU Member States.[8] Undoubtedly, the establishment of the NIS Directive has, to some extent, brought order to the EU's cybersecurity activities. However, it is possible that in the future, it will turn out that a higher level of harmonisation of Member States' obligations in this area is nevertheless desirable, resulting in the initiation of work on a new EU regulation relating to cyber security. We have seen a similar situation with regulations on personal data protection.

Organisations such as ENISA have recently been publishing on their websites short instructions addressed to different categories of actors on how to behave properly in cyberspace during a pandemic.[9] These resources include a cyber hygiene guide for small and medium enterprises, cyber security guidelines for healthcare, security indicators for IoT infrastructure. In addition to these materials, ENISA's thematic publications on various aspects of cyber security such as incident management, security implementation and vulnerability identification play an important role in the practical implementation of cyber security.

Undoubtedly, the challenge of the cyber security pandemic is the increase in the number of people using information and communication technologies. Many of these users have not previously used such solutions daily in their professional and social lives, so this group is particularly vulnerable to cyber threats due to their limited experience in this area. In such cases, adequate training for these users is important, including providing them with security knowledge to understand and enable them to practice new skills in securing their workplace. ENISA's Threat Landscape Report 2021 indicates that the main cyber security problems currently arise from ransomware attacks, which rely on unauthorised data encryption and demand payment to restore access to these resources.[10] Phishing attacks carried out by sending out crafted emails containing malicious content or attachments continue to be a significant source of malware threats. Many of these offensive actions are carried out not by individual hackers but by specialised groups whose activities are often inspired by governments and intelligence in certain countries. This reality results in attacks that are increasingly specialised and multifaceted, linked to the existence of APT-type threats, which have the character of covert, continuous, technically advanced and financially backed offensive actions using a wide range of technical (malware, bots, ICT eavesdropping) and organisational

8 D. Markopoulou, V. Papakonstantinou, P. Hert, 'The new EU cybersecurity framework: The NIS Directive, ENISA's role and the General Data Protection Regulation' (2019) 35(6) Computer Law and Security Review 1–2.

9 See more: https://www.enisa.europa.eu/topics/wfh-covid19 (01.01.2022).

10 I. Lella, M. Theocharidou, E. Tsekmezoglou, Apostolos Malatras and others, 'ENISA Threat Landscape 2021' <https://www.enisa.europa.eu/publications/enisa-threat-landscape-2021/@@download/fullReport> (31.12.2021).

(social engineering) methods.[11] The security challenges of the Internet of Things devices with their associated software cannot be overlooked either. Such solutions exchange data with the ICT systems operating them on an event or continuous basis. These devices transmit data about the time and type of activity, negatively affecting users' privacy.[12] Data subjects of Internet of Things processing are not always aware of their scope due to the technical sophistication of such processes (for example, using artificial intelligence) and the resulting difficulty in implementing the information obligation under the GDPR clearly and transparently. Certainly, particular attention should be paid to ensuring the confidentiality of such transmissions and identifying not only the users of such solutions but also the devices and software themselves involved in these processes. This will reduce the risk of unauthorised access to such systems.

The risks associated with pandemic times are linked to the occurrence of phishing attacks and ransomware. Switching to online contact without prior preparation and testing of technical solutions and procedures increases the risk of fraud and phishing. Attackers aware of the above circumstances send crafted information to users, resulting in a transfer of data to an unauthorised person or identity theft. Data encryption by ransomware malware results in loss of access to such resources. It may be impossible to recover without knowledge of an effective decryption method. Another type of attack that increases in number during epidemic threat periods is DoS. ICT systems are used more than in normal times, so the effectiveness of such a denial-of-service attack can be greater and more severe for the victim. Not to forget all other cases of loss of confidentiality of protected data using untested and inadequately secured ICT solutions. This refers to the case when the processing of information is secured by encryption, but the key used is easy to break, the algorithm no longer provides an adequate level of security or the protocol used does not use such technology throughout the life cycle of the resources we protect (end-to-end protection). It is important to emphasise that in the field of information security, we will not encounter universal and comprehensive security measures that are suitable for each case of data processing and provide protection in all its phases. It is necessary to select physical, organisational and technical protection measures adequate to the level of risk of threats related to the information resources used by the organisation.

1.5 Interoperability of data processing during a pandemic

In crisis situations, it is particularly important to exchange information effectively to achieve the objectives set. This process should be carried out in the most automated manner possible and without the need for data conversion. Art. 3 p.18

11 P. Hu et al., 'Dynamic defense strategy against advanced persistent threat with insiders. In IEEE Conference on Computer Communications (INFOCOM)', Kowloon (2015).

12 W. Iszkowski, 'Internet of Things. Systemy wbudowane' in G. Szpor (ed.), Internet rzeczy. Bezpieczeństwo w smart city (C.H. Beck 2015) 6–7.

of the Act of 17 February 2005 on Informatisation of the Activities of Entities Performing Public Tasks defines the notion of interoperability as the ability of various entities and ICT systems and public registers used by them to cooperate in order to achieve mutually beneficial and agreed objectives, taking into account the sharing of information and knowledge through business processes supported by them and implemented by means of data exchange through ICT systems used by these entities. As set out in Annex 2 to the Communication of the Commission to the European Parliament, the Council, the European Economic and Social Committee and the Committee of the Regions "Towards interoperability for European public services" (COM(2010) 744), interoperability is the ability of disparate and diverse organisations to interact towards mutually beneficial and agreed common goals, involving the sharing of information and knowledge between the organisations, through the business processes they support, by means of the exchange of data between their respective ICT systems. The sine qua non for achieving a state of interoperability is the ability to effectively achieve the objectives of delivering electronic services, by achieving an appropriate level of cooperation between ICT systems that securely and effectively exchange the necessary data to deliver specific business processes.[13] The latter concept is derived from management science and computer science, denoting a series of interrelated real-world activities that solve a specific problem or allow a specific effect that is a way to achieve a predetermined goal.[14]

The European Interoperability Framework has the following levels:

- legal – it involves adapting regulations – including procedural standards – to the challenges of the free flow of data between the EU Member States and their institutions;
- organisational – implies the harmonisation of management standards, organisational structures, policies and business processes related to information processing;
- semantic – it is understood as the establishment of agreed, consistent and unambiguous data structures at all stages of information processing;
- technological – ensuring compatibility of technical solutions (e.g., communication protocols) and software used for information processing (e.g., by formulating minimum requirements for such solutions in legal regulations or indicating the relevant technical standards that should be followed to ensure effective data exchange).

13 K. Świtała, 'Wpływ regulacji prawnej interoperacyjności na bezpieczeństwo rejestrów publicznych' in A. Gryszczyńska (ed.), Rejestry publiczne. Jawność i interoperacyjność (C.H. Beck 2016) 138.

14 F. Rahimi, Ch. Møller, L. Hvam, 'Business process management and IT management: The missing integration' (2016) 36(1) International Journal of Information Management 142.

Identifying these levels presents us with the complexity of the interoperability issue. It relates to technical problems and requires harmonisation of legal and organisational standards, which may constitute a fundamental barrier to the free flow of data. This, of course, does not happen unconditionally – as important as the unhindered exchange of information resources is ensuring their adequate security and respecting the right to privacy and personal data protection. This is confirmed by the content of Principle 8 of the Core Principle contained in the Strategy for the Implementation of the European Interoperability Framework (COM (2017) 134). Principle 11, on the other hand, points to the need to protect the information, which includes ensuring accountability of its processing. Data exchange between ICT systems should occur in a trustworthy environment based on established security policies and operating according to applicable legal regulations.

In the context of the pandemic, the exchange of data between the EU Member States on the functioning of their healthcare systems is quite limited. It is based primarily on the provisions of Directive 2011/24/EU of the European Parliament and of the Council of 9 March 2011 on applying patients' rights in cross-border healthcare. Unfortunately, the exchange of information between national contact points for cross-border healthcare in most cases is not automated. Therefore, it is proposed that regulations in this area be strengthened to create coherent and sustainable e-Health network solutions allowing the secure automated exchange between the Member States of key data relating to the operation of their healthcare systems. Of course, this should occur with due respect for patients' information autonomy.

1.6 Conclusions

During a pandemic, effective data sharing using information and communication technologies can improve decision-making based on facts and evidence. It should take place as automatically as possible. At the same time, information security and personal data protection should be duly guaranteed. The information resources processed in connection with the pandemic should be available – when the need arises – only to authorised persons (confidentiality) and be correctly structured (integrity). The implementation of data protection principles and the respect for the rights of data subjects also play an important role in this respect. This leads to increased trust of citizens in public entities and in policies and other undertakings implemented by them. In situations of epidemic threat, it is particularly important to ensure consistency of regulations related to interoperability of data sources and simultaneous provision of information security at national and European level, as well as complementarity of the adopted solutions with technical standards relating to this issue and guidelines of specialised institutions, such as ENISA. Certainly, in interoperability – especially in relation to the exchange of information on the functioning of healthcare systems in EU Member States – further harmonisation of legal regulations is desirable, streamlining the process of data exchange between Member States while maintaining information security and respect for the privacy of the individuals concerned.

Works cited

Ackerman, J.M., and Sandoval-Ballesteros, I.E., 'The Global Explosion of Freedom of Information Laws' (2006) 58(1) Administrative Law Review 85–130.

European Union Agency for Cybersecurity, *ENISA Threat Landscape Report 2021.* <https://www.enisa.europa.eu/publications/enisa-threat-landscape-2021/@@download/fullReport> (1.09.2021).

Gavison, R., 'Privacy and the Limits of Law' (1980) 89(3) The Yale Law Journal 421–471.

Hu, P., Li, H., Fu, H., and Cansever, D., 'Mohapatra Dynamic Defense Strategy against Advanced Persistent Threat with Insiders' in *IEEE Conference on Computer Communications (INFOCOM)*, Kowloon (2015), 747–755.

Iszkowski, W., 'Internet of Things. Systemy wbudowane' in ed. G. Szpor, *Internet rzeczy. Bezpieczeństwo w smart city* (C.H. Beck, Warsaw2015).

Judgment of the SAC of 3.03.2017, I OSK 1163/15, LEX nr 2260512.

Kopff, A., 'Ochrona sfery życia prywatnego jednostki w świetle doktryny i orzecznictwa, Zeszyty Naukowe Uniwersytetu Jagiellońskiego' (1982) 100 Prace Prawnicze.

Lipowicz, I., Niewiadomski, Z., Strzyczkowski, K., and Szpor, G., *Prawo administracyjne. Część materialna* (LexisNexis, Warsaw 2004).

Markopoulou, D., Papakonstantinou, V., and de Hert, P., 'The New EU Cybersecurity Framework: The NIS Directive, ENISA's Role and the General Data Protection Regulation' (2019) 35(6) Computer Law and Security Review 1–11.

Nissenbaum, H., *Privacy in Context: Technology, Policy, and the Integrity of Social Life* (Stanford University Press, Stanford 2009).

Rahimi, F., Møller, Ch, and Hvam, L., 'Business Process Management and IT Management: The Missing Integration' (2016) 36(1) International Journal of Information Management 142–154.

Świtała, K., 'Wpływ regulacji prawnej interoperacyjności na bezpieczeństwo rejestrów publicznych' in ed. A. Gryszczyńska, *Rejestry publiczne. Jawność i interoperacyjność* (C.H. Beck, Warsaw 2016).

Warren, S., and Brandeis, L., 'The Right to Privacy' (1890) 4(5) Harvard Law Review 193–220.

Westin, A., 'Science, Privacy, and Freedom: Issues and Proposals for the 1970's' (1966) 66(6) Columbia Law Review 1003–1050.

2 Countering Cybercrime during the Pandemic

Agnieszka Gryszczyńska

2.1 Introduction

The COVID-19 pandemic has significantly affected the methods of working, learning or performing public tasks. Lockdown and the associated sudden shift to performing work, delivering services and implementing public tasks online have exposed certain regulatory, technical, organisational and competency deficiencies. The above-named issues can be observed in every sector. To guarantee the continuity of economic and social processes and uninterrupted implementation of public tasks, it is crucial to have access to information resources, as well as ensure their integrity and confidentiality. The sudden increase in users' online activity is coupled with an increase in the activity of cybercriminals and groups involved in the spread of disinformation. Due to the pandemic, the effects of cyberattacks could be much more severe than before. The observed ransomware attacks on hospitals or research laboratories can involve an immediate threat to the lives and health of a number of individuals. Disinformation campaigns increase public discontent and lead not only to non-compliance with safety rules but also to physical attacks on sick or quarantined individuals, and to street riots.

The aim of the research is to verify the hypothesis on the lack of sufficient public law instruments to limit the number and adverse effects of incidents and to combat cybercrime.

2.2 The impact of digital transformation of the state and economy and the COVID-19 pandemic on cybercrime

Analysis of reports on cybersecurity indicates a steady, significant growth in the number of incidents both in Poland and across the globe. This trend is related to the global increase in the number of Internet users (in January 2021, Internet users accounted for approximately 60% of the population, social media users – 53.6%) and time spent online, which among Internet users in 2021 was already 6 h 54 m per day.[1] A shift in the scope of the provision of work, in education or leisure activ-

1 DataReportal, 'Digital 2021. Global Overview Report', <https://datareportal.com/reports/digital-2021-global-overview-report> (30.10.2021).

DOI: 10.4324/9781003263968-14

ities during the pandemic provides grounds to conduct a quantitative analysis of incidents and cybercrimes. Research on the impact of the pandemic on the number of incidents included reports prepared by CSIRT NASK and CSIRT GOV. At the same time, in the process of interpreting the results, it should be taken into consideration that in 2018 the Act on the National Cybersecurity System came into force in Poland, which introduced a legal obligation to report incidents involving essential services operators, digital services providers and incidents in a public entity to the relevant CSIRT unit. The upward trend in the number of calls resulting from the change of law is particularly visible in the statistics of CSIRT GOV.

In 2018, CSIRT NASK received 19,439 calls and recorded 3,739 security incidents, which accounts for 17.5% increase in the number of incidents compared to 2017.[2] In 2019, CSIRT NASK recorded 6,484 incidents. This represents an increase in the number of incidents by 73% compared to 2018.[3] In 2020, as many as 10,420 incidents were recorded by CSIRT NASK, which translates into an increase in the number of incidents by 61% compared to 2019 and by 179% compared to 2018.[4]

In 2018, CSIRT GOV recorded 31,865 calls, of which 6,236 were considered incidents, in 2019, 226,914 calls, of which 12,405 were considered incidents. In 2020, CSIRT GOV recorded 246,107 calls, of which 23,309 were considered incidents, an increase by about 88% compared to 2019, with a growth of calls by only about 8.5%.[5]

The structure of incidents recorded by CSIRT NASK is presented in Figure III.2.1.

The largest number of incidents were classified as "fraud," with incidents from the "phishing" subcategory comprising incidents which involve masquerading as another entity to persuade the user to reveal a private credential standing out the most from other categories. The classification adopted in the CSIRT NASK reports is based on the eCSIRT.net Incident Classification,[6] which does not reflect the meaning of fraud in criminal law. Thus, the category of "fraud" according to

2 CERT Polska, 'Security landscape of the Polish Internet 2018. Annual report on the activities of CERT Polska 2018'10, <https://www.cert.pl/wp-content/uploads/2019/05/Raport_CP_2018.pdf> (30.10.2021).

3 CERT Polska, 'Security landscape of the Polish Internet 2019. Annual report on the activities of CERT Polska 2019' 9, <https://www.cert.pl/wp-content/uploads/2020/07/Raport_CP_2019.pdf> (30.10.2021).

4 CERT Polska, 'Security landscape of the Polish Internet 2020. Annual report on the activities of CERT Polska 2020', <https://www.nask.pl/pl/raporty/raporty/4289,RAPORT-CERT-2020.html> (30.10.2021).

5 CERT GOV, 'CERT GOV Report 2020: Report on the State of Poland's Cybersecurity in 2020', <https://csirt.gov.pl/cer/publikacje/raporty-o-stanie-bezpi/974,Raport-o-stanie-bezpieczenstwa-cyberprzestrzeni-RP-w-2020-roku.html> (30.10.2021).

6 eCSIRT.net, 'Incident Classification. Incident Classification/ Incident Taxonomy according to eCSIRT.net, International Version Don Stikvoort, 11 Jan – 19 Dec 2012 (version mkVI of 31.03.2015)', <https://www.trusted-introducer.org/Incident-Classification-Taxonomy.pdf> (30.10.2021).

Incident Classification:	*Number of incidents*	*%*	*Number of incidents*	*%*	*Number of incidents*	*%*
	2018	*2018*	*2019*	*2019*	*2020*	*2020*
Abusive Content	431	11,53	812	12,52	371	3,56
Malicious Code	862	23,05	969	14,94	746	7,16
Information Gathering	101	2,70	95	1,47	60	0,58
Intrusion Attempts	153	4,09	77	1,19	174	1,67
Intrusions	125	3,34	160	2,47	317	3,04
Availability	49	1,31	57	0,88	121	1,16
Information Content Security	46	1,23	41	0,63	68	0,65
Fraud	1878	50,23	4086	63,02	8310	79,75
• including Phishing	1655	44,26	3516	54,23	7622	73,15
• including Masquerade	43	1,15	23	0,35	11	0,11
Vulnerable	69	1,85	102	1,57	211	2,02
Other	25	0,67	85	1,31	42	0,40
Total	3739	100	6484	100	10420	100

Figure III.2.1 Incidents classified by CSIRT NASK in 2018–2020 *Source: Own study based on data from CSIRT NASK (CERT Poland) reports.*

eCSIRT.net includes traditionally understood fraud within the meaning of Art. 286 § 1 of the Criminal Code (CC),[7] as well as computer fraud within the meaning of Art. 287 § 1 CC, identity theft (Art. 190 a § 2 CC), unauthorised acquisition of computer passwords or other access data (Art. 269 b § 1 CC), hacking (Art. 267 § 1 CC) and copyright infringement. The structure of incidents recorded by CSIRT GOV is presented in Figure III.2.2.

As indicated in Figure III.2.2, CSIRT GOV classifies incidents in a different manner than CSIRT NASK. Moreover, CSIRT GOV reports do not indicate whether and which taxonomy of incidents was used. In addition, the 2018–2020 reports presented data in different ways.

The lack of coherence in Incident Classification between CSIRT NASK and CSIRT GOV teams impedes quantitative research and categorisation of the most critical threats in Poland. Organisations defining a taxonomy are usually driven by different needs, and since different CSIRTs have different expectations, teams often end up developing their own incident classifications for internal use. However, the lack of a uniform and accepted classification impedes the exchange of information between CSIRTs and law enforcement agencies, as well as the research and analysis of the most critical threats. Although various initiatives are being undertaken to create new or modify existing taxonomies such as "Common Taxonomy for Law Enforcement and CSIRTs," which was set up to simplify CSIRT and

7 Criminal Code of 6.06.1997, JoL 2020, item 1444, as amended.

Incident Classification:	*Number of incidents*	*%*	*Number of incidents*	*%*	*Number of incidents*	*%*
	2018	*2018*	*2019*	*2019*	*2020*	*2020*
Malicious Code (Virus)	2448	39,26	7219	58,19	16777	71,98
Scanning	636	10,20	1878	15,14	2604	11,17
Phishing	276	4,43	1178	9,50	1396	5,99
Vulnerable	-	-	1016	8,19	1366	5,86
SPAM	-	-	210	1,69	311	1,33
Inaccessibility	275	4,41	290	2,34	254	1,09
Leakage	-	-	14	0,11	230	0,99
Attack	-	-	141	1,14	96	0,41
Masquerade	-	-	50	0,40	72	0,31
Incorrect configuration	1138	18,25	119	0,96	69	0,30
Compromising	-	-	188	1,52	66	0,28
Botnet	488	7,83	37	0,30	36	0,15
Replacement	-	-	8	0,06	13	0,06
Publication	-	-	3	0,02	11	0,05
Intrusions	-	-	44	0,35	8	0,03
DDoS	-	-	9	0,07	-	-
Breakdown	-	-	1	0,01	-	-
Total	6236	100	12405	100	23309	100

Figure III.2.2 Incidents classified by CSIRT GOV in 2018–2020 *Source: Own study based on data from CSIRT GOV reports.*

LEA cooperation, "eCSIRT.net taxonomy" which was developed in 2003 and "eCSIRT.net mkVI taxonomy" which is an adaptation of the original eCSIRT.net taxonomy, there is no uniform approach even between national CSIRTs in Poland.

The incident categories do not correspond to the normative descriptions of prohibited acts either. Not all incidents will constitute a prohibited act. Referring to the structure of a crime resulting from Art. 1 of the CC, it must be stated that a crime is such human conduct that meets the conditions allowing it to be defined as an act. The act is an unlawful act because it violates a sanctioned norm in the absence of circumstances justifying the violation due to a conflict of goods protected by law. Since the violation of the sanctioned norm is threatened by a criminal sanction, it is therefore a punishable act. In its individual assessment, it is socially harmful to a degree higher than negligible; thus, it is a culpable act. Fault may be attributed to the perpetrator of this punishable and culpable act; hence, it is a wrongful act.[8]

The quantitative study of cybercrime is by no means an easy task due to the lack of a definition of cybercrime and a catalogue of acts considered to

8 A. Zoll, *The norm from the point of view of criminal law* (Krakowskie Studia Prawnicze 1990, vol. 23) 75.

be cybercrimes.[9] Cybercrime, understood in a narrow sense, includes cyber-dependent crimes – offences that can only be committed using a computer, computer networks or another form of information communications technology (ICT), when the computer (or computer network) is the target of the criminal activity as the final goal (e.g., spamming, hacking and crimewares). These acts include the spread of viruses or other malware, hacking and distributed denial of service (DDoS) attacks. The horizontal use of hi-tech is when the computer is instead utilised as a tool to facilitate criminals' goals (e-frauds, cyber-laundering, child pornography, cyberterrorism, phishing). Such crimes are referred to as cyber-related crimes.

Criminal proceedings in Poland carried out in connection with their occurrence are instigated with the adoption of various legal qualifications of a given act, and the lists analysed in the literature focus on acts against the protection of information, not covering all categories of cases that can be considered computer-related crimes. To determine how the COVID-19 pandemic affected cybercrime in Poland, the research included both crimes against the protection of information, computer fraud, as well as traditionally understood acts of fraud that have been described in police databases as having been committed online.

As can be seen from Figure III.2.3, the predominant qualification is the act under Art. 286 CC, that is fraud, which can be described as "cyber-related crime." Analyses carried out based on data obtained from the National Police Headquarters indicate that approximately 42% of all proceedings initiated under Art. 286 CC and around 31% of offences established under Art. 286 CC concern acts committed online.

	Art. 267 § 1-4 CC	Art. 268 § 1-3 CC	Art. 268a § 1-2 CC	Art. 269 § 1-2 CC	Art. 269a CC	Art. 269b § 1 CC	Art. 286 § 1-3 CC (online frauds)	Art. 287 § 1-2 CC
2016	3401	213	499	11	44	36	27296	4103
2017	3419	190	464	13	39	28	29161	4554
2018	3676	148	382	9	51	29	30437	7402
2019	6718	182	686	17	37	55	32627	10793
2020	7017	147	764	9	33	49	35566	11219

Figure III.2.3 Cybercrime in Poland — the legal basis for initiating proceedings. *Source: Own study based on data from the National Police Headquarters.*

9 J. Kosiński, 'Cybercrime AD2020 – current status and predictions' in Gryszczyńska, Szpor, Cyberpandemic 2020 (eds.), 101–104.

This demonstrates a change in the modus operandi of the perpetrators, who use hi-tech to achieve the criminal goal of monetisation. There are far fewer acts classified as "cyber-dependent crimes" under Art. 267 § 1-4 CC (so-called hacking) or under Art. 287 § 1-2 CC, i.e., computer frauds consisting of unauthorised influence on automatic processing, storage or transmission of IT data or altering, deleting or introducing a new record of IT data with the aim of achieving a financial benefit or causing damage to another person.

As indicated in Figure III.2.4, the increase in incidents and cybercrimes has been a steady trend and during the pandemic there was no particular increase in 2020.

Research on the number of incidents and cybercrimes can also be contrasted with statistical data on the information society in Poland in 2020 (Figure III.2.5). According to research conducted by the Central Statistical Office (CSO) in 2020, 90.4% of households had access to the Internet at home (the indicator was 3.7% higher than in the previous year), 81.4% of persons aged 16–74 used the Internet on a regular basis (in 2019 it was 78.3%). As for the purposes of using the Internet in Poland, using an email as well as reading online were the most common. In the same year the share of an email users in the total population aged 16–74 amounted to 65.9%, while among Internet users 79.2%. In 2020, 60.9% of Poles purchased goods or services over the Internet, compared to 41.9% in 2016.[10]

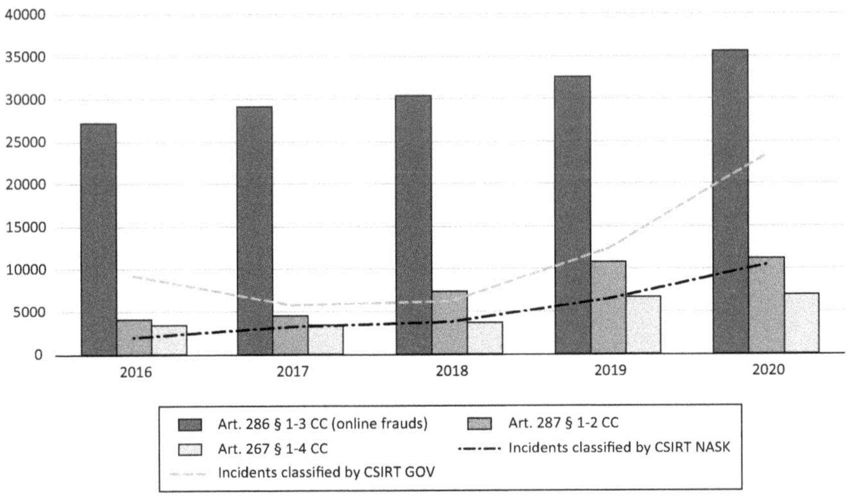

Figure III.2.4 Cybercrime and incidents classified by CSIRT NASK and CSIRT GOV in Poland. *Source: Own study based on data from the National Police Headquarters, CSIRT NASK and CSIRT GOV reports.*

10 Central Statistical Office, 'Information society in Poland in 2020', <https://stat.gov.pl/obszary-tematyczne/nauka-i-technika-spoleczenstwo-informacyjne/spoleczenstwo-informacyjne/spoleczenstwo-informacyjne-w-polsce-w-2020-roku,1,14.html> (30.10.2021).

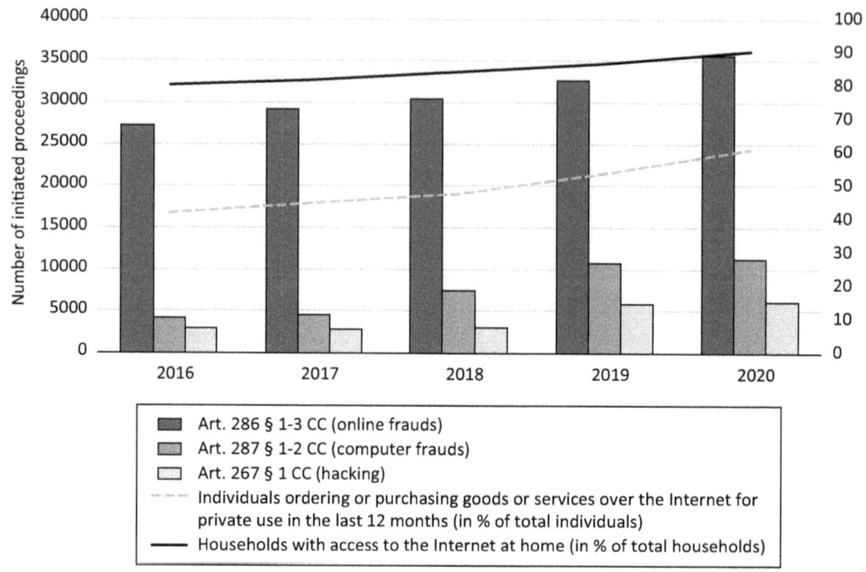

Figure III.2.5 Cybercrime and the evolution of the information society in Poland. *Source: Own study based on data from the National Police Headquarters and Central Statistical Office.*

The conducted quantitative research indicates that the growing number of incidents and cybercrimes in Poland is related to the digital transformation of society and economy. In the 2020 statistics, the impact of the pandemic is not observed. However, in order to draw unambiguous conclusions, it is advisable to conduct further quantitative research, which should also cover 2021, and compare it with statistical data from subsequent periods, after the end of the COVID-19 pandemic.[11]

2.3 Cyberattack scenarios involving COVID-19

An analysis of reports concerning network and information systems security in Poland implies a large number of incidents relating to fraud, computer fraud and malware distribution. Fake online stores and phishing-based attack scenarios are predominant among fraud-related incidents. The most common goal of the perpetrators is to get users to enter their e-banking login credentials on a fake website impersonating acquirers and banks or to get users to enter their social media login credentials. Significant damage is also caused to victims by burglaries involving

11 A. Gryszczyńska, 'The Impact of the COVID-19 Pandemic on Cybercrime' (2021) 69(4) Bulletin of the Polish Academy of Sciences: Technical Sciences.

a theft of funds from bank accounts using illegally obtained duplicate SIM cards (so-called SIM-swap-fraud) and fraud in the BEC model (business email compromise attacks). The most common types of malware used by criminals were Trojans, which make it possible to take control of an infected machine and gain access to user data, and ransomware, which blocks access to a computer system or encrypts data in order to extort a ransom. The most common attack scenarios remained sending emails with a fake invoice, payment order or information about a courier delivery.

Cybercriminals very quickly updated the previous attack scenarios to include the COVID-19 pandemic. In April, Google observed 18 million COVID-19-related phishing mailing and malware per day,[12] while a rise by 3,000% in COVID-19-themed phishing attacks was observed from mid-February to early June 2020.[13] In addition, a significant increase in the registrations of domains that use the pandemic to infect Internet users, phish for data, funds, or to create disinformation can also be observed. Both Europol, Interpol and CSIRT teams have warned about new threats and the use of the pandemic by cybercriminals.

Entities involved in cybersecurity prosecution pointed to many frauds in which perpetrators caused victims to dispose of their property in a disadvantageous manner by offering protective measures (including face masks), hygiene products, pharmaceuticals, medicines, fake COVID-19 home test kits or even vaccines for COVID-19. Paid orders were never delivered or the customer received counterfeit and/or sub-standard products.[14] Criminals are prosecuted both on national and international levels.[15]

Fraudsters also held fake fundraising campaigns for health care and hospital support and used COVID-19 in BEC attacks. For example, $7.25 million was stolen by a French pharmaceutical company via a BEC scam, in which the attacker allegedly posed as a legitimate supplier of FFP2 surgical masks and hand sanitiser.[16] Social engineering associated with COVID-19 is used in attacks targeting the unemployed as well as remote employees. Cybercriminals trick the unemployed in the United States into providing them with personal information,

12 K. Lyons, 'Google saw more than 18 million daily malware and phishing emails related to COVID-19 last week'(*The Verge*, 16.04.2020) <https://www.theverge.com/2020/4/16/21223800/google-malware-phishing-covid-19-coronavirus-scams> (30.10.2021).

13 M. Paiko, 'Phishing & BEC Scams Soar 3000%: Agari H2 2020 Email Fraud and Identity Deception Trends Report' (*Agari*, 5.08.2020) <https://www.agari.com/email-security-blog/phishing-bec-scams-soar/> (30.10.2021).

14 Europol, 'Pandemic profiteering: how criminals exploit theCOVID-19 crisis', <https://www.europol.europa.eu/publications-documents/pandemic-profiteering-how-criminals-exploit-covid-19-crisis> (30.10.2021).

15 Europol, 'Rise of fake 'corona cures' revealed in global counterfeit medicine operation, <https://www.europol.europa.eu/newsroom/news/rise-of-fake-%E2%80%98corona-cures%E2%80%99-revealed-in-global-counterfeit-medicine-operation> (30.10.2021).

16 P. Peterson, 'Phishing and BEC Scams Targeting Remote Workers are on the Rise' (*Agari*, 22.04.2020) <https://www.agari.com/email-security-blog/phishing-and-bec-scams-remote-workers/> (30.10.2021).

which they then use to extract government financial support earmarked for those in need.[17] Remote employees are at risk of being phished or infected with malware (mainly banking Trojans and ransomware) via emails containing malicious files that mimic resumes, medical leave or COVID-19-related financial support documents. Perpetrators impersonate both public entities (WHO) and globally recognisable brands, e.g., Zoom, Microsoft or Google. Ransomware attacks on healthcare facilities – hospitals and sample testing laboratories – are particularly threatening. Due to the state of the pandemic and significant risks to the lives and well-being of patients, the cyberattack on Brno University Hospital, Czechia, was considered an attack on a critical infrastructure.[18]

When discussing COVID-19-related threats, hybrid threats and disinformation need to be mentioned. As indicated by Europol, disinformation and misinformation around COVID-19 continue to proliferate around the world, with potentially harmful consequences for public health and effective crisis communication. According to the World Health Organization (WHO), the "infodemic" surrounding COVID-19 spreads just as quickly as the virus itself, with conspiracy theories, rumours and cultural stigma all contributing to deaths and injuries. Certain studies indicate that approximately 5,800 people were admitted to hospital as a result of false information on social media, at least 800 people may have died because of coronavirus-related misinformation.[19]

The COVID-19 crisis has also resulted in a surge in online distribution of child sexual abuse material. The psychological impact of isolation on children, combined with greater unsupervised Internet access, is also exploited by perpetrators committing such acts as grooming and sexual coercion and extortion.[20]

The global attacks described above are also observed in Poland in connection with COVID-19. In addition to global actors – including APT groups – the activity of Polish cybercriminals also poses a significant threat, as they use the pandemic mainly to commit fraud (fake stores and offers to sell protective products), infect Internet users with malware (at present, the number of malware infections of mobile devices with the Android system is growing dynamically), extort login credentials as well as steal funds from bank accounts. As stated in the reports of the CSIRT NASK, the most common attacks on Polish citizens are attacks

17 E. Woollacott, 'African Cybercriminals Net Millions In Fraudulent Covid-19 Government Claims' (*Forbes*, 20.05.2020) <https://www.forbes.com/sites/emmawoollacott/2020/05/20/african-cybercriminals-net-millions-in-fraudulent-covid-19-government-claims/#3eecfc35944> (30.10.2021).

18 Europol, 'Pandemic profiteering: how criminals exploit theCOVID-19 crisis', <https://www.europol.europa.eu/publications-documents/pandemic-profiteering-how-criminals-exploit-covid-19-crisis> (30.10.2021).

19 M. Saiful Islam, Tonmoy Sarkar, Sazzad Hossain Khan, et al. 'COVID-19–Related Infodemic and Its Impact on Public Health: A Global Social Media Analysis', (2020), 103(4) The American Journal of Tropical Medicine and Hygiene (30.10.2021).

20 Europol, 'Exploiting isolation: Offenders and victims of online child sexual abuse during the COVID-19 pandemic' <https://www.europol.europa.eu/publications-documents/exploiting-isolation-offenders-and-victims-of-online-child-sexual-abuse-during-covid-19-pandemic> (30.10.2021).

using scenarios in which perpetrators impersonate payment service providers and banks, and send requests to make online payments. Unauthorised acquisition of social media login credentials was also a frequently observed attack in the period between 2019 and 2021. There are numerous attack scenarios used by perpetrators, but one of the most popular is to create a website impersonating a news portal. A piece of sensational news about a kidnapping (usually of a child), a rape, a daring theft, a car accident, is posted on such a website. Below the description of the alleged incident, it is stated that surveillance video is available. Because the material is drastic and intended for adults only, it is necessary to verify the user's age to view the footage. Verification is to be done by logging into Facebook.com. After clicking the "log in" button, the victim is taken to a website impersonating a Facebook login panel. Once the victim's credentials have been taken over, their account is used to take over other accounts by sending links to phishing websites, publishing fictitious job recruitment information and to commit fraud. With the COVID-19 pandemic restrictions in place, previously used social engineering scenarios have been replaced with perpetrator-created websites containing sensational information on coronavirus. Examples of news headlines include "New facts about coronavirus" or "Child kidnapped from infectious disease hospital."

COVID-19-based social engineering is also used by groups focusing on infecting devices. On 23 September 2021, thousands of telecommunications network users in Poland received a text message with information about the imposition of quarantine and a hyperlink to download malware impersonating the official "Home Quarantine" application. The aim of the actors was to infect smartphones with the Android operating system and obtain access data to electronic banking.

The trust in the vaccination system may also be adversely affected by incidents observed in Poland and globally relating to the issuance of false COVID-19 certificates. This is carried out in several different ways. In the simplest of ways, people employed at vaccination centres, in exchange for a financial benefit, confirm false information by making an entry in the computer system about the vaccination (in November 2021, three nurses issuing false vaccination certificates were temporarily detained in Poland). Also, EU SARS-CoV-2 vaccination certificates are offered on Polish criminal forums on the DarkWeb network. Advertisements regarding official EU certificates of vaccination against SARS-CoV-2 which are valid, but contain false information, generated using cryptographic keys belonging to countries such as France, Germany, Macedonia and Poland, can also be found on international forums and groups created on instant messengers.[21]

These incidents undermine the credibility of the COVID-19 Certificate system and may also adversely affect the evaluation of the effectiveness of SARS-CoV-2 vaccine itself due to the increasing number of people with false passports confirming vaccination.

21 P. Konieczny, 'Someone has issued a valid COVID certificate for Adolf Hitler and Mickey Mouse' (*Niebezpiecznik.pl*, 28.10.2021) <https://niebezpiecznik.pl/post/falszowanie-certyfikat-covid-paszport/> (30.10.2021).

2.4 Factors impeding the identification of the perpetrators

Cybercrime in the last 20 years has become a well-organised activity. It is characterised by a division of roles and is based on business models.[22] Cybercrime marketplaces feature mechanisms that guarantee anonymity, security of payments and tools to facilitate high-risk transactions (escrow) and limit abuse (seller and buyer rating system, comments). On the DarkWeb's marketplaces, cybercriminals offer or purchase tools (exploits, malware) and data (logins and passwords, ID scans) necessary to commit crimes, provide services (renting a botnet, launching a custom attack, distributing malware) or recruit collaborators. This results in more serious and better prepared attacks causing increasingly more damage. People who work together do not know each other's personal data, image or location, and they do not exchange information about their private lives. Communication takes place with the use of encrypted messengers or email accounts that provide a high level of anonymity to their users. The perpetrators use multiple aliases, make anonymous payments – usually using cryptocurrency – and are careful to remain anonymous.

The key for the perpetrators to remain anonymous is to hide the IP address assigned by the telecommunications operator, avoid making purchases using their own data and make anonymous payments. To hinder or make it impossible to establish their own identity, cybercriminals mask the IP addresses assigned to them by using a TOR, VPN or Proxy network.

Perpetrators responsible for cyberattacks also widely exploit the lack of mechanisms to verify the identity of recipients of services delivered electronically. The infrastructure used to commit a crime is purchased by cybercriminals using fictitious data or data of other entities (both individuals and businesses) obtained from online databases – including public registers. Domain registration intermediaries rely on the data declared by the people registering domains, which leads to a situation where cybercriminals create a new identity or carry out identity theft to register a domain. Moreover, the attribution of attacks has been made significantly more difficult by the implementation of GDPR. Most online domain registers and WHOIS databases no longer publish data on Internet domain subscribers. For the purposes of attack attribution, acquiring valuable information for criminal proceedings or establishing contact with the entity whose domain is used for criminal activity, it may be recommended that information about the email address of the domain name registrant should be openly published.

Where they have been introduced, provisions on the registration of prepaid SIM cards are usually not effective. However, the goal of the regulation, i.e., to limit risks relating to the anonymity of telecommunications services, has not been achieved, because the action of confirming data may be performed by a third party on behalf of the service provider, which means that domain name registrants'

22 S.L. Moskowitz, *Cybercrime and Business: Strategies for Global Corporate Security* (Butterworth-Heinemann 2017) 3–21.

data are not properly verified. Secondly, domain name registrants are required to provide data rather than actual users of the service. As domain name registrants of prepaid services, criminals provide other people's data extracted from databases available online, both lawful (public registers) and unlawful (leaks), and trading in SIM cards registered with other people's data is common on both the DarkWeb and Clearnet.

When using e-services, most perpetrators also tend to make anonymous payments. In order to remain anonymous and ensure a safe transfer of funds derived from criminal activity, perpetrators also use bank accounts and accounts on cryptocurrency stock exchanges or online currency exchanges established using data of other people. Money laundering methods depend on the underlying act. Funds representing a ransom – in particular for decrypting ransomware-encrypted data – are to be transferred by the victims in cryptocurrency. Funds originating from fake online stores, fictitious auctions, BEC or SIM swap frauds are usually transferred to classic bank accounts, so-called money mules, in the initial phase. Only then do the perpetrators exchange them for cryptocurrency, buy precious metals (gold) or take other actions to hide their criminal origin.

The cross-border nature of cybercrime cases is also a significant factor that makes it difficult to identify perpetrators, as it requires the use of diverse tools of international cooperation and tools to secure and transfer data without delay.

2.5 De lege ferenda postulates

The dynamic development of cybercrime, observed for several years, is linked on the one hand to the increased online activity of users, and on the other to a much lower risk for perpetrators, associated with the possibility of remaining anonymous. The growing number of incidents provokes a discussion about anonymity on the Internet. Anonymity is offered to the perpetrators by DarkWeb – through the use of onion routing (TOR) and services available on the.onion domain. A significant proportion of the acts are committed using national domain names and entities providing lawful electronic services. However, the perpetrators take advantage of the lack of mechanisms enabling verification of their declared identity. To enhance the level of cybersecurity and reduce cross-cutting crime facilitators, strong action is necessary to counter identity theft and money laundering of the proceeds of cybercrime. Currently, providers of electronic services in many countries, including Poland, have no obligations relating to the collection and storage of user access logs. As a result, it is the rules and regulations of a given entity, and not a mandatory provision of law, that decide whether and from which period it is possible to obtain data concerning IP addresses from which an individual logs in to their email account. Consequently, it is not only impossible to determine who is using the email account, but it also makes it significantly more difficult or even impossible to conduct proceedings on obtaining unauthorised access to (hacking) such an account. The extent of data collected and shared as "logs" is also a serious matter. In fact, a significant number of e-service providers and banks do not collect port number information. Because operators widely use NAT in the network, and one public IP address can be assigned even to tens of thousands of users, it is impossible to determine the subscriber of the service. These issues show that mechanisms aimed at verifying the identity of service subscribers and determining the scope of data that should be collected must be introduced and the period for which they should be stored must be indicated. This will, however, require legislative changes in individual states. Data sharing between telecommunications services providers, banks and financial institutions should also be improved regarding anti-money laundering and more effective blocking of bank accounts and transactions where there is a reasonable suspicion of a prohibited act.

The growing number of phishing websites created by criminals with a view to obtaining login credentials, fake online stores and the increasing amount of misinformation related to COVID-19 make blocking websites, social media profiles or certain information an increasingly discussed issue. This discussion is inseparably linked to the debate on freedom of information, the exercise of the right to express one's opinion, or the freedom to conduct business. In the public debate, on the one hand, there are arguments relating to the need to protect Internet users from phishing and misinformation websites; on the other hand, there are fears that this will lead to censorship. There is also no general agreement on what content should be blocked and how, or labelled with additional information indicating, for example, low reliability of the quoted source. For instance, Facebook, to reduce the amount of false information on the pandemic, before allowing the user to share content about the coronavirus, is to display a special information window, where the user will see, among other things, links related to the message, sources and the date when it first appeared on the platform. Previous efforts made by the platform to block posts about coronavirus have been criticised. May 2020 also saw an interesting dispute from the legal point of view between US President Donald Trump and Twitter, after Twitter had labelled some of the President's tweets as "unverified claims" or as "misleading information."[23] What is more, in July 2020 Twitter removed a tweet that had been retweeted by President Donald Trump that falsely stated that there was a cure for the coronavirus. Moreover, the President's eldest son, Donald Trump Jr., was temporarily locked out of his Twitter account after posting the controversial video shared by Trump promoting hydroxychloroquine in COVID-19 treatment.[24] This is an important area that requires adequate regulation to be put in place. Currently, it is the rules and regulations of each website that determine the conditions of its use, including the principles of moderation and blocking posts. The introduction of such regulation may make it difficult or impossible to exercise the rights of individuals whose posts have been blocked

23 M. Kelly, 'Donald Trump escalates Twitter feud by cross-posting blocked message' (*The Verge*, 29.05.2020) <https://www.theverge.com/2020/5/29/21274493/donald-trump-twitter-feud-blocked-message-social-media-executive-order> (30.10.2021).

24 R. Shabad, 'Twitter removes tweet highlighted by Trump falsely claiming COVID-19 'cure'' (*NBC News*, 28.07.2020) <https://www.nbcnews.com/politics/donald-trump/twitter-removes-tweet-highlighted-trump-falsely-claiming-covid-cure-n1235075> (30.10.2021).

or moderated. Fortunately, there are fewer dilemmas about protecting freedom of information when it comes to blocking phishing websites aimed at obtaining login credentials. An example is an agreement concluded in Poland on 23 March 2020 on the creation of a warning list relating to domains used for extortion of data and money, the signatories of which are the Ministry of Digitalization, Research and Academic Computer Network and four major telecommunications operators. On 14 November 2021, there were 35,845 items on the list of phishing domains and 43 items contained the string "COV"; example domains include: covid-gov.pl (entered on the list of warnings on 20 August 2021), cov-19.pl (18August 2021), loterrycov.net (27 August 2021), eucovidfinances.com (27 October 2021). The impact of attacks could also be reduced by education for cybersecurity.[25]

The cross-border nature of crimes is an important factor impeding the investigation and identification of the perpetrators. It is said that electronic evidence is needed in around 85% of investigations, and in two-thirds of these investigations there is a need to obtain evidence from online service providers based in another jurisdiction. The number of requests to major online service providers grew by 84% in the period between 2013 and 2018.[26] To increase the efficiency and speed of the process of securing and retrieving electronic evidence held or possessed by service providers established in another jurisdiction in the EU, legislative action is being taken.[27] Work is also being carried out on a directive laying down harmonised rules on the appointment of legal representatives for the purpose of taking evidence in criminal proceedings.[28] The Second Additional Protocol to the Convention on Cybercrime on enhanced cooperation and disclosure of electronic evidence was also adopted in 2021 and should be opened for signature in May 2022.[29] Urgent adoption of the regulations named above is critical to ensure immediate, direct exchange of incident data. These regulations will supplement or partly replace the already existing tools for data acquisition, such as the European Investigation Order or regulations arising from the Convention or bilateral agreements relating to the execution of requests for international legal assistance in criminal cases.

25 G. Szpor, 'Legal Aspects of Education for Cybersecurity' in Gryszczyńska, Szpor, Cyberpandemic 2020 (eds.), 429–438.

26 EC, Recommendation for a Council decision authorizing the opening of negotiations in view of an agreement between the Europe an Union and the United States of America on cross-border access to electronic evidence for judicial cooperation in criminal matters, COM(2019)70 final, 5.02.2019.

27 EC, Proposal for a Regulation of the European Parliament and of the Council on European Production and Preservation Orders for electronic evidence in criminal matters, COM(2018)225 final, 17.04.2018.

28 EC, Proposal for a Directive of the European Parliament and of the Council laying down harmonised rules on the appointment of legal representatives for the purpose of gathering evidence in criminal proceedings, COM/2018/226 final, 17.04.2018.

29 Second Additional Protocol to the Convention on Cybercrime on enhanced co-operation and disclosure of electronic evidence, CM(2021)57-final, 17.11.2021.

2.6 Conclusions

The area of cybercrime is one of the crime areas most affected by the COVID-19 crisis. Social engineering-based attack scenarios, techniques, tactics and procedures used by the perpetrators of cyber-related crimes have changed in Poland, but the growth rate of incidents and cybercrimes in 2020 is similar to the level observed in 2019. Drawing unambiguous conclusions about the impact of the pandemic on the increase in cyber-dependent crimes and cyber-related crimes requires expanding the research to include data from 2021 and statistical periods following the pandemic.

The research conducted made it possible to identify regulatory gaps that facilitate committing prohibited acts. For cybercriminals, the pandemic is primarily an opportunity to increase the effectiveness of attacks based on social engineering. The actors usually remain unidentified due to the application of various methods aimed at concealing their identity and the act of money laundering. In 2020 and 2021, new tools for cooperation and disclosure of electronic evidence and combating cybercrime were discussed and worked on, but the ground for regulatory change was not the pandemic. Also, in Poland, the pandemic has not become an impulse for legislative work aimed at raising the level of cyber security. The introduced changes were not significant in their nature (such as increased lower and upper limits of the punishment provided for criminal offences of stalking and identity theft). The conducted research indicates that there are not enough legal instruments to combat cybercrime in the face of the pandemic.

Works cited

Gryszczyńska, A., 'The Impact of the COVID-19 Pandemic on Cybercrime' (2021) 69(4) Bulletin of the Polish Academy of Sciences: Technical Sciences 1–9.

Islam, M.S., Sarkar, T., Khan, S.H., et al. 'COVID-19–Related Infodemic and Its Impact on Public Health: A Global Social Media Analysis' (2020) 103(4) The American Journal of Tropical Medicine and Hygiene 1621–1629.

Kelly, M., 'Donald Trump Escalates Twitter Feud by Cross-Posting Blocked Message' *The Verge* (2020) <https://www.theverge.com/2020/5/29/21274493/donald-trump-twitter-feud-blocked-message-social-media-executive-order> (30.10.2021).

Konieczny, P., 'Someone has Issued a Valid COVID Certificate for Adolf Hitler and Mickey Mouse' Niebezpiecznik.pl (2021) <https://niebezpiecznik.pl/post/falszowanie-certyfikat-covid-paszport/> (30.10.2021).

Lyons, K., 'Google Saw More than 18 Million Daily Malware and Phishing Emails Related to COVID-19 Last Week' *The Verge* (2020) <https://www.theverge.com/2020/4/16/21223800/google-malware-phishing-covid-19-coronavirus-scams> (30.10.2021).

Moskowitz, S.L., *Cybercrime and Business: Strategies for Global Corporate Security* (Butterworth-Heinemann 2017).

Paiko, M., 'Phishing & BEC Scams Soar 3000%: Agari H2 2020 Email Fraud and Identity Deception Trends Report' Agari (2020) <https://www.agari.com/email-security-blog/phishing-bec-scams-soar/> (30.10.2021).

Peterson, P., 'Phishing and BEC Scams Targeting Remote Workers are on the Rise' *Agari* (2020) <https://www.agari.com/email-security-blog/phishing-and-bec-scams-remote-workers/> (30.10.2021).

Shabad, R., 'Twitter Removes Tweet Highlighted by Trump Falsely Claiming COVID-19 'Cure'' NBC News (2020) <https://www.nbcnews.com/politics/donald-trump/twitter-removes-tweet-highlighted-trump-falsely-claiming-covid-cure-n1235075> (30.10.2021).

Woollacott, E., 'African Cybercriminals Net Millions in Fraudulent Covid-19 Government Claims' *Forbes* (2020) <https://www.forbes.com/sites/emmawoollacott/2020/05/20/african-cybercriminals-net-millions-in-fraudulent-covid-19-government-claims/#3eecfc35944> (30.10.2021).

Zoll, A., *The Norm from the Point of View of Criminal Law* (Krakowskie Studia Prawnicze, Kraków 1990), vol. 23.

IV

Health Care and Social Security

1 Telemedicine During the Epidemic

Sebastian Sikorski

1.1 Introduction

The technical and technological progress that is taking place also affects healthcare. Not only is the level of advancement of healthcare services changing, but so is the way they are provided. An example of such a change is the provision of healthcare services within the framework of telemedicine, understood as the provision of healthcare services remotely. The World Health Organization defines telemedicine as:

> The delivery of healthcare services, where distance is a critical factor, by all healthcare professionals using information and communication technologies for the exchange of valid information for diagnosis, treatment and prevention of disease and injuries, research and evaluation and for the continuing education of healthcare providers, all in the interests of advancing the health of individuals and their communities.[1]

Telemedicine was introduced into the Polish legal order by the Act amending the Act on the Information System in Healthcare and Certain Other Acts of 9 October 2015.[2] This regulation amended the normative acts of key importance to the healthcare system. The Act on Therapeutic Activity of 15 April 2011 (ATA)[3] should primarily be mentioned here. According to the current wording of the provisions of Art. 3, para. 1 and 2a of ATA, healthcare services may be provided via ICT systems or communication systems. Changes were also introduced at the level of statutes regulating individual medical professions. This is primarily the Act on the Professions of Doctor and Dentist of 5 December 1996 (ADD),[4] according to which a doctor received the ability to provide healthcare services via ICT systems

1 WHO, Telemedicine. Opportunities and development in Member States, Report on the 2nd global survey on eHealth, 2010.
2 Act amending the Act on the Information System in Healthcare and certain other Acts of 9.10.2015 (JoL item 199).
3 The Act on Medical Activity of 15.04.2011 (JoL 2020 item 295).
4 Act on the Professions of Doctor and Dentist of 5.12.1996 (JoL 2020 item 514).

DOI: 10.4324/9781003263968-16

or communication systems (Art. 2, para. 3, item 4 of ADD). According to the provision of Art. 42, para. 1 of ADD, the doctor also decides about the patient's state of health in this form. Nurses and midwives also received solutions enabling the provision of healthcare services through telemedicine. According to the provision of Art. 11, para. 1 of the Act on the Professions of Nurse and Midwife (ANM),[5] a nurse and a midwife also perform their profession via ICT or communication systems.

1.2 Modifications introduced by the outbreak of COVID-19

A necessary condition for the extensive use of telemedicine is the classification of healthcare services provided in this way into the list of guaranteed benefits, namely healthcare services financed with public funds, the so-called basket of guaranteed benefits. The MoH makes this qualification in a regulation in accordance with the provision of Art. 31d of the Act on Healthcare Services Financed with Public Funds of 27 August 2004 (AHS).[6] The Regulation of the MoH of 31 October 2019 amending the Regulation on guaranteed primary healthcare benefits is of particular importance from the point of view of the epidemiological threat of the SARS Cov2 virus.[7] The detailed scope of these benefits was specified in the Order of the President of the National Health Fund (NHF) of 30 December 2019, no. 177/2019/DSOZ, on the conditions for the conclusion and implementation of contracts for the provision of primary healthcare services. Healthcare services provided remotely were classified on this basis as primary healthcare services financed with public funds. The method in which services were provided changed with the announcement of the state of epidemic under the Regulation of the MoH of 20 March 2020. This is because, according to the annex to the Regulation of the President of the NHF of 18 March 2020, no. 39/2020/DSOZ, an additional list of primary healthcare services was introduced, which was related to the prevention of COVID-19 (doctor's teleconsultations and nurse's teleconsultations). However, in accordance with the competence specified under Art. 8a, para. 5, item 2 of the Act on the State Sanitary Inspectorate of 14 March 1985, in view of the epidemic threat, the Chief Sanitary Inspector issued a communication (recommendation) on the method of conduct regarding primary healthcare and night-time and Christmas healthcare in connection with the spread of the new SARS-CoV-2 virus on 10 March 2020. Based on this communication, the general practice was introduced of informing patients that they should contact the clinic by telephone to arrange an appointment and to receive teleconsultations. It is this method of providing services that has been recommended to every patient,

5 Act on the Professions of Nurse and Midwife of 15.07.2011 (JoL 2020 item 562).

6 Act on Healthcare Services Financed with Public Funds of 27.08.2004 (JoL 2019 item 1373).

7 The Regulation of the MoH of 31.10.2019 amending the Regulation on guaranteed primary healthcare benefits is of particular importance from the point of view of the epidemiological threat of the SARS Cov2 virus (JoL Laws item 2120).

including those without signs of infection, requesting an appointment with a doctor.[8] Simultaneously, on 15 March 2020, the NHF issued a communication recommending the restriction of personal contacts with patients (to minimise the risk of transmission of a COVID-19 infection). It also reiterated that primary healthcare services can be provided through teleconsultations by a primary healthcare doctor, a primary healthcare nurse or a primary healthcare midwife.[9]

In the Polish healthcare system, the MoH performs, among other things, managerial, supervisory, controlling and coordinating activities with respect to its subordinate bodies.[10] Of particular importance here is the competence to issue secondary regulations to statutes. In view of such empowerment of the MoH in the system, the scope of tasks and competencies exercised by the President of the NHF gives rise to serious reservations. Some representatives of the doctrine point out that, in the case of the orders of the President of the NHF, the legislator has even allowed for the creation of a "new" unconstitutional source of law.[11] During the period of the epidemic, it is not even the orders but the announcements of the President of the NHF that largely determine the functioning of the whole of the healthcare system.

As part of the teleconsultation, the doctor can conduct an examination of the patient and gather his/her full medical history. In many clinical situations, this enables an appropriate differential diagnosis to be conducted, a diagnosis to be prepared and the appropriate treatment to be implemented. The provision of primary healthcare services in this form proved to be a factor in reducing the risk of infection of patients, who would have otherwise reported to outpatient clinics and waited in waiting rooms for an appointment, where they are highly likely to become infected with SARS-COV-2. This also significantly reduces the risk of infection of others, including the medical staff. The teleconsultations have meant that infected patients (including those infected with SARS-COV-2 or COVID-19) receive medical advice and information on where to go to confirm or rule out infection. The functionality of the system enables e-prescriptions and e-referrals to be gradually implemented. At this point, however, attention should be drawn to doubts which have arisen about the admissibility of issuing e-ZLA forms (medical certificates confirming the temporary incapacity to work) as part of the teleconsultations. This is because, according to § 6, para. 1 of the Regulation of the Minister of Labour and Social Policy of 10 November 2015 on the procedure and method of assessing the temporary incapacity to work, issuing a medical certificate and the procedure and

8 www.gov.pl/web/koronawirus/komunikat-glownego-inspektora-sanitarnego-w-sprawie-schematu -postepowania-dla-poz-i-nisoz (7.08.2020).

9 https://www.nfz.gov.pl/aktualnosci/aktualnosci-centrali/komunikat-dla swiadczeniodawcow, 7644 .html. (07.08.2020).

10 E. Knosala, Public tasks, organizational and legal forms of their performance and new concepts – scope of certain problems for discussion on the concept of the system of administrative law [in:] Concept of the system of administrative law. Convention of the Chairs of Administrative Law and Administrative Proceedings, Zakopane, 24-27/09/2006, ed. J. Zimmermann, (WolKluw.2007), 129.

11 M. Paszkowska, The health insurance system in Poland, (Difin 2015) 53–64.

method of correcting an error in a medical certificate, a medical certificate "shall only be issued after a direct examination of the insured's state of health" (§ 6, para. 1). This can simultaneously only be done by a doctor who assessed the patient's state of health, based on all the circumstances of importance to the assessment of the state of health and the impairment of bodily functions causing the temporary incapacity to work, especially with regard to its type and conditions.

It should be accepted that, in the context in question, the terms "direct" and "personal" are synonymous. Furthermore, it should be very clearly emphasised that this regulation does not specify the rules and conditions of practising the profession of a doctor. This area is regulated by a higher-ranking Act, namely the ADD. All the doctor's activities comprising diagnosis, treatment and rehabilitation, as well as issuing opinions and judgments, are performed in accordance with this regulation. It simultaneously transpires from the above provisions of Art. 2, para. 4 and Art. 42, para. 1 of ADD that a doctor can perform his duties (including issuing an opinion on the state of health) via ICT systems or communication systems. It should also be reiterated that it is the doctor who decides in every case about the possibility of diagnosing a given person using these systems. In practice, there will often be cases where a patient is referred to a standard medical appointment and a teleconsultation cannot be applied. However, in many clinical cases, such a consultation could be conducted using ICT links. Additional circumstances arising from the announced state of epidemic and the above recommendations of the Chief Sanitary Inspector to use telemedicine in primary healthcare (namely by a general practitioner) should be mentioned here. Furthermore, it arises from the wording of the provision of Art. 16, para. 1, item 1 of AHS that the assessment of the state of a patient's health, including his possible incapacity to work, is a medical procedure and the patient is entitled to receive a medical certificate. The above provision of Art. 2 of ADD also applies to medical certificates. In practice, a doubt arose during the epidemic over the wording of the above regulation of the Minister of Labour and Social Policy as to whether a doctor is authorised to issue an e-ZLA form when examining a patient using telemedicine systems. Ultimately, the practice has been generally accepted of also issuing them after the examination in this form. An additional argument was not only the announced state of epidemic – and therefore practical considerations – but also the circumstance that these certificates have only been issued in electronic form since as early as 1 July 2018. Therefore, a doctor refusing to issue a certificate confirming incapacity to work (e-ZLA) exposed him/herself to a potential charge of the improper performance of the contract with the NHF (assuming, of course, that he/she had a contract with the Fund for providing such services). However, it should be emphasised that the legal situation here has not changed, which means that there are and were no obstacles to an e-ZLA form being issued after conducting an examination with the use of telemedical systems – an e-visit, also during the epidemic.[12]

12 S. Sikorski, M. Florczak, Telemedicine helps in the battle against the pandemic, (Gazeta Prawna, 19/03/2020, B11, 2020)

The Regulation of the MoH of 12 August 2020 on the organisational standard of teleconsultations in primary healthcare also gives rise to reservations.[13] According to the empowerment set out in the provision of Art. 22, para. 5 of ATA, the MoH decided to specify the organisational standard of teleconsultations provided within the framework of primary healthcare. The authorisation alone and the need to issue such an act does not give rise to any doubts. However, the timing of issuing it, namely more than eight months after the introduction of this service into the list of guaranteed services, can already give rise to reservations. For example, because it was only in this Act that the standard of verification of the patient was determined and this is a necessary condition for the provision of correct teleconsultations (§ 3, para. 9 of the Regulation). Simultaneously, this regulation also applies to such elements of the standard, the lack of which could simply be considered a healthcare service provided in breach of the principles of practising the profession, including the profession of doctor. For example, the indication that a teleconsultation includes an examination of the person and an analysis of the patient's available medical records (§ 3, para. 7 of the Regulation). Furthermore, that the teleconsultation is to take place on conditions which guarantee confidentiality (§ 3, para. 5 of the Regulation). Also, the possibility of benefiting from healthcare services provided in direct contact with the patient if it is not possible to provide the primary healthcare service through teleconsultation because of the state of the patient's health (§ 3, para. 1, item e of the Regulation). Finally, the wording of § 3, para. 1, item a of the Regulation, which specifies the cases in which the provision of teleconsultations is ruled out, gives rise to concern. It should be reiterated here that, according to the provision of Art. 4 of ADD, a doctor is obliged to practice the profession in accordance with the guidelines of current medical knowledge, the methods and means available to him/her to prevent, diagnose and treat diseases, in accordance with the principles of professional ethics and with due diligence. However, according to the provisions of Art. 42, para. 1 of ADD, a doctor decides on the state of health of a given person after a previously examining him/her and after analysing that person's available medical records. Finally, in accordance with the provision of Art. 40, para. 1 of ADD, a doctor is obliged to maintain confidentiality of patient-related information obtained in connection with practising the profession. The question arises here of whether the restriction of the ability to provide teleconsultations breaches the statutory principles of practising the medical profession? Furthermore, doubts can also be raised as to the objective of repeating certain duties of the doctor in a sub-statutory act, the objective of which is to define the standard of providing healthcare services.

In the case of a medical emergency, which, in accordance with the provision of Art. 3, para. 8 of the Act on State Medical Rescue Services of 8 September 2006

13 Regulation of the MoH of 12.08.2020 on the organizational standard of tele-consultations in primary healthcare (JoL item 1395).

(ASMRS),[14] is defined as "a condition involving the sudden or shortly foreseeable appearance of symptoms of a deterioration of the health, the immediate result of which may be serious damage to bodily functions or injury or a loss of life, which requires immediate medical rescue actions and treatment." Such a person (including a person suffering from COVID-19 or infected with SARS-CoV-2) is transported by a medical rescue team in accordance with the provision of Art. 44, para. 1 of ASMRS to the hospital emergency ward or hospital specified by the medical dispatcher or voivodeship medical rescue coordinator, which is nearest in terms of arrival time. The provision of Art. 49a of ASMRS entered into force on 1 April 2020, allowing the voivode to conclude additional contracts on the financing of the tasks of the medical rescue teams "in the event of a state of emergency, a state of epidemic or in the event of a danger of an infection or infectious disease spreading."

However, if the patient's condition does not qualify as a sudden threat to the health and transportation within the State Medical Rescue system, it is the primary healthcare doctor who provides the treatment – mainly in the form of teleconsultations – in the case of a suspected COVID-19 or SARS-CoV-2 infection – who is obliged to assure the possibility of transportation by sanitary transport to a medical entity authorised and obliged to order a COVID-19 diagnosis, namely a hospital specialising in infections or a hospital with infection or observation/infection wards, or a hospital with an emergency ward or A&E department.[15] The sanitary transport to which the patients are entitled under Art. 41 of AHS is an accompanying service contained within the definition of a healthcare service to which patients are entitled under this provision. In principle, sanitary transport does not constitute a separate subject of contracts with healthcare providers. The exceptions are contracts concluded of the primary healthcare type and some specific types of transport financed by the Fund within the framework of the emergency assistance and sanitary transport type.[16]

From the point of view of these considerations, it is particularly important to emphasise the further expansion of the basket of guaranteed benefits to include other healthcare services provided within the framework of telemedicine. In particular, the classification of outpatient specialist care services should be emphasised here (Regulation of the MoH of 6 April 2020 amending the regulation on guaranteed benefits in outpatient specialist care)[17] according to which the provision of strictly specified healthcare services with the use of ICT or communication systems was allowed (annex 5), but only in the period of the threat of epidemic or state of epidemic. Medical rehabilitation services were also classified

14 Act on the State Medical Rescue Service of 8.09.2006 (JoL 2020 item 882).

15 https://nil.org.pl/aktualnosci/4955-podejrzenie-zakazenia-koronawirusem-wytyczne-gis (7.08.2020).

16 A. Pietraszewska-Macheta (ed.), The Act on Healthcare Services Financed with Public Funds. Commentary, publ. III, (WolKluw. 2018). LEX 2018/el.

17 Regulation of the MoH of 6.04.2020 amending the regulation on guaranteed benefits regarding outpatient specialist care (JoL item 612).

in a similar way to the guaranteed benefits provided in this form (Regulation of the MoH of 10 April 2020 amending the regulation on guaranteed benefits in medical rehabilitation).[18] However, in the case of both types of these benefits only a temporary nature of admissibility of providing benefits in this form has been introduced, i.e., for the duration of the threat of epidemic or state of epidemic.

The condition that gives rise to the greatest doubts is that specified in the Regulation of the MoH of 6 April 2020 amending the regulation on guaranteed benefits regarding outpatient specialist care. Namely, that the use of ICT systems or communication systems must not cause a threat to the patient's life or the deterioration of the patient's health, while a nurse with specific qualifications must necessarily be present with the patient. This is because a rhetorical question may be asked at this point about whether other healthcare benefits allow for the possibility of a threat to life or a deterioration of the patient's state of health arising. A similar condition has also been included in the case of guaranteed benefits in palliative and hospice care, as well as nursing and care services within the framework of long-term care (Regulation of the MoH of 16 March 2020 amending the regulation on guaranteed benefits in palliative and hospice care[19] and Regulation of the MoH of 16 March 2020 amending the regulation on guaranteed benefits in nursing and care services within the framework of long-term care), however, with the difference that the ability to provide services in this form has not been limited in time. Such limitations have also not been envisaged in the case of psychiatric care benefits and the treatment of addictions (Regulation of the MoH of 16 March 2020 amending the regulation on guaranteed benefits in psychiatric care and the treatment of addictions).[20]

It should also be reiterated at this point that, in accordance with the provision of Art. 22, para. 3b of ATA, the MoH (in consultation with the minister responsible for computerisation) has been empowered to specify the detailed requirements to be satisfied by the premises and hardware, as well as the ICT systems or communication systems of an entity providing medical services exclusively on an outpatient basis via ICT systems or communication systems at the level of a regulation. Admittedly, this is only an optional competence, which the MoH has not taken advantage of to date.[21] Currently, there are only regulations in force which specify the requirements for conducting therapeutic activities, which assume physical contact between the patient and the doctor. This is one of the factors which have resulted in health benefits provided using telemedicine essentially assuming the simplest form, namely telephone consultations with the use of the existing infra-

18 Regulation of the MoH of 10.04.2020 amending the regulation on guaranteed benefits in medical rehabilitation (JoL item 660).

19 Regulation of the MoH of 16.03.2020 amending the regulation on guaranteed benefits in palliative and hospice care (JoL item 457).

20 Regulation of the MoH of 16.03.2020 amending the regulation on guaranteed benefits in psychiatric care and the treatment of addictions (JoL item 456).

21 D. Kaczan, Telemedicine in Polish Law and comments in the light of EU law, (Zeszyty Prawnicze, 17/2017) 100.

structure and the related requirements, including the number of telephone lines, which can affect the availability of health benefits provided in this form.

Solutions introduced in accordance with the provision of Art. 7, para. 4, 7, 8, 9 and 11 of the COVID-19 Act, according to which a doctor and a dentist providing services shall keep medical records in the form of a teleconsultation card containing basic data, which is only to be stored for 30 days from the date of the teleconsultation, have also proved to be a major problem. Meanwhile, according to the provision of Art. 29, para. 1 of the Act on Patient Rights and the Patient Ombudsman,[22] an entity providing healthcare services keeps medical records for 20 years from the end of the calendar year in which the last entry was made. There are also exceptions that extend this period to 30 years in the case of the death of a patient, as well as monitoring the fate of blood and its components. These periods are also limited to 10 years in the case of X-rays kept outside the patient's medical records, 5 years in the case of referrals or doctor's orders, or 2 years where a health service has not been provided because the patient failed to show up to an agreed appointment, unless the patient has collected the referral. However, in the case of medical records regarding children under the age of 2, they are kept for 22 years. After the expiry of these periods of storage, the documentation is destroyed in a manner that prevents the identification of the patient to whom it applied. Individual internal documentation that is to be destroyed may be handed over at the request of the patient, his/her statutory representative or a person authorised by the patient to obtain the documentation both during the patient's lifetime and in the case of his death, in return for a receipt.[23] The correlates of this obligation are the patient's rights to access the information contained in the medical records regarding his/her "state of health" and "health services provided," as well as the right to "the protection of the data" contained in the medical records. As emphasised by D. Karkowska, both rights are human rights. They feature universality, durability, equality and inalienability. Certain minimum standards of protection in this respect are provided for in international and European law. As for general access to information, reference is made to Art. 12 of the UDHR,[24] according to which no one shall be subjected to arbitrary interference with his privacy, and everyone has the right to the protection of the law against such interference. According to the provision of Art. 17 of the International Covenant on Civil and Political Rights,[25] no one shall be subjected to arbitrary or unlawful interference with his privacy, and everyone has the right to the protection of the law against such interference. Protection is also afforded by the ECHR, Art. 10 of which also guarantees everyone the right to information. The European standard of the right to the protection of medical data is Art. 8 of the ECHR, which guaran-

22 Act on Patient Rights and the Patient Ombudsman (JoL of 2020 item 849).

23 D. Karkowska, The Act on Patient Rights and the Patient Rights Ombudsman. Commentary, publ. III D. Karkowska, Published (WolKluw.2016) LEX 2016/el.

24 Universal Declaration of Human Rights (Paris, 10 XII 1948)

25 International Covenant on Civil and Political Rights of 1966 (JoL 1966, No. 38, item 167).

tees everyone the right to respect for his or her private and family life. However, although this provision indicates the form in which this protection is to be implemented, any interference by the public authorities in exercising these rights is only permissible if it takes place based on the law and is necessary in a democratic society. As for health information, reference should be made to Art. 10(1)–(3) (Convention for the Protection of Human Rights and Dignity of the Human Being with regard to the Application of Biology and Medicine: Convention on Human Rights and Biomedicine).[26] Simultaneously, in accordance with the provision of Art. 26 of the Convention, no restrictions shall be placed on the exercise of the rights other than such as are prescribed by law and are necessary in a democratic society in the interest of public safety, for the prevention of crime, for the protection of public health or for the protection of the rights and freedoms of others.[27]

In view of the importance of the rights related to medical records, it should be accepted that the designated 30-day period for the storage of the teleconsultation card does not comply with the standard of protection of these rights. The intention of the legislator was probably to improve the provision of teleconsultations during the epidemic, although this should not take place with such a drastic restriction of patient rights. This problem should also be considered from a purely practical point of view, when a situation could arise in which, after 30 days, there will be no information about the teleconsultations provided, for example, regarding drug dosage, continuation of treatment, etc. Ultimately, the legislator decided to introduce a change in this area involving the storage of the teleconsultation card for a period of 30 days, measured not from the date on which the teleconsultation was provided, but from the date of cancellation of the state of epidemic threat or the state of epidemic (Art. 20, item 2 of the Act of 14 August 2020 amended by the above Act of 1 September 2020).

1.3 Conclusions

In summary, the changes introduced regarding guaranteed primary healthcare and the guidelines of the Chief Sanitary Inspector that were issued should be assessed particularly positively. Primary healthcare is the first, and consequently a very important, stage of a patient's contact with the healthcare system. The legislator defined primary healthcare in the provision of Art. 2, as "the place of the first contact of the patient, in the meaning of the provisions of the Act on Healthcare Benefits Financed with Public Funds of 27.08.2004 (JoL 2017, item 1938 and 2110),[28] hereinafter referred to as the 'patient', with the healthcare system." The specific redirection of this first level of care to the form of the provision of benefits

26 Convention for the Protection of Human Rights and Dignity of the Human Being with regard to the Application of Biology and Medicine: Convention on Human Rights and Biomedicine, Oviedo, 4.04.1997, European Treaty Series (ETS) / Série des traités européens (STE) No. 164.

27 D. Karkowska, The Act on Patient Rights and the Patient Rights Ombudsman. Commentary, publ. III D. Karkowska, (WolKluw. 2016) LEX 2016/el.

28 Act of 27.08.2004 on Healthcare Services Financed with Public Funds (JoL 2019 item 1373).

within the framework of telemedicine has significantly reduced the number of infections of both patients and staff. Although, in practice, there were difficulties in procuring the necessary protective equipment for personal appointments in outpatient clinics or at home, likewise, there were shortages in the case of infrastructure (telephone lines), which affected the availability of services. The plan to regulate the organisational standard of teleconsultations within primary healthcare at the level of a regulation should also be assessed as being positive. Emphasis should be placed on, for example, the specification of the standard of verification of the patient, which is a necessary condition for providing proper teleconsultations. Firstly, however, this initiative should be considered long overdue. Secondly, it is, to a certain extent, defective in terms of legislation because of the repetition of the statutory provisions regarding the principles of practising in the medical profession.

Another positive change is the increase in the basket of guaranteed benefits to include new benefits, in outpatient specialist care, but also in curative rehabilitation, palliative and hospice care, psychiatric care and the treatment of addictions. These last two groups of services are worth highlighting. Palliative and hospice care apply to a special group of patients who, in many cases, will not live to see the end of the epidemic. It is therefore good that the regulator has borne this group in mind. The changes in psychiatric care benefits are also important, given that the state of the epidemic has increased the demand for services of this type. However, it is incomprehensible why some of these benefits were introduced only for the duration of the epidemic. Furthermore, the provisions that the use of ICT or communication systems (telemedicine) must not cause a threat to the patient's life or a deterioration of the patient's health give rise to very serious doubts. After all, this indication should be accepted for all health benefits provided in this form. Besides, the same rules apply to practising medical professions.

The lack of appropriate regulation of the MoH specifying the detailed requirements to be satisfied by the premises and hardware, as well as the ICT systems or communication systems of an entity providing medical services exclusively on an outpatient basis via ICT systems or communication systems, also gives rise to at least doubts.

When analysing the legal regulation on epidemics, one more issue should also be raised about the quality of the legislation. The special regulation of the COVID-19 Act has amended six Acts and a total of 1,560 secondary regulations have been issued on its basis, whereby these amendments are of a block nature. One of the amending Acts strictly regarding the healthcare system, namely the Act Amending Certain Acts on the Healthcare System Related to Preventing,[29] Counteracting and Combating Covid-19 (JoL item 567) of 15 March 2020 amended a total of 15 Acts, including those which are key to the healthcare system. Five secondary regulations were issued on its basis. The scope of legislative changes illustrates,

29 The COVID-19 Act.

on the one hand, the extent of the shortcomings appearing in the legal system, and on the other, the low quality of legislation.

Finally, the scope of tasks and competencies exercised by the President of the NHF gives rise to serious reservations. According to what has been stated in the legal doctrine, some representatives of the doctrine point out that, in the case of orders of the President of the NHF, the legislator even allowed for the creation of a "new" unconstitutional source of law. The epidemic strengthened the extent of influence of the President of the NHF even further, because, during the period of the epidemic, it is not even the orders but the announcements of the President of the NHF that largely determine the functioning of the whole of the healthcare system.

Works cited

Kaczan, D., 'Telemedicine in Polish Law and Comments in the Light of EU Law' *Zeszyty Prawnicze*, 17/2017, 100.

Karkowska, D., *The Act on Patient Rights and the Patient Rights Ombudsman*. Commentary, publ. III Karkowska Dorota, published by: LEX, Warsaw 2016.

Knosala, E., 'Public Tasks, Organizational and Legal Forms of Their Performance and New Concepts – Scope of Certain Problems for Discussion on the Concept of the System of Administrative Law' in ed. J. Zimmermann, *Concept of the System of Administrative Law*. Convention of the Chairs of Administrative Law and Administrative Proceings, Zakopane, 24–27/09/2006 (WolKluw., Warsaw 2007).

Pietraszewska-Macheta, A. (ed.), *The Act on Healthcare Services Financed with Public Funds*. Commentary, publ. III, published by: LEX, Warsaw 2018.

Paszkowska, M., *The Health Insurance System in Poland* (Warsaw 2015).

Sikorski, S., *Healthcare Administration in Poland – Provision vs. Rationing* (Monografie, WolKluw., Warsaw 2021).

Sikorski, S., and Florczak, M., 'Telemedicine in Polish Administrative Law' [in:] *Telemedicine and e-Health, Legal and IT Issues*, (eds.) I. Lipowicz, G. Szpor, and M. Świerczyński (WolKluw., Warsaw 2019).

Sikorski, S., and Florczak, M., 'Telemedicine Helps in the Battle against the Pandemic' *Gazeta Prawna*, 19/03/2020.

2 Emergency Remote Teaching in the COVID-19 Pandemic Era in light of the GDPR

Piotr Drobek

2.1 Introduction

The COVID-19 pandemic has forced schools, universities and other educational institutions to work remotely. While distance education using electronic resources is not new to the educational environment, particularly for universities, the challenges faced by all educational institutions in the wake of the pandemic were qualitatively and quantitatively quite different in nature. In fact, online education, with a few exceptions, had previously been used only in an auxiliary way, if any.

In the scientific literature, the phenomenon of an abrupt shift by educational institutions from the face-to-face classes to distance learning is referred to as emergency remote teaching (ERT),[1] as opposed to online learning, which is characterised by being planned and designed to work online from the beginning. Emergency remote teaching involves temporarily moving educational activities to a remote mode due to emergency circumstances, after which they will revert to their previous mode of instruction. As indicated by Charles Hodges and others, ERT "is a way of thinking about delivery modes, methods, and media, specifically as they map to rapidly changing needs and limitations in resources, such as faculty support and training."[2] Analysing the specificity of ERT, Chiara Angiolini and others point to its three important features: first, the speed of migration due to the need for continuity of education; second, the number of activities that need to be transferred to the Internet; third, the diversity of tools and applications used in remote education. At the same time, many educational institutions or teachers themselves have been forced to combine different tools, as most schools and higher education institutions do not have an adequate technological infrastructure that fully meets their needs.[3] As a result, educational institutions, often lacking adequate infrastructure, were forced to use services of external providers avail-

1 C. B Hodges et al., 'The Difference Between Emergency Remote Teaching and Online Learning' (2020) EDUCAUSE Review. <https://er.educause.edu/articles/2020/3/the-difference-between-emergency-remote-teaching-and-online-learning> (30.11.2021).

2 Ibid.

3 C. Angiolini et al., 'Remote Teaching During the Emergency and Beyond: Four Open Privacy and Data Protection Issues of 'Platformised' Education' [2020] 1 (1) Opinio Juris in Comparatione.

DOI: 10.4324/9781003263968-17

able on the market, which were usually not adapted to the educational purposes. However, at the beginning of the COVID-19 pandemic there was a clear difference between higher education institutions, most of which had e-learning platforms in place, although without all required functionalities, and schools, most of which did not use such tools at all. As one can see, in the rapidly changing conditions of educational institutions, the operations of personal data processing have changed dramatically, causing new threats to the rights and freedoms of data subjects. It is also worth noting that the transition of schools and universities to the mode of remote work showed the previously existing problems related to personal data protection in education and highlighted completely new ones related to the risks associated with the processing of personal data in a digital environment.[4]

2.2 The legal landscape of data processing in ERT in Poland

In the absence of educational platforms or tools centrally implemented by the governmental administration, schools as well as individual teachers began to use the services and apps provided by various market players. Over time, more schools have implemented the new mode of operation in a comprehensive manner, taking more account of the need to protect personal data. However, at least at the beginning, the basic communication channel was the electronic school register[5] which was implemented earlier in most schools under the Regulation of the Minister of National Education (MoNE) of 25 August 2017 on the manner in which public kindergartens, schools and institutions keep records of the course of teaching, educational and caring activities, as well as the types of such documentation.[6] Apart from specific regulation of the electronic school register the Polish law did not provide for comprehensive regulations on the use of distance learning methods and techniques by schools and other educational institutions.

From a legal perspective, crucial for the analysis of data protection issues in the context of remote education are the legal Acts adopted since March 2020, which specify the basic framework for the operation of educational institutions during the COVID-19 pandemic. Among these pieces of legislation, it is important to note the COVID-19 Act which amends many other laws. According to the added Art. 30b of the Act of 14 December 2016 Education Law,[7] the minister competent

Studies in Comparative and National Law 47 <http://www.opiniojurisincomparatione.org/opinio/article/view/163> (30.11.2020).

4 P. Drobek, 'Zintegrowana Platforma Edukacyjna z perspektywy ochrony danych osobowych w zdalnym nauczaniu w trybie awaryjnym' in Agnieszka Gryszczyńska and Grażyna Szpor (eds.), *Internet, Cyberpandemia, Cyberpandemic* (CH. Beck 2020) 380–381.

5 See the results of the study on remote education in time of pandemic in Poland conducted by Fundacja Centrum Cyfrowe in cooperation with Centrum Edukacji Obywatelskiej and Fundacja Szkoła z klasą, 'Badanie Edukacja zdalna w czasie pandemii' (Fundacja Centrum Cyfrowe, 2020) <https://centrumcyfrowe.pl/edukacja-zdalna/> (30.11.2021).

6 JoL 2017 item 164 with amendments, para. 21.

7 JoL 2021 item 182.

for education and upbringing may temporarily restrict or suspend the operation of units of the educational system (schools and other educational institutions) in the country or its part, when this is justified by extraordinary circumstances that threaten the life or health of children and young people. The minister has also been authorised to exclude the application of certain provisions of the Education Law, the Act on the Education System and the Act on Financing Education Tasks with respect to all or some units of the education system and to introduce separate regulations in this respect to ensure the proper implementation of objectives and tasks by these units. On this legal basis, the MoNE issued a regulation on 20 March 2020 on specific solutions in the period of temporary limitation of the functioning of units of the educational system in connection with prevention, counteraction and combating COVID-19.[8] The above-mentioned legal Acts have been amended many times during the COVID-19 pandemic.[9]

The above mentioned regulation on specific solutions in the period of temporary limitation of the functioning of units of the educational system (schools and other educational institutions) in connection with prevention, counteraction and combating COVID-19 has assigned to the school principal the primary responsibility for conducting remote education and ensuring its compliance with, among other things, data protection laws. Under para. 1(1) of this regulation, the school principal is responsible for the organisation of the tasks of the school, including classes using distance learning methods and techniques or other method of delivery of these classes; in particular: determine whether students and teachers have access to IT infrastructure, software and Internet enabling interaction between students and teachers conducting classes; determine, in cooperation with teachers, the information and communication technologies used by teachers to deliver classes; determine the principles of safe participation in classes with respect to the established ICT; determine, in cooperation with teachers, the sources and materials necessary for the implementation of classes that students may use; determine with teachers the need to modify the set of pre-school education curricula or the school set of curricula, as applicable, and modify the set if necessary. According to para. 2, distance learning methods and techniques inter alia can be implemented, in particular with the use of materials and functionality of the IT tool provided by the minister competent for education and upbringing; with the use of electronic means of communication ensuring the exchange of information between the teacher, student or parent; by informing parents about available materials and possible forms of their implementation by a child or a student at home – in the case of children in pre-school education, early childhood education, early development support, remedial classes and students with moderate or severe intellectual disabilities or with multiple disabilities.

8 JoL 2020 item 493 with amendments.

9 See overview I. Staszkiewicz-Grabarczyk, 'Edukacja w czasie pandemii COVID-19 w świetle aktów prawnych / Education during the COVID-19 pandemic in the light of legal acts' [2021] 15 (2) Rozprawy Społeczne / Social Dissertations 25. (30.11.2021).

At the same time during the COVID-19 pandemic, the minister responsible for education and upbringing was developing a pre-existing IT tool dedicated to remote education originally described as an Integrated Education Platform.[10] The functioning of this platform was at the beginning regulated by the regulation of the MoNE of 20 March 2020 on specific solutions in the period of temporary limitation of the functioning of units of the educational system in connection with the prevention, counteraction and combating of COVID-19. However, this regulation was adopted as episodic. Eventually, the legal grounds for this IT tool were established in the Act of 19 November 2020 on the amendment of the Act – Teacher's Charter and some other Acts.[11] It introduces Art. 44a of the Education Law, which regulates the functioning of the Integrated Educational Platform, defining it as "an IT tool made available by the minister competent for education and upbringing."[12]

2.3 Actors involved in ERT and their responsibilities

The General Data Protection Regulation *introduces a dichotomous division between controller and processor. Assigning the primary responsibility for the processing of personal data to the controller*. According to Art. 4(7) of the GDPR, "controller" means the natural or legal person, public authority, agency or other body which, alone or jointly with others, determines the purposes and means of the processing of personal data; where the purposes and means of such processing are determined by Union or Member State law, the controller or the specific criteria for its nomination may be provided for by Union or Member State law. As already indicated, the controller may delegate the processing of data to processors who then act in the controller's name and on its behalf.[13] The controller is the entity that exercises control over the processing of personal data by deciding on the purposes and means of processing. This definition has a functional character and refers to the criterion of actual decision-making. However, when assessing whether an entity has the status of a controller one often cannot disregard legal provisions directly designating the controller or indirectly through the competences or duties of the entity, from which the status should be derived.

From this perspective, considering the current legal regulations in Poland, it should be assumed that the school is a controller with respect to the data of students, their parents, teachers and other school employees. The situation is similar with respect to higher education institutions. In the traditional view, a school or a university as a controller, when it wants to use tools or applications provided by external vendors, they will be processors acting in accordance with the controller's instructions. The consequence of this view is that such external providers are not entitled to process data for their own purposes. As indicated earlier, ERT

10 Drobek (n 4) 381–389.
11 JoL 2021 item 493, Art. 4.
12 Drobek (n 4) 385–387.
13 Article 4(8) of the GDPR.

processing shows that the landscape is more complex and dynamic. There are concerns about the intrusion into the education ecosystem of online platforms and service providers whose activities may go far beyond processing data on behalf of a controller.[14] This is of particular importance in the context of the potential treatment of entities as joint controllers, because in practice platforms and other service providers very often process personal data also for their own purposes. It should be remembered that the CJEU interprets the concept of joint controllership rather broadly, if such a situation may occur not only when decisions are made jointly, but also when they are interrelated.[15]

According to the European Data Protection Board the joint participation in the determination of purposes and means "can take the form of a common decision taken by two or more entities or result from converging decisions by two or more entities regarding the purposes and essential means."[16] This situation can lead to complex constellations where joint controllership, separate autonomous controllership or relationship based on data processing may occur. This may be particularly evident in the ERT context. However, the growing role of online platforms in educational settings may bring about a real change in the approach to data protection and privacy, deviating from its traditional framing in educational relationships involving primarily students and teachers, as has already been pointed out in the literature before.[17]

For this reason, schools, as well as higher education institutions in principle treated as controllers, should be particularly careful to assess possible situations considering all potential risks.[18] However, the circumstances of the ERT are not conducive to such in-depth assessment and selection of the partners involved in the data processing operations. Problems with classifying entities involved in data processing occur even when these issues are regulated by law. A good example of such a situation of ambiguity is the functioning of the above-mentioned IT tool made available by the minister competent for education and upbringing.

Therefore, on the one hand, there is a clear need to introduce additional regulations tailored to the specificities of educational activity, providing guarantees that the transformation towards distance learning will not diminish the protection of personal data and privacy of the persons involved. On the other hand, schools and universities need the support of the government in their relations with service

14 Angiolini (n 3) 53–57.

15 Case C-210/16 *Unabhängiges Landeszentrum für Datenschutz Schleswig-Holstein v Wirtschaftsakademie*, EU:C:2018:388; Case C-25/17 *Tietosuojavaltuutettu and Jehovan todistajat –uskonnollinen yhdyskunta*, EU:C:2018:551; Case C-40/17 *Fashion ID GmbH & Co. KG v Verbraucherzentrale NRW e.V.* ECLI:EU:C:2018:1039.

16 European Data Protection Board, Guidelines on the concepts of controller and processor in the GDPR, 07/2020 Version 2.0, 7.07.2021, 19 <https://edpb.europa.eu/system/files/2021-07/eppb_guidelines_202007_controllerprocessor_final_en.pdf> (30.11.2021).

17 Elana Zeide and Helen Nissenbaum, 'Learner Privacy in MOOCs and Virtual Education' [2018] 16 Theory and Research in Education 280.

18 Angiolini (n 3) 53.

providers, for whom often a single school or university is not a negotiating partner. It should be postulated that an attempt should be made to undertake activities at the national level to define certain framework or model agreements or conditions for provision of services, according to which the activities of educational institutions would be facilitated.

In this context, it is worth mentioning a particularly important problem related to the transfer of personal data to third countries and international organizations. It has become particularly pressing after the 16 July 2020 CJEU judgment in *Case C-311/18 Data Protection Commissioner v. Facebook Ireland Ltd., Maximilian Schrem*,[19] according to which in situations of such transfers it must be ensured that personal data will be protected in the third country in an equivalent way, even if the lack of such level of protection is due to the actions of public authorities. The support of educational institutions in this regard by the central administration, irrespective of the guidance given by data protection authorities in the context of the ERT, would be particularly welcome. Failure to do so, if the problem of the secure transfer of personal data to importers in the United States is not resolved, will increase the risks associated with the processing of personal data by these institutions.

2.4 Principles of data processing and data subjects rights

Each controller is obliged to comply with the principles of data processing listed in Art. 5 GDPR and further developed in the subsequent provisions of this regulation. These principles include fairness, lawfulness and transparency, purpose limitation, data minimisation, storage limitation, accuracy and integrity and confidentiality. The principles of data processing are of a normative nature and constitute obligations addressed to the controller[20] who, in accordance with the principle of accountability, is obliged to put these principles into practice through internal mechanisms and policies and be able to demonstrate compliance.[21]

The activities of educational institutions are largely regulated by law, both with respect to schools and universities. Sectoral legislation supplements and specifies most of the data processing principles in the context of activities of educational institutions, e.g., the legal basis of data processing operations, its scope or purpose of processing of data. It is worth mentioning that in the Polish legal system, the basis for processing of personal data of pupils or students, but also teachers, will not be a consent but legal grounds rooted in the law, as specified in Art. 6 of the GDPR, such as a legal obligation arising from the provisions of legal provisions, or the exercise of public authority or acting in the public interest. In contrast, the

19 EU:C:2020:559.

20 P. Drobek, 'Article 5' in E. Bielak-Jomaa and D. Lubasz (eds.), *RODO. Ogólne rozporządzenie o ochronie danych. Komentarz* (WolKluw. 2018) 324–325.

21 C. Docksey, 'Article 24' in C. Kuner, L. A. Bygrave and C. Docksey (eds.) *The EU General Data Protection Regulation (GDPR). A commentary* (Oxford University Press 2020) 561–563.

processing of data by a commercial vendor providing services, applications or platforms in such a context for this vendor's own purposes does not find the same legal grounds and can in principle be challenged.

The GDPR grants data subjects rights, including the right of access to data or the right to rectification. The ability to exercise these rights is, to a large extent, dependent on the controller ensuring that data processing is carried out in a transparent manner. This is of particular importance when data processing operations are complex. However, COVID-19 does not exclude the obligations of controllers to implement the principle of transparency and the fair exercise of duties in relation to the exercise of data subjects' rights.

2.5 Conclusions

The acceleration of the digital transformation of educational institutions, which occurred on an unprecedented scale in the wake of the Covid-19 pandemic outbreak, was primarily caused by the need to start remote teaching immediately without prior preparation for it. This process occurred under conditions of emergency remote teaching (ERT), revealing significant gaps in existing legal regulations, available ICT resources, and expertise as well as rising concerns relating to personal data protection and privacy. An analysis of actions taken in the education sector in relation to the COVID-19 pandemic in 2020 and 2021 in Poland allows us to draw preliminary conclusions and to propose recommendations for the implementation of appropriate public law instruments to ensure a post-pandemic model of remote teaching in accordance with the principles of data protection considering Art. 8 of CFREU, Art. 51 of the Constitution and the GDPR.

In the first place, it should be emphasised that exceptional circumstances cannot justify the exclusion of educational institutions from EU and national data protection law during and after a pandemic. Any restriction of the fundamental right to data protection should be scrutinised for proportionality and necessity, especially after the end of the pandemic threat and the possible full return to traditional forms of teaching practices.

Lessons learned from the pandemic show that although both schools and universities are bound by the general rules specified by the GDPR, the specifics of their activities require a clear sector specific legal framework for distance learning. However, there is a need to adopt separate and different regulations of these issues in relation to schools and universities considering the autonomy of the latter.

The role of public authorities is to provide systemic support for educational institutions also in relation to the necessary IT infrastructure, tools and platforms used in distance learning. An interesting attempt was made to implement an educational platform by the Minister of Education and Science. At the same time, it must be emphasised that the development of this tool should not deprive schools and institutions of the possibility of using other available tools.

In most cases, the schools and higher education institutions use tools and platforms offered by global players operating in the market. Therefore, the Polish government should support these institutions by negotiating possible framework or model agreements that they could sign with these providers, which could include, among other things, the necessary guarantees required by the CJEU judgment in case C-311/18.

Works cited

Angiolini, C., Ducato, R., Giannopoulou, A., and Schneider, G., 'Remote Teaching during the Emergency and Beyond: Four Open Privacy and Data Protection Issues of "Platformised" Education' (2020) 1(1) Opinio Juris in Comparatione. Studies in Comparative and National Law 47.

Bielak-Jomaa, E., and Lubasz, D. (eds.), *RODO. Ogólne rozporządzenie o ochronie danych. Komentarz* (WolKluw., Warsaw 2018).

Gryszczyńska, A., and Szpor, G. (eds.), *Internet, Cyberpandemia, Cyberpandemic* (CH. Beck, Warsaw 2020).

Hodges, C.B., Moore, S., Lockee, B.B., Trust, T., and Bond, M., 'The Difference between Emergency Remote Teaching and Online Learning' (2020) EDUCAUSE Review. https://er.educause.edu/articles/2020/3/the-difference-between-emergency-remote-teaching-and-online-learning

Kuner, C., Bygrave, L.A., and Docksey, Ch (eds.), *The EU General Data Protection Regulation (GDPR). A Commentary* (Oxford University Press, Oxford 2020).

Staszkiewicz-Grabarczyk, I., 'Edukacja w czasie pandemii COVID-19 w świetle aktów prawnych / Education during the COVID-19 Pandemic in the Light of Legal Acts' (2021) 15(2) Rozprawy Społeczne / Social Dissertations 25.

Zeide, E., and Nissenbaum, H., 'Learner Privacy in MOOCs and Virtual Education' (2018) 16 Theory and Research in Education 280.

3 Standards of Public Administration Services for the Elderly

A Lesson in Pandemic Time

Radosław Mędrzycki

3.1 Introduction

The state of the coronavirus pandemic is a crisis that cannot only be explained biologically. In addition, it is an eminently social and historical breakthrough on a global scale, which triggers a structural crisis in terms of the economy, politics and social relations, leading to the disintegration of previously known lifestyles.[1] Finally, this crisis also affects the law, unprepared for the challenges of an epidemic on this scale. It is pointed out that there has been a failure to respond to epidemic challenges in many countries, and it is not a case of simply being late in acting to keep people safe.

The pandemic crisis has also affected the axiological problems of contemporary societies. As Schwab and Malleret rightly point out, the platitude that the coronavirus has caused a great levelling off should be rejected; it is quite the contrary – we can see it in the class nature of societies and the translating situation of access to educational and social goods and resources. In particularly class-divided societies, the authors argue, the effects of pre-existing inequalities are visible.[2]

> COVID-19 has exacerbated pre-existing conditions of inequality wherever and whenever it strikes. As such, it is not a "leveller," neither medically nor economically, or socially or psychologically. The pandemic is a "great unequalizer" [...] that has compounded disparities in income, wealth and opportunity.[3]

As a significant social shock, the state of the pandemic has exposed weaknesses in the social and health care system concerning the elderly. How do states behave towards this social group? The general response of the administrations of European countries has been to lockdown the oldest social group (although

1 A.L. Mascaro, *Crise e pandemia* (Boitempo Editorial 2020) 6.
2 K. Schwab and Th. Mallert, *Covid-19. The Great Reset* (World Economic Forum Publishing 2020) 122.
3 Ibid., 120.

DOI: 10.4324/9781003263968-18

not only) in the name of health security and to protect overburdened health systems.[4] Soon after the positive experience of a significant reduction in the spread of coronavirus associated with locking down Chinese citizens in their homes, many European countries followed a similar path. However, this raised many questions in the initial stages because of cultural and systemic differences. Lockdown was applied, for example, in Italy, Spain, Germany, France[5] and Poland. Therefore, this has raised the legitimate question of how far such measures fall within the rule of law, including from the point of view of rights dedicated to the elderly, especially considering the international and supranational level (systemic legal context). This discussion allows us to consider the standards of public administration services for seniors in the face of a pandemic.

Assuming the need for sustainability of the legal system context, it is possible to consider what standards related to the concept of digital administration should be introduced to fully realise the assumptions of this context possible in the conditions of an epidemic (research goal). The specificity of this social group, i.e., the systemic and legal requirements and the actual conditions, should be kept in mind. Therefore, the initial assumption that introducing digital standards for the elderly should ensure social inclusion to avoid additional inequalities should not be overlooked. Because of the discussion on the notion of the standard by researchers and the lack of consensus to a single understanding of this term, for research purposes, we assume that a standard

> is such a content of a legal norm, which determines relatively measurable features, attributes of a given tangible or intangible good or describes features, attributes of some behaviour of a given subject of law about the achievements of particular fields of science in order to obtain a relatively strictly defined according to these features "product."[6]

Concerning the elderly, standards derive mainly from the experience of empirical sciences headed by medicine and biology. However, when deciding on a given social group's situation, the legislator often considers other, less apparent rationales (e.g., cultural norms).

It should also refer to the concept of a public law instrument. The object-oriented approach gives a narrower understanding of this concept, as it shows the nature of the form. As Irena Lipowicz points out in her introductory article to this monograph, the notion of public-legal instruments makes it necessary to

4 R. Armitage and L. B. Nellums, 'COVID-19 and the consequences of isolating the elderly' (2020) 5(5) The Lancet Public Health e256.

5 Q. Zhang and W. Song, 'The Challenges of the COVID-19 Pandemic: Approaches for the Elderly and those with Alzheimer's Disease' [2020] MedComm <https://www.ncbi.nlm.nih.gov/pmc/articles/PMC7262279/pdf/MCO2-1-69.pdf> (10.12.2021).

6 I. Niżnik-Dobosz, 'Pojęcie standardu w prawie administracyjnym, jego nauce i w praktyce' in Z. Duniewska, M. Stahl and A. Rabiega-Przyłęcka (eds.), *Standardy współczesnej administracji publicznej i prawa administracyjnego* (WolKluw. and Wydawnictwo Uniwersytetu Łódzkiego 2019) 40.

consider them in the category known to the science of administrative law of many European states – legal forms of administrative action. These, however, are essentially broad and may be understood subjectively and objectively. Some of them have a civil law character (contract). However, they can be used by the public administration – also as organisational activity – and they will be classified as public law instruments in subjective terms.

3.2 References

The epidemic has not rendered invalid human rights guarantees or the rule of law, which cannot be devalued because of pursuing the common good. On the contrary, human rights themselves make up a certain standard – for the law standardises specific social behaviour.

From the international legal perspective, there is yet no comprehensive specific regulation of the rights of the elderly like the rights of children or people with disabilities. However, a discussion has been undertaken around the Chicago Convention on the Rights of the Elderly.[7] Given this, it seems appropriate to refer to the European context.

The rights of older persons are explicitly referred to in Art. 23 of the Revised European Social Charter (ZEKS)[8] formulating the right of older persons to social protection, including the provision of

> adequate resources to enable them to lead a decent life and take part actively in public, social and cultural life; to provide information on services and facilities available to older persons and on the possibilities for using them;- to enable older persons, to choose their way of life freely and to live independently in a familiar environment for as long as they wish and can do so, by a. providing housing adapted to their needs and state of health or providing appropriate help to adapt their housing; b. medical care and services required by their condition; - ensuring that elderly persons in nursing homes receive support, respecting their privacy, and guaranteeing their participation in decisions concerning their living conditions in such homes.

Therefore, the international legal context is quite specific and results from the particular needs of this social group. However, because of the lack of ratification of this Act, it does not apply to Poland.[9] Although not all EU countries have bound themselves to the ZEKS, Art. 23 of this Act creates a systemic context for

7 E. Mantovani, P. Quinn and P. De Hert, 'Stereotyping and Other Forms of Discrimination in the Chicago Declaration on the Rights of Older Persons and in the Case Law of the European Court of Human Rights' in I. Doron, N. Georgantzi (eds.), *Ageing, Ageism and the Law: European Perspectives on the Rights of Older Persons* (Edward Elgar 2018).

8 Convention Revised European Social Charter (open for signature 3.05.1996, entered into force 1.07.1999 (CETS No. 163).

9 A. Ploszka, *Publicznoprawny status jednostki skrajnie ubogiej* (WolKluw. 2019) 187.

Art. 25 of the CFREU.[10] For EU legislation, the EU CFREU is relevant. Articles 25 and 21 are relevant concerning older persons: the former article guarantees older persons the right to live with dignity and independence and participate in social and cultural life. The latter prohibits discrimination on the grounds of age, among other things. These provisions have not lost their validity in the pandemic's face; the EU Agency for Fundamental Rights explicitly stresses the importance of these articles precisely in the crisis's face.[11] It is, therefore, possible to speak of a dispute of principles and attempts to weigh up values, especially the values of security and independent living. Interpreting the concept of "elderly person" within the meaning of Art. 25 of the CFREU requires considering the jurisprudence of the European Committee of Social Rights concerning the interpretation of Art. 23 of the ZEKS and the content of points 24 and 25 of the Community Social Charter on the Fundamental Rights of Workers. It should be concluded that the elderly are "persons who have reached the retirement age set by the national legislature."[12] In Poland, this age is 60 for women and 65 for men. Despite the literal wording about providing the right, Art. 25 of the CFREU falls into the category of principles, so it obliges the EU bodies and the Member States to react legislatively in the spirit of the systemic context established in the provision's text; however, it does not allow for direct claims by individuals for specific actions.[13] Legislation of Member States should therefore consider, where necessary, the creation of legislative conditions that make the requirements to live with dignity and independence and participate in social and cultural life a reality, in response to the requirements of secondary EU legislation incorporating the principles of the CFREU. It can also be argued that the provision of Art. 25 of the CFREU has a limited scope of impact. Still, its anchoring in an overarching value (protection of dignity) makes it an essential systemic reference.

> In contrast, individuals will likely be unable to rely on Art. 25 to establish that they are entitled to receive particular forms of medical or social care or to make a claim that the EU has otherwise violated their individual rights or failed to respect their subjective entitlements. However, it remains to be seen how this may limit the effect of Art. 25 in practice. As Barnard has noted, the distinction between 'rights' and 'principles' within the Charter scheme is not clear-cut […], and there may be situations where a failure to make positive provision for an individual or a group of older persons in need may constitute a failure to respect the principle of respect for the rights of older people as set out in Article 25.[14]

10 C. O'Cinneide, 'The Rights of the Elderly' in S. Peers et al. (eds.), *The EU Charter of Fundamental Rights: A Commentary* (1st edn, Hart 2014) 698.

11 FRA. European Union Agency for Fundamental Rights, *Coronavirus Pandemic in the EU-Fundamental Rights Implications: With a Focus on Older People. Bulletin #3* (1-31.03.2020) 33.

12 C. O'Cinneide, op. cit.

13 Ibid., 695, 702.

14 Ibid., 703.

As the examples of "anti-epidemic" measures show, they mainly affect the sphere of participation in the social life of older people, although with different intensity depending on the adopted state solutions. A review of the literature on more senior people shows that long-term social isolation is becoming a significant problem because of the negative consequences for older people for public health. On the one hand, a lockdown is supposed to protect the health and life of older people with multiple comorbidities. On the other, it generates additional problems by increasing the risk of cardiovascular, autoimmune, neurocognitive and mental health problems in older people.[15] The sudden interruption of contact with other people has a significantly negative impact on the psychological sphere of isolated people. It can be clear that older people are often deprived of natural stimuli forced in younger age groups by work or family activities. Even in pre-epidemic conditions, the literature has widely postulated that healthy ageing and longevity are significantly influenced by older people's social behaviour such as participation in senior citizen groups, joint outings, volunteering and even age-appropriate work activities.[16] It was also fostered by the legal mechanisms present in some EU countries, such as the possibility of establishing municipal councils of senior citizens, whose functions went beyond simply giving opinions on the shape of local legislation and otherwise involving them in decision-making processes.[17] Through isolation, natural, interpersonal bonds formed independently by older people or supported in institutions were broken. Isolation in social welfare homes, which became foci of COVID-19, was significant in its effects.

Also critical is Art. 21 of the CFREU, which prohibits discrimination based on, inter alia, age. Discrimination is one of the more complex issues mainly because of the multiplicity of possible discriminatory criteria and the fact that discrimination is sometimes justified, e.g., direct discrimination on the grounds of age allowed by law expressed in EU secondary legislation or the case-law of the European Court of Human Rights.[18] In the pandemic's face, age discrimination has played a particular role in deprioritising the treatment of older people on COVID. As a commendable example, the German Interdisciplinary Association for Intensive Care and Emergency Medicine recommends that treatment should not refer to age. The only criteria are the urgency of treatment and its chance of success.[19] An aspect of the concept of discrimination is the so-called policy of preference, which implies positive discrimination, i.e., using a differentiating

15 R.Armitage and L.B. Nellums, op. cit.

16 D.J.H. Deeg, M-L. Boertje and H. Galenkamp, 'Healthy Life Years and Social Engagement' in A. Walker (ed) *The Future of Ageing in Europe. Making an Asset of Longevity* (Palgrave Macmillan 2019) 143–176.

17 P. Olszewski, 'Aktywizacja osób starszych w Polsce i w Danii – rzecz o radach seniorów' in P. Broda-Wysocki, A. Dylus and M. Pawlus (eds.), *Dyskryminacja seniorów w Polsce. Diagnoza i przeciwdziałanie* (Wydawnictwo Naukowe UKSW 2016).

18 S. Fredman, *Discrimination law* (2nd edn, Oxford University Press 2011).

19 FRA. European Union Agency for Fundamental Rights, *Coronavirus Pandemic in the EU-Fundamental Rights Implications: With a Focus on Older People. Bulletin #3* (1-31.03.2020) 38.

criterion (e.g., age) in favour of a particular group (here: older people). It should be remembered that in each state, the systemic legal context is complemented by constitutional level regulations, sometimes directly planning the mechanisms of positive age discrimination. For example, in Poland, such regulations include the constitutional guarantee of exceptional health care for the elderly[20] and the right to social security.[21] The constitutional range of material values is further expressed in legal solutions at the statutory level.

EU law allows for positive discrimination, but as an exception to the principle of equal treatment.[22] Analysis of age discrimination shows that, in both EU and Polish national law, age discrimination is often linked to employment and labour issues. The epidemic was a new situation. However, the aim of this chapter is not to answer the question about the admissibility of lockdown in the prohibition's context of discrimination planned in Art. 21 of the CFREU, but to show the broader background of the problem resulting from specific EU regulations, especially in the possibility's context to introduce the so-called positive (privileging) discrimination.

Meanwhile, as an argument "in favour of selective" lockdown, it is pointed out that selective isolation is an adequate response to the crisis than locking up the entire population because of limited health care resources (the purpose of argument). Advocates of selective isolation argue that the elderly (as they remain in the risk group for the effects of COVID-19) gain their health security from the lockdown (they do not become infected). At the same time, the rest of the non-isolated population gains its health security (also from the point of view of access to limited medical equipment – people in younger age groups sometimes also need specialised medical care). Furthermore, economic security is also essential – it is the liquidity of payment of pensions based on contributions of working people and the financial liquidity of enterprises.

In summary, within the legal orders of countries that have adopted the CBD and ratified the CFREU, older people have a specific right to social protection in a spirit that respects their independence and autonomy of self-determination. Compensatory mechanisms (positive discrimination) are permissible to ensure equality of opportunity on an equal and fair basis with other social groups. However, one must not lose sight of the principle of the rule of law, so the administration of a state can only does what the law allows it to do. The principle of the common good must not prevail over this principle if the state is to remain in the orbit of democratic legal states.

20 Art. 68(3) Constitution.
21 Art. 67 Constitution.
22 A. Wróbel (ed), *Karta Praw Podstawowych Unii Europejskiej. Komentarz* (C.H. Beck).

3.3 ICT as a support network for mental health and general physical well-being

Communication and information technologies (ICTs) can serve to prosthesis interpersonal relationships in the face of forced or voluntary isolation associated with COVID-19.[23] They are not, of course, a substitute for one-to-one contact, but in the face of conflicting values, they can be credited with mitigating emerging social tensions.

The isolation, high mortality and uncertainty of the future associated with the coronavirus epidemic cause psychological problems. Older people, especially in the so-called IV age cohort (80 years and older), are at risk of loneliness. Singularity (not only related to the epidemic) is one factor exposing lonely older people to a lack of stimuli, medical and social support. The state of the epidemic makes it difficult to reach these people freely. Lockdown triggers the need to establish communication and monitoring platforms for the condition of the elderly. The digital exclusion of the elderly is a significant communication barrier, so it is advocated to use traditional but familiar sources of access to information such as radio and television.[24]

The literature emphasises that the digital exclusion of some older people results in the need to look for alternatives to digital solutions. This mentions interventions including more telephone contact with relatives, voluntary workers, health professionals; as such any community projects aimed at supporting older people in forced isolation are important.[25] There is a critical need for local authorities to engage in strategies to safeguard older people's mental health. Although coping with the effects of the epidemic is linked to the central government, the role of local government is to provide mental health support.

As well as stimulating contacts to maintain mental health, the need to standardise information to older people in enforced isolation because of the need to maintain physical health also seems essential.

> This exceptional situation [lockdown – annotation by the author] is having important consequences for everyone but the oldest old – those aged 85 years and older – in particular. This population segment is very vulnerable, especially under stressful situations that challenge body functional reserve. On the one hand, older adults present the greatest risk of mortality for COVID-19 (odds ratio per year increase of 1.10, 95% confidence interval 1.03 to 1.17). They, therefore, require strict protection measures against the infection. Prompting the oldest old to stay home might further increase sedentary behaviour, a situation that is likely to aggravate sarcopenia, frailty, and age-related functional decline and increase the risk of all-cause mortality. [...]

23 R. Armitage and L.B. Nellums, op. cit.
24 Q. Zhang and W. Song, op. cit.
25 R. Armitage and L.B. Nellums, op. cit.

> Ten days of bed rest suffice to result in marked impairments in muscle mass and strength, walking speed, and functional ability among individuals aged about 70 years.[26]

The research on the negative impact of isolation parallels observations made towards older people during the lockdown in France and Germany.[27] Because of the need to overcome cognitive limitations, promotional campaigns on TV or a telephone assistant should be used. Due to the digital exclusion of many older people, ICT should be less integrated into standards. However, it should not be wholly neglected, especially if there are parallel initiatives for providing basic knowledge and skills in using devices by volunteers (e.g., Somos Todos Digital in Portugal).[28] For example, a remote notification system to exercise at home could be introduced, or free and easy access to a government application for ICTs (mainly smartphones) with examples of physical exercise adapted to the needs of different age groups. This is also important given the exclusions of rehabilitation help during a lockdown. In this respect, experience with an application for recording contacts during epidemics (in Poland: ProteGO Safe) may prove helpful. Standards should be drawn mainly from medical science.

3.4 Problems of long-term institutional care (LTC) standards

We should point out that the standards of "good care" in nursing homes derive from Art. 23 of the ZEKS. This Charter, as already mentioned, deals explicitly with social issues.

> Health care services for older people should be accessible, adequate and sufficiently well resourced, while states should also take effective measures to protect the rights of older persons living in care homes or receiving home care services (which should include the establishment of suitable monitoring and inspection mechanisms).[29]

In many countries, large outbreaks in residential care homes are reported for the elderly. This situation also occurred for some time in Poland. This triggered an innate drive to discover the causes and preliminary diagnoses and remediation programmes. The crisis caused by the pandemic has led, for example, to the claim that care homes and their residents do not fit in with traditional health care and social help. Therefore, what is needed is a holistic remodelling of the system to make it more resilient than before to similar crises (so on the experience in the

26 P.L. Valanzuela and others, 'Coronavirus Lockdown: Forced Inactivity for the Oldest Old?' (2020) 21 JAMDA 988.
27 FRA. European Union Agency for Fundamental Rights, *Coronavirus Pandemic in the EU-Fundamental Rights Implications: With a Focus on Older People. Bulletin #3* (1-31.03.2020) 37.
28 Ibid., 40.
29 C.O'Cinneide, op. cit., 699.

UK).[30] Many deaths in care home residents are not only because of the vulnerability of the elderly in the face of the virus but also a consequence of failing to include care homes in pandemic response planning, including the implementation of standards of practice.[31]

Meanwhile, some guidelines have already been defined in 2011 by The EuGMS. These are recommendations for older people in care homes. They focus on ensuring the comprehensiveness of care, including collaboration between medical professions and, more broadly, psychologists. Interestingly, the use of IT tools at the time was mainly seen in the need to maintain electronic medical and nursing records tailored to the gerontological needs of the resident with the consequence of focusing on their needs rather than collecting information for reimbursement.[32]

However, the pandemic shows the need to look at IT tools differently in the face of long-term, enforced isolation in LTC. The need for isolation results in the inability of families to visit and thus the potential for abuse of nursing home residents. A similar situation could also arise in hospitals, especially in countries that have not complied with patient rights standards. So-called virtual visits could replace the lack of visits. The lack of contact between an isolated elderly patient in a hospital emergency department and his family should be something of the past – the coronavirus has shown how vital communication needs and standards are in this area. However, there is a need for standards specifying access to the Internet or, at a minimum, a telecommunications network in LTC facilities and hospitals, and an appropriate qualitative and quantitative standard of ICT and other telecommunications equipment. For example, there are no such standards in Poland, which does not mean there are no standards. These are detailed in the Minister's Regulation of Labour and Social Policy of 23 August 2012 on social welfare homes. However, the regulation contains only a general statement on the need to provide supportive services, including stimulating the establishment, maintenance, and development of contact with the family and local community (§ 5 (1)(3)(e)). Through comparison, the minimum standards for shelters for the homeless include a requirement to have a computer lab, i.e., a separate room or a part of it equipped with a computer with Internet access (however, this standard is missing regarding shelters for the homeless with care services, i.e., those in need of medical support). Considering the possibilities offered by modern technology, in those countries where no standard for remote communication has been defined, legislative and organisational work should ensure such a standard. It would be worth considering "virtual meeting rooms."

Another, although no less critical, problem during an epidemic crisis is providing alternative communication (AAC). AAC (augmentative and alternative

30 C.E. Bowman, 'Care homes after covid-19: we need a wide-ranging inquiry and reform' [2020] BMJ <https://www.bmj.com/content/bmj/369/bmj.m2105.full.pdf> (10.12.2021).

31 D. O'Neill et al., 'COVID-19 highlights the need for universal adoption of standards of medical care for physicians in nursing homes in Europe' [2020] European Geriatric Medicine <https://www.ncbi.nlm.nih.gov/pmc/articles/PMC7298916/pdf/41999_2020_Article_347.pdf> (10.12.2021).

32 Ibid.

communication) is a language that supports or replaces natural speech or writing with aided or unassisted symbols.[33] Among the various AAC communication tools are technological devices for alternative (non-verbal) communication. Lipowicz, Mędrzycki and Szmigiero[34] draw attention to the necessity of using this type of communication in specific situations caused by a pandemic condition. Standards for such communication should also be implemented in nursing homes so that the elderly, also after strokes or with medical conditions (Alzheimer's), can communicate with the staff. The problem of essential communication becomes a real challenge when faced with maintaining a sanitary regime. The standard defined in Poland, for example, is too general, as it refers to "increasing the efficiency and activating the residents of the home, including in assistive or alternative communication, with persons with verbal communication problems" (§ 5(1)(3)(b).

3.5 Technology-enabled care

Technology-enabled care (TEC) is a capacious conceptual category encompassing electronic technologies in patient care. The concept includes a variety of technological enhancements to the communication and delivery of medical services, including health care services between the recipient and the provider included in concepts such as telemedicine, telecare, m-Health.[35] One of the critical concepts of TEC is telemedicine. In its communication, the Commission of the European Communities defined it as

> the provision of healthcare services, through use of ICT, in situations where the health professional and the patient (or two health professionals) are not in the exact location. It involves the secure transmission of medical data and information through text, sound, images, or other forms needed to prevent, diagnose, treat, and follow-up patients.[36]

Telemedicine in the face of the epidemic crisis is one of the essential proxies for digital transformation, not only because it makes it possible to reduce patient-doctor contact to essential situations, but also to devote time to in-patient diagnosis for those who need it, i.e., after initial contact via the online method. Furthermore,

33 L.L. Lloyd, D.R. Fuller and H.H. Arvidson, *Augmentative and Alternative Communications: A Handbook of Principles and Practices* (1st edn, Pearson 1997).

34 I. Lipowicz, R. Mędrzycki and M. Szmigiero, 'Walka z epidemią wymaga też alternatywnych form komunikacji personelu z pacjentami' [2020] prawo.pl <https://www.prawo.pl/zdrowie/prawo-pacjenta-do-komunikacji-w-szpitalu-w-czasie-epidemi,500075.html> (10.12.2021).

35 S. Sikorski, M. Florczak, 'Telemedycyna w polskim prawie administracyjnym' in I. Lipowicz, G. Szpor and M. Świerczyński (eds.), *Temedycyna i e-zdrowie. Zagadnienia prawne i informatyczne* (WolKluw. 2019) 41.

36 Commission of the European Communities, *Communication from the Commission to the European Parliament, the Council, the European Economic, and Social Committee, and the Committee of the Regions on telemedicine for the benefit of patients, healthcare systems and society* (2008) 3.

concerning the elderly, services provided by telemedicine such as telecare, telecardiology or telediabetes are necessary.[37]

Zhang and Song write:

> The healthcare system can put aged people at risk of infection unintentionally, given the complex pathogenic environment in the healthcare setting for the elderly. Therefore, healthcare system and aged individuals should try to minimize the chance of unessential doctor visits, such as annual physical examination and dental cleaning. [...] Healthcare staffs should pay more attention to and may set aside dedicated efforts to monitor aged individuals with underlying diseases which require regular monitoring, such as hypertension. These aged patients are encouraged to contact their doctors by phone or online, and doctors can prescribe some back-up medicines for long term, which may be delivered to patients, to avoid unnecessary exposure.[38]

However, this method does not always find supporters, especially among elderly people who, without the help of IT literate people, cannot use all the telemedicine options on their own (e.g., uploading a photo online is a problem) and thus get the correct diagnosis. In Poland, in the initial period of the epidemic (March–April), after complaints to the supervisory authority mainly about the lack of availability of telemedicine, there was an increase in the number of complaints about online services.[39] Despite the existence of statutory regulations allowing the use of telemedicine advice, the matter is significantly complicated by the Code of Medical Ethics, according to which no treatment may be undertaken without first examining the patient, and such a procedure may be waived when medical advice can only be given remotely (Art. 9). With lockdown of elderly people, there should not be a problem with this – such advice can often be given just then only remotely, but in the absence of a lockdown decision – considering this regulation – the use of telemedicine as the sole method of contact with the patient seems inappropriate.[40] In extreme cases, it may even work to the detriment of the older patient. Therefore, it is a mistake to offer telemedicine advice alone, including the complete closure of outpatient clinics for those in need.

In Poland, the state of the epidemic has prompted work on a regulation on the organisational standard of telemedicine in primary care.

> The draft regulation introduces the standard of teleportation (healthcare provided at a distance using ICT systems or communication systems) in primary care (POZ), which is to ensure conditions for implementing teleportation, guaranteeing the same standard of healthcare provision by POZ

37 S. Sikorski and M. Florczak, op. cit., 43.
38 Q. Zhang and W. Song, op. cit.
39 J. Watoła, 'Diagnoza bez pacjenta' *Gazeta Wyborcza* (Warsaw, 3.08.2020).
40 Ibid.; see wider: S. Sikorski and M. Florczak, op. cit., 52.

providers while maintaining the security of medical information transmitted electronically.

The standard of teletreatment within POZ is to ensure the implementation of teletreatment, considering such elements as (1) making available and elaborating by the provider at the place of providing services and on its website information about the rules of providing teleportation; (2) confirming the identity of the beneficiary; (3) ensuring the confidentiality of the teleportation; (4) informing the beneficiary about the method of implementation of e-prescription, e-referral, certificate of temporary inability to work, if issued, and about the possibility of creating an Internet Patient Account by the beneficiary, if the beneficiary does not have such an account, in order to facilitate access to information provided under the teletrial.[41] The project on standards for teleports is probably the first legislative undertaking of this type in Poland which directly concerns the standards of public administration activities forced by the epidemic of coronavirus. Of course, there are examples of other legal solutions undertaken in the face of an epidemic (e.g., provisions of the so-called anti-crisis shields), but so far, they have concerned rights and obligations of citizens and public administration, rather than standards par excellence.

The epidemic has also highlighted problems in the lack of standards for telecare. It is part of TEC and, as such, is often combined with telemedicine. However, some variation in the forms and the telecare method distinguishes telecare from telemedicine, which is aimed directly at providing medical services. Telecare is closer to social care, although it uses medical data about the patient for this purpose. It stops or postpones the institutionalisation/deinstitutionalisation of care. Telecare is not used only for older people. Still, it is a crucial support factor in the face of the singularisation of old age, including ensuring as far as possible the independence of older people required by Art. 25 of the CRPD. Thus, telecare standards, while they can be developed alongside telemedicine standards, should nevertheless consider social functions (e.g., notification of an older person's need to move, to take medication).

3.6 Conclusions

Various predictions of the consequences of a post-pandemic world appear in the literature. Mascaro, for example, points to the effects of a pandemic: the immediate losses in the economic field are mitigated by state support, but this does not result in a social crisis caused by even more unemployment and health service troubles. The social movements of rebellion, the dysfunctionality of bare life, and the erosion of working conditions are a natural stage of the crisis of the social fabric. The deepening of the crisis will pave the way for changes in capital and

41 Explanatory Notes to the Regulation of the MoH on the organizational standard of teleporting in primary health care, p. 4.

new group, class demands seeking structural social security. Because of the phasing of the crisis and many environmental variables (including those hindering its development), various scenarios are considered, including changes with a revolutionary profile. Especially since the current crisis, unlike the one in 2008, is escaping the framework of the social status quo.[42] Others point out that the crisis will bitterly remind us that there is a profound discrepancy between the value of one's work for society and the payment for it – the epidemic clearly shows that the individuals who are least economically valued are those who do the most necessary work during the epidemic[43] – cleaners, chambermaids, nurses, medical workers, uniformed services, salespeople, social workers or rubbish waste collectors. Perhaps the growing awareness of such paradoxes is prompting a remodelling of the current view of work. However, the authors seem to agree with Mascaro that if this were to happen, "history is any guide, this optimistic scenario is unlikely to prevail without massive social turmoil first."[44]

The changes also affected public administration. The epidemic makes it explicit how important IT exclusion and the need for education in this area are. It also raises whether the older generation is really "lost" to the technological revolution or whether the state of the epidemic and specific measures will prove necessary to maintain the health of the elderly. For the time being, the pandemic is becoming a lesson in how the lack of clear standards for using information technology in older people's service negatively affects their health and even their lives. This is primarily an issue of the lack of widespread use of technology within LTC, the so-called virtual visits. Standards, in this case, should concern the speed and stability of the connection, the hardware and software environment, including ensuring intimacy with the family and protecting personal data. There is also a perceived need for an information platform on coronavirus information, including showing the need for an example set of physical exercises appropriate for the target group. Standards, in this case, result from considering gerontological and geriatric knowledge.

In addition, we should note that the legislator should pay attention to the balance between formal standards relating to the technical sphere and substantive standards of specific services. For example, we should ensure the widespread availability of applications as a formal criterion (e.g., accessible, easy to install) and communication requirements. Applications should consider Easy to Read (EtR) text requirements – for example, the standards used in the UK[45] – including facilities for people with AAC communication needs.

The analysis presented here clearly shows that the essential elements of public law instruments for digital transformation in the face of a pandemic should be normative Acts, which will plan standards and requirements. Subsequently, it

42 A. Leandro Mascaro, op. cit., 33–39.

43 K. Schwab and Th. Mallert, op. cit., 124.

44 Ibid., 127.

45 Department of Health UK, *Making written information easier for people with learning disabilities: Guidance for people who commission or produce Easy Read information – Revised Edition 2010.*

is the relevant activities of staff and social workers, i.e., public law instruments factual.

It is the standards that are to complement human rights. These – already guaranteed – should make up the development of standards and the growth of the impassable limit of the rule of law. Thus, the rule of law, especially in the face of a pandemic, should be the overriding principle because it guarantees the realisation of existing rights. Paradoxically, therefore, a pandemic can influence the development of these rights by filling them with standards.

Works cited

Armitage, R., and Nellums, L.B., 'COVID-19 and the Consequences of Isolating the Elderly' (2020) 5(5) The Lancet Public Health e256.

Bowman, C.E., 'Care Homes after Covid-19: We Need a Wide-Ranging Inquiry and Reform' (2020). https://doi.org/10.1136/bmj.m2105.

Broda-Wysocki, P., Dylus, A., and Pawlus, M. (eds.), *Dyskryminacja seniorów w Polsce. Diagnoza i przeciwdziałanie* (Wydawnictwo Naukowe UKSW, Warsaw 2016).

Doron, I., and Georgantzi, N. (eds.), *Ageing, Ageism and the Law: European Perspectives on the Rights of Older Persons* (Edward Elgar 2018).

Duniewska, Z., Stahl, M., and Rabiega-Przyłęcka, A. (eds.), *Standardy współczesnej administracji publicznej i prawa administracyjnego* (WolKluw. And Wydawnictwo Uniwersytetu Łódzkiego, Łódź 2019).

Fredman, S., *Discrimination Law* (2nd edn, Oxford University Press, Oxford 2011).

Lipowicz, I., Mędrzycki, R., and Szmigiero, M., 'Walka z epidemią wymaga też alternatywnych form komunikacji personelu z pacjentami' (09.05.2020) prawo.pl. https://www.prawo.pl/zdrowie/prawo-pacjenta-do-komunikacji-w-szpitalu-w-czasie-epidemi,500075.html.

Lipowicz, I., Szpor, G., and Świerczyński, M. (eds.), *Temedycyna i e-zdrowie. Zagadnienia prawne i informatyczne* (WolKluw., Warsaw 2019).

Lloyd, L.L., Fuller, D.R., and Arvidson, H.H., *Augmentative and Alternative Communications: A Handbook of Principles and Practices* (1st edn, Pearson 1997).

Mascaro, A.L., *Crise e pandemia* (Boitempo Editorial, São Paulo 2020).

O'Neill, D., Briggs, R., Holmerová, I., Samuelsson, O., Gordon, A.L., and Martin, F.C., 'COVID-19 Highlights the Need for Universal Adoption of Standards of Medical Care for Physicians in Nursing Homes in Europe' (2020) 11(4) European Geriatric Medicine 645–650.

Peers, S., Hervey, T., Kenner, J., and Ward, A. (eds.), *The EU Charter of Fundamental Rights: A Commentary* (1st edn, Nomos, C.H. Beck, Hart Publishing 2014).

Ploszka, A., *Publicznoprawny status jednostki skrajnie ubogiej* (WolKluw., Warsaw 2019).

Savulescu, J., and Cameron, J., 'Why Lockdown of the Elderly is not Ageist and Why Levelling Down Equality is Wrong' (2020) 46(11) Journal of Medical Ethics717–721.

Schwab, K., and Mallert, T., *Covid-19. The Great Reset* (World Economic Forum Publishing 2020).

Valanzuela, P.L., Santos-Lozano, A., Lista, S., Serra-Rexach, J.A., Emanuele, E., and Lucia, A., 'Coronavirus Lockdown: Forced Inactivity for the Oldest Old?' (2020) 21 JAMDA 988.

Walker, A. (ed.), *The Future of Ageing in Europe. Making an Asset of Longevity* (Palgrave Macmillan, Springer 2019).

Watoła, J., 'Diagnoza bez pacjenta' *Gazeta Wyborcza* (Agora SA, Warsaw 2020).
Wróbel, A. (ed.), *Karta Praw Podstawowych Unii Europejskiej. Komentarz* (C.H. Beck, Warsaw 2019).
Zhang, Q., and Song, W., 'The Challenges of the COVID-19 Pandemic: Approaches for the Elderly and Those with Alzheimer's Disease' (2020) 1(1) MedComm 69–73.

4 Public E-services for People with Disabilities during the COVID-19 Pandemic

Ewa Marzec

4.1 Introduction

The phenomenon of disability is one of the most serious social problems today. According to the WHO,[1] more than one billion people worldwide suffer from various dysfunctions that fall under the definition of a disabled person. The COVID-19 pandemic crisis affects the elderly and may increase the number of people with disabilities.

According to WHO data, the number of all coronavirus infections worldwide has exceeded 20.9 million. As a result of infections, 755,000 people have died.[2] The death rate among elderly patients with COVID-19 is as high as 15%. Statistics show that the elderly and disabled are not only more susceptible to all infections, but they also undergo more severe illness.

In Poland, there have been 56,090 confirmed cases of coronavirus infection, with 1,869 deaths and 38,853 recoveries.[3] According to the Ministry of Health, in the group of fatal cases among those infected with coronavirus, 1,319 people were 70 years and older, of which 810 people were 80 years and older.

The first studies conducted on recovering patients and the experience of previous coronavirus outbreaks indicate that the health effects of COVID-19 infection can be permanent and long-term. A study conducted on hospital patients in Hong Kong showed that half of the patients still had below-average lung function two months after treatment.

A similar study was conducted on 25 recovered patients from Wuhan.[4] In contrast, a study published in the journal Radiology indicated that a CT scan of the

1 WHO, 'World report on disability' [2013]<https://www.who.int/disabilities/world_report/2011/report.pdf> (20.11.2021).

2 WHO, '*Coronavirus disease (COVID-19) Weekly Epidemiological Update and Weekly Operational Update* '<https://www.who.int/emergencies/diseases/novel-coronavirus-2019/situation-reports> (20. 11.2021).

3 Serwis Rzeczpospolitej Polskiej, Koronawirus: informacje i zalecenia. 2020.<https://www.gov.pl/web/koronawirus/wykaz-zarazen-koronawirusem-sars-cov-2> (15.08.2020).

4 X.Wu B, '*Autopsy of COVID-19 victims in China*' [2020] https://academic.oup.com/nsr/advance-article/doi/10.1093/nsr/nwaa123/5854209 (20.11.2021).

DOI: 10.4324/9781003263968-19

lungs performed on 90 patients from Wuhan showed abnormalities of varying degrees in 66 patients.[5] Furthermore, analysis of medical data collected during the SARS outbreak indicates that the recovered patients may be suffering from chronic cardiovascular disorders due to long-term inflammation.

Access to public e-services in administration and medicine plays an important role in meeting the needs of people with disabilities. Additionally, the COVID-19 pandemic era will minimise the risk of infections among the elderly and people with disabilities.[6]

This chapter aims to analyse the importance of e-services provided by the public administration in Poland in the era of the pandemic and discuss issues concerning the design of public services for people with disabilities. The chapter tries to answer whether e-services can be optimised to consider the needs of people with different dysfunctions and thus increase the accessibility of public services. The study's methodology is based on the theoretical analysis of the phenomenon of disability and e-services in Poland, the analysis of own research results and the analysis of legal Acts and official documents.

This chapter aims to analyse the importance of e-services provided by the public administration in Poland in the era of the pandemic and discuss issues concerning the design of public services for people with disabilities. The chapter tries to answer whether e-services can be optimised to consider the needs of people with different dysfunctions and thus increase the accessibility of public services.

4.2 A situation of people with disabilities

There are many definitions of disability constructed within different sciences: pedagogy, psychology, sociology, medicine, social sciences or law. A review of definitions of disability as seen by various fields of science is presented, among others, by A. Bieganowska.[7]

In the Polish legal system in the 1970s, there was a visible distinction between the concept of an invalid and a disabled person. These differences were highlighted in several legal acts, for example, in the Act of 29 May 1974 on provision for war and military invalids and their families, the Act of 27 August 1997 on vocational rehabilitation and employment of the disabled, and in numerous executive regulations. Under Polish legislation, the two terms were mutually exclusive, and obtaining an invalid status excluded the application of regulations intended for persons with a disability.

This situation was changed on the day the Act of 28 June 1996 amending some Acts on old-age provision and social insurance came into force; according to the

5 T. Foster, *COVID-19* <https://radiopaedia.org/articles/covid-19-4> (20.11.2021).

6 *GOV.PL Koronawirus: informacje i zalecenia.* 2020. <https://www.gov.pl/web/koronawirus/wykaz-zarazen-koronawirusem-sars-cov-2> (15.08.2020).

7 A. Bieganowska, *Przekaz medialny w modyfikowaniu postaw studentów pedagogiki wobec niepełnosprawności* (Wydawnictwo UMCS, 2015) 121.

amendment, the concept of disability was replaced with the concept of inability to work.

The Polish legislature has not developed a single legal definition of the term "disability." The legal Acts that address this issue use a whole set of different notions, such as "disability," "disabled person," "person with disability," as well as those of an outdated or pejorative character: "handicap," "retardation," "dis-ability," e.g. Arts. 19, 20 of the Act of 18 February 1994 on pension provision for officers of the Police, the Internal Security Agency, the Intelligence Agency, the Military Counterintelligence Service, the Military Intelligence Service, the Central Anti-Corruption Bureau, the Border Guard, the Government Protection Bureau, the State Fire Service and the Prison Service and their families, "invalid," "severe disability," e.g., Art. 156 of the Penal Code, "clumsiness," "inability to make an independent decision," "total inability to live independently," "chronically ill."

It should also be noted that most legal acts do not define these terms, and if they do, they are often general, unclear and give some freedom of interpretation. It also happens that different terms are assigned the same meaning.[8]

4.3 Public e-service

An electronic service (e-service) is a service provided in an automated manner using information technology, using ICT systems in public telecommunication networks, at the individual request of the service recipient, without the simultaneous presence of the parties in the same location.[9]

The definition of public service as a service dedicated to all citizens points to such important attributes that distinguish it from other types of services, as universality and accessibility. Therefore, every citizen is entitled to free access to public services, including e-services. However, it turns out that this right is often violated by excluding certain social groups from using public services. These groups include people with disabilities whose specific needs have not been considered in shaping and implementing services.

The need for new solutions to reduce discrimination is a natural consequence of the increasingly intense struggle against marginalisation, social exclusion, including digital exclusion. It results from the formal obligation imposed by the CRPD ratified by Poland in 2012. This document specifically notes the need to ensure access to information and communication, including information and communication technologies and systems, including the Internet and services provided by both public and commercial service providers. Fulfilling the provisions of the Convention guidelines for non-discriminatory solutions that fall within the

8 D. Kurzyna-Chmiel, *Podstawy prawne i organizacyjne oświaty. Prawo oświatowe w zarysie* (WolKluw. 2009).

9 Cz. Martysz, G. Szpor, K. Wojsyk, *Ustawa o informatyzacji działalności podmiotów realizujących zadania publiczne.* Komentarz (WolKluw. 2015).

scope of broadly understood universal design, i.e., such that will be useful to everyone to the greatest possible extent without the need for adaptation or specialised design. Such action also applies to the design of websites that mediate public e-services.[10]

Web accessibility means designing user-friendly interfaces with all Internet users in mind – both computer savvy and those with limited cognitive abilities. It is a very important concept in the context of every user, and in the case of disabled users, it plays a particularly important role. We can distinguish different types of accessibility restrictions of websites. These include functional, cognitive, motor or sensory limitations for the elderly and disabled. People with disabilities can easily use websites designed according to accessibility principles. This makes intuitive navigation of websites even more important, as it improves communication with the user and facilitates searching and retrieving data.

To meet the needs of people with disabilities to access websites, which are often their only source of information and intermediary with the outside world, the EU has recommended Web Content Accessibility Guidelines (WCAG)[11] accessibility standards for websites developed by the World Wide Web Consortium (W3C).

4.4 Barriers to accessing public services

Removing barriers and ensuring accessibility for all citizens, including, above all, people with mobility or perception difficulties, is one of the key tasks of a state realising the principles of social justice. Meanwhile, social isolation, exclusion and discrimination of people with disabilities, the elderly and other groups who, due to their characteristics, have a permanent or temporary impairment remains a problem of the Polish society.

Despite many efforts and considerable outlays made to improve the living conditions of people with disabilities and the elderly, in terms of work or exercising basic civil rights and freedoms, several of them still experience many barriers that make it difficult or impossible for them to function in society. The CRPD states that "accessibility refers to ensuring that persons with disabilities can participate on an equal basis with others in every sphere of society." However, activities undertaken in this area so far have mostly been of an interventionist, ad hoc or even incoherent nature and, despite often significant financial outlays, have ultimately failed to produce the socially expected results.

The NIK report "Accessibility of public space for the elderly and persons with disabilities." shows that the state of accessibility of public space in Poland is unsatisfactory.[12] The report indicates that "none of the 94 facilities in the

10 I. Mościchowska, B. Rogoś-Turek, '*Badania jako Podstawa Projektowania User Experience.* [PWN, 2019] 73.

11 W3C. 'Web Content Accessibility Guidelines (WCAG) 2.1' <https://www.w3.org/TR/2018/REC-WCAG21-20180605/#sotd> (20.11.2021).

12 SAO, '*Dostępność przestrzeni publicznej dla osób starszych i niepełnosprawnych*' [2018] <https://www.nik.gov.pl/kontrole/P/17/094/> (19.12. 2021).

24 municipalities audited was free of barriers or non-functional solutions that prevented people with disabilities from freely using these facilities." The sites were also tested by public space accessibility specialists, including people with various disabilities. NIK pointed out that already at the stage of preparation and design of some activities and investments, there were no solutions to improve the accessibility of public space. Moreover, in almost 40% of cases, design, technical or tender documentation did not consider solutions for persons with various disabilities, and concepts of improvements concerned mainly persons with motor disabilities, neglecting other types of disabilities or the needs of the elderly. The above confirms how an insignificant percentage of infrastructure in Poland meets the conditions of accessibility and is available for people with special needs. People with disabilities also face many barriers in public institutions and places that, according to their statutes, should support groups at risk of social marginalisation.

4.5 Analysis of the needs of people with disabilities in terms of access to public e-services

Statistical studies show that many people with disabilities are older people. Despite having good intellectual capacity, most of these people have limitations in mobility, which often result from the reduced perception of senses: e.g., hearing, sight. It is estimated that about 30% of the population over 60 years of age are people with various disabilities.[13]

Considering this data, the need of shaping a broadly defined public space has become particularly important.[14] Currently, public space goes beyond the physical environment, such as urbanised areas, housing estates, cities and green areas for recreation and leisure. Digital space as an element of public space is gaining particular importance. Digital space, properly adjusted to the needs of people with disabilities, makes it possible to realise their social and professional activity. It translates into the quality of life of people with disabilities. People with disabilities, including older people, should use digital space on equal terms with others. Adaptation of digital space to the diverse needs of people with disabilities and older people requires design activities based on the principles of accessibility and universal design.

The Act of 4 April 2019 on digital accessibility of websites and mobile applications of public entities, on the one hand, implements the obligation to implement Directive 2016/2102 into the Polish legal order, on the other hand – it is also in line with the assumptions of the governmental programme, Accessibility Plus.[15] All e-services, websites and mobile applications must be adapted, i.e., they

13 <https://www.who.int/news-room/fact-sheets/detail/ageing-and-health> (19.12.2021).

14 M. Wysocki, 'Przestrzeń publiczna przyjazna seniorom' (*Polityka Senioralna*, 3(4) 2017) 91.

15 *GOV.PL Program Dostępność Plus - Przyjazna Polska.* <https://www.gov.pl/web/archiwum-inwestycje-rozwoj/program-dostepnosc-plus-przyjazna-polska> (14.12. 2021).

must become fully accessible to everyone, including people with disabilities, by 23 September 2020 at the latest.

The provision of digital accessibility by public entities is based on their website, or mobile application meets the requirements set out in the Annex to the Act. Accessibility means the principles and techniques that should be applied in designing, creating, maintaining and updating websites and mobile applications to make them more accessible. Digital accessibility of a website and mobile application is about ensuring perceivability, functionality, understandability and compatibility. The functionality of a website or mobile application is to ensure that the information presented is fully accessible both through classical methods, such as being displayed on a computer screen but also read in its entirety through the widest possible number of tools. Perceptibility is about presenting information in a way that allows it to be perceived by different senses (not all website users use the same reasons). Comprehensibility is ensuring that all information presented, as well as the way to get there, is understandable for every user. The user must not be surprised by the way the information is presented. In the case of information of particular importance, the user must be given all advice and additional information to enable the possible use of functionalities related to the presented data (e.g., in the case of bank forms, forms related to personal data, etc.).[16]

The NIK report on the implementation by entities performing public tasks obligated to adapt their websites to the needs of persons with disabilities shows that only two out of 23 audited websites (8.7%) were properly adapted. The NIK found significant errors in the case of the remaining 21 (91.3%) audited websites, including three websites assessed negatively (13.0%). According to the NIK, the irregularities found may make it difficult or impossible for people with disabilities to use the content on websites.[17]

As part of an audit conducted in 2014. "Implementation of selected requirements for ICT systems, exchange of information in electronic form and the National Interoperability Framework on the example of some offices of municipalities and cities with county rights."[18] The NIK checked the adaptation of the way information is presented by IT systems to the needs of persons with disabilities only in terms of the occurrence of HTML syntax errors on the websites of offices, but without assessing the activities of the audited entities in this area, given that the adaptation of the existing ICT systems to the requirements of WCAG 2.0 should

16 G. Szpor, K. Czaplicki (eds.) *Ustawa o dostępności cyfrowej stron internetowych i aplikacji mobilnych podmiotów publicznych. Komentarz* (WolKluw. 2020).

17 SAO, 'Realizacja przez podmioty wykonujące zadania publiczne obowiązku dostosowania ich stron internetowych do potrzeb osób niepełnosprawnych [2016]. https://www.nik.gov.pl/kontrole/D/15/505/ (19.12.2021).

18 SAO, 'Wdrażanie wybranych wymagań dotyczących systemów teleinformatycznych, wymiany informacji w postaci elektronicznej oraz Krajowych Ram Interoperacyjności na przykładzie niektórych urzędów gmin miejskich i miast na prawach powiatu' https://www.nik.gov.pl/kontrole/P/14/004/LPO/ (20.11.2021).

have taken place by 31 May 2015. During the audit, several errors were found in the presentation of content on the websites of offices.

The NIK conducted in 2014 an audit of the Provision of public services to persons using sign language.[19] It checked, among others, the availability of information for the deaf on the websites of selected public entities. The findings of the audit show, among other things, that the information posted on the websites of the audited entities were addressed to the public and mostly did not meet the criterion of accessibility, especially for deaf persons.

According to the Accessibility Report of the Widzialni Foundation 2019,[20] e-services have not changed significantly in comparison to the 2018 study. On a scale of up to 21 points, the highest score was given to the obywatel.gov.pl website – 17 points, the lowest – to the following websites: epuap.gov.pl – 6 ceidg.gov .pl – 7 points. Examples of errors include: a blind user could not fill in an application for 500+ on the "Emp@tia" website, where the form did not have text labels. Another problem was with PUE ZUS, checking information about insurance and contributions and filling in the application form on the praca.gov.pl website. A blind user was not able to obtain information about insurance and contributions. PUE ZUS seemed to him a chaotic portal. Interaction with navigation elements was a barrier for the consultant, as there was a fear of unintentionally changing one's data in the system.

The mobile app accessibility survey showed that the quality of app accessibility had increased slightly compared to the 2018 survey results. Care was taken to improve functionality and efficient exchange of information (e.g., mObywatel). The mObywatel app makes it possible to create an account and navigate the app efficiently without much difficulty. In the context of people using screen readers, the biggest problems of the application are labels/text descriptions of active elements. When searching for the nearest outpatient unit, the results presented in the app did not take geolocation into account.[21]

The Act of 4 April 2019 on digital accessibility of websites and mobile applications of public entities together with the Act on Ensuring Accessibility for Persons with Special Need also provide an important foundation for the international obligation under the CRPD to ensure accessibility for persons with disabilities. The Convention emphasises the importance of accessibility not only of the physical environment, but also of the social, economic and cultural environment, the availability of goods, services, new technologies, including their affordability and ensuring the availability of information about them, access to health care and education, and to information and means of communication. The lasting effect

19 SAO, 'Wdrażanie wybranych wymagań dotyczących systemów teleinformatycznych, wymiany informacji w postaci elektronicznej oraz Krajowych Ram Interoperacyjności na przykładzie niektórych urzędów gmin miejskich i miast na prawach powiatu' https://www.nik.gov.pl/kontrole/P/14/004/LPO/ (20.11.2021).

20 P. Marcinkowski, M. Luboń, 'Raport dostępności 2019' <https://www.widzialni.org/container/raport-dostepnosci-2019.pdf> (20.11.2021).

21 P. Marcinkowski P, Luboń M, op. cit.

of the Accessibility Plus programme,[22] an element of which is the Act on Digital Accessibility of Websites and Mobile Applications of Public Entities, is to be the integration of accessibility issues into all public policies, into the practice of planning, implementation and evaluation of the functioning of the state, through investments (construction, transport, technology) in existing public buildings and multi-family housing stock, space, means of transport, websites or services of a universal nature, and even activities that strengthen the producers of adaptive and compensatory technologies.

4.6 Analysis of selected public e-services in the era of COVID-19

The coronavirus pandemic has caused significant changes in the education system. School closures have affected 1.3 billion children worldwide,[23] so the problem is widespread and particularly affects students with disabilities.

On 8 July 2020, the European Parliament adopted a resolution on the rights of people with intellectual disabilities and their families during the COVID-19 pandemic crisis.[24] In the document, members of Parliament expressed "deep concern about the disproportionate impact of the COVID-19 pandemic crisis on people with intellectual disabilities and other mental health problems and their families." They strongly condemned "any medical discrimination against people with intellectual disabilities," recalling that "appropriate measures adopted by the Member States must be consistent with the CRPD and ensure equal and non-discriminatory access to health care and social services." It also emphasised that "people with intellectual disabilities or mental illness should be provided with the same treatment as any other person with COVID-19, including intensive therapy."[25]

In addition, the European Parliament resolution of 8 July 2020 on the rights of people with intellectual disabilities and their families in the COVID-19 pandemic crisis also stresses "the need to adhere to the principles of universal design, taking into account the opportunities offered by innovative technologies and digital applications when developing accessible resources for learners with intellectual disabilities, and the need to enable distance learning."

22 *GOV.PL Program Dostępność Plus - Przyjazna Polska.* <https://www.gov.pl/web/archiwum-inwestycje-rozwoj/program-dostepnosc-plus-przyjazna-polska> (14.12.2021).

23 E. Akbari, 'Coronavirus school closures could widen inequities for our youngest students. The Conversation' <https://theconversation.com/coronavirus-school-closures-could-widen-inequities-for-our-youngest-students-136669> (19.12.2021).

24 European Parliament, Resolution on the rights of persons with intellectual disabilities in the COVID-19 crisis (2020/2680(RSP)) <https://www.europarl.europa.eu/doceo/document/B-9-2020-0204_EN.html> (20.11.2021).

25 European Parliament, Resolution on the rights of persons with intellectual disabilities in the COVID-19 crisis (2020/2680(RSP)) <https://www.europarl.europa.eu/doceo/document/B-9-2020-0204_EN.html> (20.11.2021)/

The crisis caused by the COVID-19 pandemic has shown that "the concept of inclusive education has not yet materialized" and

> in the many Member States, students with intellectual disabilities have not been able to continue their education while in isolation, and families do not have support for the education of people with intellectual disabilities, especially when it comes to access to innovative digital technologies and distance learning applications.

The U.S. Government Accountability Office (GAO) (U.S. Government Accountability Office no date)[26] indicates in its report that the COVID-19 pandemic forced schools to move quickly to distance learning. This presented significant challenges, especially for English language learners and students with disabilities. Special education services for students with disabilities such as occupational and speech therapy and rehabilitation were difficult to provide remotely. A major factor that hindered this process was the wide range of needs of students with disabilities as identified in the Individuals with Disabilities Act (IDEA), including services specified in their individualised education programmes; and the ability of parents or guardians to assist teachers and service providers in providing general education, special education and related services to their children.[27] Providing occupational therapy, physical therapy or speech therapy to students with special needs was particularly difficult to do remotely. School district officials participating in the study indicated that they met some of the challenges by modifying instruction, holding virtual meetings with parents and encouraging collaboration between general and special education teachers. For example, some districts changed student goals and services in interim distance learning plans.[28]

In Poland, students, parents and teachers negatively evaluate the remote learning experience. Apart from the guidebook's recommendations,[29] no coherent, comprehensive solution was prepared, resulting in schools individually determining how to implement the core curriculum at a distance. The pandemic exposed weaknesses in the level of digitisation of the school system, important from the point of view of the functioning of educational institutions. The main issue is the insufficient level of digital competence of teachers, a large proportion of whom had problems with planning and conducting lessons remotely, using appropriate software. One in ten of the surveyed directors of rural schools stated that it was

26 *U.S. Government Accountability Office*, <https://www.gao.gov> (20.11. 2021).

27 C. Christensen, J. Schurz, N. Malkus, *School district responses to the COVID-19 pandemic: Round 6, ending the year of school closures,* (American Enterprise Institute, 2020).

28 Congressional Committees. *Distance Learning: Challenges Providing Services to K-12 English Learners and Students with Disabilities during COVID-19.* Report to Congressional Committees. (United State Government Accountability Office, 2020).

29 MEiN, '*Kształcenie na odległość – poradnik dla szkół*' [2020] <https://www.gov.pl/web/edukacja/ksztalcenie-na-odleglosc--poradnik-dla-szkol> (19.12. 2021).

impossible to make lessons remotely in their institution. Another major limitation is the availability of equipment.[30]

With the COVID-19 epidemic affecting every citizen, solutions dedicated to people with disabilities and their caregivers have been introduced. Their purpose is to facilitate the daily functioning of this group of our society.

An example is the video hotline introduced by the Ignacy Łukasiewicz PGNiG Foundation and the Polish Association of the Deaf. The tool was created under the Accessibility Plus programme. It is dedicated to deaf people who need information about the COVID-19 epidemic. It can be used through popular instant messengers and the online sign language interpreter application.[31]

The Support Service System (SOW) is a nationwide, free-of-charge, dedicated IT system maintained by PFRON, through which persons with disabilities and entities acting on their behalf may apply online for support financed by PFRON. The publication of information on services provided by the SOW system on the GOV.PL website means that the beneficiaries of support funded by PFRON will handle their official matters more conveniently. The website contains all forms of support distributed by local governments, which can be applied electronically, without leaving home, using the SOW system.[32]

The publication of information directly in the Service of the Republic of Poland will contribute to the implementation of the postulate of a single place to obtain information by Polish citizens, entrepreneurs and civil servants on assistance provided to people with disabilities. It will increase the visibility of the SOW system's e-services in the digital space. Every citizen or entrepreneur looking for information on government administration has one complete and exhaustive source of knowledge at their disposal – the website – where they can quickly find all the information they need, presented in a uniform and standardised way.

They are making information on e-services offered by PFRON available on the GOV.PL website will translate into increased knowledge about forms of support prepared for people with disabilities, their employers and institutions acting on their behalf. A greater awareness in this area will allow every person who needs such assistance to apply for it electronically.

On 27 January 2021, the eHealth Network adopted guidelines on proof of vaccination issued for medical purposes, updated on 12 March 2021. These guidelines define the main interoperability elements, the minimum data set on vaccination certificates, and the unique identifier (Digital Green Certificate). The eHealth Network and the Health Security Committee established by the provisions of Art.

30 P. Sobiesiak-Penszko, F. Pazderski, '*Dyrektorzy do zadań specjalnych - edukacja zdalna w czasach izolacji. Raport'* [2020] <https://lekcjaenter.pl/strona/28/raport-%22dyrektorzy-do-zadan-specjalnych---edukacja-zdalna-w-czasach-izolacji%22> (20.11.2021).

31 Polski Związek Głuchych, *Koronawirus – Tłumacz PJM dla całej Polski.* [2020] https://www.pzg.org.pl/2020/07/koronawirus-tlumacz-pjm-dla-calej-polski-2/ (20.11.2021).

32 Państwowy Fundusz Rehabilitacji Osób Niepełnosprawnych '*Cała Polska objęta wsparciem SOW!'* [2020] <https://www.pfron.org.pl/aktualnosci/szczegoly-aktualnosci/news/cala-polska-objeta-wsparciem-sow/> (20/ 11.2021).

17 of Decision No. 1082/2013/EU of the European Parliament and the Council,[33] have also worked on the preparation of a common standardised data set for the use of COVID-19 test result certificates, guidelines for recovery certificates and relevant data sets, and an outline of elements for health certificate interoperability.[34]

Building on the work done so far, the Digital Green Certificate. Ultimately, after amendments by the European Parliament EU COVID-19 Certificate[35] was adopted.

The COVID-19 Certificate regulation has been used in the EU since July. The COVID-19 Certificate includes three types of certificates: vaccination certificates, test result certificates and certificates for people who have recovered from COVID-19.[36]

The main objective is to provide an easy-to-use, non-discriminatory and secure tool that guarantees full respect for data protection principles. Certificates are issued in digital or paper form. Both are accompanied by a QR code that contains the most important information and a digital signature confirming that the certificate is authentic.[37]

The COVID-19 Certificate can be downloaded through your IKP Online Patient Account. Log in and under the "Certificates" tab, select the type of certificate and click “Download QR Code”. Then save the document on your device or print it. The certificate can be downloaded from the Patient's Internet Account or printed at the clinic or vaccination centre. It will also be available in the “My IKP” mobile application (Patient’s Internet Account) and in mObywatel.

The information contained in the certificate should also be edited in a human-readable format, printed, or displayed in plain text (Digital Green Certificate). The layout of attestations should be easy to understand, simple and user-friendly. The information and layout should be presented in a manner accessible to persons with disabilities in accordance with the requirements for accessibility of information, including digital data, set out in Directive (EU) 2019/882.[38]

The EU e-service COVID-19 Certificate includes the following websites: gov.p l. login.gov.pl, pz.gov.pl, patient.gov.pl. The EU e-service COVID-19 Certificate analysis shows that there are errors on login.gov.pl and pz.gov.pl. Links to banks’ login pages were still not embedded inside the list of elements, and there were errors with character encoding in their alternative images. In the form for entering

33 Ibid.

34 EC ‘eHealth Network. Interoperability of health certificates Trust framework’ <https://ec.europa.eu/health/sites/default/files/ehealth/docs/trust-framework_interoperability_certificates_en.pdf> (20.11.2021).

35 European Parliament, Resolution on the rights of persons with intellectual disabilities in the COVID-19 crisis (2020/2680(RSP)) <https://www.europarl.europa.eu/doceo/document/B-9-2020-0204_EN.html> (20.11.2021).

36 GOV.UK < https://www.gov.uk/coronavirus> (20.12.2021).

37 GOV.PL Unijny Certyfikat Covid. <https://www.gov.pl/web/certyfikat/o-certyfikacie-informacje> (20.11.2021).

38 Directive (EU) 2019/882 of the European Parliament and of the Council of 17.04.2019 on the accessibility requirements for products and services.

personal data, there is no information about the required fields in the text layer, and in its last step, the hierarchy of headers has not been preserved. The problems with the patient.gov.pl login page are identical to those with pz.pl.gov.pl and gov .pl. An additional difficulty after logging in to the Patient's Internet Account is the lack of intuitive focus on the appropriate elements after loading a new view, which gives the impression of a non-functioning page. The hierarchy and header structure is properly designed.

4.7 Conclusions

The coronavirus pandemic proved that it is necessary to quickly adapt the standards of functioning of individual offices and state bodies to the requirements of modernity, using new forms of communication.

At the same time, the overall system of digital services for citizens remains too complicated and dispersed.[39] It, in turn, causes difficulties in using e-services by people with disabilities. There are too many platforms and interfaces, and some of them remain unintuitive. Newly built services should present a higher level of maturity, i.e., they should be analysed for the possibility to automate processes and eliminate the participation of a clerk (transactional services, services for self-downloading of documents, electronic payment of possible fees). The existing services should also be reviewed from this point of view.

There is a need to unify and systematise the existing platforms, which is particularly important for disabled users. A user who communicates remotely with public entities must get acquainted with many websites with different interfaces and functionalities.

When carrying out digitisation activities, one should remember the risk of digital exclusion of specific social groups and care should be taken to ensure the availability of computer equipment and systematically increase digital competence, particularly of disabled persons and the elderly. Public e-services should be prepared under the principles of universal design. Websites and mobile applications should be made accessible by WCAG 2.1. It can be assumed that the COVID-19 pandemic will accelerate the digitisation process.

Works cited

Akbari, E., 'Coronavirus School Closures Could Widen Inequities for Our Youngest Students' *The Conversation* (2020), <https://theconversation.com/coronavirus-school-closures-could-widen-inequities-for-our-youngest-students-136669> (19.12.2021).

Bieganowska, A., *Przekaz medialny w modyfikowaniu postaw studentów pedagogiki wobec niepełnosprawności* (Wydawnictwo UMCS, Lublin 2015).

39 K. Roszewska, 'The concept of an active social service platform' 26th Geographic Information Systems Conference and Exhibition "GIS ODYSSEY 2019" (Croatian Information Technology Society – GIS Forum, 2019).

Christensen, C., Schurz, J., and Malkus, N. (eds.), *School District Responses to the COVID-19 Pandemic: Round 6, Ending the Year of School Closures* (American Enterprise Institute 2020).

Garlicki, L., and Szmyt, A. (eds.), *Sześć lat Konstytucji Rzeczypospolitej Polskiej. Doświadczenia i inspiracje* (Wydawnictwo Sejmowe, Warsaw 2003).

Kurzyna-Chmiel, D., *Podstawy prawne i organizacyjne oświaty. Prawo oświatowe w zarysie* (WolKluw., Warsaw 2009).

Marcinkowski, P., and Luboń, M., 'Raport dostępności 2019' (2019) <https://www.widzialni.org/container/raport-dostepnosci-2019.pdf> (20.11.2021).

Martysz, Cz, and Szpor, G., *Wojsyk K, Ustawa o informatyzacji działalności podmiotów realizujących zadania publiczne* (WolKluw., Warsaw 2015).

Mościchowska, I., and Rogoś-Turek, B., *Badania jako Podstawa Projektowania User Experience* (PWN, Warsaw 2019).

Roszewska, K., 'The Concept of an Active Social Service Platform' 26th Geographic Information Systems Conference and Exhibition "GIS ODYSSEY 2019" (CITS– GIS Forum, 2019).

Sobiesiak-Penszko, P., and Pazderski, F., 'Dyrektorzy do zadań specjalnych – edukacja zdalna w czasach izolacji. Raport' [2020] <https://lekcjaenter.pl/strona/28/raport-%22dyrektorzy-do-zadan-specjalnych---edukacja-zdalna-w-czasach-izolacji%22> (20.11.2021).

Szpor, G., and Czaplicki, K. (eds.), *Ustawa o dostępności cyfrowej stron internetowych i aplikacji mobilnych podmiotów publicznych. Komentarz* (WolKluw., Warsaw 2020).

Szpor, G., and Gryszczyńska, A. (eds.), *Access to Spatial Data and its Limitations. Legal Aspects* (Nacionalna knjižnica, Zagreb 2015).

Wiśniewski, L. (ed.), *Wolności i prawa jednostki oraz ich gwarancje w praktyce* (Wydawnictwo Sejmowe, Warsaw 2006).

Wysocki, M., 'Przestrzeń publiczna przyjazna seniorom' (2017) 3(4) Polityka Senioralna 91.

Xiu-Wu, B., 'Autopsy of COVID-19 Victims in China' (2020) 7(9) Natl. Sci. Rev. 1414–1418.

V

Administration in a Pandemic

1 Access to Public Information in a Pandemic

Agnieszka Piskorz-Ryń

1.1 Introduction

Europe has been hit by various crises over the last 50 years. However, these have not been associated with widespread threats to the life and health of citizens because of infectious diseases. It has been exactly 100 years since the end of the Spanish flu pandemic.[1] For public authorities around the world, the COVID-19 pandemic implies the need to redefine the ways in which public authorities behave and act and involves the use of various public law mechanisms. This chapter will analyze legal solutions concerning making public information available in the Republic of Poland in the first period of the pandemic. The choice of this issue is based on the following grounds. Informing citizens does not directly serve to protect the most important values in the time of a pandemic, such as life and health; however, it indirectly has a significant impact on their protection. This is so for several reasons. Firstly, information is an intangible good that reduces uncertainty.[2] With the high level of uncertainty that accompanied the first months of the pandemic, providing reliable information was very important. Human health depends not only on easily accessible health care. It is also affected by ensuring access to reliable information about the nature of the risks and how to protect yourself and your family.[3] Secondly, in Poland, access to public information is provided on analo-

1 A. Erkoreka, 'The Spanish influenza pandemic in occidental Europe (1918–1920) and victim age' (2010) 4 (2) Influenza and Other Respiratory Viruses 81; A. Crosby, *America's Forgotten Pandemic. The Influenza of 1918* (Cambridge University Press 2003); L. Cilek, G. Chowell and D.R. Fariñas, 'Age-Specific Excess Mortality Patterns During the 1918–1920 Influenza Pandemic in Madrid, Spain" (2018)187 (12) *American Journal of Epidemiology* 2511.

2 G. Szpor, 'Administracyjnoprawne problemy informatyzacji' in, J. Supernat (ed), *Między tradycją a przyszłością w nauce prawa administracyjnego. Księga jubileuszowa dedykowana Profesorowi Janowi Bociowi* (Wydawnictwo Uniwersytetu Wrocławskiego 2009).

3 COVID-19: Governments must promote and protect access to and free flow of information during pandemic – International expert. <https://www.ohchr.org/EN/NewsEvents/Pages/DisplayNews.aspx?NewsID=25729> (29.10.2021); Inter-American Commission on Human Rights, Resolution No. 1/2020, Pandemic and Human Rights in the Americas, 10.04.2020; UNESCO, 'The Right to Information in Times of Crisis' (UNESCO 2020) <https://en.unesco.org/sites/default/files/unesco_ati_iduai2020_english_sep_24.pdf> (29.10.2021) Economic and Social Council, 'Social and Cul-

DOI: 10.4324/9781003263968-21

gous terms by everyone, this includes journalists. In turn, they have an important role in informing the public and monitoring the work of the government. This role was particularly important in the first period of the pandemic. Thirdly, one of the objectives of access to information on the activities of public authorities is to increase citizens' trust in the state. Access to public information and open operation of public administration are not a remedy for the problems of modern democracies.[4] However, the lack of reliable knowledge may exacerbate certain processes. This is more important given that acceptance of government action during the first period of the pandemic was not very high in Europe. An opinion poll conducted in May 2020 for Le Figaro and FranceInfo among 1,000 French, 500 British, 500 Italian, 500 Spanish and 500 German citizens showed that only 51% of respondents from five European countries (Germany, France, Spain, Italy and the UK) believed that the government "rose to the occasion" (63% of British citizens, 60% of German citizens, 50% of Italian citizens, 34% of French citizens, 32% of Spanish citizens). Claims "the government told the people the truth," "it made the right decisions at the right time," "it did what needed to be done to equip hospitals and health workers," "it showed it knew where it was going" met with approval from 43–46% of European respondents.[5] On the other hand, citizens who place their trust in their governments more easily comply with onerous bans, which in the case of COVID-19 is crucial. Igor Krastev links this trust to the effectiveness of public administration in the fight against the SARS-CoV-2 virus. He points out that in this fight the attitude towards democracy is not important. There are democracies that have failed in this area, as well as those that have succeeded. A similar situation applies to non-democratic governments. What is crucial in his assessment is trust in public authority.[6] The overt action of the state is of course only one of the mechanisms for building it. Trust is needed not only to respect prohibitions, but also to respect their negative social and economic effects. The fight against a pandemic has required and will continue to require many areas of decision-making with negative economic impacts, which creates impatience and opposition in society. In addition to concerns about their own health, people are also afraid of the economic crisis and its consequences. Therefore, it is so important to have access to reliable information on the state of the country and its preparedness to face the next wave of pandemics. Fear, uncertainty and mis-

---

tural Rights, General Comment No. 14: The Right to the Highest Attainable Standard of Health (Art. 12)', 11.08.2000<https://undocs.org/E/C.12/2000/4> (29.10.2021).

4 R. Davis, 'Public access to community documents: a fundamental human right?'(1999), 3(8) EIoP 1; F. Bannister and R. Connolly, 'The Trouble with Transparency: A Critical. Review of Openness in e-Government' (2011) 3(1) P & I 10; B. Finel and K. Lord, 'The Surprising Logic of Transparency' (1999) *43(2)* ISQ 315; P. Birkinshaw, *Freedom of Information – The Law, the Practice and the Ideal*, (2th end, Butteworths 1996).

5 'Les Français beaucoup plus critiques envers le gouvernement que leurs voisins, selon un sondage' La Point Politique [2020] https://www.lepoint.fr/politique/les-francais-beaucoup-plus-critiques-envers-le-gouvernement-que-leurs-voisins-selon-un-sondage-10-05-2020-2374910_20.php (29.10.2021).

6 I. Krastew, *Is It Tomorrow Yet?: Paradoxes of the Pandemic* (Penguin Books Ltd2020), 22.

information have a negative impact on social cohesion and solidarity. These are two essential elements for successfully overcoming any crisis. The best antidote to these threats is informed, responsible and active citizenship.[7] Thus, recognising the vital importance of information for the preservation of social peace in an emergency, it was decided to select this reference area. Within this framework, the chapter will describe the increased legislative activity and its impact on ensuring access to information of a public nature during the first period of the pandemic, also evaluating the solutions adopted from a constitutional perspective. The considerations undertaken in this study are based on several methodological assumptions. Firstly, the provision of information in connection with the SARS-CoV-2 pandemic can be considered beyond the aspect established above also in the context of freedom of speech, proactive information policy of the state, but also its role in counteracting disinformation and infodemia can be analysed. The indicated issues are very important but will not be covered here due to the limited framework of this chapter. Secondly, providing public information is a subsidiary task. The public administration in a situation of a serious threat should, in the first place, act directly to protect the health and life of citizens. Protecting public health and ensuring access to public information are not in natural conflict, as is the case with protecting health and privacy. It is therefore not a conflict between the general interest and the welfare of the individual. And, more importantly, it is possible to realise both these rights in the case of an efficient organisation of the state. Therefore, it was decided to determine whether the state of digital transformation before the pandemic had an impact on the implementation of the information obligations of the public authority and whether the pandemic accelerated the process of digital transformation in the information sphere.

1.2 Principles of access to public information in the Republic of Poland

The principles of providing information on the activities of public authorities in the Republic of Poland derive from Art. 61 of the Constitution. Pursuant to this provision, citizens have the right to obtain information on the activities of public authorities and persons performing public functions. The right to obtain information shall include access to documents and entry to sittings of collective organs of public authority coming from universal elections.[8] The right guaranteed by Art. 61(1) and (2) of the Constitution may be restricted only in view of the protection, as provided by statutes, of the freedoms and rights of other persons and economic entities, as well as the protection of public order, security or an important economic interest of the state.[9] The principles of restricting the use of consti-

7 I. Montero de Espinosa Candau et. al., Transparencia, el acceso a la información y la protección de datos personales ante la emergencia sanitaria COVID-19' Herramientas Eurosocial (2020) No 48.

8 Art. 61 clause 2 Constitution.

9 Art. 61(3) Constitution.

tutional freedoms and rights are also regulated in Art. 31(3) of the Constitution. Pursuant to this provision, limitations to the exercise of constitutional freedoms and rights may be established only by statute and only when they are necessary in a democratic state for its security or public order, or for the protection of the environment, health and public morals, or the freedoms and rights of others. Such limitations may not affect the essence of the freedoms and rights. The regulation of limitations to the right to public information in Art. 61(3) of the Constitution does not mean the exclusion of the application of Art. 31(3). The limitations set out in both these provisions are of a complementary nature. This means that Art. 31(3) is modified by the normative content of Art. 61(3) in the scope, in which it regulates (more narrowly) the direct prerequisites of interference, while the application of the remaining elements of proportionality not expressed in Art. 61(3) (such as the necessity conditioned by the standard of a democratic state and the prohibition of interference with the essence of the right) remains fully relevant. The right guaranteed by Art. 61(1) and (2) of the Constitution may be restricted only in view of the protection, as provided by statutes, of the freedoms and rights of other persons and economic entities, as well as the protection of public order, security or an important economic interest of the state.[10] The principles of restricting the use of constitutional freedoms and rights are also regulated in Art. 31(3) of the Constitution. Pursuant to this provision, limitations to the exercise of constitutional freedoms and rights may be established only by statute and only when they are necessary in a democratic state for its security or public order, or for the protection of the environment, health and public morals, or the freedoms and rights of others. Such limitations may not affect the essence of the freedoms and rights. The regulation of limitations to the right to public information in Art. 61(3) of the Constitution does not mean the exclusion of the application of Art. 31(3).

The Access Act is an elaboration of the provisions of Art. 61 of the Constitution. It guarantees everyone the right to information on public matters (public information) (Art. 1). A person exercising this right may not be required to demonstrate a legal or factual interest (Art. 2(2)). The request thus does not require justification. The right to public information includes the entitlement to obtain public information, including to obtain processed information to the extent that it is of particular importance for the public interest; to inspect official documents; to access meetings of collective bodies of public authority coming from universal elections (Art. 3(1)). The right to public information includes the right to obtain public information containing up-to-date knowledge of public matters without delay (Art. 3(2)).

The Act also specifies the forms in which the information is to be made available. The basic form is the Public Information Bulletin (BIP). It is a teleinformatic publication. The Act on Access to public information as well as specific Acts determine information that must be obligatorily published therein. Apart from that, other public information (optional information) may be published in the BIP.

10 Art. 61(3) Constitution.

Furthermore, public information may be made available upon request or by displaying or posting it in generally accessible places or by means of devices installed in these places, which make it possible to familiarise oneself with this information (Art. 10–11). Moreover, the right to information may also be realised through the right of access to meetings of collective bodies of public authority coming from universal elections and providing access to materials, including audiovisual and ICT materials, documenting such meetings (Art. 7(1)(3)). BIP is of fundamental importance for ensuring access to public information. This results primarily from the fact that only public information that has not been made available in the BIP or data portal is made available upon request (Art. 10(1)). Making information available in the BIP means, therefore, that the obliged entity is not obliged to make it available upon request, but only to inform, by means of an ordinary letter, where in the BIP it can be found.

The Access Act defines the procedure of access to public information. It stipulates that information should be provided immediately, not later than within 14 days, with the possibility of extending the deadline to two months (Art. 13). However, this provision applies in principle only to the exercise of the right to information in the form of an application. In the case of non-request forms, it is assumed that information should be provided without undue delay. These regulations are important because the Code of Administrative Procedure does not apply to the procedure for providing public information. Only the refusal to provide public information and discontinuation of the proceedings for providing access to information by the public authority take the form of a decision to which the Code of Administrative Procedure applies (Art. 16).

1.3 Modification of regulations in the first period of the pandemic

In connection with the threat of the SARS-CoV-2 virus on the territory of Poland, a state of epidemic emergency was introduced from 14 March 2020, and then on 20 March 2020 an epidemic state was declared. However, one of the states of emergency provided for in the Constitution has not been introduced. Similar legal solutions adapting the functioning of the state to the state of pandemic have been introduced in many European and non-European countries.[11] Under the COVID-19 Act, both administrative and procedural deadlines were suspended during the period in which an epidemic emergency or state of epidemic is in force. This was one of the legal solutions following the reduction in the work of public administration offices and the courts resulting from the extensive efforts to slow down the virus. In a situation where the general good (health, life of individuals) must be protected, the authorities cannot be required to function normally and

11 The Covid Pandemic The Time Capsule of the First 6 Months An International Perspective' (2020) 39 (2) M&L 89; I. Montero de Espinosa Candau et al., op. cit.

conduct proceedings in compliance with statutory deadlines, the administrative court noted.[12]

The suspension or suspension of the administrative time limits lasted in Poland from 14 March 2020 until 23 May 2020. The course of administrative time limits was governed by Art. 15 of the Zzr the COVID-19 Act. According to this provision,

> during the period in which a state of epidemic emergency or a state of epidemic declared on account of the COVID-19 is in force, the course of the time limits provided for by administrative law: 1) on the observance of which the granting of legal protection before a court or authority depends on […] shall not commence, and those commenced shall be suspended for that period.

The time limit referred to in Art. 13 of the Act on Access (the time limit for providing public information upon request) may fall into this category. In the event of its exceeding, the applicant is entitled to lodge a complaint for inaction with an administrative court. Pursuant to Art. 15 zzr Sec. 5, actions performed to exercise a right or obligation during the period of suspension of the commencement or suspension of the time limits referred to in Art. 15 zzr Sec. 1 are effective. This meant that obliged entities could provide public information despite the suspension of the deadlines. Suspension did not apply to all time limits. Exceptions to this were set out in sections 15 zzr(2) to (5) of the COVID-19 Act. These did not provide for preferential treatment of time limits under the Access Act. The next article dealt with the suspension of procedural and judicial time limits. According to Art. 15 zzs (11) of the COVID-19 Act, during the period of an epidemic emergency or a state of epidemic declared because of COVID-19, the running of procedural and judicial time limits in judicial proceedings, including judicial-administrative proceedings (s. 1), and other proceedings conducted under the Acts shall not commence, and those commenced shall be suspended for that period (s. 10). Cessation of activities by a court, authority or entity conducting proceedings or inspection, respectively, within the period referred to in para. 1 may not be the basis for legal remedies concerning inaction, protraction or violation of a party's right to have a case heard without undue delay. It means that the indicated provisions prolonged the activity of entities obliged to make public information available as well as the control of decisions made by them both within the framework of administrative control and court control.

The provisions of the COVID-19 Act are not an example of good legislation. This is evident in the numbering of the articles themselves, where Art. 15 of the COVID-19 Act is followed by Arts. 15a to 15 zzzzzze, or 232 provisions. This is made possible by adding letters to the number 15 and using leading indices. However, the criticisms do not only relate to the systematics of the Act. The hasty legislation is also evident in the legal solutions introduced. Doubts concern,

12 Judgment of the Provincial Administrative Court of 30/06/2020, II SAB/Op 32/20.

inter alia, the legal basis for the suspension of the running of time limits in the Access Act. Interpretation difficulties in this respect were aggravated by the lack of clear rules in the doctrine for qualifying time limits as material and procedural. Despite the fact that administrative deadlines were referred to in Art. 15 zzsr(1), the basis for suspending or not commencing the running of deadlines could also be Art. 15 zzsr(1)(10) of the COVID-19 Act. This is because a deadline for providing public information can be qualified as a procedural deadline in proceedings other than those listed in Art. 15 zzsr(1)(1–9) conducted under other Acts. This is justified by the fact that pursuant to Art. 16 of the Access Act the Administrative Procedure Code applies only to the issuance of a decision to refuse access to public information, which has already been mentioned. Thus, the process of granting public information itself does not take place based on the Code of Administrative Procedure. In the jurisprudence of the administrative courts, this very provision has, in principle, been recognised as the basis for the suspension of the time limits referred to in Art. 13 of the Act on Access. However, the opposite position may be encountered. In those judgments, although the Court referred to Art. 15zs (1)(10) of the COVID-19 Act it held that this provision was not applicable in view of the wording of Art. 15zs(2). This provision indicates that the suspension of the commencement and running of time limits referred to in para. (1) does not apply to time limits in cases referred to in Art. 14a(4) and (5) before the courts. The latter provision, in turn, specifies cases considered urgent by the legislature, which are not affected by the suspension of the commencement and running of time limits. Pursuant to Art. 14a(5) of the COVID-19 Act, urgent cases are those cases for which the law sets a time limit for their consideration by the court. Pursuant to Art. 21 of the Act on Access, the provisions of the Law on Administrative Court Proceedings apply to complaints examined in proceedings for access to public information, except that: transmission of the file and the response to the complaint shall take place within 15 days from the date of receipt of the complaint; the complaint shall be examined within 30 days from the date of receipt of the file together with the response to the complaint. It follows from the above, in the courts' view, that cases concerning access to public information constitute a category of urgent cases, in relation to which the regulation of Art. 15zzs(1) of the COVID-19 Act is excluded.[13] The described difficulties in identifying the legal basis for the suspension of time limits are also evident in the case law. Most of the panels of judges are in favour of the possibility of suspending time limits, apart from the exceptions indicated.

The suspension or suspension of the running of time limits lasted until 23 May 2020. Both provisions of Art. 15 zzs and Art. 15 zzr concerning the running of time limits were repealed by Art. 46(20) of the Act of 14 May 2020 on amending certain Acts in respect of protective measures in connection with the spread of the SARS-CoV-2 virus (JoL 2020, item 875). The repealing provision entered

13 Judgment of the Provincial Administrative Court of 10/08/2020 r., II SAB/Op 40/20; Judgment of the Provincial Administrative Court of 3/08/2020 r., II SA/Gd 247/20.

into force on 16 May 2020, however, by virtue of Art. 68(1) and (6) thereof, the time limits in the proceedings referred to in Art. 15zzs and Art. 15 zzr which have not begun to run began to run 7 days after the entry into force of this Act. In the case of deadlines that have been suspended, they have begun to run again after the lapse of 7 days from the date of entry into force of this Act (Art. 68, ss. 2 and 7).

1.4 Assessment of legal solutions for limiting the right to information in the first pandemic period

The introduced solutions gave the possibility not to provide public information. This lasted for over two months. Poland was not an exception in this respect. Only a few countries chose to exempt access to information cases from the suspension of deadlines or to give preferential treatment to requests for access to information on pandemic control.[14] The importance of the right to public information in this important period for the state and society has already been written about in the introduction. For access to public information, the timing of the request is crucial. Most often, information is relevant to the recipient only when it has the attribute of being up to date. Thus, if the primary purpose of this right is to control public authorities, obtaining information on their actions with considerable delay reduces the significance of this information. Suspension of the running of time limits or failure to start them resulted, in practice, in the impossibility to file a complaint about inaction. Everyone entitled between 14 March 2020 and 23 May 2020 was temporarily deprived of the possibility to exercise this right. In accordance with the Council of Europe Convention on Access to Official Documents, hereinafter referred to as the Tromsø Convention, an application for access to such documents shall be handled promptly. A decision shall be taken, and the applicant informed as soon as possible or within a reasonable time. Above all, timeliness is linked to the possibility of challenging an authority's failure to act. Safeguarding the right to public information is of fundamental importance. Without such security it is impossible to speak of the right to information as a public subjective right. Providing public information is an obligation of the obliged entity, the fulfilment of which may be asserted. In Poland the right to information is secured through administrative and judicial control. According to the already cited Tromsø Convention, an applicant who has been refused an official document, explicitly or implicitly, in part or in whole, should be guaranteed access to a review procedure before a court or other independent and impartial body established by law (Art. 8). In the case of the right to information, the suspension of time limits under Law COVID-19 resulted in a temporary restriction on the implementation of access to information. During this period, under the indicated law, the inaction of the obliged entity was lawful (legal). However, this does not change the fact that the obliged entity could and should provide, reliable and up-to-date information on public affairs. By implementing Art. 3.2 of the Access to Information Act, it could

14 I. Montero de Espinosa Candau et al., op. cit.

publish important information. The most important issues could be made public in the BIP. The administration could also use other less formalised tools to make information available, such as Twitter or websites. It could also actively cooperate with journalists.

The aim of this chapter, however, is not to assess the state of information of citizens during a pandemic as an active form of policy implementation but the execution of a legal obligation incumbent on public authorities. Indeed, access to information in the form of a request serves to control the authority and to verify its official communications. Therefore, access to information on request is so important. In view of the above, the assessment of the solutions introduced in the COVID-19 Act should be made based on the provisions of the Constitution. However, the considerations that follow are not intended to assess to the extent indicated the constitutionality of the COVID-19 Act. This is the role of a duly constituted CT.

Art. 61(3) and 31(3) of the Constitution, already discussed above, formulate cumulatively included prerequisites for restricting access to public information in the Republic of Poland, thus defining an impassable limit of the lawmaker's interference with the right guaranteed by the Constitution. The issue that needs to be determined is whether suspension (non-starting) of deadlines may be treated as a limitation of the constitutionally guaranteed right to information. Art. 31(3) allows for the establishment of limitations "to the enjoyment of constitutional freedoms and rights." Indeed, the exercise of a given constitutional right or freedom is a process that is immanently linked to the constitutional right or freedom as such and cannot be structurally separated from that right or freedom. Interference in the manner or scope of exercising constitutional rights or freedoms inevitably harms the constitutional right or freedom as such.[15] The formulations quoted above justify the qualification of the temporary suspension of the running of time limits as a limitation of the right to public information.

The right to public information, pursuant to the above-mentioned provisions, may be restricted: firstly, by way of a statute; secondly, when there is a functional connection between the restriction and the realisation of the values indicated in Art. 61(3) and Art. 31(3) of the Constitution; thirdly, when there exists in a democratic state a necessity to introduce such a restriction; fourthly, it does not violate the essence of the constitutional right and freedom. These premises require a brief discussion. There is no doubt as to the fulfilment of the first of them, which boils down to the requirement of preserving the statutory form of the restriction. With respect to the second one, the restrictions introduced by the COVID-19 Act were established for the protection of order and security, which should be deemed to be in line with Art. 61(3) of the Constitution. Indeed, there was a functional relationship between these restrictions and the protection of the values indicated in that provision. This issue does not require further analysis. The next

15 L. Bosek, M. Szydło, 'Komentarz do art. 31 Konstytucji', in M. Safjan and L. Bosek, (eds.) *Konstytucja RP. Tom I. Komentarz do art. 87-243*, (C.H.Beck 2016).

premise concerns the principle of proportionality *sensu largo*. It consists of three components, namely the imperatives of usefulness, necessity and the principle of proportionality *sensu stricto*. The first of these requires the legislator to always ascertain the real need for interference with an individual right in each situation (the applicability requirement). It is therefore necessary to determine the purpose of a given legal regulation, on the assumption that it is itself only an instrumental purpose, which is intended to achieve an aim. In this case, the intrinsic objective was the protection of citizens' health by slowing down the virus as part of the protection of public safety. In this respect, the utility imperative is at least partly fulfilled. Another element of the principle of proportionality is the imperative of necessity, which is understood as the requirement to apply such legal measures that will be effective, i.e., serve to achieve the goals intended by the legislator. It seems that the regulation introduced by the the COVID-19 Act, to the extent to which it concerned the right to public information, does not meet the requirement of necessity in relation to those offices which could work remotely (they implemented the system of electronic document management, hereinafter referred to as EZD). As regards applications sent in electronic form, their positive consideration could have taken place within the framework of remote work. It was different in the case of refusal of access to information and applications submitted in paper form. Here it was necessary to print out the reply, sign it and send it by post. It should be noted that most requests for access to public information in Poland are submitted by email or e-PUAP. Thus, it can be concluded that the legislator did not consider the possibility of remote work of offices. "In seeking an answer to the question of whether interference in the sphere of an individual's constitutional right is consistent with the principle of necessity, one should consider whether the aim pursued by the legislator can be achieved by equally effective means, but less burdensome for the individual."[16] It seems that those entities, where the EZD system was introduced, there was a possibility to fulfil the aim of the Act by a less burdensome measure. The action of the legislature, in relation to those offices which were able to work remotely, does not meet the imperative of necessity. It should suspend the running of time limits or suspend their commencement regarding access to public information only to the extent that the work could not be performed remotely.

Finally, it is necessary to consider the fundamental issue of whether the established limitations do not infringe the essence of the right to public information guaranteed in Art. 61 of the Constitution. The analysis of the essence of the right to information is based on an absolute approach. According to it, in the case of each constitutional right and freedom, it is possible to identify *in abstracto* a specific inviolable core (nucleus) of this right or freedom, into which the public authorities may not encroach under any circumstances, even for the purpose of protecting the values indicated in Art. 31(3) Constitution.[17] The essence of a given

16 Judgment of the Provincial Administrative Court of 30.06.2020 r., II SAB/Op 32/20.
17 L. Bosek, M. Szydło, op. cit.

constitutional right or freedom is the element determining the identity of the right or freedom in question. A violation of the essence of a right or freedom occurs when the introduced restriction concerns the fundamental rights constituting the content of a given right and prevents the right from performing the function it is supposed to perform in the legal order.[18] As regards the right to information, as it has already been written, the timeliness of its realisation and the possibility to appeal against the failure to provide information make it impossible for this right to fulfil the function entrusted to it in the Constitution. The right to appeal against failure to provide information should be regarded as a component part of the content of this right. Without it we can only talk about a semblance of the right to information. Significant concerns can therefore be formulated as to whether the provisions of COVID-19, insofar as they related to the right to information, violated the essence of that right.

It should also be noted that the Constitution allows for the use of specific mechanisms of limiting the rights guaranteed therein of a temporal nature. This concerns the introduction of states of emergency. It provides for three states of emergency: martial law, state of emergency and state of natural disaster. In accordance with Art. 228(1) of the Constitution, their introduction requires the occurrence of an exceptional situation. They can be introduced in situations of special threat when ordinary constitutional means are insufficient. The premise of a situation of special dangers that cannot be removed by ordinary constitutional means expresses the principle of exceptionality (subsidiarity) of states of emergency.[19]

There must therefore be a situation in which it is not possible to counter the threat without deviating from the application of constitutional norms in force in the "normal situation," including using the possibility of limiting individual rights and freedoms in accordance with Art. 31(3) of the Constitution.[20] As indicated earlier, there are doubts about the possibility of limiting the right to information through the COVID-19 Act based on Art. 31(3) of the Constitution. It is undisputed that the right to public information could be temporarily restricted to the extent provided for in this Act in the situation of the introduction of a state of emergency due to a threat to the security of citizens (Art. 230(1) of the Constitution). When it is introduced, in accordance with Art. 21(8) of the Act of 21 June 2002 on the state of emergency, during its duration, restrictions may be imposed on human and civil liberties and rights, inter alia, regarding access to public information. The right to public information is one of the rights and freedoms that may be restricted during the state of emergency. The Constitution in Art. 233(1) defines the rights and freedoms that are not subject to limitations during states of emergency.

18 Judgment of CT of 12.01.1999 r., P 2/98, OTK 1999 Nr 1 poz. 2.

19 S. Steinborn, 'Komentarz do art. 228 Konstytucji', in Marek Safjan and Lech Bosek (eds.), *Konstytucja RP. Tom I. Komentarz do art. 87-243* (C.H. Beck 2016).

20 K. Wojtyczek, Granice ingerencji ustawodawczej w sferę praw człowieka w Konstytucji RP (WolKluw.1999) 199.

Concluding the considerations relating to the implementation of the right to information in the first stage of the pandemic, it is proposed to formulate recommendations for public authorities. These also consider the experience of other countries.[21] Firstly, due to the importance of information in the modern world, plans should be created to make public information available in crisis situations. It is worth creating emergency procedures for providing public information, based on the experience within the organisation, considering the circumstances of the SARS-CoV-2 threat, but also other threats. The described risk-based procedures should be adapted to possible threats. Secondly, it is worth including proactive information of public authorities in the procedures. This can at least partly neutralise the lack of implementation of the right to information on request in a threatening situation. Thirdly, it is worth reviewing the activities related to the implementation of the right to public information during the first wave of the pandemic and assessing the status of the use of available digital technologies. As part of the procedures being prepared, consider and exploit the potential of the digital solutions available to provide information in the event of crises.

1.5 Conclusion

The provisions introduced in the the COVID-19 Act concerning the suspension or suspension of deadlines in matters of access to public information sanctioned the inaction of the obliged entities (legislative, executive and judicial authorities) causing a temporary suspension of the right to public information. Their aim was to avert threats by taking actions aimed at preventing the spread of the SARS-CoV-2 virus. The assessment of the described limitation made based on Art. 31(3) of the Constitution is a source of doubts as to the degree of the legislator's interference with the right to information referred to in Art. 61 of the Constitution. It seems that the ordinary legislator excessively interfered with the essence of this right, infringing its core, i.e., the possibility to appeal against inaction. Such interference would be justified in the case of the introduction of a state of emergency. There are also doubts as to whether the imperative of necessity as an element of the principle of proportionality *sensu largo* is met, insofar as the legislator did not consider the possibility of remote working as a measure that is equally effective and less severe for the individual. It should be stressed that a state of emergency does not exempt public authorities from compliance with the principle of legality and the rule of law. This is one of the basic criteria for the assessment of regulations on access to information in connection with the COVID-19 pandemic.

Moreover, it must be stated that the state of digital transformation before the pandemic had no influence on the shaping of the obligation to implement access

21 I. Montero de Espinosa Candau et al., op. cit.; International Conference of Information Commissioner, 'Access to Information in the context of a global pandemic Statement' (International Conference of Information Commissioner 2020) <https://www.informationcommissioners.org/covid-19> (29.10.2021).

to public information in the legislation in the first period of the pandemic. The legislator did not consider that the objective of social isolation could have been achieved by means other than suspension or suspension of deadlines. Remote working was at least in part as effective as the measure adopted by the legislature. The legislator should at least, where possible, have authorised or imposed teleworking while resolving the doubts which arose in this regard. In the future, more emphasis should be placed on protocols for transition to remote working and electronic document flow in a public entity. In terms of access to public information, this would require the elimination of problems related to the delivery of written correspondence. From the point of view of preparing the administration for future threats, it is essential where an electronic document management system has been introduced and to adapt this system, as far as it is possible, to the remote work of officials. It is also necessary to assess the technical resources of employees for the implementation of a remote working system.

Works cited

Bannister, F., and Connolly, R., 'The Trouble with Transparency: A Critical. Review of Openness in e-Government' (2011) 3(1) P & I 10.

Birkinshaw, P., *Freedom of Information – The Law, the Practice and the Ideal* (2nd edn, Butteworths 1996).

Cilek, L., Chowell, G., and Fariñas, D.R., 'Age-Specific Excess Mortality Patterns during the 1918–1920 Influenza Pandemic in Madrid, Spain' (2018) 187(12) American Journal of Epidemiology 2511.

Crosby, A.W., *America's Forgotten Pandemic. The Influenza of 1918* (Cambridge University Press, Cambridge 2003).

Davis, R., 'Public Access to Community Documents: A Fundamental Human Right?'(1999) 3(8) EIoP 1.

Erkoreka, A., 'The Spanish Influenza Pandemic in Occidental Europe (1918–1920) and Victim Age' (2010) 4(2) Influenza and Other Respiratory Viruses 81.

Finel, B., and Lord, M., 'The Surprising Logic of Transparency' (1999) 43(2) ISQ 315.

Krastew, I., *Is It Tomorrow Yet?: Paradoxes of the Pandemic* (Penguin Books Ltd. 2020).

'Les Français beaucoup plus critiques envers le gouvernement que leurs voisins, selon un sondage' *La Point Politique* (2020). https://www.nouvelobs.com/politique/20200510.AFP6468/les-francais-beaucoup-plus-critiques-envers-le-gouvernement-que-leurs-voisins-selon-un-sondage.html.

Montero de Espinosa Candau, I., Carneiro Freire, M., Cordero Sanz, C., and Cordero Sanz, J., 'Transparencia, el acceso a la información y la protección de datos personales ante la emergencia sanitaria COVID-19' (2020) 48 Herramientas Eurosocial.

Safjan, M., and Bosek, L. (eds.), *Konstytucja RP. Tom I. Komentarz do art. 87–243* (C H Beck 2016).

Supernat, J. (ed.), *Między tradycją a przyszłością w nauce prawa administracyjnego. Księga jubileuszowa dedykowana Profesorowi Janowi Bociowi*' (Wydawnictwo Uniwersytetu Wrocławskiego, Wrocław 2009).

'The Covid Pandemic: The Time Capsule of the First 6 Months: An International Perspective' (2020) 39(2) M&L 89.

Wojtyczek, K., *Granice ingerencji ustawodawczej w sferę praw człowieka w Konstytucji RP* (Zakamycze, Kraków 1999).

2 Common Remote Access to Public Spatial Data in a Pandemic Situation on the Example of the Geoportal

Mateusz Badowski

2.1 Introduction

The sanitary-epidemiological rules introduced in the wake of the COVID-19 pandemic have reformulated the conditions for direct human interactions. The pandemic also led to difficulties in accessing various types of data, both private and public, including spatial data. The study aims to evaluate the effectiveness of the adopted technical and legal solutions to ensure common remote access to spatial data through the Geoportal (geoportal.gov.pl) during the pandemic.

Spatial data is a term defined among others by the so-called INSPIRE-Directive.[1] Spatial data means any data directly or indirectly referenced to a specific location or geographical area.[2] In other words, spatial data can be shown on a map. As the name suggests, their most important feature is the spatial reference.[3] The time-consuming and costly task of searching for existing spatial data or checking whether it can be used for a particular purpose was identified as the main obstacle to making full use of available data (No. 15 of Preamble of INSPIRE-Directive). The main goal of the INSPIRE-Directive is to counteract obstacles to access to specific spatial data.[4]

The distinction between public and private spatial data is fundamental. This division is dichotomous. Public data is data processed in connection with the performance of public tasks. Other data is private data. Therefore, all data available through public registers or public infrastructure (e.g., through the Geoportal), even created by private entities and voluntarily provided to the entity performing

1 Directive (EU) No 2007/2/EC establishing an Infrastructure for Spatial Information in the European Community (INSPIRE) [2007] OJ L 108/1.

2 Art. 3(2) INSPIRE-Directive and Art. 3 (1) Law of 4.03.2010 on spatial information infrastructure, JoL item 214, further uiip.

3 S. Markus, *Wissenschaftlicher Beitrag für den Aufbau einer Geodateninfrastruktur zur Lösung von Aufgaben des E-Government* (ETH Zurich 2008) 20.

4 M. Badowski, 'Legal limitations of public access to spatial data in Germany' in G. Szpor, A. Gryszczyńska (eds.), *Access to spatial data and its limitations. Legal* aspects (GIS Forum. Croatia 2015), 40–49.

DOI: 10.4324/9781003263968-22

public tasks, are public data. At the same time, such provision does not affect the private legal protection of such data and the right to it.[5]

Access to private data is not a homogeneous category. Unless a specific provision so provides, private data holders are not obliged to make the data available or otherwise disclose it. This principle follows, for example, from Art. 51(1) Constitution, according to which no one may be obliged otherwise than by law to disclose information concerning his or her person. However, nothing stands in the way of providing access to data collected (or more broadly processed) by private entities without an explicit obligation as part of their business activities (cf. services provided, e.g., by Google Maps), or without a purpose explicitly aimed at obtaining a financial benefit (e.g., exchange of interesting trails by members of off-road groups and associations, cf. the existing Facebook group "Szlaki OFF ROAD").[6] Thus, an entity can effectively commit to disclosing certain data about itself.[7]

Consequently, private data may be disclosed based on mandatory law (when a specific provision so provides) or under civil law and freedom of contract.[8] Voluntary access rules may apply to the conclusion of the contract, the freedom of choice of the contracting party and the form of the transaction.[9] Therefore, they may also be included in soft law regulations, such as codes of good practice. An example of such a regulation is the German Code of Personal Data Protection in Spatial Data Services.[10]

Data are available to the public (common availability) if an indefinite group of people has more than a purely theoretical right to get acquainted with them. At the same time, it should be noted that the right of public access does not necessarily imply the right to disseminate or use the acquired data.[11] The obligation to make public data available consists not only in the availability of certain data to the recipient, but at least – as a rule – implies the necessity for active action on the part of the providing body, which consists in providing a certain scope of data to the interested party, upon his/her request.[12]

5 M. Badowski,' Dostęp i wykorzystywanie publicznych danych przestrzennych w świetle prawa niemieckiego' in G. Szpor, K. Czaplicki, *Internet. Informacja przestrzenna. Spatial information* (C.H. Beck 2018), 17.

6 <https://www.facebook.com/groups/1414156225341430> (1.11.2021).

7 M. Wild, 'Art. 51' in M. Safjan, L. Bosek (eds.), *Konstytucja RP. Tom I. Komentarz do art. 1–86* (C.H. Beck 2016), 15.

8 Art. 353[1] of the Act of 23.04.1964 Civil Code, JoL 2020 item 1740.

9 K. Pietrzykowski, *Kodeks cywilny. T. I. Komentarz. Art. 1–449* (10th edn, C.H. Beck 2020), Art. 353[1] no. 1.

10 Datenschutzkodex für Geodatendienste <https://geodatenkodex.de/> (1.11.2021); M. Badowski,' Niemiecki Kodeks ochrony danych osobowych w usługach danych przestrzennych' in J. Gołaczyński (ed), *Wybrane dobre praktyki w zakresie usług elektronicznyc* (C.H. Beck 2016), 131–152.

11 R. Püschel, H. Sigmar, *Handbuch zu Grundbuch und Liegenschaftskataster. Leitfaden für die bayerischen Kommunen mit zahlreichen Beispielen und Praxishinweisen* (IBOORBERG 2008), 101.

12 Cf. Judgment of SAC of 12.09.2013, I OSK 777/13, Legalis 1330467.

Public data are made available in two ways: passive or active. Passive access is understood as making data available upon request after it has been prepared for the recipient, if only in the form of a statement, an answer to a question in the mode of access to public information[13] or environmental information.[14] Active sharing is understood as the preparation of data to be made available in the form of registers or infrastructures, even if the data sharing process itself is of a request nature. As an example, it can be mentioned the application for access to the data contained in the cadastral survey from the Register of Land and Buildings.[15] An example of remote access to public data without an application can be access to the service of viewing maps of Register of Land and Buildings located on the Geoportal.[16]

This chapter examines the activities of the Central Office of Geodesy and Cartography under conditions of the ongoing pandemic from the point of view of common remote access to spatial data through Geoportal. The pandemic's initial time, March–July 2020, was taken as the reference period and compared with the current state. The analysis concerns data and services made available through this service, both related to the development of the pandemic (data on infections, inspectorates of the National Sanitary Inspectorate, or infectious hospitals) and data not related to this phenomenon (making new data or services available during the pandemic). The scope of the study also included activities to promote the use of Geoportal (publication of instructional videos on YouTube, updating the website, or launching a new version of the mobile application Geoportal Mobile), in the context of record hits to the portal and the already planned legal changes that came into force in and affect the availability of public spatial data. The analysis was conducted using empirical, dogmatic and historical methods.

Conducted research serves to verify the thesis that significant computerisation of public administration units' activities in the field of common automated access to spatial data and services and the introduced changes in legal regulations allowed avoiding negative effects of COVID-19 pandemic on accessibility to public spatial data through the Geoportal.

2.2 Geoportal as a point of common access to public data

The project of creating the Geoportal dates to 2005 when the Geoportal.gov.pl project was launched. The project was implemented under the Sectoral Operational Program – Improvement of the Competitiveness of Enterprises 2004–2006. Its main goal was to improve the competitiveness of enterprises by providing online

13 Art. 2(1) of the Access Act.

14 Art. 4 of the Act of 3.10.2008 on providing information on the environment and its protection, public participation in environmental protection and environmental impact assessments, JoL 2021, item 247.

15 Art. 24 (4) of the Act of 17.05.1989 Geodetic and Cartographic Law, JoL 2021, item 1990, further pgik).

16 <geoportal.gov.pl>, 1.11.2021.

services based on spatial data, including cadastral data and metadata ("metadata" is defined in Art. 3 no. 4 uiip, as data that describe data sets and services, e.g., spatial data, and make it possible to discover, inventory and use these data and services). Other important objectives included developing entrepreneurship, improving innovativeness and competitiveness of enterprises, streamlining of decision-making processes, and modernisation of public administration work resulting in time and cost savings both in the public and private sector.[17]

The continuation and extension of the Geoportal project is Geoportal 2 (now commonly known as Geoportal), which was started in 2009. This project's scope included work related to the implementation of the INSPIRE-Directive, as required by the Spatial Information Infrastructure Law. Geoportal acts as a central access point to search services for viewing, downloading, transformation, and services that allow running these services on INSPIRE spatial data. INSPIRE spatial data processed within the Geoportal to refer to (or are related to) the territory of Poland, are in electronic form, are maintained by (or on behalf of) a public administration body or a third party which has been given the opportunity to be included in the infrastructure for spatial information and belong to one of the spatial data themes defined in the annex to the law on spatial information infrastructure (cf. Art. 4 sec. 1 uiip). The Chief Geodesist of Poland is responsible for creating and maintaining the Geoportal (cf. Art. 13 sec. 1 uiip).

Geoportal remains the fourth most visited public portal.[18] On its maps one can find, among other things, layers of the State Register of Borders, addresses and streets, land and building registry data, data on land development, topographic objects, spatial development plans, real estate prices, public utilities, land relief as well as data obtained from other institutions regarding e.g., existing flood risks and threats. A new layer "Coronavirus" was added during the COVID-19 pandemic.

As of early 2020 the Geoportal enjoyed a high interest of about 600,000 page views per month, when in 2021 it increased by about 30% to 800,000 page views per month. November 2020 saw the year's highest monthly visitation rate of nearly 718,000, and in 2021, the portal was visited nearly 1 million times e.g., in April (as of 1 November 2021). Subsequent months during the pandemic period clearly show unabated, significantly higher interest in the portal continuing even during the holiday break.[19] Increased traffic was observed already from March 2020, when the previous record of visits to the portal was broken for the first time.[20] These data only confirm how important it is to have common access to public spatial data, regardless of the duration of the pandemic.

17 <https://www.geoportal.gov.pl/o-geoportalu/informacje-o-projekcie>, (1.11.2021).

18 <https://widok.gov.pl/statistics/>, (1.11.2021).

19 <https://widok.gov.pl/statistics/geoportal-krajowy/>, (1.11.2021).

20 'Rekordowa liczba odwiedzin serwisu geoportal.gov.pl – Aktualności z 03.04.2020' <www.geoportal.gov.pl>, (1.11.2021).

2.3 Data shared in the Geoportal during the pandemic

2.3.1 Coronavirus-related data, services and recommendations made available on the Geoportal

On 13 March 2020, a new publicly accessible "Coronavirus" layer was added to the Geoportal with data pertaining to the fight against COVID-19. It began by publishing information on the location of infectious disease hospitals.[21] The tab included existing infectious diseases hospitals, hospitals with infectious diseases wards and hospitals planned for conversion into infectious diseases hospitals – further subdivided into existing infectious diseases hospitals, hospitals adapted to this purpose and hospitals with infectious diseases wards. After selecting a particular institution, basic object data retrieved from the Healthcare Information Systems Center were displayed, including the name of the institution, its address and contact phone numbers. Two days later, in the "Coronavirus" layer, further functionalities were added (the "Infections" tab), which made it possible to see the map of hourly updated COVID-19 infection status at the level of provinces and individual districts.[22] On 16 March 2020, the Geoportal included the location of State Sanitary Inspection facilities, also accessible from the "Coronavirus" layer.[23] Currently, the service is no longer available to the same extent. The functionality of this "Coronavirus layer" is currently limited only to information about large-format stores.

On 19 March 2020, the guidelines of the Chief Geodesist of the Country recommending the implementation of preventive measures for surveyors when performing geodetic and cartographic work and for employees of the Geodetic and Cartographic Service maintaining the National Geodetic and Cartographic Resource, which were agreed with the Chief Sanitary Inspector, were communicated through the Geoportal website. The introduced rules corresponded to the principles of the so-called "social distance."[24] At the same time, the bodies of the Geodetic and Cartographic Service managing the state geodetic and cartographic resource were instructed, with respect to maintaining and providing access to the state geodetic and cartographic resource, to undertake technical and organisational actions concerning providing access to the materials of the state geodetic and cartographic resource and verification of the results of geodetic work in such a manner that it would not cause administrative barriers in the investment process, real estate trade or business activity. In particular, this concerned:

- launching all possible ways of receiving applications and making data available through e-services;

21 'Warstwa „Koronawirus" w Geoportalu – Aktualności z dnia 13.03.2020' <www.geoportal.gov.pl> (1.11.2021).

22 'Mapa aktualnego stanu zakażeń wirusem COVID-19 w geoportalu – Aktualności z 15.03.2020' <www.geoportal.gov.pl> (1.11.2021).

23 'W Geoportalu lokalizacje placówek Państwowej Inspekcji Sanitarnej – Aktualności z 16.03.2020' <www.geoportal.gov.pl> (1.11.2021).

24 'Wytyczne GGK w związku z rozprzestrzenianiem się koronawirusa – Aktualności z 19.03.2020' <www.geoportal.gov.pl> (1.11.2021).

- ensuring the widest possible access to data contained in the National Geodetic and Cartographic Resource by means of e-services;
- with regard to the commenced modernisation of the land and building register, for procedural activities (notifications, submitting comments, filing objections) using e-services in a supportive manner, as well as the starosty's websites, and enabling the extension of deadlines for these works;
- taking other technical and organisational measures aimed at counteracting the spread of COVID-19 in cooperation with the contractors for surveying works. If the need arose, it was necessary to introduce, in consultation with the contractors for geodetic works, annexes to the contracts concluded for the execution of public procurement.[25]

The implemented recommendations were not always carried out as expected, therefore in connection with signals of major difficulties in servicing geodetic work related to the coronavirus pandemic, the Chief Surveyor of Poland issued a letter to Heads of District and City Presidents asking them to make every effort to support geodetic contractors in carrying out their tasks, which would lead to streamlining the work of documentation centres in such difficult circumstances. Particular attention was drawn to the necessity of launching all possible computerised access to the geodetic and cartographic resource and organising remote work for employees of geodetic and cartographic documentation centres.[26]

2.3.2 Accessibility to the new data

Despite existing difficulties, the pandemic did not cause discontinuation of access to new data not related to epidemiological situation. For example, the "Major Groundwater Reservoirs" layer was added to supplement the data available from the Polish Geological Institute,[27] the layer "Register of Applications, Decisions and Notifications" indicating the location and data on applications, decisions and notifications in construction matters,[28] within the group of layer "Archival data" a new subgroup "Thematic maps" has been added (in subgroup "Thematic maps" there are five layers: administrative, landscape, hydrographic, sozologic, general geographic maps),[29] while in the group of layer "Specialized geodetic information" a new subgroup "ZSIN" (**Z**integrowany **S**ystem **I**nformacji o **N**ieruchomościach – Integrated Property Information System) was added, and in it the layer "State Treasury Land" presenting the location of the State Treasury

25 <Https://www.geoportal.gov.pl/documents/10179/1041743/Wytyczne+GGK+w+zwi%C4%85zku+z+rozprzestrzenianiem+si%C4%99+koronawirusa.pdf/d6ff5696-d87f-4f6a-b329-86366845929a>, (1.11.2021).

26 'GGK apeluje do powiatów o usprawnienie pracy ośrodków dokumentacji – Aktualności z 24.03.2020' <www.geoportal.gov.pl> (1.11.2021).

27 'Główne zbiorniki wód podziemnych w Geoportalu – Aktualności z 27.03.2020' <www.geoportal.gov.pl> (1.11.2021).

28 'Pozwolenia na budowę w Geoportalu – Aktualności z 17.04.2020' <www.geoportal.gov.pl> (1.11.2021).

29 Cf. 'Archiwalne mapy tematyczne w Geoportalu – Aktualności z 12.05.2020 <www.geoportal.gov.pl> (1.11.2021).

Land.[30] In the Integrated Property Information System, two new layers "Land Use" and "Classification Contours" were added within the layer group "National Land Records Integration."[31] The basic altitude matrix data for a large part of the counties were also updated[32] and new orthophotos have been added.[33] Some available services have also been updated, e.g., BDOT10k datasets for 20 counties.[34] New contracts for updating the BDOT10k database were also signed.[35] The functionality of some services, e.g., the service of Numerical Terrain Model was extended by presentation of information concerning coordinates of a point in the WGS84 system[36] and the Universal Geocoding Service has been supplemented with a new feature that enables users to locate geographic objects from the National Register of Geographic Names.[37]

The search engine for the points of the basic geodesic network was also launched[38] and land parcel search engine, thanks to which the users have gained the possibility of easier search (location) of land parcels based on all county land and building registry databases.[39] Contracts were also signed for the development of new data, e.g., contracts for the development of an orthophotomap[40] or airborne laser scanning data acquisition contracts.[41]

During the pandemic the land register numbers available on the Geoportal were removed. It is worth noting this fact, even though the cause was not the virus itself, and the change introduced was aimed at broader protection of personal data. In connection with the order of the President of the Office for Personal Data Protection of 6 April 2020,[42] according to which it is forbidden to disclose land and mortgage register numbers in the geoportal.gov.pl service, despite the appeal of the above mentioned decision to the administrative court, on the website in the

30 'Grunty Skarbu Państwa w Geoportalu – Aktualności z 05.06.2020' <www.geoportal.gov.pl> (1.11.2021).

31 'Użytki gruntowe i kontury klasyfikacyjne z KIEG widoczne także w ZSIN – Aktualności z 19.06.2020' <www.geoportal.gov.pl> (1.11.2021).

32 'Aktualizacja danych podstawowej osnowy wysokościowej dla 256 powiatów – Aktualności z18.06.2020' <www.geoportal.gov.pl> (1.11.2021).

33 'Nowe ortofotomapy w PZGIK – Aktualności z 30.06.2020' <www.geoportal.gov.pl> (1.11.2021).

34 'Aktualizacja baz BDOT10k – Aktualności z 07.04.2020' <www.geoportal.gov.pl> (1.11.2021).

35 'Umowy GUGiK na aktualizację BDOT10k w 2020 roku – Aktualności z 15.04.2020' <www.geoportal.gov.pl> (1.11.2021).

36 'Rozszerzenie funkcjonalności usługi NMT – Aktualności z 23.04.2020' <www.geoportal.gov.pl> (1.11.2021).

37 'Nowa funkcjonalność w Uniwersalnej Usłudze Geokodowania – Aktualności z 22.05.2020' <www.geoportal.gov.pl> (1.11.2021).

38 'Wyszukiwanie punktów osnowy geodezyjnej dostępne w Geoportalu Krajowym – Aktualności z 31.03.2020' <www.geoportal.gov.pl> (1.11.2021).

39 'Ulepszone wyszukiwanie działek w portalu ZSIN – Aktualności z 08.05.2020' <www.geoportal.gov.pl> (1.11.2021).

40 'Umowy GUGIK na opracowanie ortofotomapy w 2020 roku – Aktualności z 07.04.2020' <www.geoportal.gov.pl> (1.11.2021).

41 'Umowy GUGIK na skanowanie laserowe – Aktualności z 16.04.2020' <www.geoportal.gov.pl> (1.11.2021).

42 No. DKN.5112.13.2020 <https://www.uodo.gov.pl/pl/file/2819> (1.11.2021).

place of the land and mortgage register number the following information was displayed: "The numbers of the land and mortgage registers have been hidden on the basis of the decision of the President of the Office for Personal Data Protection of 6.04.2020 until an administrative decision is issued in the pending proceedings." The Chief Land Surveyor appealed against the decision of the President of the Office for Harmonisation in the Internal Market prohibiting access to land and mortgage register numbers, however, the Voivodship Administrative Court in Warsaw refused to suspend the execution of the appealed decision restricting the processing of personal data in the scope of land and mortgage register numbers. The dispute over this issue has not yet been definitively concluded.

2.4 The use of the Geoportal and activities promoting it

Geoportal, on one hand a source of commonly used data, on the other hand, however, multi-layered specialised data, is still not the most intuitive service for an inexperienced user, among various public and private services. The use of the service still requires some preparation, both technical and substantive. Although the situation is improving and to facilitate and improve the operation of the geoportal .gov.pl homepage it is being updated.

Common access to search and browsing services using a standard web browser, without any additional plugins, using computers, tablets or smartphones should be considered as desirable. However, the intuitiveness of the service from the point of view of a common user needs still improvement. There are other services, which of course do not contain as much data, but also provide other spatial data services, which manage to provide spatial data in a more user-friendly way for the non-advanced user. We are talking here about a global player like Google and its map service. As an example, let's use probably the most frequently used address search service. In the Google Maps service, it is enough to enter even a part of the address and the system finds the searched city or street without any problem. Finding a city or a specific street through the Geoportal has recently been significantly facilitated, but until now it required the use of appropriate formulas, otherwise the search result did not give a result. It is still necessary to select the appropriate search range from the search of territorial units. The service was made available in October 2021. It allows to find units of the basic, three-level territorial division of the country (municipalities, counties, provinces) along with their spatial location,[43] place names and physiographic objects – this service also became available at the beginning of October 2021 and makes it possible to find objects in the National Register of Geographic Names (PRNG) database along with their spatial location.[44] The search mechanism is now much more intuitive, and it is

43 Wyszukiwanie jednostek terytorialnych w serwisie www.geoportal.gov.pl – Aktualności z 7.10.2021' <www.geoportal.gov.pl> (1.11.2021).

44 'Nowe wyszukiwania na podstawie PRNG w serwisie www.geoportal.gov.pl – Aktualności z 5.10.2021' <www.geoportal.gov.pl> (1.11.2021).

now possible to search for a particular street without specifying the building number. Although there is still an obligation to use the appropriate search formula, e.g., for exact addresses (town, street number), but without providing the number now the street will be found.

After almost a year since the previous publication, from 16 March 2020, more instructional videos were added to YouTube to make using the Geoportal easier and clearer. A total of 22 videos were added in 2020 and 2021, which cover some of the Geoportal's functionalities such as searching by coordinates, adding a link to the composition of a specific map, printing a map, determining the terrain profile, comparing orthophotos over time, determining the volume of land masses, basic information about searching in the Geoportal (general, addresses and parcels), checking the zoning arrangements, analysing visibility along a set line and area visibility, as well as instruction for downloading some data.[45]

A new version of Geoportal Mobile application has also been made available – for users of mobile devices with Android operating systems, adapted to the 64-bit version of the operating systems. The main functionality of the new viewer is the full use of the application to access spatial data services provided by the Head Office of Geodesy and Cartography.[46] A new map composition of www.geoportal.gov.pl has also been launched, adjusted to Android and iOS mobile devices. The composition starts automatically when accessing www.geoportal.gov.pl from such a device and can always be launched independently at https://mapy.geoportal.gov.pl/mobile.[47]

2.5 Changes in existing regulations and common availability of public spatial data

2.5.1 Changes made by the Shield 4.0

The provisions of Shield 4.0 were included in the Law of 19 June 2020 on interest subsidies for bank loans granted to entrepreneurs affected by COVID-19 and on simplified proceedings for approval of the arrangement in connection with the occurrence of COVID-19.[48] The Act amended 55 laws, but its main objectives were the introduction of interest rate subsidies for bank loans granted to entrepreneurs who find themselves in a difficult financial situation due to bearing the negative economic consequences resulting from the spread of the COVID-19 infectious disease, actions taken to prevent, prevent and combat it, and changes in commercial law as regards the rules for conducting simplified restructuring proceedings in connection with the occurrence of COVID-19 (Art. 1 Shield 4.0).

45 <https://www.youtube.com/user/GUGiKPL> (1.11.2021).

46 <https://play.google.com/store/apps/details?id=pl.gispartner.imapmobile>, 15.11.2021, although the app itself gets a rather average rating of 3.4 out of 5 out of 3,316 ratings.

47 'Uruchomienie nowej aplikacji mapowej przystosowanej do obsługi na urządzeniach mobilnych – Aktualności z 26.06 <www.geoportal.gov.pl> (1.11.2021).

48 JoL 2020, item 1086, (Shield 4.0).

From the standpoint of the Geodetic and Cartographic Law and availability of spatial data, the discussed Act introduced two key changes. First, it allows individuals performing independent functions in the field of geodesy and cartography to certify as true to the original copies of protocols, maps, and other documents that they prepare and submit to the state geodetic and cartographic resource together with the results of geodetic work (Art. 29 of Shield 4.0, conferring such powers based on Art. 42 sec. 4 pgik). Such authorisation is a key element allowing surveyors to submit electronic documentation as part of the results of surveying work and makes it possible for a surveyor to prepare a completely electronic, consistent document, authenticated in its entirety by the work contractor. The introduced change unifies procedures used in various offices and allows for far-reaching automation of processes.[49] These provisions will remain in effect even after the COVID-19 pandemic ends, and their long-awaited introduction should be considered an important step towards digitising investment processes.

Second, to facilitate investment processes during an epidemic threat or outbreak, the obligation to report surveying works and communicate the results of surveying works related to the delineation of a building or land development network was suspended. The deadline for notification of surveying works has been extended to ten working days from the date of commencement of the works. An obligation was imposed on administrative bodies to provide information on the verification of surveying works by electronic means of communication. Moreover, the collection of fees for accessing data sets, such as orthophotomaps, data from the state register of basic geodetic, gravimetric and magnetic grids, detailed geodetic grids, data concerning registered land plots as regards their identifiers and geometry, and concerning buildings as regards their identifiers, geometry and type according to the Classification of Fixed Assets, was suspended (Art. 77 sec. 49 of Shield 4.0, introducing Art. 15zzzia in the COVID-19 Act). The introduction of the changes in question was intended to streamline the operation of surveying in the situation caused by the COVID-19 outbreak. It also had the effect of ensuring that businesses continue to operate, and jobs are maintained, with the intention of limiting the negative effects of the pandemic.[50] This is the first stage of the “release” of geodetic and cartographic data. The next stage began on 31 July 2020 and stems from a law primarily amending the Geodetic and Cartographic Law.

2.5.2 Amendments to the Geodetic and Cartographic Law

During the COVID-19 pandemic, the Geodetic and Cartographic Law was amended several times. The amendment concerned the certification of conformity with the original of documents to be transferred to the National Geodetic and

49 Justification of the Shield 4.0, Sejm, Druk no. 382, 22.5.2020, p. 19 <https://www.sejm.gov.pl/Sejm9.nsf/druk.xsp?nr=382> (1.11.2021).

50 Justification (n 53), 72–73.

Cartographic Resource together with the results of geodetic work by persons performing independent functions in the field of geodesy and cartography and was introduced by the Shield 4.0 Act.

The purpose of the following, among others, introduced by the Act of 16 April 2020 amending the Act – Geodetic and Cartographic Law and certain other Acts.[51] The purpose of the Act is to eliminate excessive constraints, including bureaucratic ones, in the process of geodetic and cartographic works, related to, among others, reporting of geodetic and cartographic works, providing access to the materials of the state geodetic and cartographic resource (pzgik), fees for the said access, submission of results of geodetic and cartographic works, and their verification. In addition, the Act introduced changes in the procedure for obtaining professional licences in the field of geodesy and cartography and contains new provisions to speed up the investment process by regulating the legal grounds for providing access to planning documents using geoinformation techniques.[52] However, this change was planned even before the epidemiological emergency was conducted. Indeed, the draft of this law was submitted to the Sejm on 20 December 2019.

From the standpoint of remote access to public spatial data, the most significant changes introduced by the Act amending the Polish Geodetic and Cartographic Law involve expanding the catalogue of data from the national geodetic and cartographic resource, which are available free of charge. Pursuant to the principle set forth in Art. 40a sec. 1 of the Polish Geodetic and Cartographic Act, authorities maintaining the National Geodetic and Cartographic Resource register provide access to the resource material against a fee. However, as of 31 July 2020 the catalogue of data available free of charge has been significantly extended. There has been introduced resignation from paying for access to the pzgik data concerning basic and detailed matrixes, orthophotomap, digital terrain model, as well as the data from the database of topographic objects of the level of detail that enables creation of standard cartographic studies, data sets concerning registered land parcels as regards their identifiers and geometry, datasets relating to buildings in terms of their identifiers, geometry and type according to the Classification of Fixed Assets, making available collective datasets of data covered by the land and building register, as well as special cartographic studies in the form of e-typological maps (cf. Art. 40a sec. 2 no. 1 lit. c–j, Art. 40c sec. 5 and attachment – table no. 1, no. 3–5, no. 14 and no. 17 pos. 4–5 pgik). In addition, it is worth noting that the exemption from the charges for the services of "ASG-EUPOS" system in the field of development of satellite observation data was introduced. Entities included in the educational system and universities for educational purposes received subjective exemption from the fees for services of the "ASG-EUPOS" system (Art. 40b sec. 1a no. 1-2 pgik). Such actions should be unequivocally supported, as the data collected by the public administration, which is made available free of charge, can thus be used by other entities to create innovative services. These data

51 JoL 2020, item 782, further the Act amending pgik.

52 Justification (n 53), 1.

can also provide a foundation for the creation of innovative goods and products that stimulate the economy by creating new jobs and encouraging investment in industry and business.[53]

2.6 Conclusions

The study examined the activities of the Central Office of Geodesy and Cartography in conditions of the ongoing pandemic from the perspective of common remote access to spatial data through the Geoportal. The analysis concerned data and services made available through this service, both related to the development of the pandemic (data about infections, inspectorates of the National Sanitary Inspectorate, or infectious diseases hospitals), and data not related to this phenomenon (making available new data or services during the pandemic). The scope of the study also included activities to promote the use of Geoportal (publication of instructional videos on YouTube, updating the website, or launching a new version of the mobile application Geoportal Mobile) in the context of record hits to the portal. Also analysed were the legal changes (Shield 4.0 and the Act amending the Geodetic and Cartographic Law) that came into force in the reference period during the pandemic.

Conducted research states that thanks to the promoted computerisation of public administration units' activities in the field of common automated access to spatial data and services, the pandemic period did not have a significant negative impact on the remote common accessibility to public spatial data. Analysed statistical data allows even to state that this period contributed to the popularisation of geoportal.gov.pl service among Internet users, thus increasing the availability of public spatial data. Short research period does not allow to analysis continuity of this phenomenon, but it can be assumed that the mentioned popularisation will have a permanent character. Certainly, charges for downloading some data were also abolished during the pandemic will contribute to this process. An important part of data necessary in practice was made permanently available free of charge, however, this fact cannot be associated with the ongoing pandemic, but with the already planned deliberate action of the legislator.

Geoportal, as a service commonly used also by persons not professionally engaged in geodesy and cartography could be made more intuitive. Despite the ever-increasing amount of data available through this portal, using search engines on this site is quite difficult, and geoportal.gov.pl itself seems to be quite complicated for the untrained user. Although the GUGiK boasts about the training courses organised by the Office, they were conducted only for the employees of various ministries[54] and other levels of government.[55] At the same time, it

53 Justification (n 53), 17.

54 'Blisko 400 osób wzięło już udział w szkoleniach z Geoportalu – Aktualności z 25.05.2020' <www.geoportal.gov .pl>, (1.11.2021).

55 'Szósta już sesja szkoleniowa Projektu POWER zakończona – Aktualności z 7.08.2020'.

should be mentioned that the information campaign containing answers to questions posed during the videoconference on the changes in the Polish Geodetic and Cartographic Code for representatives of the Geodetic and Cartographic Service and geodetic contractors. Approximately 1,800 participants took part in the videoconference, and 170 questions were answered in 17 sessions.[56]

However, there is no widespread information campaign about the opportunities offered by the spatial data services available through the Geoportal, for example through instructional videos describing the basic functionality or webinars. This is not changed by the inclusion of videos related to changes in the law regarding the investment and construction process, because of changes in the geodesic and cartographic law.[57] These are strictly training publications posted on social media that are more accessible than a multi-page user manual, which, it should be noted, was not updated the last time the website was refreshed.[58] However, a step in the right direction has been made by publishing videos on YouTube.

Works cited

Badowski, M., 'Dostęp i wykorzystywanie publicznych danych przestrzennych w świetle prawa niemieckiego' in (eds.) Grażyna Szpor and Kamil Czaplicki, *Internet. Informacja przestrzenna. Spatial information* (C.H. Beck, Warsaw 2018), 15–23.

Badowski, M., 'Niemiecki Kodeks ochrony danych osobowych w usługach danych przestrzennych' in ed. Jacek Gołaczyński, *Wybrane dobre praktyki w zakresie usług elektronicznych* (C.H. Beck 2016), 131–152.

Pietrzykowski, K., *Kodeks cywilny. T. I. Komentarz. Art. 1–449* (10 ed. C.H. Beck 2020).

Püschel, R., and Harreiter, S., *Handbuch zu Grundbuch und Liegenschaftskataster. Leitfaden für die bayerischen Kommunen mit zahlreichen Beispielen und Praxishinweisen* (Boorberg, Stuttgart 2008).

Safjan, M., and Bosek, L., *Konstytucja RP. Tom I. Komentarz do art. 1–86* (C.H. Beck 2016).

Seifert, M., *Wissenschaftlicher Beitrag für den Aufbau einer Geodateninfrastruktur zur Lösung von Aufgaben des E-Government* (ETH Zürich 2008).

Szpor, G., and Gryszczyńska, A., *Access to spatial Data and its Limitations. Legal Aspects* (Croatian Information Technology Society 2015).

56 'Siedemnasta i ostatnia część odpowiedzi na pytania zadane podczas wideokonferencji – Aktualności z 11.08.2020' <www.geoportal.gov.pl> (1.11.2021).

57 <https://www.youtube.com/watch?v=U_4v7BR9lJ4> (1.11.2021).

58 <https://opendata.geoportal.gov.pl/geoportal/Geoportal_MaterialySzkoleniowe.pdf> (1.11.2021).

3 Verification of Identity in a Pandemic

Kamil Czaplicki

3.1 Introduction

The purpose of this chapter is to analyse techniques and methods for identifying identity under pandemic conditions. The SARS-CoV-2 virus has affected every area of human activity unprecedentedly. It has also affected the process of identity verification and is associated with the mandated coverage of the nose and mouth public places. The fight against the COVID-19 pandemic and the so-called lockdown of many countries and societies did not limit the processes of identity confirmation but strengthened them even more. Widespread monitoring of people in public places, registration of exits from home, control of movement or reasons for leaving home have never been used in the EU countries. State-of-the-art devices such as drones or mobile applications were used for this purpose. The words of J.G. Fichte from 1796 about identification ring true:

> the basic principle of a state well run by the police is that every citizen should be recognized at every place and at every time as a particular person, is current. No one can be unknown to the police. The above goal can only be achieved in the following ways. Everyone should always carry with him a document signed by the nearest government representative in which his person will be carefully described. No one should therefore be admitted in any place without disclosing based on the document his name and his last place of residence.[1]

The ubiquitous control associated with the movement of populations during a pandemic had a profound effect on many and was the cause of much anxiety and even mental health problems. European societies, weaned from strict controls, suddenly had to submit to the rigours of lockdown. The impact was also noticeable in the summer of 2020 and 2021 when many countries began to loosen restrictions, and part of the population started to behave irrationally, leading to the re-development of the pandemic.

This chapter characterises and evaluates the validity of basic ID methods and techniques.

DOI: 10.4324/9781003263968-23

Unfortunately, as shown by the experience of several months of combating the pandemic, as well as the organisation of elections or protests at that time, not all methods and techniques of identity identification used in different countries meet the standards of correct, safe and effective identity identification. In this chapter, we assume that identity verification based on biometric techniques is the safest method of identity verification during a pandemic. The chapter uses comparative and dogmatic methods.

3.2 The concept and meaning of identity identification

The term "identification" is ambiguous, differently understood in different scientific fields. It can be found in psychology, sociology, engineering and legal sciences. Although the term appears in many legal acts of the EU and is one of the basic terms of law, it has not been officially defined in legal acts of the EU so far. The e-IDAS defines the term "electronic identification" as the process of using data in an electronic form identifying a person, uniquely representing a natural or legal person, or a natural person representing a legal person. The term "electronic identification" means as a tangible or intangible entity containing data identifying a person, i.e., a set of data enabling the identification of that person and used for authentication purposes for an online service.

In this chapter, the term "identification" will be understood as a multi-level process to recognise a particular person from a group of other people.[2]

It is also worth noting that the concept of identification is often confused with the concept of authentication. However, these are not synonyms and should not be used interchangeably. Identification is the process of automated recognition of a specific user, and authentication is the action of verifying the declared identity of the individual. The identification and authentication process requires the involvement of at least two entities – the identified (authenticated) and the identifier (authenticator). The identified (authenticated) is a person subject to the identification (authentication) process, and the identifier (authenticator) is an entity that, based on legal regulations or a contract, is entitled to carry out the identification (authentication) process. It should also be noted that authentication belongs to IT terminology and is usually used in the context of IT systems. We should share the view expressed by G. Szpor that IT terminology is difficult for lawyers to understand due to IT professionalism.[3]

Identification of identity and its authentication is based on three methods – based on what we know, based on what we have and based on who we are.[4] Methods based on what we know are methods based on PINs, codes, passwords, which confirms our identity. Methods based on what we have are identification methods based, for example, on cards or identity documents whose possession confirms our identity, and methods based on who we are biometric methods that use biometric data to verify identity.

Nowadays, more and more often, multimodal systems are used, i.e., systems that combine two or three methods of identification and authentication – e.g., a combination of a technique based on what we know and what we have. Such solutions provide more security than single-component systems[5] Today, most identification and authentication systems based on what we have also referred to as a knowledge element (e.g., PIN) without which it is not possible, for example, to use the electronic signature certificate stored on a processor card or the signature stored on electronic identity cards implemented in many EU countries. Multi-component identification is increasingly used on the Internet. The existing PIN verification is enriched by, e.g., an SMS sent to a smartphone. It is increasingly used on social networking sites and auction portals. Despite some inconvenience, this method provides much higher security. The inconvenience consists mainly in the impossibility of logging in, e.g., to a social networking site in case of lack of access to the phone (e.g., its discharging or theft). However, it is worth noting that the positive sides of multi-component identification related to increasing its security level outweigh its inconvenience many times over. Multi-component identification protects against identity theft and impersonation. It also provides greater privacy and control over access to resources. The legislation most broadly regulating identification and authentication is the e-IDAS. The e-IDAS Regulation identifies three levels of security for electronic identification systems – low, medium and high. Security levels mean the degree to which an electronic identification means can be trusted to establish a person's identity, thereby providing confidence that the person providing the identity is the person to whom the identity has been assigned. A security level depends on the degree of confidence that an electronic identification medium offers as to the identity of a person being provided or reported, considering the processes, management activities and technical safeguards in place. Low-security level refers, in the context of an electronic identification system, to an electronic identification means that provides a limited degree of confidence in a person's claimed or reported identity and is characterised in terms of the technical specifications, standards and procedures associated with it, including technical safeguards designed to reduce the risk of identity impersonation or modification. Medium security level refers, in the context of an electronic identification system, to an electronic identification means that provides a medium degree of confidence in a person's asserted or claimed identity and is characterised concerning technical specifications, standards and procedures associated with it, including technical safeguards designed to reduce the risk of identity impersonation or modification significantly, and high level of security refers, in the context of an electronic identification scheme, to an electronic identification means that provides a higher degree of confidence in the person's asserted or claimed identity than an electronic identification means with a medium level of assurance and is characterised in terms of the technical specifications, standards and procedures associated with it, including technical safeguards designed to prevent identity impersonation or modification. Multimodal identification methods provide the highest level of security.[6]

3.3 The impact of a pandemic on the identification process

The COVID-19 pandemic highlighted previously unknown flaws in standard identification methods.[7] The widespread use of masks covering the mouth and nose, in addition to the glasses worn by some individuals, essentially completely masked the person's image, making it impossible for both controllers and remote ID systems to recognise the image. As indicated in the literature, wearing masks had a negative impact on biometric systems recognising the face, and imposing facial exposure in the identity identification process raised security concerns. On the other hand, however, the pandemic period contributed to the spread of remote identity identification methods, that is, methods based on what we have and what we know. In many cases, identification of a smartphone and assigning it to a specific person replaced the traditional method of identification – for example, verification of eligibility to receive a courier package by PIN code received on the cell phone or authorisation of transactions SMS code at the bank. Remote identity verification has also been used in telemedicine or universities during exams. Gradual getting used to remote identity identification will positively impact the post-pandemic period and may reduce the costs of operation of some enterprises, offices and universities. In the case of well-designed systems that meet the legal and technical requirements, the security of remote identification guarantees a high level of security. It should not cause concern in their use. Some companies had plans and scenarios in place if a situation requiring remote working arises. Still, most companies, and thus their systems, were not prepared for this, and the hurriedly implemented systems had many security gaps, which criminals meticulously exploited.

In EU countries, it has also become common to use applications that monitor the movement of citizens and warn in case of being near a person infected with the coronavirus. Applications such as ProteGo Safe (Poland), COVID Tracker Ireland (Ireland), Corona Warn App (Germany), CoronaMelder (Netherlands), SwissCivid App (Switzerland), eRouska (Czech Republic) and Smittestopp (Norway) contribute to reducing the scale of the spread of the virus by warning about contact with a sick person. The application identifies users, and in case of detecting contact with an infected person, it sends a message about the potential infection. Importantly, such applications are free and completely voluntary, and their effectiveness depends largely on the number of people who use them. It is also worth noting that many organisations defending human rights, privacy and protection of personal data criticise applications, pointing to too great interference in privacy. Many people, due to the threat of a pandemic, voluntarily give up their privacy to fight a common threat. There may be concern about using such apps after the pandemic is over. Hence, many organisations call coronavirus apps to be uninstalled once the pandemic period is over.

Many countries also used apps to confirm attendance at home during quarantine. Such apps were mandatory and made it easier to monitor quarantine compliance by those in quarantine. The apps located the phone and confirmed the identity of the user. The applications used the so-called selfie photo that each user had to take during the registration process. During the quarantine period, the application user was asked several times a day to take a similar photo and share their location. The application facilitated the functioning of services that did not have to control persons who correctly performed the commands and tasks from the home quarantine application.

Remote identification can be used to a limited extent. It isn't easy to consider it sufficient to all conditions and needs because de facto it confirms more the presence of the device (phone, card) in the right place than the person assigned to it. This problem concerns both the method based on knowledge and the method based on what we have. Although popular, fast and easy to implement, both these methods do not guarantee the highest level of security. In case of acquiring, e.g., a password, a card or a phone, the system will effectively recognise the identifier and consequently identify the user, who will be charged with the consequences of the identification. However, the authorised holder is not in the given place at all and is not aware of the identification by the given system. The consequence of increasing the convenience and speed of identification is to decrease its security.

The process in which remote identification is not sufficient is the confirmation of identity by public entities, state protection services, including epidemiological services. In this case, full confirmation of the identity of the controlled person is required. Standards and procedures for identity identification require confirmation of identity clearly, based not only on the devices used by the person but also on the characteristics directly associated with the person being verified. The most common method of confirming identity is by using identity documents and ensuring the holder's identity concerning the data contained in the identity document. Although this method is the most popular, it proved to be too invasive and feared during a pandemic. It requires passing the document to another person (which can promote the spread of the virus) and exposing the entire face to compare the image contained in the document with that of the person using it. Taking off the mask or even touching it with your hand can expose you to danger and contribute to spreading the virus. It is hard to imagine that in the case of verifying a person's identity using an identity card, not to verify the image of the person using it. This could contribute to an increase in identity theft and overall crime. Identity theft associated with using someone else's identity document is a constant and extremely dangerous phenomenon. Identity theft, also known as identity fraud or identity crime[8], uses another person's personal information to falsely claim to be someone else.[9] The definition of identity theft is contained, among others, in the EC's document "Towards a general policy on the fight against cybercrime" of 22 May 2007, where identity theft is defined as the use of personal identifying information, such as a credit card number, as a tool to commit other crimes. Among the numerous methods of identity theft, we can point to those specific only to the digital environment and those that occur in both digital and virtual environments. Analogically to all cybercrime, we can distinguish two approaches to identity theft – vertical and horizontal. Vertical approach to identity theft concerns crimes that occur only in the virtual sphere, while the horizontal approach concerns methods that occur both in the virtual and real sphere. One example of identity theft in real life is using someone else's identity document. It is facilitated by the construction of the document, i.e., the adoption of a standard format of ID1 document, blurs the image of the document, making it of little use in the identification process. As a rule, the photo on identity documents is reduced twice in size to that provided on the application.

A major change in the use of identity documents has been the introduction of electronic (biometric) identity documents, equipped with an electronic microchip with data stored in electronic form. Such documents extend the possibility of identification through automatic scanners or the ability to display data (including a photo) on a computer monitor.

Almost all countries have implemented electronic identity cards (within the EU, only Denmark and Ireland do not issue national identity cards). Out of the 27 EU member states, 14 are issuing biometric documents (Belgium, Cyprus, Germany, Hungary, Ireland, Italy, Latvia, Lithuania, Luxembourg, Netherlands, Poland, Portugal, Spain and Sweden). Unlike the electronic document, the biometric document is equipped with biometric identifiers and allows automatic verification of these identifiers.

Identity verification based on an ID card is extremely popular and occurs not only in the case of public entities and services but also in banks, at the post office, or in private companies (e.g., entrance of visitors to the office building). During wave 1 of the pandemic, national elections were also held (e.g., in France (15 March 2020), Germany (15 March 2020), Moldova (15 March 2020), Poland (22 March, 28 June and 12 July 2020), Switzerland (5 April 2020), as well as Australia (29 March 2020), South Korea (15 April 2020), Iceland (27 June 2020) or New Zealand (19 September 2020). Identity verification procedures during elections require proof of identity and thus verification of the person's image entitled to vote. Since most elections are held in closed premises, removing masks and goggles may contribute to the spread of the SARS-CoV-2 virus. Communications from state election authorities and health officials have generally indicated that briefly removing masks to confirm identity is not associated with a high risk of infection.[10] Later, when other virus variants began to appear (mainly the Delta variant), these recommendations were no longer so unambiguous. There appeared information that a few seconds of contact is enough to get infected in the media.

3.4 Biometric identification during a pandemic

Given the controversy over existing identity verification methods and techniques, it seems important to develop new identity verification methods or modify existing ones so that they are more secure for the person verifying and the person being confirmed.

Among the methods that seem to meet security conditions and at the same time are characterised by the highest level of identification are biometric identification methods – the third model of identification based on what we have. The word "biometrics" is derived from Greek words: bios – life and metron – measure. The term is commonly defined as a technique for measuring living beings, targeting methods for automatically recognising people based on their physical characteristics.[11] Biometrics is based on the processing of biometric data, which are defined as data that can directly and unambiguously identify an individual based on the personal characteristics of their body.[12] The legal definition of biometric data is contained in GDPR. According to Art. 4(14) of the Regulation, biometric data are personal data that result from specific technical processing, concern physical, physiological or behavioural characteristics of a natural person and allow or confirm the unambiguous identification of that person such as a facial image or dactyloscopy data.

Biometrics allows a person to be uniquely linked to their identity and is often referred to as an electronic code of their physical characteristics.[13] Biometrics has an extremely wide range of applications. It is used, e.g., for securing electronic devices (e.g., computers and smartphones), as an element of an access control system or for securing access to data and servers. For several years, it is also gaining popularity as an element of identification of the identity document holder – obligatorily in passport documents and optionally in national identity cards. Identity verification based on electronic identity documents requires specialised equipment and software. The identity verification process begins with reading a special MRZ (Machine Readable Zone) using an OCR scanner and determining the access control protocol key. After verifying the access right, electronic data stored in the microprocessor are read, and the authenticity of the document is verified by checking electronic signatures and the issuer's authentication certificate. In the next step, biometric samples are taken: a facial image and fingerprints. Identity is verified by comparing the biometric data read from the chip with the data taken from the holder. However, biometrics is not widely used in European Union countries. Undoubtedly, it had not gained the popularity predicted back in 2001 when biometrics was named by the influential American technology magazine *MIT Technology Review* as one of the top ten new technologies that will change the world.[14] Perhaps a pandemic will contribute to its development and widespread adoption.

The literature indicates many classifications of biometrics, including those based on anatomical and behavioural, passive and active, static and dynamic, and multimodal features and how they are created. The most common and comprehensive classification is based on anatomical and behavioural features. Anatomical features include fingerprint, iris, hand or wrist vein pattern, voice tone, odour, facial geometry, hand geometry, facial temperature distribution, retina, DNA identification, ear geometry and skin surface analysis. On the other hand, behavioural traits include mouth movement, eye movement, typing, including the way and speed of typing on a keyboard, voice characteristics or the way one walks.

Within the European Union, biometric passports with two biometric features – a biometric facial image and a fingerprint – were introduced in 2006. In the case of national ID cards, the most common feature is the biometric facial image and less common is the fingerprint image. Unlike their traditional counterparts, Biometric documents are equipped with an electronic chip with data stored. Such a document allows the implementation of automatic identity verification that ensures effective and rapid verification of the person's identity using the document. The identification process checks the conformity of the biometric features possessed by the person using the document with the features recorded on the document. The verification is extremely fast and efficient. However, in times of pandemic, a biometric document is not a secure source of identity verification because, as in the case of standard documents, it requires the holder to unveil his face and put his fingerprints on the reader. Of course, procedures can be implemented to increase security – such as wiping the reader after using an anti-virus agent or setting the camera away from the operator. However, this may prove not easy to implement in practice.

The pandemic period may therefore contribute to the search and spread of new methods of identification and proof of identity. The public sector should take advantage of the banking sector's experience, which for many years has been implementing identification based on the vein pattern of the finger (palm) or the iris of the eye. The French Data Privacy Institute (CNIL) has identified these methods as the safest techniques of so-called non-traceable biometrics, i.e., techniques that cannot be traced, copied or replicated. However, what is important from a pandemic point of view is that they do not require direct contact with the operator or touch any readers or devices. In the case of vein pattern biometric identification, confirmation of a person's identity is done by recognising the pattern of a vein pattern, such as the hand. The blood vessel pattern of the hand, finger or even the whole body of each person is unique. A biometric system that verifies identity using the palm vein pattern uses near-infrared light. Near-infrared light (e.g., from LEDs) is transmitted through the palm, finger or wrist and is partially absorbed by the haemoglobin in the veins. This makes it possible to obtain an image of the structure below the outer layer of the skin, giving a unique pattern of the blood vessel system. This pattern is extremely difficult to capture and counterfeit. The recognition algorithm analyses the number of veins, their positions and the points at which the veins cross. The entire scanning process takes very little time, and authentication is done based on the comparison[15]

And in the case of iris biometric identification, the system first measures the face and locates the iris on it. Then, they take a detailed photo of the iris with very high resolution. The system determines the pupil border and the outer border of the iris, eliminating the effects of eyelid closure and light reflections. The image is then converted to be identical for each eye, regardless of the degree of pupil dilation or the scale of the object in the image. The iris pattern thus determined is converted into a mathematical code and used for identity verification[16]

So far, due to financial constraints, both vein pattern biometrics and iris biometric identification have not been implemented in identity documents. However, it is worth noticing that placing iris patterns in biometric documents is provided by ICAO documents, especially Machine Readable Travel Documents, Development of a logical data structure – LDS from 18 May 2004. It describes technical requirements to be met by the iris image. Both the facial image and fingerprint have fully satisfied the identification needs. Still, now much more emphasis should be placed on non-contact and non-invasive methods of identity verification, which at the same time provide the highest level of security for citizens to guarantee their privacy. Biometric traits that are the basis for identification are personal data and must be processed in compliance with the principles and rules set out in GDPR. The European legislator has introduced as many as ten principles of personal data protection. These principles are set out in Art. 5 of Regulation 2016/679, distinguishing between lawfulness, fairness, transparency, purpose limitation, data minimisation, data accuracy, storage limitation, integrity, confidentiality and accountability. These principles reflect values of a fundamental nature, defining the so-called data quality principles, which have an overriding force over the rest of the data protection legislation[17] Principles are non-merely ideas, values or postulates, but have a normative character[18] Other provisions of Regulation 2016/679 should be considered from the point of view of implementing the principles, which in this context are referred to as interpretative directives[19] The principles concerning data processing, due to their essence, are general, thanks to which they remain relevant in changing conditions.

3.5 Conclusions

The chapter presented an analysis of basic methods of identification and identity verification. Due to their invasiveness, the need to expose the face and eyes, and the fact that the fingerprint is placed on the reader, current methods do not guarantee full security and can contribute to the spread of the virus. Therefore, it seems reasonable to look for remote and secure identity verification methods. Currently, the most promising method is vein biometrics and iris biometrics. These methods are successfully implemented in the banking sector and should be considered part of identification in biometric identity documents.[20]

The pandemic period may prompt many entities, including public security services, to look for solutions based on automatic identity identification methods, modelled, for example, on the "social control system" solutions used in China. Current technology enables remote, automatic and contactless identification of identity. Basing identification on multiple features, including from surveillance, cellular networks or GPS transmitters, enables constant surveillance of society. However, fighting a pandemic cannot be an excuse for the widespread invasion of privacy. Control in Western societies should respect basic human rights, including dignity. Biometric identification based on the features described in this chapter, although it can be carried out automatically and without contact, requires the participation of the holder of the feature in the identification process. The holder must consciously hold the ID document to the reader and then place his hand over the reader or look in a certain way into the lens of an iris camera.

Works cited

Fichte, J. G., 'Fundamenty prawa naturalnego według zasad teorii nauki. Publikacja z 1796r przytoczone za: E. Mordini, Biometria a biopolityka, w "Człowiek i dokumenty", 2007, nr 7, 21.

Adams, C., 'Identification' in ed. H.C.A. van Tilborg, *Encyclopedia of Cryptography and Security* (Springer, Boston, MA 2005).

Szpor, G., Martysz, C., and Wojsyk, K., *Ustawa o informatyzacji działalności podmiotów realizujących zadania publiczne* (Komentarz and WolKluw., Warszawa 2007), 39.

Walter, W., *Security for Service Oriented Architectures* (Auerbach Publications 2014), 48.

Sengar, S.S., Hariharan, U., and Rajkumar, K., 'Multimodal Biometric Authentication System using Deep Learning Method' in 2020 International Conference on Emerging Smart Computing and Informatics (ESCI) AISSMS Institute of Information Technology, Pune, March, 12–14, 2020.

Lodder, A.R., and Murray, A.D., *EU Regulation of E-Commerce, A Commentary* (Elgar, Amsterdam 2017).

Czaplicki, K., 'Standardy identyfikacji tożsamości, wyzwanie dla administracji' in (eds.) Z. Duniewska, A. Rabiega-Przyłęcka, and M. Stahl, *Standardy współczesnej administracji i prawa administracyjnego* (WolKluw., Warsaw 2019), 506–521.

Sullivan, C., 'Is Identity Theft Really Theft' (2009) 23(1–2) International Review of Law, Computers & Technology 77–88.

Koops, B., and Leenes, R., 'Identity Theft, Identity Fraud and/or Identity-Related Crime' (2006) 30 DuD Datenschutz und Datensicherheit 553–554.

Toby, S.J., 'New Development: Running Elections during a Pandemic' (2020) 41(1) Public Money & Management 65–68.

Vacca, J., *Biometric Technologies and Verification System* (Elsevier 2007), 3.

Czaplicki, K., *Dokumenty tożsamości. Jawność i bezpieczeństwo* (C.H. Beck, Warsaw 2016), 235.

Redei, G.P., *Encyclopedia of Genetics, Genomics, Proteomics and Informatics* (Springer, Dordrecht 2008).

Pugliese, J., *Biometrics, Bodies, Technologies, Biopolitics* (Routledge, New York 2010), 1.

Wagh, D.P., Fadewar, H.S., and Shinde, G.N., 'Biometric Finger Vein Recognition Methods for Authentication' in (eds.) B. Iyer, P. Deshpande, S. Sharma, and U. Shiurkar, *Computing in Engineering and Technology. Advances in Intelligent Systems and Computing*, vol 1025 (Springer, Singapore 2020).

Tambouratzis, T., and Masouris, M., 'GA-Based Iris/Sclera Boundary Detection for Biometric Iris Identification' in (eds.) B. Beliczynski, A. Dzielinski, M. Iwanowski, and B. Ribeiro, *Adaptive and Natural Computing Algorithms*. 8th International Conference, ICANNGA 2007, Warsaw, Poland, April 11–14, Springer 2007.).

Drobek, P., 'Zasada celowości w dobie wielkich zbiorów danych (Big Data)' *Monitor Prawniczy* 2014/9, 22.

Fajgielski, P., *Ogólne rozporządzenie o ochronie danych, ustawa o ochronie danych osobowych* (Komentarz, WolKluw., Warszawa 2018) 143.

Banaś, T.A.J., 'Zasady prawa ochrony danych osobowych' in (eds.) T.A.J. Banaś, E. Bielak-Jomaa, M. Kuba, and J. Łuczak, *Prawo ochrony danych osobowych. Podręcznik dla studentów i praktyków* (Difin, Warsaw 2016), 22.

Chkhartishvili, A., Gubanov, D., and Novikov, D., *Social Networks: Models of Information Influence, Control and Confrontation* (Springer 2019).

4 Remote Working in Public Administration during a Pandemic versus Data Protection

Beata Konieczna-Drzewiecka

4.1 Introduction

Following the emergence of a new acute respiratory infectious disease caused by SARS-CoV-2 virus infection, also known as COVID-19 or "coronavirus," in the public space in late December 2019, on 30 January 2020, the WHO declared a public health emergency of international concern, and then on 11 March 2020, WHO declared the series of COVID-19 cases occurring since December 2019 as a pandemic.

One of the many solutions adopted by the legislator in the COVID-19 Act was the possibility of the employer to order the employee to perform, for a definite period, work specified in the employment contract, outside the place of its regular performance, called in parentheses remote work (Art. 3).

This legal solution introduced by the law was aimed at achieving a specific goal, namely the protection of health and life.

Subsequently, the amendment of 31 March 2020 added a provision on the possibility of issuing an order to perform work remotely to, respectively, officers of the services listed in the provisions on retirement benefits for officers of the Police, the Internal Security Agency, the Intelligence Agency, the Military Counterintelligence Service, the Military Intelligence Service, the Central Anti-Corruption Bureau, the Border Guard, the State Protection Service, the State Fire Service, the Customs and Penitentiary Service and their families.

The subsequent amendment of the COVID-19 Act dated 19 June 2020 is significant not only because of the changes it introduced, but also because it filled a gap in the rules for remote working that existed between 31 March and 19 June.

The amendment added six paragraphs to Art. 3 of the COVID-19 Act, which set forth the rules for performing remote work. Accordingly:

1. the performance of remote work may be ordered if the employee has the technical skills and possibilities and premises for performing such work and the nature of the work makes this possible. In particular, remote work may be performed by means of direct remote communication or concern the performance of manufacturing parts or material services;

DOI: 10.4324/9781003263968-24

2. the employer is to provide the tools and materials needed to perform remote work;
3. when performing remote work, an employee may use tools or materials not provided by the employer, provided that this allows for the respect and protection of confidential information and other legally protected secrets, including business secrets or personal data, as well as information the disclosure of which could expose the employer to damage;
4. upon the employer's order, an employee performing remote work is obligated to keep a record of the performed actions, including a description of these actions, as well as the date and time of their performance. Moreover, the employer is obligated to determine in the order the form and frequency of drawing up records of actions by the employee;
5. the employer may revoke the remote work order at any time.

It should be noted that the concept of remote work was introduced into the Polish legal order by the COVID-19 Act and does not constitute telework within the meaning of Arts. 67^5–67^{17} of the Labour Code. Telework, according to the code definition (Art. 67^5 Labour Code), should be understood as work performed regularly outside the workplace, with the use of electronic means of communication within the meaning of the provisions on the provision of electronic services, and a teleworker is an employee who performs work in the above manner and transmits the results of work to the employer, in particular by means of electronic communication such as email. Comparatively, remote work does not require that work results be communicated via electronic communication, so it can be more widely used than telework. Additionally, remote work in its definition has no requirement to use electronic communication means, which in turn is a prerequisite for recognising work as telework.

Between March and June 2020, it was up to the employer to determine the rules for remote working, and in doing so, the employer could refer to the general rules under employment law, including telecommuting, and consider its policies on secure information management in the organisation.

Art. 67^{11} of the Labour Code indicates that the employer shall provide the teleworker with the equipment necessary to perform work in the form of telework, meeting the requirements specified in Chapter IV, Section 10 of the Labour Code, on health and safety at work, insure the equipment, cover the costs associated with the installation, servicing, operation and maintenance of the equipment, provide the teleworker with technical assistance and necessary training on the use of the equipment – unless the employer and teleworker decide otherwise, in a separate agreement.

However, considering the circumstances surrounding the introduction of regulations giving the possibility to work remotely and the clear message that from the first days of the epidemic to maintain a social distance, the employer's decision was and should be to give the order to carry out work in the form of remote working, considering the need to ensure the continuity of the organisation and ensure secure flow of information. The employer was therefore obliged to weigh the interests, between the good which is the life and health of its employees/stakeholders, the organisational and technical capabilities of the organisation itself to order the remote work of more staff, in the face of knowledge concerning:

- the sensitivity of the information resources processed as part of the tasks performed by employees;
- the need to access systems using only fixed data communications equipment; and
- inability to provide remote workers with the necessary equipment to perform their work safely.

Listed above are only examples of issues that should be subject to careful analysis, including risk analysis for the protection of personal data as referred to in the provisions of General Data Protection Regulation.

Pursuant to the provision of Art. 24 of the GDPR, it is the controller's responsibility, having regard to the nature, scope and purposes of the processing and to the risks of violations of the rights or freedoms of natural persons of varying degrees of probability and seriousness, to implement appropriate technical and organisational measures so that the processing of personal data respects the principles arising from the GDPR. Furthermore, according to the principle of data protection by design arising from Art. 25 GDPR, the controller, when determining the means of processing as well as at the time of the processing itself, is to implement appropriate technical and organisational measures designed to effectively implement data protection principles, such as data minimisation, and to give the processing the necessary safeguards to meet the requirements of Regulation 2016/679 and to protect the rights of data subjects.

Therefore, an employer should perform the appropriate analysis before ordering its employees to perform work remotely:

- one in terms of being able to process the personal data of its employees for purposes such as communication and, if necessary, admittance to the organisation (body temperature measurement);
- second in terms of the ability to access the organisation's information resources, including personal data, of a remote employee performing his job.

4.2 Processing of employees' personal data in the context of remote working

An employer should process an employee's personal data – depending on the type of employment – based on one of the grounds for processing personal data regulated by the GDPR. Pursuant to Art. 6(1) of the GDPR, the processing of personal data shall be lawful only in the cases listed in this provision in points (a) to (f) and to the extent resulting therefrom. Such cases include, among others, when the processing is necessary for the performance of a contract to which the data subject is a party or to take steps at the request of the data subject prior to entering a contract (Art. 6(1)(b) GDPR) and when it is necessary for compliance with a legal obligation incumbent on the controller (Art. 6(1)(c) GDPR).

In the public administration, an employee may be hired both based on civil law contracts and employment contracts, which are governed by the Labour Code. While the provisions of the Labour Code strictly define the scope of personal data which may be requested by the employer in connection with the employment of an employee, there are no provisions which would regulate this issue in relation to civil law contracts. In practice this means that in the first case the employer is obliged to process such a volume of personal data as is adequately specified in Art. 22^1 of the Labour Code. In the second case it is the employer himself who must decide what data he will ask the person to provide when concluding an agreement with him.

The above argument is a background for the employer to analyse whether in a situation when an employee is allowed to work remotely, the catalogue of data processed about the employee will not be expanded.

In case of the Labour Code regulations, what should be paid attention to, in the author's opinion, is the employee's contact details. In Art. 22^1 § 1 of the Labour Code, the employer has the right to demand from a person applying for employment personal data including "contact details indicated by the person." On the other hand, Art. 22^1 § 3 of the Labour Code indicates a catalogue of data that the employer may additionally demand from the employee. Therefore, it should be noted that it is the candidate who independently chooses the way of contact, which has a direct impact on the personal data he/she provides. He can also freely decide to provide more than one piece of information in this regard (phone number, email). Therefore, if the employer would like to be contacted in a different way than the candidate decided, the collection of such additional data can only take place with the consent of the person applying for employment.

Referring the above to the situation of ordering the employees to work remotely, with the necessity to stay in constant contact with them by phone, in the absence of the possibility to provide e.g. company cell phones, the basis for asking the employee to provide a private phone number should be found in the disposition of art. 22^1 § 4 of the Labour Code, according to which the employer demands the provision of personal data other than those specified in § 1 and 3, if it is necessary for the realisation of a right or fulfilment of an obligation arising from a rule of law. However, when obtaining such personal data, considering the change of the basis, purpose and new circumstances surrounding the processing of the employee's personal data, the employer should also ensure that the employee is properly informed about the above, thus fulfilling the information obligation arising from the disposition of Art. 13 GDPR.

Also, when the employer introduces new communication solutions based on external solutions, after checking them from the security point of view, which will be discussed later in this article, he should inform the employee about the rules of their use. It should provide information, e.g., on the functions of a given solution in terms of protecting the privacy of an employee who connects via videoconference from his or her place of residence. An example of a solution offered on the market is a tool that allows blurring the background or switching off the camera during real-time calls.

Another issue that was unlikely to be used in government prior to the introduction of remote working legislation is the performance of work by an employee on private equipment, using private internet.

From the provisions of the Labour Code, the employer's obligation under telework is to provide the employee with the equipment necessary to perform work in the form of telework, ensure the equipment, cover the costs associated with the installation service, operation and maintenance of the equipment, provide the employee with technical assistance and necessary training in the use of the equipment. Allowing at the same time the possibility of determining other provisions in this regard between the employer and the employee under a separate agreement. In this regard, pursuant to Art. 67^{11} §2 of the Labour Code, the employer and the teleworker may determine in the agreement the scope of insurance and rules for use by the teleworker of equipment necessary to perform work in the form of telework, which is the property of the teleworker.

In the case of remote work, in the initial period the regulations did not set out such detailed rules for the use of private equipment for remote work. It was not until the June amendment of the COVID-19 Act that provisions were introduced under which, in performing remote work, an employee may use tools or materials not provided by the employer, if it enables respect for and protection of confidential information and other legally protected secrets, including business secrets or personal data, as well as information the disclosure of which could expose the employer to harm. The adoption of the above solution by the employer, however, should become the subject of careful analysis before allowing it. This type of work model, also known as "BOYD" (Bring Your Own Device), which has been used in the private sector for years, consists in using employees' private computers and mobile devices to process company data, including personal data, on such devices. The application of this kind of solution should be preceded by analyses showing in which areas, for example, the organisation cannot apply this model, and in which areas it is allowed, after the application of many technical solutions for the security of data processed in this model. Also, for employees who are to use the BOYD model for remote work, principles should be prepared, e.g., security policy, with which they should be acquainted before starting to work in this model.

In addition, it also remains equitable, given the vague wording of s. 3(5) of the COVID-19 Act, to obtain the employee's consent to use his or her private equipment for remote work.

Another issue that the employer had to analyse in the first weeks of the so-called "lock down" was the issue of rotating work. Some tasks of the public administration unfortunately cannot be performed by remote working. So, another issue that needed to be recognised was the legal possibility of measuring the body temperature of people entering the organisation, including employees. In the face of this practical problem and the dynamically changing situation, the employer, as a data controller, was obliged to take only such actions which remained adequate and correct from the legal point of view.

The regulations do not explicitly authorise temperature testing in the workplace. Nor do the regulations issued during epidemics address this issue. Opinions on the subject raised doubts about the possibility of allowing body temperature testing due to the need to comply with the principles of health and safety at work arising from Art. 207 of the Labour Code,[1] where life and health in conditions of real danger would have priority over the protection of privacy. On 5 May 2020, the President of the Office for Personal Data Protection also joined the discussion and published his position on the website, clearly stating that "in a situation where, for example, a person's body temperature is measured or data concerning his or her health is collected, and then the information is recorded, transmitted and collected, then a special category of personal data is processed."[2] At this point we may only recall the discussions on the admissibility of breath alcohol testing of employees. At that time, it was argued that breathalyser tests are used to comply with health and safety rules and are aimed at protecting the lives and health of employees. Despite such arguments, there was no consensus among experts as to the admissibility of such actions[3] (Labor Code amendment did not give employers the right to breathalszer tests).

The above statement ended the discussion on whether measuring a person's body temperature involves the processing of personal data, i.e., collecting, recording, transmitting and storing. In the opinion of the President of the Office for Personal Data Protection, measuring body temperature involves the processing of personal data, including data belonging to a special category, the processing of which under the GDPR is subject to many limitations. Pursuant to the GDPR, processing of data concerning health, and as such should be considered the result of measuring body temperature, is prohibited as a matter of principle, and is permitted only under the conditions set forth in Art. 9(4) of the GDPR.

The President of the Office of Personal Data Protection, held that the data protection regulations do not object to the processing of data of employees and visitors about, for example, measuring temperature or implementing a questionnaire with medical symptoms. As raised, Art. 9(2)(i) of the GDPR indicates that special categories of data (concerning health) may be processed when this is necessary for reasons of public interest in the field of public health, such as protection against serious cross-border health threats, if this is provided by law. This provision could be considered to correspond to national regulations in the field of COVID-19 pandemic control.

1 Guidelines for measuring temperature at the back of the law, <https://www.prawo.pl/kadry/pomiar-temperatury-czy-i-jak-pracodawcy-moga-to-robic-czy-mozna,500489.html> (14.12.2021).

2 Temperature check to prevent the spread of COVID-19, <https://uodo.gov.pl/pl/138/1516> (14.12.2021).

3 Labor Code amendment did not give employers the right to breathalyzer tests, <https://uodo.gov.pl/pl/138/1076> (14.12.2021), Doubts about the position of the President of the Office for Personal Data Protection with respect to carrying out sobriety checks on employees, <https://odo24.pl/blog-post.watpliwosci-dotyczace-stanowiska-prezesa-uodo-w-zakresie-przeprowadzania-kontroli-trzezwosci-pracownikow> (14.12.2021).

In his position, The President of the Office of Personal Data Protection, also indicated that "in accordance with Art. 17 of the COVID-19 Act, the Chief Sanitary Inspector has the power to influence other entities and changes in the existing legislation, as well as to indicate the adoption of appropriate solutions."[4] Further, the Act gives the Chief Sanitary Inspector several possibilities of performing tasks by the Chief Sanitary Inspector, who determines the general directions of actions of sanitary authorities. Under the new regulations, the sanitary inspector also has the authority to introduce additional solutions – bearing in mind the need to regulate certain issues and take necessary actions related to combating the epidemic. In the opinion of the President of the Office of Personal Data Protection, Art. 17 of the Act does not preclude employers or entrepreneurs from introducing the above-mentioned solutions aimed at combating COVID-19. Therefore, if a sanitary inspector finds it necessary to adopt a solution in the form of taking the temperature of employees and so-called visitors entering the workplace or collecting statements from employees concerning their health condition, he can use his legal powers, because of which an obligation will be imposed on the workplace in the form of a decision to take temperature measurements or to collect statements from employees concerning their health condition. "The sanitary services may also decide to measure the body temperature of visitors who enter the building to do business."[5]

In conclusion, the President of the Office of Personal Data Protection indicated that

> all actions that will be taken by the sanitary inspector and the entities it will affect will be based on the provisions of the law that regulate its actions and on the above-mentioned decisions, guidelines, and recommendations – i.e., the powers under the Act. These measures will provide the legal basis for these actions, including the basis for processing personal health data.[6]

Notwithstanding the above, in the above-mentioned communication, the President of the Office of Personal Data Protection also drew attention to the issue of processing of sensitive data in the workplace, claiming that "the legal basis for processing health data in the employment sector, i.e., in the employer-employee relationship and in the relationship with a public entity, cannot be Art. 9(2)(a) of the GDPR, i.e., the consent of the data subject." As also argued in the literature, consent should not constitute a valid legal basis for the processing of personal data in a particular situation where there is a clear imbalance between the data

4 Temperature check to prevent the spread of COVID-19, <https://uodo.gov.pl/pl/138/1516> (14.12.2021).

5 Taking body temperature was allowed in airports based on the guidelines issued by GIS "Rules of conduct in air travel and at airports in connection with the risk of eradication in the area of Poland of coronavirus (SARS-Co-V-2), 1.03.2020, <https://gis.gov.pl/wp-content/uploads/2020/03/03-SAMOLOTY-i-LOTNISKA_01.03.2020.pdf> (14.12.2021).

6 Ibid.

subject and the controller, where the controller is a public authority and therefore it is unlikely that in this situation consent would be freely given in all cases.[7] It should be noted that in the employer-employee relationship there is also an inequality between the two entities. The employer also cannot order employees and so-called visitors entering the workplace to take temperature measurements. In any event, he must show a legal basis that would give such authority.

Therefore, the analyses and findings made at the beginning of the COVID-19 pandemic, in the light of the presented position of the President of the Office of Personal Data Protection, needed to be verified in terms of the possible existence of regulations/decisions legalising the processing of sensitive data within the framework of measuring body temperature of a given person. It was also crucial for the issue of fulfilling the information obligation. According to the President of the Office of Personal Data Protection, "the controller is obliged to provide the persons whose personal data it processes with all the necessary information in the information clause." The content of the information clause should contain the elements indicated by GDPR and be conveyed to such persons. The information obligation should be fulfilled by the controller in such a way that the data subject can directly acquaint himself/herself with all the information. The clause may be included e.g., in the questionnaire, as well as it may be available in the workplace or in the office, e.g., at the reception desk, on the notice board or on the website. Nevertheless, the data subject should be informed about the basic issues related to the processing of his/her personal data (controller's data, purpose of the processing, legal basis, data scope) at the latest at the time of data collection, and then possibly referred to the full content of the clause which can be found in the above-mentioned places.[8]

The above issues, subjected to a reliable analysis by the employer, are part of the implementation of the principle of accountability arising from Art. 5 GDPR. Indeed, the employer is obliged to be able to demonstrate at each stage of the processing of personal data that the personal data are:

1. processed lawfully, fairly and in a manner transparent to the data subject ("lawfulness, fairness and transparency");
2. collected for specified, explicit and legitimate purposes and not further processed in a way incompatible with those purposes ("purpose limitation");
3. adequate, relevant and limited to what is necessary for the purposes for which they are processed ("data minimisation");
4. correct and updated as necessary ("correctness");

7 P. Fajgielski, *Commentary on Regulation 2016/679 on the protection of individuals with regard to the processing of personal data and on the free movement of such data and repealing Directive 95/46/EC (General Data Protection Regulation), [in:] General Data Protection Regulation. Personal Data Protection Act. Commentary* (WolKluw. 2018) 163.

8 Temperature check to prevent the spread of COVID-19, op. cit.

5. kept in a form which permits identification of the data subject for no longer than is necessary for the purposes for which the data are processed ("retention restriction");
6. processed in a manner that ensures appropriate security of personal data, including protection against unauthorised or unlawful processing and accidental loss, destruction or damage, by means of appropriate technical or organisational measures ("integrity and confidentiality").

4.3 Processing of personal data in remote working

Preparing an organisation for the transition to remote working requires employers to make several organisational and technical changes that should be subject to extensive analysis before they are applied, including as part of a data protection risk analysis.

Employer-side knowledge of the information resources processed by the organisation, in terms of their "sensitivity" [sensibility], is the starting point for further discussion.

Given that public sector bodies process various types of data, including personal data, in different systems during their activities, they should decide as to whether, to what extent and with what tools their employees will be able to work remotely, including connecting to systems used in their daily work. Therefore, to organise a secure environment and maintain business continuity by public sector entities, appropriate organisational and technical measures should be taken. The literature indicates that negative features of remote work include loss of organisational culture, alienation of employees, cyber threats, harm to those who cannot take advantage of remote work.[9]

4.3.1 Organisational resources

When preparing an organisation for the transition to a remote working model, in addition to the technical aspects, the informational aspect is important. Before moving to remote working, the employee should be reminded of the security rules in force in the organisation, also in the context of personal data processing. It is, of course, up to the employer to verify in advance that they are up to date in terms of the new conditions. However, in the case of maintaining the organisation's existing information security management principles, the employee should be reminded of them.

A good practice may be to conduct e-learning training, using for example a presentation sent to all employees on the principles of secure information processing,

9 B. Orell and M. Lager, *The Trade-Offs of Remote Work: Building a More Resilient Workplace for the Post-COVID-19 World* (Workforce 2020) <https://www.aei.org/research-products/report/the-trade-offs-of-remote-work-building-a-more-resilient-workplace-for-the-post-covid-19-world/> (14.12.2021).

including personal data. It should be noted that the rights and obligations of the employer as a data controller during the performance of remote work by employees are not essentially different from those during work in the office. This also applies to the situation of hiring new employees, who also require training in the principles of personal data protection in force in the organisation. Consider that the organisation's data protection management should function while working remotely in accordance with regulations. This means, among other things, completing and updating as necessary:

1. a register of processing operations;
2. register of categories of processing activities;
3. register of infringements;
4. register of data subject's rights requests;
5. registers of issued and withdrawn authorisations.

The employee should also be advised of the channels of communication with the employer in the event of an incident that may constitute a breach of personal data protection. As a rule, the employer should make employees aware that remote work should, as far as possible, be performed in a part of the private environment (e.g., an apartment) to which outsiders (family members, acquaintances, etc.) will have limited access. Situations which in a private environment may cause potential breaches of personal data protection can be, for example: unintentional flooding of equipment or documents by household members or unauthorised access to a computer.

4.3.2 Technical resources

Bearing in mind the analyses of the type of data processed as part of the activities carried out by public sector entities, remote working should be based, as a rule, on equipping employees with mobile business devices, e.g., laptops, smartphones, tablets, previously properly configured, e.g., through:

- encrypting discs, memory cards or other electronic information carriers;
- granting employees access rights adequate to their role in the organisation (as users by default);
- installing anti-virus systems;
- enabling all security features (e.g., passwords, automatic screen locks, remote deletion of hardware contents);
- enabling all automatic updates for the operating system, applications and anti-virus system.

When an organisation needs to adopt the BOYD model of using private devices for work, the organisation should first conduct risk analyses, considering numerous risks, which may include:

1. loss of business data, including personal data (leaked, stolen, destroyed – ransomware);
2. breaking company security measures;
3. spreading the infection to the company's network;
4. loss of employee data.

For instance, an INTERPOL assessment of the impact of COVID-19 on cyber-crime has shown a significant target shift from individuals and small businesses to major corporations, governments and critical infrastructure. As indicated in the report: two-thirds of member countries from Europe reported a significant increase in the malicious domains registered with the key words "COVID" or "Corona" aiming to take advantage of the growing number of people searching for information about COVID-19 online. Cybercriminals are taking advantage of the pandemic to deploy ransomware against critical infrastructure and healthcare institutions responsible for COVID-19 response. Cloning of official government websites is increasingly occurring to steal sensitive user data, which can later be used in further cyberattacks. Widespread phishing campaigns are being registered by European law enforcement agencies.[10]

The risk analysis should address the following aspects:

1. What type of information could be processed in the execution of work from the BOYD model, with the categorical exclusion of the ability to process information critical to the organisation. As part of the access to information, would access to personal data also be allowed. During the first week of the pandemic in the United States, more than half of employees used personal computers to work from home. What's more, nearly a quarter of employees had "frequent WIFI problems at home, which limits the ability of antivirus software to protect your computer from cyber intrusions."[11] Also in Croatia, among the many recommendations and guidelines issued to combat the health and other impacts of COVID-19, cyber threats were not included.[12]
2. Whether the organisation can adequately prepare/check employees' private equipment.
3. If an employee's private equipment cannot be prepared/checked, to what extent does the organisation agree to allow its use for remote work.

10 INTERPOL report shows alarming rate of cyberattacks during COVID-19, Cybercrime: COVID-19 Impact – Interpol <https://www.interpol.int/News-and-Events/News/2020/INTERPOL-report-shows-alarming-rate-of-cyberattacks-during-COVID-19> (14.12.2021).

11 Security „Increasing Cybersecurity Gaps and Vulnerabilities Due to Remote Work During COVID-19" <https://www.securitymagazine.com/articles/92571-increasing-cybersecurity-gaps-and-vulnerabilities-due-to-remote-work-during-covid-19; Morphisec's 2020 WFH Employee Cybersecurity Threat Index> (14.12.2021).

12 A. Škiljić, *Cybersecurity and remote working: Croatia's (non-)response to increased cyber threats* (International Cybersecurity Law Review 2020) <https://link.springer.com/article/10.1365/s43439-020-00014-3> (14.12.2021).

Security of an organisation's information resources, including personal data processed by it, will largely depend on the adopted IT solutions and the indicated principles of performing remote work. For instance, in Morphisec's Cybersecurity Threat Index for Workers Working from Home, for example, they indicated that "working remotely was a completely new experience for 49% of employees." 75% of employees working from home say they usually or almost always follow their IT team's advice on cybersecurity protocols. The most common tip employees received from their IT department regarding the transition to working from home was to be wary of suspicious emails, attachments, or pop-ups (56%). This was followed by making sure anti-virus software is active (48%) and updating software frequently (46%). Worryingly, 20% of employees said their IT team did not give them any guidance when they switched to working from home. Business chat apps, such as Slack and Microsoft Teams, were rated by employees working from home as the second most necessary tool for remote work. However, employees admitted that they were the least cautious about using these types of services.[13]

Therefore, the employee should be provided with the guidelines necessary for the employee to implement and follow when working remotely. both using company equipment and private equipment (under the BOYD model). The guidelines should include the following:

4. information about the methods of communication between the employee and the employer, with information about allowing private phones in addition to company phones;
5. information about the organisation's systems and work mail login policies. Employees should use two-factor authentication when logging into their work mailboxes. The greater the number of additional security features, the less likely cybercriminals are to get into systems;
6. information about the rules of using encrypted USB flash drives, indicating the impossibility of using company equipment for private purposes;
7. information about the rules of using the Internet, first of all the company Internet (from the company phone), and if this is not possible, about the rules of using the private Internet, e.g. after changing the default password for the home router so that it corresponds to the security rules established in the organisation;
8. obliging employees to connect to a VPN before logging on to the organisation's systems, and if it is not possible to establish such a connection, for example, to work exclusively by means of business email;
9. requiring employees to log out of their work account and computer/laptop each time they leave their post;
10. requiring employees to store all information created on the organisation's servers. If this is not possible, temporarily storing business information on

13 Security "Increasing Cybersecurity Gaps and Vulnerabilities Due to Remote Work During COVID-19" op. cit.

password-protected and encrypted mobile devices (e.g., laptop, portable drive) with prior approval from the IT department;
11. if an employee uses private equipment – in addition, an obligation for employees to:
    - have up-to-date, secure anti-virus software,
    - create a separate user account used for work, secured with a password, known only to the employee
12. information about the rules of users' access to videoconferencing, in particular:
    - regarding the technical conditions for the equipment and the connection,
    - in terms of rules of installing software on private hardware and rules of use,
    - in terms of the principles of secure information processing, including personal data during the videoconference.

The solutions offered on the market that allow conducting video meetings and videoconferences are cloud-based. Therefore, also this aspect in terms of the processing of personal data by such solutions should be analysed by the employer. Due to the very complex issues related to cloud computing, it should be noted that public administration has its own regulations[14] and standards that should be considered and met before implementing solutions based on a cloud environment in an organisation.[15]

A topic that should also be analysed within the organisation, and which relates to both organisational and technical aspects of work, is the issue of taking out paper documents, along with the personal data they contain. According to Art. 32 of the GDPR, adequate technical and organisational security measures should be used regardless of where the work is performed. The GDPR does not impose specific solutions and their selection is at the discretion of the controller. The COVID-19 Act also did not introduce specific regulations in this respect, which allows the claim that this was an intentional action dictated by the purpose, so that the employer has the possibility of shaping the manner of performance of work under the employee's subordination, by issuing orders on an ongoing basis. Moreover, the concept of remote work cannot be narrowed only to remote use of the employer's digitised resources (especially files), to the exclusion of the possibility of using files in another form, i.e., traditional (paper), at one's place of residence. It should be noted that in the provision on remote work the phrase "outside the place of its permanent performance" is included, which not only defines remote work (regardless of whether it is performed with the use of digital documentation in its entirety or also in traditional (paper) form), but also proves that

14 Resolution No. 97 of the Council of Ministers on the initiative "Common Information Infrastructure of the State", The Legal Monitor 2019 position 862.

15 Cloud Computing Cyber Security Standards, <https://chmura.gov.pl/informacje/scco/>, (14.12.2021).

the legislature recognised the place of performance of work outside the place of its permanent performance also on an ad hoc basis as the place of work. However, in the absence of specific regulations, especially statutory ones, the solution adopted by the employer should be analysed from the point of view of managing and minimising risks in connection with, for example, transporting files to a place of residence, storing them temporarily in a place of residence, or in connection with accidental loss and unauthorised disclosure. Developing a policy in this field in an organisation should also be accompanied by an analysis of the risks associated with possibly allowing company documents to be printed on private printers or saved on USB flash drives. An employer should consider the risk that the private equipment used may save printed documents, and that they may not be properly disposed of using paper shredders.

4.4 Conclusions

The COVID-19 Act did not introduce specific regulations, creating only a space for the employer to adequately and currently shape the way of providing work, including the development of rules to ensure that the provision of remote work takes place in compliance with applicable laws, in particular data protection law. As has also been shown, data protection regulations at the time of the pandemic were not helpful in answering many questions related to the processing of personal data. Therefore, the lack of statutory regulations or guidelines on the organisation of remote working, especially with the need to use private equipment, were and still are a challenge for the proper organisation of information security management in organisations, not only in the public sector, but also in the private sector. Changing work habits and practices, along with the use of the remote working model will have to involve an emphasis on data security.[16] The role of IT teams in ensuring business continuity has never been more important.[17]

The coronavirus pandemic has shown that in the face of a threat to life and limb, the value of privacy recedes into the background. Moreover, it has become apparent that the legal standards governing the data protection sector are so general and underdefined that various new and additional ways of processing personal data can be justified to "pursue the public interest."

Works cited

Babbs, A., *How to Leverage Data Security in a Post-Covid World* (Computer Fraud & Security 2020), 8–11.

16 A. Babbs, *How to leverage data security in a post-Covid world* (Computer Fraud & Security 2020) 8–11; K. Curran, *Cyber security and the remote workforce* (Computer Fraud & Security 2020) 11–12.

17 F. Malecki, *Overcoming the security risks of remote working* (Computer Fraud & Security 2020) 10–12.

Curran, K., *Cyber Security and the Remote Workforce* (Computer Fraud & Security 2020), 11–12.

Fajgielski, P., *Commentary on Regulation 2016/679 on the Protection of Individuals with Regard to the Processing of Personal Data and on the Free Movement of such Data and Repealing Directive 95/46/EC (General Data Protection Regulation), [in:] General Data Protection Regulation. Personal Data Protection Act. Commentary* (WolKluw., Warsaw 2018), 163.

Malecki, F., *Overcoming the Security Risks of Remote Working* (Computer Fraud & Security 2020), 10–12.

Orell, B., and Lager, M., *The Trade-Offs of Remote Work: Building a More Resilient Workplace for the Post-COVID-19 World* (Workforce 2020).

Škiljić, A., *Cybersecurity and Remote Working: Croatia's (Non-)Response to Increased Cyber Threats* (International Cybersecurity Law Review 2020).

VI

Economic Activity and Financial System during a Pandemic

1 Supporting Entrepreneurship during the COVID-19 Pandemic

Mariusz Szyrski

1.1 Introduction

In the wake of the so-called COVID-19 pandemic, the policy of support for market players and entrepreneurship more broadly has changed significantly. We are witnessing a phenomenon where support for high innovation in the economy is being pushed aside in favour of support for enterprises to counter the problem of bankruptcy. During the COVID-19 pandemic, companies focused on obtaining grants and funds for working activities and providing salaries for their employees rather than preparing new innovative R&D projects. This can also be seen in the normative sphere – several legal acts have emerged with the primary aim of adopting solutions to mitigate the negative effects of the COVID-19 pandemic. From the point of view of legal science, these solutions can be classified in various ways, which will, among other things, be the subject of this chapter. The main research question, around which the considerations will be carried out, is in what direction is the state aid in supporting entrepreneurship in times of the COVID-19 pandemic heading, and what forms does this aid take? This analysis will be carried out on the example of the situation in Poland.

1.2 Freedom of establishment and entrepreneurship

Art. 20 of the Constitution states that a social market economy based on freedom of economic activity, private property and solidarity, dialogue and cooperation between social partners constitutes the basis of the economic system of the Republic of Poland. As rightly noted in the literature, the principle of a social market economy is first and foremost a principle of state policy. It sets the framework within which that policy should be pursued. Although long known in economics and legal sciences, the very definition of a social market economy has no unambiguous normative content. The interpretation of Art. 20 of the Constitution is determined by the basic elements of the market, which are economic freedom and private property, and by the desirable elements of the social order, which are

DOI: 10.4324/9781003263968-26

social solidarity, social dialogue and cooperation of social partners.[1] The social market economy is currently not subject to any legal definition. Its content has been repeatedly derived by the CT.[2] It is worth noting an interesting statement by A. Powałowski that a special role in the course of implementation of the principle of a social market economy falls to the state itself, which should appear in the economy as an entity representing social interest because it is the state that constitutes a superior, formalised institution created by a particular society, a global institution on the scale of a given country, which is supposed to *de jure* and *de facto* represent the nation, a community consisting not only of citizens (natural persons) but also organisations and various collective entities established by them.[3]

According to the constitutional regulation, the essence of the social market economy is economic freedom. One may refer here to an interesting formulation found in the preamble to the Act of 6 March 2018 Entrepreneurs' Law,[4] where it is written that guided by the constitutional principle of freedom of economic activity, as well as by other constitutional principles relevant to entrepreneurs and the economic activity they carry out, including the principles of the rule of law, legal certainty, non-discrimination and sustainable development, recognising that the protection and promotion of freedom of economic activity contribute to the development of the economy and the growth of social welfare, striving to guarantee the rights of entrepreneurs and taking into account the need to ensure continuous development of economic activity in conditions of free competition, the Entrepreneurs' Law is enacted. It expresses basic axiological values important for business functioning in Poland and its environment. It is also worth noting that certain notions and legal definitions have been put in order in the act, defining, inter alia, what business activity is (business activity is organised profit-making activity, performed on its behalf and in a continuous manner). The regulation itself consisting in the definition of economic activity or the freedom of economic activity is not sufficient. These definitions – implementing the postulate of supporting economic development – must also be followed by public administration forms and specific forms of support for future economic activity. *Ratio legis* of the new law should be assessed positively, although it has been criticised.[5] Indeed, many ambiguities have recently arisen in relation to the functioning of the previous legislation, i.e., the Act on Freedom of Economic Activity. With some shortcomings of the new Act, however, it must be said that it regulates more comprehensively the process of registering a business, running it and finally end-

1 P. Tuleja, 'Commentary to article 20 of the Constitution of the Republic of Poland' in P. Tuleja (ed.) Constitution of the Republic of Poland. Commentary (WolKluw. Lex., Warsaw 2019).

2 A. Rychtel-Warzocha, 'Freedom of economic activity in the light of the jurisprudence of the Polish Constitutional Tribunal' (2017) 1 GSP 155.

3 A. Powałowski, 'Social market economy in Polish law' (2018) 1 GSP 51.

4 JoL 2021 item 162 with amendments.

5 M. Woch, 'Business Constitution. Political declaration, enactment of laws, and implementation' (2020) 7-8 PPP 90.

ing it. It also includes regulations that will positively impact cooperation between business and public administration.

The concept of entrepreneurship is related to the concept of an entrepreneur. The term "entrepreneur" appeared in economic literature at the turn of the 17th and 18th centuries and is derived from the French word "*entrepreneur*," describing a person who undertakes some activity or project.[6] The term entrepreneur was used, for example, to refer to suppliers, intermediaries or contractors. The word "*entreprendre*," also derived from French, means *to undertake*. The French word "*entreprenant*" is also used to describe a bold, self-confident person and has entrepreneurial qualities.

In contrast, the English word "*entrepreneurship*" has no direct translation into French.[7] Currently, in economic literature, entrepreneurship is most often equated with starting and running a business. This applies to the establishment of small, family businesses and medium-sized enterprises.[8]

Recently, the term "start-up" has also become very popular. In Poland, it is a form that has not yet been regulated by law. The Polish Agency for Enterprise Development assumes that a start-up is an entity represented by a person who is at the stage of establishing a company or who has been running it for up to 3.5 years and uses technologies/work methods available on the market for no longer than five years to produce its products/services[9]. An interesting analysis was made by A. Grycuk, indicating that the most frequently postulated characteristics of start-ups include:

- the use of modern technologies in the products offered (services provided) and/or in the way they are delivered;
- operating in conditions of high risk – it results from the development of a new product or service, an untested business model, the unpredictable behaviour of customers or the actions of current and future competitors (other entities from the same sector, the threat of the emergence of substitutes);
- short period of operation (usually less than 5 years);
- seeking or having a repeatable, scalable (allowing the business to scale up easily) and profitable business model, aiming for rapid growth.[10]

However, the postulate of a short period of activity indicated above cannot be regarded as an element characterising a start-up. It is rather a statistic referring to the "survival" in market conditions of a given project – also resulting from the period of financing in subsidy programmes. It would be wrong to say that start-ups are created only for such short periods of time. Following R. Białek and

6 D. Łochnicka, 'Employee entrepreneurship and its impact on organizational effective' (Wydawnictwo Uniwersytetu Łódzkiego 2016) 11.

7 Ibid.

8 Ibid. 12.

9 M. Nieć, Startups in Poland. Report (PFR 2019) 4.

10 A. Grycuk, 'Selected tools for supporting startups in Poland' (2019) 2 Studia BAS 153.

R. Nowak, we can agree that start-ups are characterised by innovation, they are companies introducing new technologies or using them, high risk and variable growth rate (few manage to "launch", most fail after the start), youth – with short tenure and are generally founded by young people, public trust – pursuing the goals of the state and using public subsidies and funds, connection with the R and D sector – a relatively large share of people with academic status among founders or, financing by *venture capital* funds and business angels – which entities verify the presented ideas from the perspective of efficiency and profitability.[11] Some normative guidance for understanding the concept of a start-up may be the content of Art. 2(1) of the Act of 10.05.2018 on supporting new investments,[12] which introduces the concept of "new investment". This notion is to mean an investment in tangible or intangible assets related to the establishment of a new enterprise, an increase in the production capacity of an existing enterprise, the diversification of an enterprise's production by introducing products not previously produced in the enterprise or a fundamental change concerning the production process of a current enterprise, excluding an enterprise against which bankruptcy proceedings have been initiated, or an application for bankruptcy has been filed with the court. Currently, a trend has arisen for practically every new business idea to be called a start-up, and the main determinant here is the age of the person starting the business. This is a trend that will continue in our country's business environment soon.

It should be noted that we do not find a definition of the notion of "entrepreneurship" in the Polish legal system. However, it appears in the text of the normative acts themselves. An example is the content of Art. 4.1.1 of the Act of 9 November 2000 on the establishment of the Polish Agency for Enterprise Development.[13] It is stipulated that the Agency implements state tasks in the development of entrepreneurship. On the grounds of this Act, however, we do not find a broader explanation of this notion, although it should be associated with the content of further paragraphs of this editorial unit, where it is stated that the Agency also implements state tasks within the scope of development of innovation, including technological progress; internationalisation of the economy, including export; information society; labour market and human capital; regional.

However, there is a definition of an entrepreneur – and it is a natural person, legal person or organisational unit not being a legal person, to which a separate Act grants legal capacity, performing a business activity. Business activity is an organised profit-making activity conducted on one's behalf and continuously.

European law, on the other hand, talks about freedom of establishment. Freedom of establishment covers the taking-up and pursuit of activities as a self-employed person and the setting up and management of undertakings, in particular

11 R. Białek and R. Nowak, 'Determinants of startup development in Poland' (2018) 15 Zeszyty Naukowe WSEI 43.

12 JoL 2020 item 1752 with amendments.

13 JoL 2020 item 299 with amendments.

companies within the meaning of the second para of Art. 54 of the TFEU, under the conditions laid down for its nationals by the law of the host state. The freedom of establishment which the TFEU confers on citizens of the Union includes the right conferred on companies, formed under the law of a Member State and having their registered office, central administration or principal place of business within the Union, to carry on their activities in the other Member States through a subsidiary, a branch or an agency. The provisions of Union law on freedom of establishment are intended to ensure the possibility of benefiting from national treatment in the host Member State.[14]

1.3 Forms of support for entrepreneurship

Bearing the above in mind, we should consider what support for entrepreneurship in Poland currently consists of? If we accept the definition that entrepreneurship is related to undertaking and carrying out activities on one's account – it would be important to remove barriers that limit these opportunities, and on the other hand, to actively support these activities – also in the financial aspect. This is particularly important for activities related to limiting the effects of the COVID-19 pandemic. As is rightly indicated in the literature, the impact of this pandemic on the Polish economy began to be felt almost immediately after the epidemic was declared.[15] Despite introducing the so-called anti-crisis shield in several stages, there is no doubt that a significant group of enterprises will not be able to continue their economic activity. And although in the first weeks of the epidemic, public attention was primarily focused on industries which, due to legal or actual restrictions, could not generate revenue at all (e.g., tenants of commercial space in shopping malls, the following industries: tourism, sports, catering, hairdressers, physiotherapists, some manufacturers), the long-term impact of COVID-19 will be severe for most enterprises.[16]

The first statutory Act to appear in legal circulation in this respect was the COVID-19 Act. As indicated in the explanatory memorandum to this Act – the Act specifies, in particular, the principles and procedure for preventing and combating infection and the spread of a contagious disease in humans caused by the SARS-CoV-2 virus, including the principles and procedure for taking anti-epidemic and preventive measures to inactivate the sources of infection and cut the pathways of the disease, the tasks of public administration bodies in preventing and combating the disease, rights and obligations of beneficiaries, healthcare providers and persons residing on the territory of the Republic of Poland within the scope of prevention and eradication of the disease, as well as the principles of covering the costs of performing tasks related to counteracting COVID-19,

14 J. Fiema-Kurek, 'Freedom of establishment and tax loss deductibility' (2020) 5 MP 8.

15 R. Cieślak, 'The impact of COVID-19 pandemic on project implementation in the public-private partnership model and concessions for works or services' (2020) 3 FK 42.

16 Ibid. 43.

in particular the mode of financing healthcare services for persons suspected of being infected or infected with the disease to ensure these persons adequate access to diagnostics and treatment.

From the point of view of entrepreneurship, however – of particular importance is the content of the Shield 2. The Act defines the term "support," which is to mean all forms of offering entrepreneurs on market terms repayable financial support instruments granted by the Institution to entrepreneurs, including loans, guarantees, sureties and other tools, the object of which is to finance business activity, excluding instruments reserved for entities performing banking and insurance activities. Support may also be provided in other repayable financial debt instruments if the parties to the agreement agree. The following forms of support have been specified here: loans, guarantees or sureties, as well as leasing or other instruments related to financing economic activity, under market conditions.

As one can see, this law provides primarily for the support of a financial nature, which is not always crucial. It seems that it would be desirable to find a balance between organisational, financial and substantive support for market players – particularly at this time of the COVID-19 pandemic. This issue will be topical in relation to the analysis of the COVID-19 pandemic situation and will have a much more universal significance.

Organisational support is primarily related to forms of activity that entrepreneurs may undertake on the Polish market. It is about the state supporting such solutions that may potentially influence a better position of Polish entrepreneurs in the international arena and internally. Particular attention should be paid to the new regulation concerning the so-called simple joint-stock company. In the justification of the act on amendments to the Commercial Companies Code and certain other acts, it was indicated that the bill proposes regulation of a new type of capital company: a simple joint-stock company (SKA). A PSA is a modern form of a non-public capital company intended for innovative undertakings. It is supposed to combine the corporate character of a company as a legal person and its basic manifestation, i.e. the exclusion of the personal liability of shareholders for its obligations, with considerable freedom in shaping the company's relationship, both in terms of mutual relations between shareholders and the system of management and supervision over that process. This new company structure is distinguished, on the one hand, by the admission of new categories of contributions to cover membership rights and, on the other hand, by a modern mechanism of protection of the company's creditors, abandoning the construction of share capital in favour of flexible limitations on distributions to shareholders, considering both the size of the company's aggregate indebtedness and its degree of solvency. The simple *joint*-stock company is suited to various roles, including that of a start-up vehicle, a *joint venture* vehicle, a single-member company participating in a grouping of companies and a special purpose vehicle (SPV) (*special purpose vehicle*). The legislator does not limit the purposes for which simple joint-stock companies may be established. An important motive behind the design of the PSA legislation was the desire to create a company model that meets the needs of the digital age economy, based on innovation, knowledge, and technology, and to a lesser extent on the company's ownership of (substantial) assets, permanently tied up in its assets.[17] This change – seen by some as revolutionary – will indeed increase the percentage of company incorporation, mainly due to the reduction in the initial capital required. It is a formula that is primarily intended to open up the "organisational" spectrum of possibilities for creating so-called start-ups. A simple joint-stock company may be established by one or more persons for any legally permissible purpose unless the law provides otherwise. In such a company, a share capital expressed in zlotys shall be created, to which monetary and non-monetary contributions made shall be allocated, and the share capital shall amount to at least 1 zloty. A non-monetary contribution to cover shares may be any contribution having material value, particularly the provision of work or services.

Organisational support should also mean infrastructural support. The so-called technology parks have been operating and developing for some time. The basis for the operation of such areas is primarily Art. 7 of the Act on supporting new investments.[18] Here we have several forms of support. The Act states that the tasks of the area manager include carrying out activities aimed at the creation of new investments and their development in the areas assigned to the management, including:

- making available to economic operators, on a contractual basis, items of property of which the area manager is the owner, a dependent holder or has been given the management thereof;
- the management of assets which the area manager owns holds in trust or has under his management, in such a way as to facilitate business;
- providing free of charge information services for entrepreneurs applying for support and those benefiting from support, as well as other services indicated in the investment development plan;
- carrying out activities promoting economic activity and new investments;
- providing entrepreneurs with information obtained from Poviat Labour Offices and social partners functioning in the area assigned to the area manager, relevant to the realisation of new investment;
- taking action to improve cooperation between entrepreneurs, the local community and the social partners;
- assistance to entrepreneurs in dealing with public administration;
- cooperation in respect of taking into account the needs of the labour market in the education process: with secondary schools, in particular with schools providing vocational education and lifelong learning establishments, with practical training establishments and with centres for further education and vocational development, with universities;

17 A. Opalski, 'Simple joint-stock company – a new type of commercial company (Part I)' (2019) 11 PPH 5.

18 JoL 2020 item 1752 with amendments.

- creating tools for the development of an innovative economy;
- recommending to entrepreneurs the optimal location for new investments.

The financial aspect is highly complex, especially in the current environment. Currently, there are many forms of support for entrepreneurship – and at different "life stages" of projects. This aspect's difficulty lies primarily in the fact that currently, one of the most important groups of entities – grantors – is private funds on the Polish market. These, in turn, are targeted primarily at highly innovative projects with the fastest possible rate of return. Therefore, there is no room for projects that do not meet the characteristics of high innovation but could potentially bring profit. Unfortunately, the problem is also exacerbated by the allocation mechanisms of public administration. The high innovation factor for a product or service is very highly scored here. Again, this results in the marginalisation of projects that cannot demonstrate novelty but could potentially contribute positively to the economic development of a given region. It could be concluded that after several years of this kind of policy, a certain impasse has been created, especially in the aspect of the content of the regulation in Art. 21a of the Act on some forms of support for innovative activity,[19] which indicates that the minister competent for economy establishes programmes in innovativeness of the economy implementing the innovation policy of the state, concerning in particular innovative products, services and markets; pro-innovative competencies of the society; competencies of personnel in creating and managing innovations; skills of entrepreneurs in intellectual property protection; internationalisation of innovative activity; links between science and economy. It would be good if the innovative activity were treated as part of a complete policy and not just as its predominant element, as is currently the case.

Currently, within the framework of financial support, new solutions are being implemented concerning reducing ZUS contributions and other benefits for entrepreneurs starting up a business. A very important regulation in this respect is the content of Art. 18 of the Act – Entrepreneurs' Law,[20] according to which an entrepreneur who is a natural person, who takes up business activity for the first time or takes it up again after at least 60 months from the date of its last suspension or termination and does not perform it for a former employer, for whom before the day of taking up a business activity in the current or previous calendar year he performed within the framework of an employment relationship or a cooperative employment relationship activities included in the performed business activity, is not subject to compulsory social insurance for six months from the date of taking up business activity. As rightly pointed out in the literature – the provision refers directly to obligatory social insurances. Thus, the relief for a start does not apply to health insurance. Therefore, in a situation where an entrepreneur decides to take advantage of the relief and does not pay social insurance contributions, he or she

19 JoL 2020 item 1752 with amendments.
20 JoL 2021 item 162 with amendments.

is obliged to register for health insurance and pay a monthly health contribution.[21] An entrepreneur who continues to operate a business after the 6 months of the start-up relief for the next 24 months will be entitled to benefit from the preference commonly referred to as small ZUS. In the case of this relief, the minimum basis for the assessment of contributions for pension insurance, disability insurance, accident insurance, as well as contributions for sickness insurance, if the entrepreneur joins voluntary sickness insurance, may be an amount not lower than 30% of the amount of the minimum wage.[22] Importantly, the so-called small ZUS can be used by an entrepreneur who has resigned from the relief for starting at all or before six months. Because the so-called "small ZUS" is counted for full 24 months, it is in a situation when the entrepreneur resigns from the relief for a start, e.g., on the tenth day of a given month – the period of the "small ZUS" should be counted only from the next month.[23]

The financial aspect brings another extremely important element: the entrepreneur's situation in the labour market. If we analyse the statistics, we find that most business activities are undertaken in sole proprietorships. Here, the issue of research financing itself or financing of non-scientific projects remains in the background – what comes to the fore are the practical aspects related to running a business and the lack of application *per analogiam of the* rules resulting from the Act of 26 June 1974 of the Labour Code[24] to the situation of the owner of such a company. Very high labour costs in the Polish reality caused that in the recent years such forms as managerial contracts or contracts resulting from the Act of 23 April 1964 – Civil Code,[25] also called contracts of employment – have become popular. – Civil Code, also known as junk contracts.[26] Such a situation often causes pathologies in which people are forced to set up one-person businesses so that the employer can pass the costs to the employee. This is a comfortable situation for the employer because he is relieved of the obligation to pay, for example, social security contributions or accountancy services. The situation becomes even more complicated in situations where the employer does not want, for example, to recognise the right to leave arising from the employment relationship under the Labour Code. The same situation may apply to other benefits (e.g., leave on demand, additional components of remuneration). Here, however, in the court jurisprudence, there is, unfortunately, no uniform position on the relationship between economic activity and the performance of work under an employment relationship. When analysing a similar case with respect to VAT, the Court of Appeals in Warsaw noted that by practising the profession of an architect and conducting business activities on his own account, the plaintiff has sufficient knowledge, experience and familiarity with the rules of

21 M. Korzeniewski, 'Commentary to Article 18 of the Entrepreneurs' Law' in A. Pietrzak (ed.), Entrepreneurs' Law. Commentary (WolKluw. Lex, Warsaw 2019).
22 Ibid.
23 Ibid.
24 JoL 2020 item 1320 with amendments.
25 JoL 2020 item 1740 with amendments.
26 M. Mędrala, 'Junk contracts – selected problems' (2012) 25 ZNWSZiBK 99.

conducting these activities to know that by presenting the defendant with documentation concerning his business activities and agreeing to receive remuneration plus due VAT, he establishes with the defendant a civil law relationship, and not an employment relationship within the meaning of the Labour Code (judgment of the Court of Appeals in Warsaw of 19 June 2002, Case No. III APa 197/01, p. 22). III APa 197/01, Lex No 74579). It was further argued that it is commonly known that remuneration paid based on an employment relationship is not subject to VAT, unlike services provided on the basis of a civil law relationship. In this situation it is obvious that the claimant, when concluding the agreement with the respondent, knew he was concluding a civil law agreement and not establishing an employment relationship within the meaning of Art. 22(1) of the Labour Code (judgment of the Court of Appeal in Warsaw of 19 June 2002, III APa 197/01, Lex No 74579). The Supreme Court, in turn, for example, stated that reporting in the register of business activity in the municipal office the running of one's own business activity consisting in the provision of sales agency services (and obtaining an entry in this register) and then concluding an agreement on the provision of sales agency services does not exclude the establishment and assessment that the parties to the agreement were in fact linked by the employment relationship under the employment contract for the position of a salesperson (judgment of the Supreme Court of 24.07.2001, I PKN 560/00, OSP 2002/5/70).

In recent months – as reported earlier in this article – there have been several financial solutions for entrepreneurs in the wake of the COVID-19 pandemic. Among the most common are:

- exemption from ZUS contributions for three months (March–May 2020) covering: companies which report up to 9 people for insurance, self-employed who pay contributions only for themselves, with income up to 3 times the average salary, social cooperatives, clergy;
- exemption from ZUS contributions for two months (April–May 2020) covering the self-employed who pay contributions only for themselves, with income above 3 times the average wage and income lower than PLN 7,000;
- exemption from half of the contributions to ZUS for three months (March–May 2020) covering companies that report between 10 and 49 people for insurance;
- parking allowance of up to about PLN 2,000 – for commissioned employees (contract of mandate, agency agreement, contract of specific work) with income below 3 times the average remuneration, and also for self-employed persons, regardless of the amount of income, whose income in the month preceding the submission of the application decreased by at least 15% with respect to the preceding month; the above-mentioned persons are entitled to no more than three times the amount of the benefit; for self-employed persons on a tax card the benefit will amount to PLN 1,300, while for contractors whose total income from civil law contracts is less than PLN 1,300 – the amount of lost income;
- subsidising workers' salaries.

The benefits mentioned above are based primarily on mechanisms in which the Social Insurance Institution participates – so their main element are exemptions or transfers of payments of contributions for various types of insurance. This in turn can be associated with the sphere of the so-called benefit administration. Another important field are also facilitations related to the tax system. One of such mechanisms in the legislation related to COVID-19 is the postponement of payment of tax advances or taxes themselves.

Looking into the near future – it seems that soon there will be a visible collision on the axiological level. This concerns the adopted provisions of the package known as the "Constitution for Business" – specifically, Art. 10 of the Act – Entrepreneurs' Law,[27] which provides that the authority is guided in its actions by the principle of confidence in the entrepreneur, assuming that he acts under the law, honestly and with respect for good practice, and the content of Art. 11 of this Act,[28] according to which if the subject of the proceedings before the authority is the imposition of an obligation on the entrepreneur or limitation or withdrawal of an entitlement, and in the case there are doubts as to the content of the legal norm, these doubts are resolved in favour of the entrepreneur, unless it is opposed by the disputable interests of the parties or the interests of third parties directly affected by the outcome of the proceedings. Soon, numerous inspections are to be carried out by the Social Insurance Institution (ZUS) and by tax offices regarding the way in which aid funds granted to entrepreneurs in connection with COVID-19 pandemic are used. It should be ensured that these inspections are carried out in accordance with the content of the regulations above, which the business community has highly anticipated.

1.4 Conclusions

The chapter began with the question of in what direction is state aid for supporting entrepreneurship in times of the COVID-19 pandemic heading and what forms does this aid take? The analysis carried out in this article allows us to accept the statement that it is, above all, currently financial aid, which depends to a large extent on the current market situation of the entity in question. Additionally, it must be stated that the rules connected with financial aid are not too restrictive, and what relates to this – many economic entities have received it. In the nearest future we can expect numerous inspections on the part of ZUS and tax offices regarding the collected funds and their use. Therefore, it will be crucial not to shake the trust gained based on the previously adopted Constitution for Business and the principle of trust in the entrepreneur. It seems that state aid should not focus as strongly on financial aspects as it does now. Monetary benefits from the administration are important, but there is a lack of comprehensive support using other forms, especially in the COVID-19 pandemic. The article points to the

27 JoL 2021 item 162 with amendments.
28 JoL 2021 item 162 with amendments.

existence in the legal regulation of a simple joint-stock company or forms offered by the Social Insurance Institution. These are the right directions, which in the future may allow the development of entrepreneurship in Poland, especially at the level of small and micro entities, including start-ups. At the axiological level, it is important to ensure the survival of market entities and to support their multidirectional development. One of such forms should be mentoring and organisational support. Unfortunately, financial forms are among the simplest solutions, which is why they have recently been so eagerly used and implemented.

Works cited

Białek, R., and Nowak, R., 'Determinants of Startup Development in Poland' (2018) 15 Zeszyty Naukowe WSEI 43.

Cieślak, R., 'The Impact of COVID-19 Pandemic on Project Implementation in the Public-Private Partnership Model and Concessions for Works or Services' (2020) 3 FK 42.

Fiema-Kurek, J., 'Freedom of Establishment and Tax Loss Deductibility' (2020) 5 MP 8.

Grycuk, A., 'Selected Tools for Supporting Startups in Poland' (2019) 2 Studia BAS 153.

Łochnicka, D., *Employee Entrepreneurship and its Impact on Organizational Effectiveness* (Wydawnictwo Uniwersytetu Łódzkiego, Łódź 2016).

Mędrala, M., 'Junk Contracts – Selected Problems' (2012) 25 ZNWSZiBK 99.

Nieć, M., *Startups in Poland.* Report (PFR, Warsaw 2019), 4.

Opalski, A., 'Simple Joint-Stock Company - A New Type of Commercial Company (Part I)' (2019) 11 PPH 5.

Pietrzak, A. (ed.), *Entrepreneurs' Law. Commentary* (WolKluw.Lex, Warsaw 2019).

Powałowski, A., 'Social Market Economy in Polish Law' (2018) 1 GSP 51.

Rychtel-Warzocha, A., 'Freedom of Economic Activity in the Light of the Jurisprudence of the Polish Constitutional Tribunal' (2017) 1 GSP 155.

Tuleja, P. (ed.), *Constitution of the Republic of Poland. Commentary* (WolKulw. Lex, Warsaw 2019).

Woch, M., 'Business Constitution. Political Declaration, Enactment of Laws, and Implementation' (2020) 7–8 PPP 90.

2 Improving the Electronic Communication of the Taxpayer with the Tax Authorities during the Pandemic

Aneta Szymczak

2.1 Introduction

There has been a dynamic development of e-services in taxation in recent years. Although the first normative regulations in this respect were introduced in 2002, disseminating such services in society was initially quite slow. Although taxpayers were able to use more and more electronic forms, available on the websites of tax administration bodies, year by year, paper forms of tax settlements prevailed. Over time, however, this trend began to change. The increasing number of new electronic instruments, covering not only the sphere related to the disclosure of the tax base and tax calculation but also used in tax proceedings and other forms of communication of taxpayers, paying agents and collectors with the tax authorities, meant that the scope of matters requiring personal contact with the office was decreasing. In some taxes, the obligation to use electronic forms was introduced in place of the previous right to settle taxes and submit reports in electronic form.

Activities related to preventing, counteracting and combating COVID-19 coincided with the intensification of work of the central administration on the implementation of other solutions for electronic communication between the taxpayer and the tax authorities. The events resulting from the pandemic only accelerated the introduction of new tools, which have been successively extended with new types of forms and e-services for some time now. On the other hand, the taxpayers have started to use electronic contact forms with the tax administration authorities. The introduction of restrictions on direct contact between taxpayers and tax authorities during the pandemic period did not significantly hamper communication during that time. Previous experience and systematic encouragement of taxpayers to use electronic tools meant that they did not have major problems using several new instruments and improvements implemented during this period by the Ministry of Finance and the National Tax Administration.

2.2 Legal basis for obligations and powers to file tax returns electronically

In the tax law, the possibility to file returns electronically was introduced by the Act of 12 September 2002, amending the Tax Ordinance Act and certain other

DOI: 10.4324/9781003263968-27

acts (JoL No. 169, item 1387). Art. 3a was added to the Tax Ordinance (the Act of 29 August 1997, JoL 2020, item 1325; hereinafter: the Tax Ordinance), which authorises to send declarations by electronic means of communication. However, it entered into force only as of 1 January 2004. As of that date, taxpayers in Poland may file returns and any declarations, lists, statements, reports and information they are obliged to submit under tax law by electronic means of communication. This right also applies to paying agents and collectors. For this purpose, taxpayers, paying agents and collectors are obliged to use electronic forms. They must contain data specified in separate regulations (appropriate for a specific, settled tax) and an electronic signature. The Ordinance of the Minister of Development and Finance of 19 September 2017 on the manner of sending declarations and applications and the types of electronic signature with which they should be affixed (JoL item 1802, as amended; the 2017 Ordinance) contains implementing provisions to the Tax Ordinance, specifying the manner of sending declarations and applications using electronic communication and the types of electronic signature with which particular kinds of declarations or applications should be affixed.

In the initial period, the use of the electronic form of settlements had to be preceded by a notification to the head of the tax office responsible for keeping records of taxpayers and paying agents and indicating a person authorised to submit declarations in this form and to sign them with an electronic signature. Only a confirmation of the notification by the head of the tax office entitles the taxpayer to settle tax in this form. In 2009, the notification obligation was abolished. The popularisation of the electronic form of settlements caused this obligation to be perceived by taxpayers as a barrier impeding the contact of taxpayers, paying agents and collectors with the tax authority in electronic form.

The Tax Ordinance does not regulate issues related to the form of filing tax returns. In this respect, it refers to individual tax acts. However, specimens of forms are specified in implementing regulations issued based on these acts.

An obligation to submit declarations, statements, lists, statements, reports and information in electronic form has been introduced in some taxes. In contrast, in others, it is the right of taxpayers, paying agents and collectors, who may also use other forms, including paper forms. As of 2015, this obligation applies to most forms submitted under the Corporate Income Tax Act of 15 February 1992.[1] The same is true for VAT (the Law of 11 March 2004 on Goods and Services Tax, JoL 2020, item 106). As of 2018, the obligation to send VAT returns electronically has been extended to all taxpayers registered as active VAT taxpayers. This obligation also applies to the electronic submission of corrections to declarations and returns. VAT records must also be kept electronically, and from October 2020, this data must be sent on a new JPK_VAT form with the return, which includes two parts. The VAT record (information about purchases and sales, which results from the trader's VAT records for a given period) and the VAT return. The obligation to

1 JoL 2020, item 1406.

send tax forms electronically also applies to most entities covered by the Personal Income Tax Act of 26 July1991.

On the other hand, taxpayers have left how to submit their tax forms. Taxpayers of personal income tax, corporate income tax, tax on goods and services, inheritance and gift tax, tax on civil law transactions, tax on certain financial institutions, tax on gambling, tonnage tax, tax on the extraction of certain minerals may use interactive forms, the so-called e-declarations. Appropriate e-declarations have also been prepared for paying agents and inherited enterprises.

However, in taxes such as agricultural, forestry and real estate tax, the proceeds from which constitute revenues of local government units, the possibility of filing electronic forms depends on whether the municipal council has adopted a resolution on this matter.

The obligation to send forms electronically has also been imposed on pension authorities submitting annual tax returns for pensioners and other persons receiving income from these authorities. The forms are transmitted using interface software made available to that authority by the minister responsible for public finance, secured by a dedicated certificate issued by the office serving that minister, given to the pension authority (§ 2(3) of the 2017 Regulation).

Another group of regulations governs the powers of tax authorities to communicate with taxpayers using electronic communication. Under Art. 3e of the Tax Ordinance, a tax authority may serve letters in the form of an electronic document in all tax matters handled by the authority only after obtaining consent from the taxpayer, paying agent and collector. For this purpose, the authority must request such consent from these entities. The entities, as mentioned earlier, also have the right to opt-out of the service of letters using electronic communication.

The possibility of filing applications (requests, explanations, appeals, complaints, reminders, requests) electronically in tax proceedings is also regulated separately. According to Art. 168 of the Tax Ordinance, they may be submitted via electronic communication via the tax authority's electronic mailbox. If the regulations require that a specific template submit applications, they should contain data in a fixed format. They must be signed with a qualified electronic signature, a trusted signature or a personal signature and include the electronic address of the submitter.

2.3 Tax portals of tax administration bodies

In Poland, the main tax portal handling most tax matters is the website of the Ministry of Finance – podatki.gov.pl. It contains a range of information to help taxpayers correctly fulfil their tax obligations. The website contains instruments necessary for settling tax liabilities, including, above all, e-declarations, electronic forms for tax declarations and returns, a tax calculator and a tax calendar. The portal also enables the electronic submission and receipt of letters and handling of certain matters. It also contains instructions on how to file e-declarations, including who can file such a declaration, sign e-declarations and obtain an official acknowledgement of receipt. At the e-mail address: info.e-deklaracje@mf.go v.pl, you can get assistance in case of technical problems with the operation of the Tax Portal, including the e-Declarations system.

The clear and functional layout of the website ensures easy access to, and use of the tools provided. Separate tabs for individual taxes have been created on the portal, where taxpayers, in addition to basic information on the tax, will find current legal acts, announcements and explanations. The tabs were created for personal income tax (PIT), corporate income tax (CIT), value-added tax (VAT), excise tax and customs duty. A common tab has been created for tax on civil law transactions and tax on inheritance and donations. The same applies to local taxes and fees, including tax on transport, real estate tax, agricultural tax, forest tax and local fees. The last summary tab is – other taxes, which includes: tax on gambling, tax on shipbuilding, tonnage tax, tax on certain financial institutions, tax on the extraction of certain minerals and stamp duty.

In taxes, where e-declarations have been created, the possibility to settle the tax directly using the platform has been ensured. In the remaining taxes, forms have been provided to download in electronic or paper versions. Separate COVID-19 tabs have been created for each tax where amendments have been made related to the emergency measures taken in connection with the pandemic, providing information on the amendments and actions brought for the specific tax. Most of these relate to the protection of taxpayers from liquidity loss. If a taxpayer needs to benefit from the measures introduced, the site also provides specimen forms for downloading electronically or for printing.

The *Twój e-PIT tab*, where tax returns completed for the taxpayer have been prepared, has become very popular. It was one of the biggest improvements introduced by the National Tax Administration (KAS) in 2019 and 2020. In the run-up to the pandemic, settlement points in shopping malls, a special National Tax Information (KIS) hotline for Twój e-PIT, and hundreds of computer workstations in tax offices were set up to publicise the service and help taxpayers settle their taxes. Taxpayers could also obtain information on all activities related to the PIT settlement in social media on the FB profile of the action, Instagram and the MF and KAS profiles on Twitter.

The tax administration is responsible for the tax return prepared by the system. At the same time, the previous forms of settlements, i.e., electronic and paper, have been preserved. The taxpayer himself chooses whether to use Twój e-PIT prepared by the tax administration or fill in the tax return by himself. This service relates to a time-saving guarantee of security and a lack of risk of late settlement. To strengthen data security, taxpayers can use the login history preview, which allows them to check all attempts to enter the system. It contains precise information on the dates and methods of logging in.

In 2017, for the first time, the number of PIT returns filed electronically (10.1 million) was higher than the number of returns filed on paper (8.7 million).[2]

2 Data from the website of the Ministry of Finance: <https://www.gov.pl/web/kas/twoj-e-pit-nowa-jakosc-w-rozliczeniu-podatku>.

However, in 2019, taxpayers settling their income tax for 2018 filed approximately 16 million returns electronically, more than 4 million more than in the previous year (almost 11.4 million in 2018).[3] The Ministry of Digitalisation (MC) research has shown that the Twój e-PIT service is known to 83% of surveyed Internet users. That e-filing of tax returns is the most popular e-service in the administration.[4]

In 2019, the Twój e-PIT service could be used by personal income taxpayers who do not conduct business activity (PIT-37) and taxpayers who receive income from cash capitals PIT-38. The following year, new types of returns completed for the taxpayer were added, i.e. In the next year, new types of returns filled in for the taxpayer were added, i.e., PIT-28 e-declaration (for persons, who settle, e.g., income from lease, tenancy or other contracts of similar nature, as well as from the sale of processed plant and animal products), as well as PIT-36 e-declaration (for persons, who, e.g., settle income from lease, from retirement and disability pensions from abroad). The service was not available to taxpayers who are entrepreneurs. According to the Ministry of Finance announcements, taxpayers who conduct business activity will have e-declarations prepared in 2021. Therefore, they will settle their tax for 2020 using tax returns prepared by KAS in the Twój e-PIT service.

The data based on which KAS determines the tax payable or overpaid come from declarations submitted by tax remitters (PIT 11), who are obliged, by 31.01, to provide the tax office with electronic forms containing information about income from other sources, as well as about income and collected advances for income tax. Art is the basis for the obligation to provide declarations only in an electronic form using appropriate forms. 45ba of the Personal Income Tax Act of 26 July.

Based on the available data from the state registers, when preparing e-PIT, the tax administration also considers the majority of tax preferences to which a particular taxpayer is entitled, such as a single parent, joint settlement with a spouse, allowances for children over the age of 18 (if the child is a student or a doctoral student), or the so-called youth allowance.

Taxpayers log in to the Twój e-PIT service using their tax data (authorisation data) or the trusted profile.

The returns prepared by KAS in the Twój e-PIT service are subject to verification by the taxpayer, who may amend, accept or reject them. Because the returns do not consider all allowances and deductions to which a particular taxpayer is entitled, the form can introduce appropriate changes. There is also a possibility to indicate the public benefit organisation to which the taxpayer wants to allocate 1% of the tax each year.

3 Data from the website of the Ministry of Finance: <https://www.gov.pl/web/kas/nowy-rekord-okolo-16-mln-pit-ow-zlozonych-przez-internet-za-2018-r>.

4 Data from the website of the Ministry of Finance: <https://www.gov.pl/web/finanse/pit-przez-internet-najpopularniejsza-usluga>.

Persons (old-age pensioners and disability pensioners) for whom disability pension funds submit the returns may transfer 1% of their tax to a selected public benefit organisation using the e-service PIT-OP statement.

If a taxpayer does not use the statement in the Twój e-PIT service or does not settle the tax in another acceptable form (electronic or paper), the statement prepared for them after 30 April is automatically deemed to have been filed. The exceptions are annual tax returns on PIT-28 and PIT-36 forms. Unlike PIT-37 or PIT-38, these are not subject to automatic acceptance on 30 April.

Thanks to the automatic acceptance of tax returns, taxpayers who fail to file their tax returns are not liable for failure to meet the deadline. In such a situation, if the automatically accepted return shows the amount of tax due, the taxpayer will receive a piece of appropriate information from the tax office by 31 May, indicating the amount of tax to be paid. The deadline for payment of this amount is seven days from the date of delivery of the information. Until the deadline for payment expires, the taxpayer will not be charged default interest. Interest will interest be charged only after the deadline has passed, but not before 1 June.

On the other hand, if the prepared return reveals an overpayment (in any case, regardless of whether the taxpayer accepted the return himself or whether it was accepted automatically), the taxpayer will receive a refund within a shorter period. The deadline for electronic returns is 45 days (instead of 3 months) – (Art. 77 § 1-point 5a of the PIT). However, the deadline for reimbursement of the overpayment is calculated from the date of filing the return. This means that in the case of automatic acceptance, it is counted from 1 May. Self-filed tax returns have priority over tax returns automatically accepted through the Twój e-PIT service.

Automatic acceptance of the return on 30 April does not mean that the taxpayer is prevented from making corrections. For this purpose, he may use the Twój e-PIT service and submit a correction in any legally acceptable form, including paper.

In 2020, due to the pandemic period, the legislator introduced a new regulation allowing the filing of annual PIT returns for 2019 later without incurring consequences on this account. According to 15 zzj of the COVID-19 Act, if the taxpayer submits the return on the amount of income earned (loss incurred) for 2019 and pays the due personal income tax after the deadline, but no later than by 1 June 2020, he will not incur liability on this account. The legislator treated this action as an institution of active contrition referred to in Art. 16 § 4 of the Act of 10.09.999 Fiscal Penal Code.[5] The same consequences apply to submitting a declaration on the amount of the solidarity contribution and its payment in the period between 30 April and 1 June. Thus, the legislator did not explicitly extend the deadline for filing tax returns by 1 month but proposed a solution whereby submitting the recovery after the deadline, i.e., between 30 April and 1 June, would not entail any consequences that no default interest would be charged on taxes not paid on time.

5 JoL 2020, item 19, 568, 695 and 1106.

For persons who wanted to use the Twój e-PIT service but did not have a trusted profile (e.g., due to the lack of a bank account), the Ministry of Digitalisation prepared the so-called temporary trusted profile. Under Art. 33 of the Act of 31 March 2020 amending the COVID-19 Act, the profile was to be valid for three months. Still, the minister responsible for IT was authorised to extend the period of its validity. The interim trusted profile is an instrument prepared only for the period of a pandemic.

In 2020, the Twój e-PIT service was extended to include full access to previous PIT returns, information on the status of overpayment refunds and a substituted tax micro-account. A micro-account is a single, permanent, individual taxpayer account into which PIT, CIT and VAT tax payments are made. Taxpayers who use the Twój e-PIT service when settling their tax can pay their tax online to an automatically added micro-account. Other taxpayers may check their micro-account number in the generator available on the podatki.gov.pl website.

For taxpayers whose tax return reveals an overpayment, a new e-service has been created containing information on the status of the overpayment refund by the tax office.

In 2020, e-declarations in corporate income tax (CIT) were introduced. Also, in this tax, due to the pandemic period, the Ordinance of the Minister of Finance of 27 March 2020 on extending the deadline for filing the return on the amount of income earned (loss incurred) and payment of due tax by taxpayers of corporate income tax (JoL item 542), the period for filing the return and payment of tax was extended until 31 May 2020.

In cases where appropriate electronic forms have not been placed on the tax portal, taxpayers may use the e-PUAP. Using this platform, they can submit applications, explanations, appeals, complaints and reminders, signing them with a trusted profile or qualified electronic signature.

This platform enables the electronic submission of applications for certificates issued by tax authorities. Using e-PUAP, it is possible to obtain a certificate of no arrears in taxes or the status of arrears, as well as fees and fines, a certificate of VAT taxpayer status. Taxpayers may also apply for the issue of critical information on rates (WIS) or essential excise information (WIA).

The portal also allows for the submission and revocation of powers of attorney to represent taxpayers before tax authorities and to handle tax matters on behalf of the taxpayer, including the submission of declarations, statements and other electronic tax documents.

In addition, the platform enables the online submission of so-called general letters, i.e., letters for which no specimen document is required. The condition for available letters to be effective is the existence of an appropriate legal basis applicable to a given type of proceedings. In cases where taxpayers cannot communicate via the tax portal of the Ministry of Finance, they may submit letters to tax offices or local tax authorities using this platform.

Another service that taxpayers can use is biznes.gov.pl. It is primarily dedicated to entrepreneurs (entities intending to start a business and those conducting business). In addition to assistance in setting up and running a business, business entities will also find links to tax forms. Because many of the introduced tax law regulations concerned entrepreneurs in the pandemic period, information and electronic application forms were posted on the website.

A special service dedicated to excise taxpayers and entities obliged to pay customs duties is the Platform of Electronic Services for Taxes and Customs (PUESC). The platform makes it possible to use e-services in handling and controlling trade in goods with third countries and work in excise goods.

2.4 New e-services introduced in the pandemic period

The electronic tools used by taxpayers in the run-up to the pandemic made it possible to handle tax matters without having to visit a tax office. On the other hand, the introduction of new regulations related to preventing, counteracting and combating COVID-19 was accompanied by creating new electronic instruments enabling taxpayers to submit relevant applications via the Internet.

In taxation, the largest number of regulations were aimed at easing taxpayers' difficulties with timely paying liabilities and other instrumental obligations. To this end, deadlines for payment of taxes and submission of returns and declarations were extended. The consequences of failure to meet tax obligations on time were also abolished.

New facilities were introduced for taxpayers with difficulties in timely payment of tax obligations during the pandemic period, using the so-called reliefs to repay tax obligations (Art. 67a and Art. 67b of the Tax Ordinance). A taxpayer who applies for the remission of tax arrears, for the tax to be paid in instalments, or for a deferral of the tax payment deadline during a pandemic or within 30 days of its cancellation, if the tax authority issues a positive decision, will not have to pay a prolongation fee. Following the new regulations, a new simplified application form has been developed. Taxpayers can submit applications online via the biznes.gov.pl portal. Creating an account on this portal and sending documents require a qualified electronic signature or a trusted e-PUAP profile.

The same improvements have been introduced in local taxes constituting municipalities' income, for which the competent authorities are heads of villages, mayors and presidents. Taxpayers of those taxes may also use the institution of reliefs in repayment of tax liabilities. Relevant information in this regard has been posted on the websites of individual local government units. In addition, in the Act of 31 March 2020 amending the COVID-19 Act and in the Shield 2, additional powers were provided for the commune authorities in property tax. The municipal council may adopt a resolution on introducing, for a part of the year 2020, exemption from property tax: land, buildings and structures related to conducting business activity for those groups of entrepreneurs whose financial liquidity has deteriorated due to negative economic consequences due to COVID-19. This exemption may also cover non-governmental organisations. By way of a resolution, the municipal council may also extend for the above groups of entrepreneurs the deadlines for payment of those property tax instalments whose payment falls in April, May and June 2020. The deadline may be extended until 30 September 2020 at the latest.

Municipalities' new financial policy tools leave a considerable margin of political discretion both as to the application of these extraordinary instruments and their scope. To deformalise the procedure related to the use of the support granted to taxpayers, it is not required to attach to the application statements the deterioration of financial liquidity due to the pandemic. Indeed, municipalities must consider the need to support business taxpayers and their financial situation and their fiscal policy in this regard. Verification of taxpayers will be possible at a later stage using the tools provided for tax authorities in the Tax Ordinance Act.

The use of the exemption and the extension of the deadline for payment of property tax does not require an application. Resolutions adopted by the municipal council on introducing exemptions or new deadlines for payment of tax instalments constitute acts of local law. They are generally binding in the municipality's territory, the bodies of which adopted a resolution in this regard. The cities in which such resolutions have been passed have posted them on their websites. Therefore, it was possible to take advantage of the exemption and the extended deadline without the need to introduce new electronic tools.

For VAT taxpayers struggling with liquidity due to a pandemic situation, the possibility of releasing funds held in a VAT account was allowed. The obligation to have such an account was introduced in 2018 to present the so-called split payment mechanism, which aimed to prevent evasion of VAT. Funds accumulated in this account can only be spent on the payment of public-law liabilities. Once the funds are released in a pandemic situation, they can be used for any purpose, including the taxpayer's current activities. At the same time, a possibility has been created for taxpayers to submit applications for releasing funds from the VAT account electronically via the website biznes.gov.pl with a trusted e-PUAP profile signature or a qualified electronic signature.

2.5 Other forms of communication between taxpayers and tax authorities

As of March 2020, the National Fiscal Administration appealed and encouraged the use of primarily remote forms of contact: by e-mail or through an e-PUAP mailbox and to handle matters by phone. Questions can be asked electronically using a form available on the tax portal and via a chat with a consultant of the National Fiscal Information using a special form available on the portal.

Traditional forms of settling issues have not been completely abandoned. However, a visit to the office was possible after making a prior reservation of an appointment. For that purpose, a new service was launched, making it possible to make an appointment using an electronic form available on the website podatki .gov.pl. It was also possible to make an appointment by phone.

The Ministry of Finance has also announced works on developing and implementing the e-Tax Office project, which will be a service analogous to the Twój e-PIT service.

According to the ministry's announcement, it is an effective online tool of an informational and transactional nature, making it possible to handle complex matters, primarily those concerning VAT, PIT and CIT. The service will make available five groups of services: e-Taxpayer, e-Paying Agent, e-Attorney, e-Collector and e-Notary channel. Taxpayers will have access to tax information that concerns them and to cases of other taxpayers for which they have obtained appropriate authorisation. Paying agents, attorneys, bailiffs and notaries will also have access to e-services in this service. These entities will be able to track information on the status of their settlements, the status of cases or submitted documents.

The project also provides the possibility of paying tax and making other transactions related to the available e-services, thanks to online electronic payment. The service creates a wide catalogue of e-services of the National Fiscal Administration available and provides IT support for KAS clients.

2.6 Conclusions

The digital transformation in taxation has gained momentum in recent years. More and more tools for communication with taxpayers are successively appearing, accompanied by the extension of obligations to use electronic instruments in particular taxes. Apart from the advantages for taxpayers in the form of simplifying settlements with the tax office and taking over some of the duties that have been imposed on taxpayers by the tax authorities, e-services allow for better and faster control of irregularities that occur. Thanks to electronic tools, the tax authorities have access to increasing information and taxpayer data. It, in turn, translates into a "tightening" of the system and a reduction in the number of inspections that are burdensome for taxpayers. It is because tax authorities control only those entities whose data disclosed in this way indicate irregularities.

The available e-services and new, additional tools placed on tax portals work very well in the pandemic period. They make it possible to handle all tax matters, including tax proceedings, without the need for direct contact with the tax authorities. Meanwhile, the Twój e-PIT service, through which the National Tax Administration prepared PIT returns for taxpayers, enjoyed record interest.

Work cited

GOV, 'Data from the Website of the Ministry of Finance' https://www.gov.pl/web/kas/twoj-e-pit-nowa-jakosc-w-rozliczeniu-podatku (14.02.2019).

GOV, 'Data from the Website of the Ministry of Finance' https://www.gov.pl/web/kas/nowy-rekord-okolo-16-mln-pit-ow-zlozonych-przez-internet-za-2018-r (07.05.2019).

GOV, 'Data from the Website of the Ministry of Finance' https://www.gov.pl/web/finanse/pit-przez-internet-najpopularniejsza-usluga (02.07.2019).

VII

Education in a Pandemic

1 Problems of Digital Transformation of Universities in Times of Pandemic

First Experiences

Beata Zbarachewicz

1.1 Introduction

Due to the spread of the SARS-CoV-21 virus and the introduction of a temporary restriction on university functioning to the prevention, counteraction and eradication of COVID-19, the work of universities has changed from March 2020. The situation forced universities to search and introduce digital solutions to organise their work on an ongoing basis. According to UNESCO statistics, schools and universities in China and Mongolia were closed on 21 February 2020 due to the coronavirus. Four months later, educational institutions were closed in 123 countries, culminating (data from 1 April) in 193. It meant that the epidemic situation affected the functioning of 91% of pupils and students worldwide. By May 2020, the number had fallen to 139.[1] The data shows the dynamics of the pandemic in 2020 and the global problem concerning the sphere of education. When making decisions on restrictions, the countries' authorities were guided by the safety of pupils, students, teachers and employees of schools and universities.

The aim of the study is to present the introduced statutory and regulatory solutions and to assess their implementation and the effectiveness of the solutions applied in 2020. The thesis is verified that the legal regulations enable the implementation of the university's objectives, and their evolution and application are adequate to the threats. In the research, the dogmatic method was used as the main method and the empirical method as an auxiliary one.

Standardised rules unify the processes, and the way universities operate. Still, applying parts of the regulations in non-standard situations like the COVID-19 epidemic emergency may cause problems or be impossible. The pandemic made it necessary to adapt statutory regulations and internal university regulations to the new conditions. The analysis will be the regulations generally applicable to Polish HEIs concerning the organisation of their work in the first year of the pandemic.

1 *COVID-19 Impact on Education* <https://en.unesco.org/covid19/educationresponse>.

DOI: 10.4324/9781003263968-29

1.2 Legal basis for the functioning of polish universities during the pandemic

In the area of higher education, pandemic solutions were introduced by laws and regulations.[2]

The rules for documenting the studies course are set out in the Regulation of the Minister of Science and Higher Education (MoSHE) of 27 September 2018 on studies.[3] However, the pandemic situation caused numerous amendments to the existing regulation.

- Regulation of the MoSHE of 12.03. 2020 amending the regulation on studies;[4]
- Regulation of the MoSHE of 12.05.2020 amending the regulation on studies;[5]
- Regulation of the MoSHE of 14.08.2020 amending the regulation on studies;[6]
- Regulation of the MoSHE of 29.09.2020 amending the regulation on studies;[7]
- Regulation of the MoSHE of 29.10.2020 amending the regulation on studies;[8]
- Regulation of the MoSHE of 8.01.2021 amending the regulation on studies.[9]

Detailed solutions for the functioning of HEIs are set out in the Regulation of the MoSHE of 11 March 2020 on the temporary restriction of the functioning of certain entities of the system of higher education and science in connection with preventing, counteracting and combating COVID-19[10] and subsequent ones: Regulation of the MoSHE of 16 March 2020 amending the Regulation on the temporary restriction of the functioning of certain entities of the system of higher education and science in connection with preventing, counteracting and combating COVID-19;[11] the Regulation of the MoSHE of 23 March 2020 on the temporary restriction of the functioning of certain entities of the system of higher education and science in connection with preventing, counteracting and combating COVID-19;[12] Regulation of the Ministry of Science and Higher Education of 25 March 2020 amending the Regulation on the temporary restriction of the functioning of certain entities of the system of higher education and science in connection with preventing, counteracting and combating COVID-19;[13] Regulation of the Ministry of Science and Higher Education of 9 April 2020 amending the Regulation on the

2 Act of 31.03.2020 on amending the Act on combating COVID-19 and some other acts (JoL 2020 item 568, Shield 1.0); Shield 2.0; Shield 4.0.
3 JoL 2018 item 1861 with amendments.
4 JoL 2020 item 420.
5 JoL 2020 item 853.
6 JoL 2020 item 1411.
7 JoL 2020 item 1679.
8 JoL 2020 item 1908.
9 JoL 2021 item 62.
10 JoL 2020 item 405.
11 JoL 2020 item 455.
12 JoL 2020 item 511.
13 JoL 2020 item 528.

temporary restriction of the functioning of certain entities of the system of higher education and science in connection with preventing, counteracting and combating COVID-19;[14] Regulation of the Ministry of Science and Higher Education of 24 April 2020 amending the Regulation on the temporary restriction of the functioning of certain entities of the system of higher education and science in connection with preventing, counteracting and combating COVID-19;[15] Regulation of the Ministry of Science and Higher Education of 14 May 2020 amending the Regulation on the temporary restriction of the functioning of certain entities of the system of higher education and science in connection with preventing, counteracting and combating COVID-19;[16] Regulation of the Ministry of Science and Higher Education of 21 May 2020 on temporary restrictions on the functioning of scientific institutes of the Polish Academy of Sciences in connection with preventing, counteracting and combating COVID-19.[17]

Medical schools, schools supervised by the Minister of Defence and art schools had different regulations for the time of the pandemic.

1.3 The role of Shield 2.0 and Shield 4.0 to the functioning of universities in times of pandemic

According to the Law on Higher Education and Science provisions, the rector of a university, within the autonomy to which he is entitled, is responsible for ensuring safe and hygienic working and educational conditions at the university. However, the special situation caused by the pandemic required nationwide action. For this reason, the so-called first anti-crisis shield included a provision allowing the relevant ministers to temporarily restrict or suspend the education of students and doctoral students. Such a decision could be taken only in cases justified by extraordinary circumstances threatening life or health.[18]

The exceptional circumstances associated with the pandemic required specific measures. The response came in the form of the Shield 2.0 and Shield 4.0 crisis shields, which, in addition to solutions for the entire economy, also included science and higher education regulations. The entire academic and scientific community received support. The changes covered lecturers, scientists, students tied to the prevention, counteraction and eradication of COVID-19, other infectious diseases and crisis situations caused by them, the Act of 31 March 2020 on amending certain acts in the health care system related to the prevention, counteraction and eradication of COVID-19 and the Act of 31 March 2020 on amending the Act on specific solutions related to the prevention, counteraction and eradication of COVID-19, other infectious diseases and crisis situations caused by them.

14 JoL 2020 item 643.
15 JoL 2020 item 741.
16 JoL 2020 item 861.
17 JoL 2020 item 911.
18 Shield 1.0.

During the pandemic, university authorities, university employees and students faced numerous organisational problems related to reducing university activities. The universities, to ensure the fulfilment of their tasks, look for the administrative and technical solution.

The solutions introduced by the "Shields" covered the bodies of HEIs primarily, and the amendments to the Act on Higher Education and Science allowed for the transfer of competencies. Rectors gained greater powers to issue orders in matters belonging to the competencies of the university senate in cases where the action of this body is not possible, and decision-making is necessary to ensure the continuity of the university's functioning.[19] For example, if the university senate cannot perform its tasks, the rector may issue orders on matters that are the senate's competencies. Suppose it is the rector who cannot perform his/her tasks. In that case, they shall be performed by a member of the community of the respective higher education institution, indicated by the minister supervising the institution. However, the senate of the higher education institution must approve, at its next meeting, orders issued in such a manner.[20]

The Law on Higher Education and Science introduced provisions allowing for remote meetings of university councils and senates. The sessions could be conducted using IT technologies, ensuring their control and registration, and ensuring votes' secrecy.[21]

The defence of the doctoral dissertation may be conducted outside the seat of the doctoral subject using information technology, ensuring control and registration of the dissertation. Also, the postdoctoral dissertation colloquium may be conducted outside the seat of the postdoctoral provider using information technology, ensuring control of its progress and registration. The provisions also apply to doctoral dissertations, habilitation proceedings and proceedings for the conferment of the title of professor initiated before 1 May 2019. Meetings of the competent authority may be conducted using information technology to ensure that they are monitored and recorded and that votes are secret.

Shield 2.0 introduced the extension of the period of evaluation of scientific activity by one year. In the evaluation, scientific categories will be granted in individual science disciplines, which will translate into the possibility of conducting studies with a general academic profile and granting scientific degrees. The first evaluation of the quality of scientific activity was to cover the years 2017–2020. After the change, it will cover 2017–2021 and start on 1 January 2022.

Shield 2.0 assumes the possibility of obtaining funds for research with the omission of the competition procedure when it concerns scientific research or development works on methods of preventing the spread, infection or combating

19 <https://www.gov.pl/web/nauka/rozwiazania-dla-szkolnictwa-wyzszego-i-nauki-w-drugiej-tarczy-antykryzysowej> (22.04.2020).

20 Tarcze dla środowiska naukowego i akademickiego – podsumowanie zmian <https://www.gov.pl/web/nauka/tarcze-dla-srodowiska-naukowego-i-akademickiego--podsumowanie-zmian> (03.09.2020).

21 Shield 2.0.

infection or infectious disease being the cause of declaring an epidemic threat or epidemic state.

The Act also concerns other financial issues covering the area of science and higher education. Financial resources for higher education and science are granted in the form of a specific subsidy for implementing tasks related to, inter alia, education and support for the implementation of tasks of NAWA, NCN, NCBR and the Łukasiewicz Centre did not use this year may be used in 2021.

During the period of restriction or suspension of the functioning of a higher education institution, periodic evaluations of the academic staff shall not be carried out, and academic staff shall not be referred for periodic examinations and for examinations to issue a decision on the need to grant leave for health reasons.[22] The service credentials of the academic staff shall remain valid, without the need for renewal, during the period of university restriction or suspension and for 60 days thereafter.[23]

The rector may change the organisation of the 2019/2020 academic year as defined in the internal acts of the University. Until 30 September 2020, the doctoral training provider may change the organisation of doctoral training as regulated in the internal acts of the provider.[24]

During the period of restriction or suspension of the functioning of a higher education institution, it will also be possible to grant aid payments to students and doctoral students without the obligation to apply the Code of Administrative Procedure.

Current student affairs should be resolved. According to the regulations, Student ID cards remained valid until 31 March 2020. It was necessary to look for solutions related to the limitations resulting from COVID-19. The Regulation of the Ministry of Science and Higher Education of 12 March 2020 amending the regulation on studies in § 45 extended by law the validity of electronic student cards whose validity was confirmed in the first semester of the academic year 2019/2020. The ID cards remained valid until 31 May 2020, without confirmation. Due to the continuing epidemic condition, further amendments were necessary. The Shield 2 introduced amendments to the Act of 20 July 2018 Law on Higher Education and Science and the Law of 3.07.2018 Introducing the Act – Law on Higher Education and Science. Article 1b(4) added to the Law on Higher Education and Science provides for the extension by the law of the validity of student cards during the period of restriction or suspension of the institution's functioning and 60 days after the end of the period of restriction or suspension. The regulation explicitly emphasises that there is no need to confirm the validity of student identity cards. The provision in question also applies in each case to student IDs whose validity has expired within 30 days preceding the restriction or suspension of the institution's functioning. The above regulations are of key

22 Shield 4.0.
23 Ibid.
24 Shield 2.0.

importance, particularly for students, because of their special rights resulting from student rights, including entitlement to discounts in public transport.[25]

The Ministry of Digitalisation recommended that universities and students use the student mLegitimation, i.e., a mobile application accessible using the mObywatel profile.[26]

Shield 4.0 also introduces the extension of the validity of doctoral cards without confirming their validity for the duration of the suspension of doctoral education and 60 days after its completion. The provision also applies to ID cards that have expired in the 30 days preceding the suspension of doctoral training.[27]

Another solution for HEIs arising from Shield 2.0 is the possibility of carrying out verification of achieved learning outcomes. A higher education institution may conduct credit and final course examinations and diploma examinations outside the institution's headquarters, using information technology ensuring their control and registration. It applies to subject credit, semester examinations and diploma examinations.[28] The university makes the rules for verifying achieved learning outcomes available in the Public Information Bulletin. The provisions of Shield 4.0 abolish the obligation to register examinations, and the change in the provision does not apply only to epidemic situations.

Another change resulting from Shield 4.0 concerns enrolment in second-cycle studies. The provision stipulates that

> for second-cycle studies starting in the academic year 2020/2021, a person may be admitted who presents a certificate of completion of studies containing information on the level, field and profile of studies, the degree obtained and the verbal result of studies. The certificate should be submitted to the university within 30 days from the date of issuing the diploma of graduation, under pain of removal from the list of students.[29]

1.4 Specific solutions resulting from the regulations of the MoSHE for the functioning of HEIs during a pandemic

The first regulation of the MoSHE on temporary restrictions on the functioning of certain entities of the system of higher education and science in connection with preventing, counteracting and combating COVID-19 was issued on 11.03.2020. The scope of the regulation covered higher education institutions supervised by

25 'Komentarz do wybranych przepisów tzw. 'Tarczy antykryzysowej 2.0' dotyczących szkół wyższych (Instytut Rozwoju Szkolnictwa Wyższego (Parlament Studentów Rzeczypospolitej Polskiej 2020) 14 <https://psrp.org.pl/komentarz-do-wybranych-przepisow-tzw-tarczy-antykryzysowej-2-0-dotyczacy-szkol-wyzszych">https://psrp.org.pl/komentarz-do-wybranych-przepisow-tzw-tarczy-antykryzysowej-2-0-dotyczacy-szkol-wyzszych/.

26 <https://www.gov.pl/web/mobywatel/mlegitymacja-studencka>.

27 Shield 4.0.

28 Shield 2.0.

29 Shield 4.0.

the minister in charge of higher education and science. A restriction was introduced on the activities of HEIs, by suspending education in the period from 12 March 2020 to 25 March 2020 in the whole country. The education provided in degree programmes, postgraduate programmes, in other forms and the education of doctoral students provided as part of their courses has been suspended. According to the regulation, during education suspension, classes may be conducted using distance learning methods and techniques, regardless of whether this has been provided for in the curriculum.

The Regulation of 16 March 2020 stipulated that in the period from 18 March 2020 to 25 March 2020, the functioning of higher education institutions supervised by the minister responsible for higher education and science shall be restricted in the territory of the country by limiting the obligation to provide work by their employees on their premises, except when it is necessary to ensure continuity of the functioning of the institution.

The deadline for restricting the functioning of higher education institutions, suspending education, and limiting the obligation to provide work by employees of higher education institutions on their premises in higher education institutions supervised by the minister responsible for higher education and science was extended to 10 April 2020.

According to § 2 of the Regulation of the Minister of Higher Education and Science of 23 March 2020, higher education institutions which during the period of suspension of university education provided classes using distance education methods and techniques may continue to provide courses using these methods and techniques after the end of the period of suspension, but no longer than until 30 September 2020. Due to the continuing epidemic condition, the regulations extended the time for restricting the functioning of HEIs. The next deadline was 24 May 2020.

The necessary conditions for the verification of the achieved learning outcomes were clarified, particularly the conduct of credit and examinations at the end of specific courses and diploma examinations. It was emphasised that credit and examinations might take place outside the headquarters of the institution or its branch using information technology but under the condition of ensuring control of the process of verification of the achieved learning outcomes and its registration.

The Regulation of the Ministry of Science and Higher Education of 14 May 2020 repealed the restriction on the obligation to provide work by HEI employees on their premises. Earlier regulations provided for the exclusion of the limitation on work when it was necessary to ensure the continuity of the functioning of a higher education institution.

The Regulation of the Ministry of Science and Higher Education of 21 May 2020 maintained the restriction on the functioning of higher education institutions supervised by the minister responsible for higher education and science by suspending education and extended the deadline to 30 September 2020 on the territory of Poland. Until 30 September 2020, classes can only be taught using distance learning methods and techniques regardless of whether this has been provided for in the curriculum of the education in question. Higher education institutions may conduct classes at their seats or branches provided for in the study programme to be realised during the final year of study. The rector or the head of another entity providing doctoral education shall give such courses. The rector shall take and determine the conditions for the delivery of courses and the use of the infrastructure of the higher education institution or other entity, as appropriate, ensuring the safety of persons conducting and participating in courses.

The proposed solutions were searching for answers to emerging problems resulting from the introduced restrictions. IT solutions were sought to meet the statutory requirements and enable remote meetings of the senate, university councils, and proceedings granting the degree of doctor, habilitation colloquies. As far as the course of studies is concerned, solutions streamlining the activities of higher education institutions included: conducting classes, conducting examinations and final course tests online, extending the validity of student ID cards without the need to appear in person at the university, electronic diploma theses, replacing the signature on protocols with the authentication of these persons in the ICT system, under the rules of functioning of the system used in a higher education institution to keep records of the course of studies in electronic form.

Higher education institutions may conduct credit and final course examinations and diploma examinations using information technology, ensuring control and registration thereof. It is possible thanks to the changes introduced to the Act on special support instruments in connection with the spread of the SARS-CoV-2 virus, which allowed universities to use electronic means of communication and electronic solutions to a greater extent than before. Shield 2.0 solutions make it possible to verify achieved learning outcomes using information technology to ensure their control and recording. Examinations can be online with the obligation to register for the examination course, and it applies to both semester examinations and diploma examinations.[30]

The provisions of Shield 4.0 abolish the obligation to register examinations, and the change in the provision does not apply only to epidemic situations. The introduced solutions make it possible to conduct examinations using electronic tools of communication, ensuring in particular: real-time transmission of the diploma examination between its participants, multilateral real-time communication in which the participants of the diploma examination may express themselves during the examination while observing the necessary security rules.[31]

1.5 Distance learning using distance education methods and techniques

Before the pandemic, e-learning and distance learning were treated by universities as tools to support the teaching process. The 2014 study E-learning in European

30 Shield 2.0.
31 Shield 4.0.

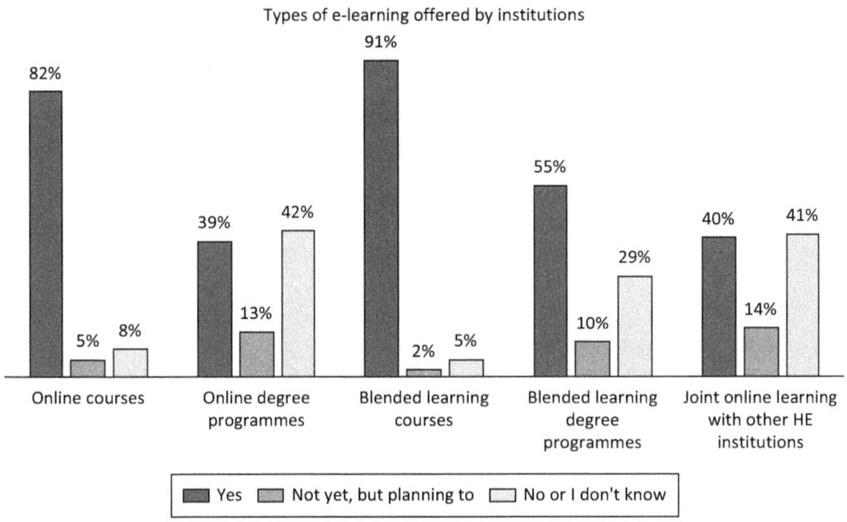

Figure VII.1.1 E-learning offered by universities in 2013. Source: Gaebel 2013. (See note 32).

Higher Education Institutions shows that virtually all participating higher education institutions offered some digital learning, and more than half offered – or at least planned – online study programmes.[32] It is presented in Figure VII.1.1. Ten Polish universities participated in the study, including four polytechnics, two economics universities, two universities and two natural science universities.

As shown in Figure VII.1.2, the choice of e-learning was most often related to the desire to combine studies with work.

The reduction in the university's functioning in connection with COVID introduced significant changes in the organisation of the educational process. The teaching process functioned remotely, and schools at all levels switched to pandemic-era remote learning. They conducted classes using distance learning methods and techniques regardless of whether this was provided for in the curriculum of a particular course.

It is not only schools and universities that differ in their level of preparation for remote learning. As noted by the Conference of Rectors of Academic Schools in Poland, teachers, pupils and students are ready for remote learning to varying degrees. It concerns their skills and equipment, and access to the Internet. The Minister of National Education admits that 92% of students have access to the Internet, which means that 8% of students are excluded from obligatory remote learning. In this respect, the actual percentage of students excluded is much higher

32 M. Goebel, V. Kupriyanova, R. Morais, E. Colucci, 'E-learning in European Higher Education Institutions November 2014, Results of a mapping survey conducted in October-December 2013' (2014) 29.

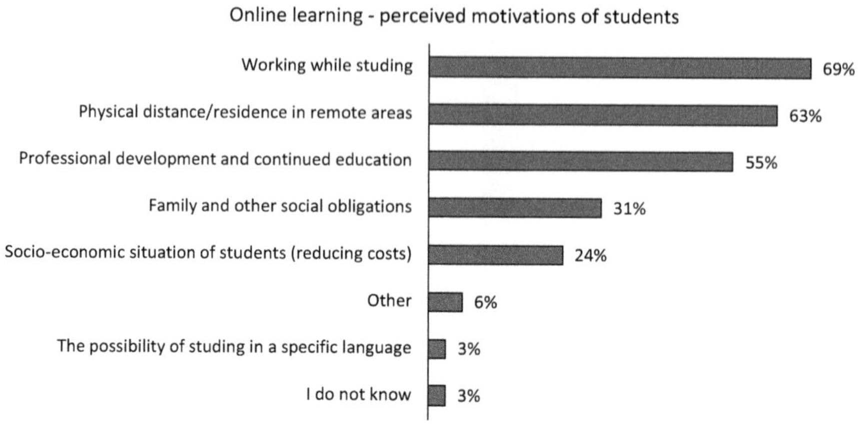

Figure VII.1.2 Reasons for choosing e-learning 2013. Source: Gaebel 2013. (See note 32).

due to other deficiencies. KRASP stresses that it is the state's responsibility to ensure that all children have access to education.[33]

Distance learning at the level of the Law of 20.07.2018. Law on Higher Education and Science[34] is regulated in Art. 67, para 4, which states that: if the specificity of education in a degree programme in a particular field of study allows it, part of the learning outcomes covered by the study programme may be obtained through classes conducted using distance education methods and techniques with the use of infrastructure and software ensuring synchronous and asynchronous interaction between students and academic teachers.

The legislator allowed for the realisation of part of the learning outcomes provided for a given field of study. This dimension was defined in the regulation of the MoSHE of 27 September 2018 on studies. Under §13 of this regulation, the number of ECTS credits obtained through distance learning methods and techniques cannot be higher than 50% of the number of ECTS credits required for graduation at a given level. For degree programmes with a general academic profile, starting from the academic year 2020/2021, it will be 75% of the number of ECTS points.

Due to the restrictions on the functioning of HEIs until 30 September 2020, full-time education has been suspended in the territory of the country, HEIs provide lectures using distance learning methods and techniques regardless of whether this has been provided for in the curriculum of a given education. In the case of the provision of distance education, there shall be no limitation on the

33 Stanowisko komisji ds. komunikacji i odpowiedzialności społecznej KRASP z 6 kwietnia 2020 roku <https://www.krasp.org.pl/pl/Aktualnosci/?id=21200/Stanowisko_dotyczace_dostepu_do_edukacji_w_czasie_epidemii>.

34 JoL 2018 item 1668.

number of ECTS credits that may be obtained through distance education using methods and techniques specified in the study programmes.

The provision of Art. 67(4) of the UPSWiN[35] contains another important normative content. It is about linking distance education with the use of IT infrastructure ensuring synchronous and asynchronous contact between lecturer and student. Synchronous contact involves real-time communication, asynchronous contact involves the delivery of teaching materials to the student without maintaining unity of time (and place) in the teaching process[36]. The Ministry of Science and Higher Education did not recommend the platform for remote education. Universities independently searched for solutions and made use of previous experiences. For example, classes in various forms of distance learning at the Cardinal Stefan Wyszyński University in Warsaw are conducted through the university's YouTube channel, the Moodle platform (e.uksw.edu.pl), the MS Teams application (office365.uksw.edu.pl), Umail in the USOSweb system, Skype communicator, Zoom.us application, Google Classroom application.

The advantages of remote learning are flexibility, availability of didactic materials, the possibility of feedback between trainer and trainee.[37]

The remote form concerned the classes and the control of the achieved learning outcomes. The university was obliged to publish the rules of conducting them in the Public Information Bulletin.[38]

The Ministry of Science and Higher Education on 2 September published Recommendations for university authorities on the organisation of the academic year 2020/2021 Organisation of education in the new academic year.[39] Decisions on the choice of the teaching model were left to the rectors. The recommended way of organising education is a mixed model. A large part of lecture, conversation and seminar classes, and some exercise and project classes are held using distance learning methods and techniques. On the other hand, the remaining courses take place in a stationary format.

The coronavirus pandemic requires special safety rules to be observed. Therefore, in a situation where the university will carry out classes in a face-to-face form, it is necessary to remember about such organisation that will minimise the risk of infection – e.g., by reducing the size of groups, as well as such changes in the timetable that will not allow the simultaneous accumulation of too many

35 JoL 2018 item 1686.

36 *Rekomendacja ws. zmian w przepisach dotyczących wykorzystania w* procesie kształcenia akademickiego metod i technik kształcenia na odległość przygotowana na zlecenie Centrum Analiz Legislacyjnych i Gospodarczych, 2020, p. 4.

37 Monarcha-Matlak, A. 'E-learning w administracji publicznej' in Grażyna Szpor, Wojciech Wiewiórowski (eds.), *Internet. Prawno-informatyczne problemy sieci, portali i e-usług* (C.H. Beck, 2012) 374.

38 Shield 4.0.

39 *Rekomendacje dla uczelni Organizacja kształcenia w nowym roku akademickim* <https://www.gov.pl/web/nauka/organizacja-ksztalcenia-w-nowym-roku-akademickim-rekomendacje-dla-wladz-uczelni> (02.09.2020)

people. (Ministry of Science and Higher Education, 2020). When organising education, Rectors of universities are obliged to consider the assumptions from the letter of the Chief Sanitary Inspector of 12 May 2020 to the MoSHE,[40] they should also consider the Environmental Guidelines in connection with the partial restoration of university activities.[41]

1.6 Digital transformation – a challenge for universities

The pandemic has highlighted the importance of digital infrastructure and has also drawn attention to digital competencies and continuous improvement of competencies and qualifications.

Quoting from the Commission's proposal for a Regulation of the European Parliament and of the Council establishing the Digital Europe programme for 2021–2027:

> Digital transformation is affecting all sectors of the economy and changing the way we live, work and communicate. Future prosperity will be underpinned by investment in strategic digital capabilities and strategic digital infrastructure, upgrading skills and modernising the interface between government and citizens.[42]

Digital transformation and green transformation will play a central and priority role in the successful recovery of the economy.[43]

The Communication on the future of research and innovation and the European Research Area to define a new approach to innovation and ensure optimal use of the EU budget highlights the need to launch public-private partnerships in Horizon Europe.[44] For the success of the digital transformation, it is essential to develop skills and the opportunities they can create for society. There are 1 million job vacancies for digital experts in Europe. At the same time, 70% of companies indicate that they are delaying their investments because they cannot find employees with the right skills. It is an opportunity for universities to offer new courses to develop digital competencies and new skills. There is also a task

40 Pismo Głównego Inspektora Sanitarnego z 12 maja 2020 roku do Ministra Nauki i Szkolnictwa Wyższego (EP.NE.743.64.2020). Letter GIS 2020.

41 *Środowiskowe wytyczne w związku z częściowym przywracaniem działalności uczelni* <https://www.gov.pl/web/nauka/srodowiskowe-wytyczne-w-zwiazku-z-czesciowym-przywracaniem-dzialalnosci-uczelni> 18.05.2020.

42 COM/2018/434 final - 2018/0227 (COD) <https://eur-lex.europa.eu/legal-content/PL/TXT/?qid=1591479211249&uri=CELEX:52018PC0434#footnote7>.

43 G. Szpor, 'Jawność i jej ograniczenia. T.1 Idee i pojęcia' (Wyd C.H.Beck 2016) 125–129.

44 Communication p. 12: *Zmiany w tymczasowych ramach środków pomocy państwa w celu wsparcia gospodarki w kontekście trwającej epidemii COVID-19*. Dz Urz UE 2020 C 164/3 <https://eur-lex.europa.eu/legal-content/PL/TXT/?qid=1591479211249&uri=CELEX:52020XC0513(01)> <https://eur-lex.europa.eu/content/news/index.html>.

for higher education. Our higher education and vocational education and training systems should train more scientists, engineers and technicians that the labour market needs.

Digitisation, automation, and advances in the development of artificial intelligence will require an unprecedented shift in skills for industrial workers. The acquisition of new professional skills and retraining should be an important part of our social market economy. Investment in skills should be increased, and lifelong learning should become a common way of acquiring knowledge. It will require concerted action by industry, Member States, social partners, and universities through a new skills pact to contribute to upgrading or re-skilling and unlock public and private investment. The agreement will focus on sectors with high growth potential for Europe and on sectors undergoing the most significant change. It is a great opportunity for the European education area. Universities should offer courses equipping graduates with digital competencies.

1.7 Conclusions

As the International Association of Universities (IAU) notes, the coronavirus crisis has drawn attention to, and at the same time posed many new and unexpected challenges for, higher education institutions. Universities can forge new paths for crisis management, and researchers should make efforts to better understand the virus and slow its spread. The pandemic situation creates challenges but also opportunities for European universities, regarding digitisation and digital learning and teaching, open science, research, quality assurance, university autonomy, funding and citizen engagement.[45]

The COVID-19 pandemic emergency caused constraints on the day-to-day of universities and caused the law and its application to change. The work of the universities during the pandemic was not suspended, further restrictions were gradually lifted, and current activities were restored. The universities were forced to develop new solutions, which enabled education and day-to-day university work to be carried out remotely, while maintaining the requirements arising from the regulations of the Ministry of Science and Higher Education and sanitary requirements.

Based on the analysis carried out, it can be concluded that the epidemic threat forced the introduction of new solutions and issuance of legal acts defining other than previously applicable rules for the functioning of HEIs during the pandemic. Numerous solutions intensifying digitisation of documentation and the use of electronic communication in its processing, introduced in connection with the restrictions on the activities of HEIs during the pandemic, were not limited only to the time of the pandemic. It can be assumed that most of the solutions introduced during the pandemic will enter permanently into the procedures and organisation of university work.

45 *Covid-19 and universities* <https://eua.eu/issues/27.html>.

Empirical studies involving document analysis and participant observation have shown that in non-standard situations, such as the current COVID-19 epidemic emergency, the application of some regulations is problematic or even impossible. The pandemic made it necessary to establish new regulations, both statutory and company-specific, and to change the application of the law. Based on the analysis carried out, it was indicated that changes were necessary in the organisation of the university's work regarding the education process, which from March 2020 is carried out exclusively online, examinations, including diploma examinations online (diploma theses and documentation are kept in electronic form). Electronic solutions required securing appropriate computer equipment, equipped with webcams and microphones, and an efficient Internet connection. It also required students and university staff to acquire new digital competences. Some of the solutions introduced during the pandemic will probably also be used after the pandemic has ended. The changes that occurred during the pandemic demonstrated the need for new competences. New fields of study including digital competences are an opportunity and a task for universities.

Works cited

Goebel, M., Kupriyanova, V., Morais R., and Colucci, E., *E-Learning in European Higher Education Institutions*, results of a mapping survey conducted in October–December 2013 (2014), 29.

Komentarz do wybranych przepisów tzw., *"Tarczy antykryzysowej 2.0" dotyczących szkół wyższych*, Instytut Rozwoju Szkolnictwa Wyższego, Parlament Studentów Rzeczypospolitej Polskiej (Kwiecień, Warsaw 2020), 14.

Monarcha-Matlak, A., 'E-Learning w administracji publicznej' in (eds.) G. Szpor and W. Wiewiórowski, *Internet. Prawno-informatyczne problemy sieci, portali i e-usług* (C.H. Beck, Warsaw 2012), 374.

Kotowski, A., Michalski, M., and Syryt, A., *Rekomendacja ws. zmian w przepisach dotyczących wykorzystania w*, procesie kształcenia akademickiego metod i technik kształcenia na odległość przygotowana na zlecenie (Centrum Analiz Legislacyjnych i Gospodarczych, Warsaw 2020).

Szpor, G., *Jawność i jej ograniczenia. T.1 Idee i pojęcia* (C. H. Beck, Warsaw 2016), 125–129.

2 Use of Educational Applications, Including Video Games, by Public Entities during the Pandemic

Konrad Radomiński

2.1 Introduction

The coronavirus pandemic has rapidly accelerated the digital transformation of education, work, commerce, and social and family life. As a result, public entities have faced many challenges in carrying out their actions. This chapter focuses on activities belonging to non-imperative public law instruments, especially on social-organisational action of administration in the scope of the provision of information to citizens (information provision). Within this scope, the specific types of information provided to citizens, such as educational and preventive information (public warnings) designated to support remote education and to limit the rapid and uncontrolled spread of coronavirus, were taken as the research area. Because the providing of educational and preventive information had to be done remotely during the pandemic, it was decided to explore a specific type of measures that could increase the effectiveness of information provision, such as video games and educational applications.

This chapter aims to verify the thesis of video games and educational applications, and the empirical method was used to verify this thesis.

The first part of the chapter presents the results of a query of the "Serwis Rzeczpospolitej GOV.pl" (Polish Republic Service GOV.pl). The question aimed to determine the scope in which public entities supplemented information provision by educational applications and video games.

The second part of the chapter analyses formal and informal public-private video game involving actions intended to increase the effectiveness of the information provision that support lockdown maintenance.

The third part of the chapter analyses the popularity of video games in Poland in different age groups. It also explores the impact of tightening and loosening the lockdown on the number of players, using the example of the game *World of Tanks*. This analysis aims to determine whether the information provision through video games and educational applications could meet with public approval.

DOI: 10.4324/9781003263968-30

2.2 Video games and educational apps as tools to support non-manual information instruments of public actors in education

A query of the portal "Serwis Rzeczypospolitej GOV.pl" (which integrates the websites of all government administration entities) by the keyword "games" returned 1,016 results. Of these, 303 results were related to video games. Other results included information on gambling games, playing on the musical instruments, staff games, sports games, family picnics, board games, etc. Some results were even unrelated to the keyword of the query and appeared in the results because the "games" keyword was within other words. It seemed reasonable to make the query criterion more specific by using the phrase "video games". However, this led to an increase of the results to 1996, caused by the query-engine defects. Despite putting both keywords in inverted commas, the query returned results in which at least one of the keywords, i.e., "games" or "video," was used. Moreover, due to the limited possibilities of filtering tools and the lack of sorting tools, the analysis of all 1,016 results had to be carried out manually. Despite the difficulties, public entities actions on information provision involving video games from the pandemic period were identified.

The first identified public entity action is conducted based on the Resolution of the Council of Ministers No. 43/2019 of 28 May 2019 on the establishment of the multi-year programme "IT Talent Development Program for 2019–2029" (M. P. of 2019, item 571, as amended), the "Let's Code" campaign. During the pandemic period, to make remote learning more effective and attractive, the campaign's educational offerings were supplemented with 22 video games and educational applications for programming learning for the youngest, prepared by commercial entities. These include a special edition of the popular game Minecraft and games with characters from Disney cartoons such as Moana or Frozen and other movies such as Star Wars or Wonder Woman.[1] This selection of games seems attractive to children. A small disadvantage of this action is the fact that the organisers of the campaign only collected in one place links to games created by commercial studios instead of preparing their public products. On the other hand, the need for rapid action to provide children with attractive and educationally valuable ways of spending their time during a pandemic ruled out the development of attractive video games and educational applications by public entities by themselves. However, it should be postulated to develop public video games and educational applications instead of using only commercial ones.

The second public action is a pilot study on video games in schools, which started on 8 September 2020. This is intended to implement the core curriculum for developing students' digital competencies. The study is to result in creating a database of video games and educational applications on the Integrated

1 GOV, 'Gry i aplikacje online' (*Serwis Rzeczypospolitej Polskiej*) <https://www.gov.pl/web/koduj/gry-i-zabawy> (17.08.2021).

Educational Platform epodreczniki.pl.[2] So far, six educational games tailored for primary school pupils have been made available in the so-called Games Zone.[3] In addition, the portal includes educational mathematical applications prepared by the University of Łódź and a link to educational applications "Godność, wolność i niepodległość" ("Dignity, Freedom and Independence") and "Dziedzictwo kulturowe Jana Pawla II" ("the Cultural Heritage of John Paul II"). The pilot study is still ongoing, so more video games and educational applications are expected to be made available gradually.

The third public action involving video games and educational application is the Ministry of Science and Higher Education's "Remote Lessons" campaign, which has been running from March 2020 to February 2021.[4] Its aim was to increase the effectiveness of remote learning and student engagement in the classroom by providing attractive multimedia materials. Among them, many video games and educational applications for primary and pre-school students have also been made available. The significant number of these is indicated by the fact that the campaign appeared 144 times in the query results. Most of the video games and educational applications which has been made available were commercial works. The fact that games and educational applications intended to support the educational process were quickly collected and made available in one place is positive. However, it should be postulated to develop public video games and educational applications in the future instead of using only commercial ones (as in the case of the "Let's Code" campaign).

As a fourth action, it was decided to collectively analyse the support given by different public entities to the "Remote Lessons" campaign in the framework of their other projects on video games and educational applications developed.

Before the outbreak of the pandemic, the Ministry of Education and Science planned to develop two educational applications for schoolchildren as part of the "Niepodległa" ("Independent") programme (to mark the centenary of Poland's independence). At the end of 2019, the "Dignity, Freedom and Independence" and in February 2021, the "Cultural Heritage of John Paul II" applications have been released. Both applications provide supportive teaching material for primary and secondary school students.[5]

2 GOV, 'Gry komputerowe i wideo w szkołach – rusza pilotaż programu' (*Serwis Rzeczypospolitej Polskiej*, 08.09.2020) <https://www.gov.pl/web/edukacja-i-nauka/gry-komputerowe-i-wideo-w-szkolach-rusza-pilotaz-programu> (18.08.2021).

3 Ministry of Science and Higher Education, 'Strefa Gier' (*Strefa Gier,*) <https://zpe.gov.pl/a/stefa-gier/DxuxDTnQJ> (12.08.2021).

4 GOV, 'Zdalne lekcje' (*Serwis Rzeczypospolitej Polskiej*) <https://www.gov.pl/web/zdalnelekcje> (17.08.2021).

5 GOV, 'Innowacyjne narzędzie dla nauczycieli historii – gra edukacyjna „Godność, wolność i niepodległość" wchodzi w fazę pilotażu' (*Serwis Rzeczypospolitej Polskiej*, 20.12.2019) <https://www.gov.pl/web/edukacja-i-nauka/gra-edukacyjna-niepodlegla> (18.08.2021); GOV, 'Gra edukacyjna „Dziedzictwo kulturowe Jana Pawła II"' (*Serwis Rzeczypospolitej Polskiej*, 16.02.2021) <https://www.gov.pl/web/edukacja-i-nauka/gra-edukacyjna-dziedzictwo-kulturowe-jana-pawla-ii> (20.08.2021).

In 2021, the educational platform "Ekoesperymentarium" ("Eco-experimentarium") has been released in cooperation with the Ministry of Climate and Environment. Educational applications for children aged 5–10 have been made available on this platform.[6]

In December 2020. The National Heritage Institute has launched an online educational application, "Zabytek" ("Monument") that allowed, among other things, to view virtual 3D models of 603,530 Polish monuments. This allowed students to learn about their country's most important monuments without leaving home and exposing themselves to coronavirus infection.[7]

In October 2020, Statistics Poland released Census of Agriculture educational apps aimed at primary school students.[8]

In September 2020, the joint-stock company of the State Treasury "Polska Grupa Energetyczna" (PGE) (Polish Energy Group) has prepared a platform containing educational video games and educational applications for primary school students entitled "Przygody Kota Ciepłosława" ("The Adventures of Ciepłosław the Cat").[9]

In April 2020, the Ministry of Infrastructure in cooperation with the General Inspection of Road Transport (GITD) and the Railway Transport Office (UTK) also joined the action of supporting the "Remote lessons" campaign.[10] GITD has prepared an educational platform entitled "Bezpieczna Szkoła Krokodyla Tirka" ("TIR the Crocodile Safe School"), where educational materials for children were place.[11] UTK has prepared an educational platform "Railway ABC" and an educational mobile platform game under the same title.[12]

6 GOV, 'Edukacja ekologiczna' (*Serwis Rzeczypospolitej Polskiej*) <https://www.gov.pl/web/klimat/edukacja-ekologiczna> (17.08.2021); Mamy Projekt, 'Graj' (*Graj*) < https://ekoeksperymentarium.pl/graj> (17.08.2021).

7 GOV, 'Materiały edukacyjne Narodowego Instytutu Dziedzictwa' (*Serwis Rzeczypospolitej Polskiej*, 11.12.2020) <https://www.gov.pl/web/edukacja-i-nauka/materialy-edukacyjne-narodowego-instytutu-dziedzictwa> (19.08.2021); National Institute of Cultural Heritage, 'Obiekty 3D' (Obiekty 3D) <https://zabytek.pl/pl/obiekty?media=3d&strona=2> (19.08.2021).

8 GOV, 'Materiały edukacyjne dotyczące Spisu Rolnego – zachęcamy do pobrania' (*Serwis Rzeczypospolitej Polskiej*, 29.10.2020) <https://www.gov.pl/web/edukacja-i-nauka/materialy-edukacyjne-dotyczace-spisu-rolnego--zachecamy-do-pobrania> (19.08.2021; Statistics Poland, 'Materiały edukacyjne' (*Powszechny Spis Rolny 2020*) <https://spisrolny.gov.pl/materialy-edukacyjne> (19.08.2021).

9 GOV, 'Przygody Kota Ciepłosława – projekt edukacyjny PGE Energia Ciepła' (*Serwis Rzeczypospolitej Polskiej*, 23.09.2020) <https://www.gov.pl/web/edukacja-i-nauka/przygody-kota-cieploslawa> (18.08.2021); PGE Group, 'Poznaj Kota Ciepłosława' (*Poznaj Kota Ciepłosława*) <https://kotcieploslaw.pl/dla-uczniow/gry> (18.08.2021).

10 GOV, 'Edukacja o bezpieczeństwie online' (*Serwis Rzeczypospolitej Polskiej*, 08.04.2020) <https://www.gov.pl/web/infrastruktura/edukacja-o-bezpieczenstwie-online> (18.08.2021).

11 General Inspection of Road Transport, 'Bezpieczna Szkoła Krokodyla Tirka' (*Bezpieczna Szkoła Krokodyla Tirka*) <https://gitd.gov.pl/edukacja/materialy-edukacyjne> (18.08.2021).

12 Railway Transport Office, 'KolejoweABC – Peronowo' (*Peronowo*) <https://kolejoweabc.pl/peronowo> (18.08.2021).

In April 2020, the Research and Academic Computer Network (NASK) launched the "Akademia NASK" ("NASK Academy") platform, which makes available an educational role-playing game "Rufus w opałach" ("Rufus in trouble") created a few years earlier. Its aim is to prepare children for the threats they may face both in the virtual and real world.[13]

In February 2020, the Institute of National Remembrance has released an educational video game "Polish Underground State," based on the mechanics of the popular board game "Memo." The game is designed to help students acquire knowledge about the heroes of the Polish independence underground.[14]

Polish State Railways (PKP), within the framework of the "Safe crossing" campaign, has made available an educational platform with educational games for children, "The safe crossing VR" application, allowing children to learn appropriate behaviour around railways in a safe virtual environment, and the game "Safe crossing – challenge," available for personal computers and mobile devices.[15]

The National Museum in Katowice has also published its educational application with quizzes to support the "Remote Learning" campaign.[16]

Some of the above-mentioned video games and educational applications were used during the actions of the Chancellery of the Prime Minister "Children's e-Day 2020" and "Winter holidays 2021," which were designed to provide children with interesting and safe forms of spending time in isolation.

Through the "GOV.pl" portal public entities have promoted also video games and educational applications developed by non-governmental or supranational entities, including the "Cyberchronix" game developed by EU bodies to make it easier to learn and understand the provisions of the GDPR,[17] and the application developed by the non-governmental organisation "Demagog" intended to teach how to recognise fake news in the Internet. The six thematic categories were

13 GOV, 'Poznaj cykl zabaw edukacyjnych o bezpieczeństwie w sieci – #zostanwdomu bezpiecznie z Akademią NASK' (*Serwis Rzeczypospolitej Polskiej*, 10.04.2020) <https://www.gov.pl/web/koduj/poznaj-cykl-zabaw-edukacyjnych-o-bezpieczenstwie-w-sieci--zostanwdomu-bezpiecznie-z-akademia-nask> (19.08. 2021); Research and Academic Computer Network, 'Rufus w Opałach' (*Rufus w Opałach*) <https://akademia.nask.pl/gra.html> (19.08.2021).

14 GOV, 'Aplikacja „Polskie Państwo Podziemne" – zachęcamy do pobrania' (*Serwis Rzeczypospolitej Polskiej*, 14.02.2020) <https://www.gov.pl/web/edukacja-i-nauka/aplikacja-polskie-panstwo-podziemne--zachecamy-do-pobrania> (18.08.2021); Institute of National Remembrance, 'Polskie Państwo Podziemne" – do pobrania' (*Instytut Pamięci Narodowej*) <https://ipn.gov.pl/pl/aktualnosci/88767,Aplikacja-Polskie-Panstwo-Podziemne-do-pobrania.html> (19.08.2021).

15 Polish State Railways, '#Zostańwdomu – edukacja poprzez zabawę z kampanią społeczną „Bezpieczny przejazd…"' (*Bezpieczny przejazd*, 07.04.020) <https://www.bezpieczny-przejazd.pl/aktualnosci/detail/zostanwdomu-edukacja-poprzez-zabawe-z-kampania-spoleczna-bezpieczny-przejazd> (11.08.2021).

16 National Museum in Kielce, 'Quizy' (*Quizy*) <https://mnki.pl/pl/edukacja/quizy/quizy> (12.08.2021).

17 EU Science Hub, 'Cyber Chronix' (*Cyber Chronix*, 19.04.2021) <https://ec.europa.eu/jrc/en/research-topic/security-privacy-and-data-protection/cyber-chronix> (11.08.2021).

also the topic of vaccination, particularly topical during a pandemic (GOV 2021a, Demagog.org 2021).[18]

Further actions identified by the query relate to cooperation between public and commercial entities in the scope of using video games to support information provision, primarily information helpful in preventing the rapid and uncontrolled spread of coronavirus. For this reason, they will be addressed in the next sub-chapter.

2.3 Cooperation between public and commercial entities in the scope of using video games to prevent the rapid and uncontrolled spread of the coronavirus

Successfully maintaining lockdown has proven challenging for public entities. Repressive instruments in fines and administrative penalties have not always been effective. Consequently, public entities have – within the framework of the non-imperative public law instruments at their disposal – established cooperation with entrepreneurs or non-governmental organisations to promote safe time spent at home. This cooperation has been focused in Poland under the slogan #Zostańwdomu (#StayHome). What greatly facilitated the possibility of public-private cooperation was the exemption of supplies and services necessary to prevent the rapid and uncontrolled spread of coronavirus from the public procurement procedure. The only requirement was the disclosure of information about the date of conclusion of the agreement, its subject and value, as well as information about the counterparties and indication of the circumstances justifying its conclusion in this special mode.[19] This has made it possible to significantly reduce the time taken to establish collaborations, also involving the video games industry.

The most important public-private initiative implemented by the Ministry of Digital Affairs under the patronage of the President of the Republic of Poland in cooperation with the video game industry was "Grarantanna" (word play containing words "game" and "quarantine") organised in spring 2020. During "Grarantanna" there were, among the others, "Grarantanna Cup" eSports tournaments in the most popular multiplayer games, organised in cooperation with ESL Poland and well-known Youtubers. 78,542 players actively participated in these tournaments. In addition, webinar RPG sessions were held, with over 4,000 players participating. 14,000 people attended webinars on video game development. From those participants 40 teams has been created and qualified to the 2020 game design competition. Over 9,000 people attended the webinars and competitions on the game "Minecraft." In total, the presented event engaged around 100,000

18 GOV, 'Aplikacja umożliwiająca rozpoznawanie fake newsów w internecie' (*Serwis Rzeczypospolitej Polskiej*, 10.02.2021) <https://www.gov.pl/web/krrit/aplikacja-umozliwiajaca-rozpoznawanie-fake-newsow-w-internecie> (20.08.2021); Demagog.org, 'Nie daj się wkręcić w fake newsy!' (*Fajnie, że wiesz!*) < https://aplikacja.fajniezewiesz.pl > (20.08.2021).

19 Art. 6 COVID-19 Act.

people and around 300,000 people visited the event website itself.[20] The success of this campaign has resulted not only in the transfer of attractive knowledge and skills to thousands of people, but also in making it easier to maintain lockdown without the need for use of repressive public law instruments.

Video game design championships accompanied "Grarantanna." In June 2020, a game design championship commemorating the 100th anniversary of the Battle of Warsaw was held, co-organised by KGHM, the Krakow Technology Park and Game Planet.[21] In June 2021, the Chancellery of the Prime Minister organised another game design championship, for pupils and students.[22]

In addition, the #stayathome campaign was also accompanied by broadcasts of eSports tournaments on public television (online and on air). These included Polish and European World of Tanks league tournaments held in March, April and June 2020.[23] Further broadcasts took place in November/December 2020[24] January/April[25] and May/June 2021.[26] Parallel to the UEFA Euro 2020 finals, the publicly televised eEuro 2021 finals took place using the PES 2021 game and other games using the FIFA 2021 game.

20 GOV, 'Czy jesteście gotowi na GRARANTANNĘ?' (*Serwis Rzeczypospolitej Polskiej*, 08.03.2020) <https://www.gov.pl/web/cyfryzacja/czy-jestescie-gotowi-na-grarantanne> (8.08.2020); GOV, 'Poznaj mistrzów Grarantanny Cup!' (*Serwis Rzeczypospolitej Polskiej*, 20.05.2020) <https://www.gov.pl/web/cyfryzacja/poznaj-mistrzow-grarantanny-cup> (8.08.2020); Ministry of Digital Affairs and Teatrikon, 'Grarantanna Game Jam' (*Grarantanna Game Jam*) <https://itch.io/jam/grarantanna-game-jam/entries> (8.08.2020); Ministry of Digital Affairs and Teatrikon, 'Grarantanna' (*Grarantanna*) <https://www.grarantanna.pl/#strona-glowna> (8.08.2021).

21 Krakow Technology Park, '1920 Jam Bitwa Warszawska' (*1920 Jam Bitwa Warszawska*) <http://1920jam.pl/gry/> (15.08.2021).

22 GOV, 'Mistrzostwa w projektowaniu gier – przedłużamy konkurs!' (*Serwis Rzeczypospolitej Polskiej*, 17 Jun 2021) <https://www.gov.pl/web/cyfryzacja/mistrzostwa-w-projektowaniu-gier--przedluzamy-konkurs> (20.08.2021).

23 TVP Sport.pl, 'Za nami emocjonujący dzień Polskiej Ligi World of Tanks' (*TVP Sport eSport*, 26.03.2020) <https://sport.tvp.pl/47294983/za-nami-emocjonujacy-dzien-polskiej-ligi-world-of-tanks> (07.08.2020); TVP Sport.pl, 'Esport, Europejska Liga World of Tanks na twitchu TVP Sport [transmisja, live, online, stream]' (*TVP Sport eSport*, 22.04.2020) <https://sport.tvp.pl/47260035/esport-europejska-liga-world-of-tanks-na-twitch-tvp-sport-transmisja-live-online-stream-na-zywo> (07.08.2020; TVP Sport.pl, 'Polska Liga World of Tanks znów w TVP Sport! Czas na drugą edycję' (*TVP Sport eSport*, 16.07.2020) https://sport.tvp.pl/48995929/polska-liga-world-of-tanks-znow-w-tvp-sport-czas-na-druga-edycje (07.08.2020).

24 TVP Sport.pl, 'World of Tanks: Aż 9 drużyn zawalczy w Europejskiej Lidze' (*TVP Sport eSport*, 30.11.2020) <https://sport.tvp.pl/51101184/europejska-liga-world-of-tanks-ponownie-w-tvp-sport> (15.08.2021).

25 TVP Sport.pl, 'Esport, Europejska Liga World of Tanks - 2. turniej kwalifikacyjny, 2. Dzień. [ZAPIS]' (*TVP Sport eSport*, 06.01.2021) <https://sport.tvp.pl/51664042/europejska-liga-world-of-tanks-2-turniej-kwalifikacyjny-2-dzien-zapis> (15.08.2021); TVP Sport.pl, 'Esport: nadciąga kolejny sezon Europejskiej Ligi World of Tanks w TVP Sport!' (*TVP Sport eSport*, 05.04.2021) <https://sport.tvp.pl/53142855/esport-nadciaga-kolejny-sezon-europejskiej-ligi-world-of-tanks-w-tvp-sport> (15.08.2021).

26 TVP Sport.pl, 'Esport: 8 polskich drużyn zagra o 10000 zł w World of Tanks Polish Tournament 7/70!' (*TVP Sport eSport*, 26.05.2021) <https://sport.tvp.pl/53998051/esport-8-polskich-druzyn-zagra-o-10000-zl-w-world-of-tanks-polish-tournament-770> (15.08.2021).

In addition to formalised public-private actions involving games, the video game industry has taken many private initiatives to join the #StayHome campaign. Youtubers and streamers, came out with the #gamersvsCOVID2019 initiative, in which during their streams they promoted safe behaviours. Moreover, they prepared a website with the same name as their action, where they made available the text of a declaration for gamers and employers in the video games sector. The signatories committed to maintaining and promoting health and safety rules during a pandemic (Gamersvscovid19 2020a-b).[27]

The activities of the world's largest video game developers were focused under the slogan #PlayApartTogether and received the support of Raymond Chambers, WHO Ambassador for Global Strategy, and WHO Director-General Tedros Adhanom Ghebreyesus, who, through social media, encouraged people to respect isolation and play video games together in order to flatten the disease curve while staying save at home but connected to other people – through games.[28] As part of this campaign, game developers and digital game distribution platforms undertook a range of activities including promoting the WHO recommendations, systematically making games available for free, granting premium accounts for massively multiplayer online games (MMOs), organising community events or selling games at reduced prices. An interesting example was the action taken by Niantic, producer of the game Pokémon GO®, whose mechanics involve players moving around in the real world.

Niantic adapted the mechanics of its game to lockdown by, among other things, allowing players to play together regardless of the distance separating them (by default, players had to gather in one place to play together), more frequent Pokémon and opponents appearance around the player location and increasing the accuracy of tracking the device's movement, and even the ability to connect device to a stationary sport device like treadmill, so players could move and play without having to move off-site.[29] Some developers, such as CD PROJEKT RED,

27 Gamersvscovid19, 'gamersvscovid19' (*gamersvscovid19*) <https://gamersvscovid19.com/> (10.08.2020); Gamersvscovid19, 'Stay home. Play games. Join #gamersvsCOVID19 & take the pledge. http://gamersvscovid19.com' (Twitter, 19.03.2020) <https://mobile.twitter.com/gamersvscovid19> (10.08.2020).

28 R. Chambers, 'We're at a crucial moment in defining outcomes of this pandemic. Games industry companies have a global audience - we encourage all to #PlayApartTogether' (Twitter, 28.03.2020) <https://twitter.com/RaymondChambers/status/1244011120551022594> (05.08.2020); Tedros Ghebreyesus, 'While we are all #TogetherAtHome: Listen to music, read a book or play a game' (Twitter, 20.03.2020) <https://twitter.com/drtedros/status/1241110858694000643> (05.08.2020);

T. Ghebreyesus, 'Thank you @RaymondChambers for mobilizing the gaming industry to feature @WHO advice on #COVID19 to their users. We all must #PlayApartTogether' (Twitter, 28.03.2020) <https://twitter.com/drtedros/status/1244036436493557761> (05.08.2020); Businesswire, 'Games Industry Unites to Promote World Health Organization Messages Against COVID-19; Launch #PlayApartTogether Campaign' (*businesswire.com*, 28.03.2020) <https://www.businesswire.com/news/home/20200328005018/en/> (06.08.2020).

29 Niantic, 'Embracing real-world gaming from home' (*Niantic Labs*, 30.03.2020) <https://nianticlabs.com/blog/stay-safe/> (06.08.2020).

have combined the reduction of their games with a donation to the fight against pandemics.[30]

The above-mentioned actions should be a guideline for the public entities in carrying out their non-imperative actions, especially information provision. Those actions have shown that video games, thanks to their popularity, can be used as effective tools to – in this case – promote lockdown compliance. However, apart from the active cooperation between public television and representatives of video games, the interest of public entities in such cooperation, which could be observed during the first wave of the pandemic, did not spill over into the following waves. This must be considered negatively, as the experience of Grarantanna has shown that public-private cooperation using video games has great potential to increase the effectiveness of the information provision. Therefore, it is difficult to explain the absence of such cooperation during subsequent pandemic waves.

2.4 The social significance of video games before and during a pandemic in Poland

Conducted during the pandemic period, Polish Gamers Research 2020 surveyed Internet users between 15 and 65. Respondents were asked what activities they were undertaking in May 2020. In the survey group thus outlined, the percentage of gamers was 76%. On this basis, it has been estimated that Poland's total number of players is around 16 million people.[31] Only 19.9% of these players were between 15 and 24 years old. The majority, 80.1%, of the players were adults between 25 and 65 years of age (respectively 25–34: 25.7%; 35–44: 24.2%; 45–54:16.4% 55–65: 13.6%,).[32] In Polish Gamers Research 2019, the main research group consisted of Internet users in the 15–55 age range; the percentage of gamers in this group was also 76%. The group of Internet users between 56–65 ("Silver gamers") years old was studied separately;[33] the percentage of gamers in this group was 52%. Despite the "addition" of Silver gamers to the main research group in 2020, the percentage of gamers among Internet users has not decreased and has remained constant at 76%. This allows us to make two assumptions. The first is that both before and during the pandemic, the social importance of

30 CD Projekt Red, 'Dziś przekazaliśmy 4 miliony złotych na walkę z koronawirusem' (*CD Projekt Red*, 25.03.2020) <https://www.facebook.com/CDPROJEKTRED/photos/a.299352593514281/2843995749049940/?type=3&theater> (06.08.2020).

31 Polish Gamers Observatory, 'Polish Gamers Research 2020' (*Polish Gamers Observatory*, 2020) <https://polishgamers.com/pgr/polish-gamers-research-2020/the-demographical-profile-of-polish-gamers/how-many-gamers-are-there-among-polish-internet-users/> (07.08.2021); Eryk Rutkowski, Jakub Marszałkowski and Sławomir Biedermann, 'The game industry of Poland — Report 2020' (*European Games Developer Federation*, 2020) 7 <http://www.egdf.eu/wp-content/uploads/2020/09/PPE_PL_The-Game-Industry-of-Poland-report-2020v4.pdf>, (10.08.2021).

32 Polish Gamers Observatory (n 30).

33 Polish Gamers Observatory, 'Polish Gamers Research 2019' (*Polish Gamers Observatory*, 2020) <https://polishgamers.com/pgr/polish-gamers-research-2019/the-demographical-profile-of-polish-gamers/number-of-polish-gamers-by-platforms> (10.08.2020).

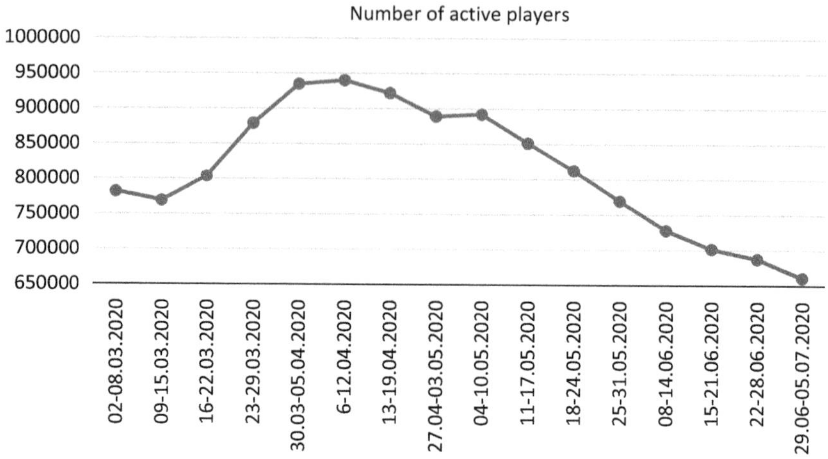

Figure VII.2.1 Number of active World of Tanks players before, during and after the first lockdown. DoM1N, 'Statystyki serwera' (*DoM1N.com*) <https://www.dom1n.com/?s=statystyki+serwera> (10.08.2020).

gaming in Poland was and remains high. The second is that the number of gamers increased during the pandemic. Similarly, in the Report "Condition of the Polish Games Industry 2020," it was indicated that the number of people interested in video games has increased and will continue to increase because of the pandemic (Krampus-Siepielak et al. 2019).[34] The time spent playing video games has also increased. 31% of respondents said they spend more time playing games; it was 39% for children. However, what is most important for the topic of this chapter is that about one-third of gamers admitted that they play video games to learn something new or to develop their skills.[35]

In addition to the research results presented above, the number of active players on European servers of the game World of Tanks®, which is very popular in Poland, was also analysed on a weekly basis between 2 March 2020 and 5 July 2020 (fist pandemic wave) – Figure VII.2.1.

As illustrated in Figure VII.2.1, the first large increase – by 75,000 – in the number of active players occurred during the week of 23 to 29 March 2020. This was the first week after the epidemic state was declared in Poland[36] (20 March 2020) and, at the same time, the first week in which classes in schools and universities were suspended and moved online, and the week in which severe restrictions

34 Krakow Technology Park, 'The State of Polish Video Games Industry 2020' (*Polish Gamers Observatory*, 2020) <https://polishgamers.com/wp-content/uploads/2021/04/Raport_2021_long_FINAL_EN_WEB.pdf> (10. 08.2021).

35 Polish Gamers Observatory (n 30).

36 GOV, 'Wprowadzamy stan epidemii w Polsce' (*Serwis Rzeczypospolitej Polskiej*, 23.03.2020) <https://www.gov.pl/web/koronawirus/wprowadzamy-stan-epidemii-w-polsce> (07.08.2020).

were placed on movement, limiting it to travel to and from work, volunteering to fight the coronavirus, and essentials of daily life.[37] Further restrictions introduced by the government included a prohibition of the independent movement of minors and the closure of parks, boulevards and other public places where many people congregated, introduced from 1 April 2020.[38] Also that restriction reflected in Figure VII.2.1 as an increase of approximately 60,000 active players for the two weeks from 30 March to 12 April 2020, the period immediately following the introduction of the new movement restrictions. From around 13 April, the start of a downward trend is evident (the number of active players has fallen below 900,000 for the first time since the start of the pandemic, with a brief increase in the week of 4 to 10 May 2020 due to the commemoration of the anniversary of the end of World War II, accompanied by in-game events and promotions)[39] in terms of the number of active players, which coincides with the first phase of lockdown abolition, under which parks and forests were made available and people over the age of 13 were allowed to move independently (GOV 2020k).[40] Further large declines (of around 40,000 players per week) in the two weeks between 11 and 24 May 2020 coincide with the next phase of lifting restrictions, with restaurants and cafes opening from 18 May 2020,[41] and hotels and shopping centres opening earlier on 4 May 2020.[42] The next decline of a further 40,000 active players for the first two weeks of June 2020, which are the weeks following 30 May 2020 when cinemas, theatres and gyms were opened.[43] The last period – from 15 June 2020 – shown in Figure VII.2.1 is a systematic decline in the number of active players associated with the opening of borders within the EU and the start of the holiday season.[44] The success of the promotion "supporting" players during lockdown is also evident in

37 GOV, 'Wprowadzamy nowe zasady bezpieczeństwa w związku z koronawirusem' (*Serwis Rzeczypospolitej Polskiej*, 24.03.2020) <https://www.gov.pl/web/koronawirus/wprowadzamy-nowe-zasady-bezpieczenstwa-w-zwiazku-z-koronawirusem> (07.08.2020).

38 GOV, 'Kolejne kroki w walce z koronawirusem – w sklepie mniej osób, ograniczenia w poruszaniu nieletnich, a parki, plaże i bulwary zamknięte' (*Serwis Rzeczypospolitej Polskiej*, 31.03.2020) <https://www.gov.pl/web/koronawirus/kolejne-kroki> (08.08.2020).

39 World of Tanks, 'Take the Road to Berlin and Reap the Rewards!' (*World of Tanks.eu*, 04.05.2020) <https://worldoftanks.eu/pl/news/general-news/road-to-berlin-regulations> (05.08.2020).

40 GOV, 'Nowa normalność: etapy znoszenia ograniczeń związanych z COVID-19' (*Serwis Rzeczypospolitej Polskiej*, 16.04.2020) <https://www.gov.pl/web/koronawirus/nowa-normalnosc-etapy> (09.08.2020).

41 GOV, 'Znosimy kolejne ograniczenia – 18 maja pójdziesz do fryzjera, kosmetyczki i restauracji' (*Serwis Rzeczypospolitej Polskiej*, 13.05.2020) <https://www.gov.pl/web/koronawirus/3etap> (10.08.2020).

42 GOV, '4 maja ruszą hotele, centra handlowe i rehabilitacja lecznicza' (*Serwis Rzeczypospolitej Polskiej*, 29.04.2020) <https://www.gov.pl/web/koronawirus/kolejny-etap> (10.08.2020).

43 GOV, 'Nowe zasady zasłaniania nosa i ust, otwarte kina i siłownie – wchodzimy w kolejny etap odmrażania' (*Serwis Rzeczypospolitej Polskiej*, 27.05.2020) <https://www.gov.pl/web/koronawirus/4-etap-odmrazania> (10.08.2020).

44 GOV, '13 czerwca otwieramy granice – kontrole tylko wyrywkowo' (*Serwis Rzeczypospolitej Polskiej*, 10 Jun 2020) <https://www.gov.pl/web/koronawirus/13-czerwca-otwieramy-granice--kontrole-tylko-wyrywkowo> (10. 08.2020).

Figure 1. The developer of the World of Tanks granted a 14-day premium account between 20 March and 3 April 2020, so players who activated the promotion on the last possible day, i.e., 3 April, ended their premium account period on 17 April 2020.[45] (World of Tanks 2020a). The period between 20 March and 17 April 2020 overlaps with the peak of interest in the game seen in Figure VII.2.1.

2.5 Conclusions

The research results cited in this chapter indicate that video games, including educational ones, are very popular in Poland. This argues in favour of their use as tools supporting non-imperative legal instruments of public entities, especially in the field of information provision. The popularity of video games makes them a medium of information of a wide range. The results of the query of the "GOV. PL" portal indicate that, during the pandemic period, public entities used mentioned above potential of video games and other educational applications. In comparison to the pre-pandemic period, use of the video games and other educational applications by the public entities to support their information provision activities significantly increased. This was particularly visible in the area of supporting education, especially of the youngest students. Most of the identified actions where public entities used video games and educational applications were in fact related to educational campaigns such as "Let's code" or "Remote lessons." Also, the individual activities of various public entities (as part of their other projects) have focused primarily on the educational use of these multimedia products. The query also shows that video games' educational use and applications is still being developed. New multimedia products are still being developed, especially as part of pilot studies on the use of video games in education. Some of the new games already seem to go beyond the pandemic issue. Indeed, in August 2021, the Polish Embassy in Dublin released a retro video game to popularise and encourage people to visit Poland.[46]

The use of video games for public-private actions to prevent the rapid and uncontrolled spread of coronavirus seems to be slightly less popular among public entities. In fact, only during the first wave of the coronavirus pandemic such initiatives were conducted (and attracted much interest). The exception is still public television, which continued such public-private cooperation throughout the coronavirus pandemic.

From the information cited in the first and second sub-chapters, it appears that public actions with the use of video games have primarily targeted children and young people. This appears to be inaccurate. Indeed, the statistics quoted in the

45 World of Tanks, 'You Are Not Alone During Trying Times!' (*World of Tanks.eu*, 20.03.2020) <https://worldoftanks.eu/pl/news/general-news/be-safe-2020> (05.08.2020).

46 GOV, 'Joxer Goes to Poland - nowa gra video, która zawładnie Twoją wyobraźnią!' (*Serwis Rzeczypospolitej Polskiej*, 09.08,021) <https://www.gov.pl/web/irlandia/joxer-goes-to-poland---nowa-gra-video-ktora-zawladnie-twoja-wyobraznia> (21.08.2021).

third sub-chapter show that video games are more popular among young adults and middle-aged people (25–44) than among children. In the post-pandemic period, public entities should make use of the experience gained by supporting the education of children with video games to extend this concept to the training of adults. This applies to training in areas where trainees' successful acquisition of skills depends on training which, however, in the real world, could be dangerous for the trainee himself, his organisation or his environment. In this regard, attention should be drawn to the undoubted problem that relates to the use of video games and educational applications by public bodies. This problem is funding. A query has shown that most video games and educational applications used during the pandemic period were commercial. This is primarily due to the long process of granting funding for such products. Time which, especially in the early stages of the coronavirus pandemic, was not available. Despite this long time and other difficulties, however, it should be postulated that public entities should use the commercial video games and engage in the development of their own solutions. Indeed, the coronavirus pandemic showed that such products are sorely needed.

Works cited

Rutkowski, E., Marszałkowski, J., and Biedermann, S., *The Game Industry of Poland — Report 2020* (European Games Developer Federation, Warsaw 2020).

Chambers, R., 'We're at a Crucial Moment in Defining Outcomes of This Pandemic. Games Industry Companies Have a Global Audience - We Encourage All to #PlayApartTogether' (Twitter, 28.03.2020).

Ghebreyesus, T., 'While We Are All #TogetherAtHome: Listen to Music, Read a Book or Play a Game' (Twitter, 20.03.2020).

Ghebreyesus, T., 'Thank You @RaymondChambers for Mobilizing the Gaming Industry to Feature @WHO Advice on #COVID19 to Their Users. We All Must #PlayApartTogether' (Twitter, 28.03.2020).

3 The Role of Infographics in Reducing Uncertainty in a Pandemic Situation

Wawrzyniec Święcicki

3.1 Introduction

A pandemic state is a formal-legal or factual emergency.[1] It is a surprising and new situation for everyone, changing dynamically and evoking strong emotions related to the sense of real danger. An increased sense of anxiety is fostered by lack of knowledge and uncertainty. Access to reliable and comprehensive information becomes a priority need in such exceptional circumstances.

Citizens are looking for up-to-date data on the scale of the epidemiological threat and clear guidance on how to protect themselves against infection. In turn, those responsible for pandemic management have an interest in ensuring that citizens have widespread access to necessary, reliable and accurate information.

As a rule, all available information channels are used for this purpose, ranging from notices and posters displayed in public spaces, through the press, radio and television, to Internet portals and social media. The key issue, however, is not the presence of information but its accessibility and usability. In this case, accessibility should be understood as those features of the message that ensure that it is clear and understandable to everyone, regardless of their knowledge, predispositions or habits. On the other hand, the usefulness of information is determined by its practical relevance affecting the knowledge or quality of life of the recipient, but also by the ease of its further dissemination.

The aim of this chapter is to verify the hypothesis on the rationality of the widespread use of infographics as an optimal way to effectively reduce uncertainty in pandemic conditions.

3.2 Forms of uncertainty reduction in the information society

The development of information technology and the Internet has resulted in a huge increase in media users' expectations with a simultaneous tendency to minimise their own cognitive load and process information in an increasingly shallow

1 A. Monarcha-Matlak "States of emergency and cyberpandemics" in G. Szpor, A. Gryszczyńska (eds.), *Internet Cyberpandemia, Cyberpandemic* (C.H.Beck 2020).

DOI: 10.4324/9781003263968-31

way. This is because living in information societies, characterised in the literature as societies focused on reducing uncertainty,[2] we encounter a huge number of stimuli daily, which may lead to a phenomenon referred to in psychology as "information overload." There is a situation in which there is difficulty understanding a particular issue due to an excessive number of available data. This, in turn, may lead to the so-called "paradox of choice" described by Barry Schwartz, the author of the theory according to which too many options make it difficult to decide and increase the perceived stress.[3]

Media users therefore try to minimise their cognitive load by avoiding complex reasoning, memorising and decision-making. At the same time, they are characterised by impatience and orientation to quick gratification in the form of an easy solution to a problem, intensified, for example, by the widespread use of "intelligent" algorithms adjusting information to users' preferences. In practice, this means that most people do not actively seek the best answer to their doubts but settle for the first solution that seems good enough. To effectively inform as many people as possible, we must consider the habits and limitations of media users. Therefore, it is important that in addition to the reliability of the message, its form should be attractive, concise and legible to guarantee understanding.

The Internet is the most popular of all information media. It is a medium that is available all the time and continuously via mobile devices, which most people always carry with them. Therefore, it is only natural that, when in doubt or in need of information, one's first instinct is to consult the Internet. This is done by means of an Internet search engine, i.e., a programme or a website finding information on the Internet according to key words or phrases formulated in natural language.[4] From the thousands of indications obtained, most users open at most the first few links. Therefore, from the author's point of view, search engine optimisation (SEO), understood as a set of actions aimed at achieving by the website the highest possible position in search engine results for selected key words and phrases, is particularly important. The search engine algorithm responsible for presenting results in the appropriate positions analyses several hundred different features of the website, including its individual elements. The most important of these are related to user activity, e.g., number of entries, time spent on the site, number of clicks or links to other websites. Social media such as Facebook or Twitter play a particularly important role in the website positioning process (for this reason, they are often integrated with the website).

To encourage users to enter a website, stay on it for as long as possible and share a link to it with other social media users, it is necessary to have attractive content that arouses interest, evokes emotions and meets people's current needs.[5]

2 G. Szpor "Openness and its limitations t.1 Ideas and concepts" (C. H. Beck 2016).

3 B.Schwartz "The paradox of choice. Why more means less?" (Wydawnictwo Naukowe PWN 2020).

4 W. Babik "Słownik encyklopedyczny informacji, języków i systemów informacyjno-wyszukiwawczych" (Association of Polish Librarian, series: Nauka, Dydaktyka, Praktyka 2002) 305.

5 T. Karkowski and K. Korczak "Zarządzanie wiedzą w ochronie zdrowia z wykorzystaniem wybranych rozwiązań ICT" (WolKluw. Polska 2016)

Content with high viral potential is a particularly valuable online resource. A viral is a work, most often a short film, a photo or a graphic, containing an intriguing message, instantly gaining popularity because it is willingly shared on social media.[6] Internet users like to send or share this type of information with their friends, who in turn pass it on to other people in their personal networks of friends (personal networks). The mechanism resembles a virus, which infects subsequent recipients. The similarity is not accidental – viral is a form of viral marketing. This type of marketing consists in initiating a situation in which users voluntarily disseminate information among themselves, considering it worthy.[7]

Most of the virals functioning on the Internet start their existence on the website or social media profile of a given company or institution. They may also disseminate them on sites such as YouTube. Users, deciding that the content is worth using, may use a link to the website or copy the whole element (e.g., an illustration) and send it by email, post it on their blog, website or social media profile. Due to the distributed nature of this form of marketing, it is difficult to measure its effectiveness accurately. Measurements such as the number of impressions, clicks and hits for specific content, as well as the number of social media shares such as likes on Facebook or retweets on Twitter are included.

According to Jonah Berger,[8] there are six factors that drive viral campaigns:

1. Image – the better something affects our image, the more willing we are to share it;
2. Current topics – we like to share what we are passionate about now;
3. Emotions – if we care, we want to share it;
4. Popularity – the more often we share something, the more likely we are to follow it;
5. Practical value – people share useful information to help others;
6. Interesting stories – like a Trojan horse, they can smuggle additional information or ideas under an attractive form.

All the above-mentioned characteristics are demonstrated by infographics and therefore, as a versatile information tool, in many respects it is superior to other forms of communication (text, image, film). The utilitarian dimension of infographics has been recognised and considered by governing bodies and institutions during the pandemic, finding its place in specific legal Acts.[9] According to these guidelines, "Guests should be informed through specific signage before entering the establishment (infographics, also adapted for people with visual impairments)

6 P. Bucki "VIRAL. Jak zarażać ideami i tworzyć wirusowe treści" (Wydawnictwo Naukowe PWN 2019).

7 "Virals - what are they and what role do they play in marketing?" (Poradnik Przedsiębiorcy 2017) <https://www.poradnikprzedsiebiorcy.pl/-czym-sa-virale>.

8 J. Berger, "Contagious: Why Things Catch On" (Simon & Schuster 2016).

9 EU guidelines for the gradual resumption of services to tourists and health protocols in hospitality establishments – COVID-19. Official Journal of the European Union 2020/C 169.1 of 13.05.2020.

about the symptoms of COVID-19, what to do in case of symptoms during their stay or within 14 days after departure." These guidelines consider the provision of accessible information for people with disabilities, which – regarding websites and mobile applications, including the infographics posted there – is an obligation of public entities regulated by EU and Polish law.[10]

3.3 Characteristics of infographics and their usefulness during a pandemic

An infographic is a graphical representation of information with the necessary explanation. In the study of the copyright character of infographics, it is understood as "visual elements such as signs, charts, maps and diagrams that are intended to help understand the given textual content."[11] It follows from the definition that infographics operate mainly with images. Text is only a necessary explanation. This makes infographics universally understandable. It works on the principle of picture writing using universal symbols, based on associations and intuition. This reduces the time taken to perceive and analyse the data to a minimum, enabling a quick understanding of the problem. In addition, thanks to the emotions evoked by the image, it engages the observers' attention more and is therefore well remembered.

The use of images affects the visual attractiveness of infographics. A well-designed infographic advantageously stands out from other forms of communication and focuses attention on itself.

A very important advantage of infographics is its conciseness. The brief form of the message increases the likelihood that more people will read it in its entirety. What is important in this case is the proper selection of content. Limiting the amount of information to an essential minimum has a positive effect on the recipient, protecting him from unnecessary information overload and, as a result, increasing his satisfaction.

Infographics, by definition, aims to focus attention on information that is relevant. Thanks to this, it clearly shows, sometimes not obvious, connections between information. This, in turn, makes it possible to explain even very complicated issues in a simple and effective way.

Infographics are one of the most valuable resources on the Internet. As a carrier of information that attracts attention with an attractive graphic form, operating with a universal language of images and containing optimally processed data highlighting relationships and facilitating the drawing of conclusions, it seems to be an ideal solution for communicating with the public in a crisis such as a pandemic. Additionally, thanks to its unique features, it has a high viral potential.

10 G. Szpor, K. Czaplicki [eds.] "Law on digital accessibility of websites and mobile applications" (WolKluw. Polska 2019).

11 A. Nowak-Gruca "Infographics as an object of copyright protection" (Zeszyty Naukowe Uniwersytetu Jagiellońskiego 2017/1) 5-23.

This means that it can spread itself online through frequent sharing via social media and thus actively reach a wide audience.

A quantitative study of the use of infographics on Polish websites (Table VII.3.1) confirms this statement. It is worth noting here that the Google search engine indicates the most positions when the second – next to infographics – keyword is COVID-19. Slightly fewer indications were obtained for the word – coronavirus, and the least – pandemic. For phrases using the keywords "COVID-19" and "coronavirus," most results overlapped, while for the word "pandemic" the results were mostly different.

3.4 The themes of the infographics

Analysis of the first 30 search results for the phrases "infographics pandemic" and "infographics coronavirus" reveals clear differences in the indicated infographics' dominant themes and the functions they perform.

Many infographics searched for the phrase "infographics pandemic" (nearly 70%) are about the impact of the pandemic on the daily and professional lives of citizens. These are mainly the results of surveys describing changes in leisure, communication, learning or environmental habits. A separate group consists of infographics describing the impact of the pandemic on work organisation and communication within companies, the current situation of industries, or predicted economic and social consequences related to the situation.

The second most numerous groups are infographics concerning health. In addition to basic education on hygiene principles, more specific topics appear, e.g., coping with stress.

The third group consists of general studies comparing pandemics in a historical perspective, presenting data on the response of selected institutions to a pandemic or the impact of a pandemic on the environment.

On the other hand, a search for the phrase "coronavirus infographics" yields a set of infographics in which health care-related topics clearly dominate. In this case, nearly 67% of the results relate to basic behavioural rules that reduce the possibility of infection, such as instructions on how to wash hands thoroughly, keep social distance, store food, etc.

Table VII.3.1 Quantitative analysis of infographics related to the pandemic

Search term	*Number of indicated searches*
Infographics pandemic	277 000
Coronavirus infographic	740 000
Infographics COVID-19	855 000

Source: Own compilation based on the results of a search of Polish-language sites in the Google browser on 17 August 2020.

Table VII.3.2 Analysis of search results for the phrase "pandemic infographic"

Infographic title	*Publisher*	*Data source*	*Function*	*Potentialviral*	*Format graphics*	*Link*
Pandemics around the world	Onet.pl	Gisanddata.maps,The World Economic Forum, Centersfor Disease Control and Prevention, WHO	Popular Science	only the original	Vertical	https://ocdn.eu/pulscms-transforms/1/wCfk9kpTURBXy8xNDk3YTdhNmY2MDY4YTZhNjNjZDJmZmY2YTA2YjZmYy5qcGeRlQLNAtAAwsOBoTAF
What good practices does business follow in a pandemic	Forum Odpowiedzialnego Biznesu	Forum Odpowie-dzialnego Biznesu	Marketing	8+ oryginał	Level	https://api.ngo.pl/media/get/134336?w=1527&h=1080
Everyday life in Poland during the SARS-CoV-2 coronavirus pandemic	Uniwersytet im. Adama Mickiewicza w Poznaniu	Badanie zrealizowane przez Zakład Teoriii Badań Praktyk Społecznych Wydziału Socjologii UAM	Informational	5+ oryginał	Level	https://amu.edu.pl/__data/assets/image/0016/111526/varieties/h600.jpg
The media situation during the COVID-19 pandemic	PAP	PAP, ankieta wśród 34 dziennikarzy największych redakcji w Polsce,2-6.06.2020	Informational	only the original	Vertical	https://www.pap.pl/sites/default/files/202007/Sytuacja%20w%20mediach%20w%20czasie%20pandemii_green_0.jpg
How do Poles help during a pandemic?	Orange Polska	Badanie "Dobroczyn-ność a COVID-19," Havas Media na zlecenie Orange Polska	Informational	only the original	Vertical	https://biuroprasowe.orange.pl/wp-content/uploads/2020/07/office/COVID_19_pomaganie_infografika.jpg

(*Continued*)

Table VII.3.2 Continued

Infographic title	*Publisher*	*Data source*	*Function*	*Potentialviral*	*Format graphics*	*Link*
How does the pandemic affect the environment	IMPEL GROUP	Rozproszone, opracowanie własne	Popular Science	only the original	Vertical	https://www.impel.pl/images/INSIGHT_GRAFIKA/Infografiki/IMPEL-infografika-Covid19_eko.jpg
How social organisations get involved in the fight against a pandemic	Forum Odpowiedzialnego Biznesu	FOB	Marketing	7+ oryginał	Level	https://api.ngo.pl/media/get/132532?w=1199&h=848
Different faces of a pandemic	Dziennik Gazeta Prawna	John Hopkins University Coronavirus Resource Center, Worldo-meters.info	Informacyjna	2+ oryginał	Level	https://ocdn.eu/images/pulscms/YmQ7MDA_/f014f955-29d8-4abd-a260-20ef6e9f87dd.jpeg
CORONavirus 2019-nCoV	Enel-zdrowie	brak danych	Educational	32+ oryginał	Level	https://enel.pl/zdrowie/Infografiki/koronawirus_infografika.jpg
COVID-19: Number of confirmed cases per million population	Mariusz Gromada	Opracowanie własne na podstawie google.com/covid19-map	Informational	only the original	Level	https://cdn.galleries.smcloud.net/t/galleries/gf-pyfe-UmNj-KFt2_pandemia-koronawirusa-1920x1080-nocrop.jpg
Pandemic Archive A.D. 2020	Archiwa Rodzinne Niepodległej, Archiwa Państwowe, Narodowa	Archiwa Rodzinne Niepodległej, Archiwa Państwowe, Polska Fundacja Narodowa	Marketing	only the original	Vertical	https://www.archiwa.gov.pl/images/Archium_Pandemii_infografika_v3-gotowe-01(1).jpg
Plans of Poles after the pandemic	Provident	Barometr Providenta	Informational	only the original	Vertical	https://d2xhqqdaxyaju6.cloudfront.net/file/attachment-s/1626492/77/s-778-x.png

Poles' leisure time during coronavirus	Prezent marzeń	Prezentmarzeń, ankieta, marzec 2020 r.	Informational	only the original	Vertical	https://brief.pl/wp-content/uploads/2020/04/czas_wolny_polakow_podczas_koronawirusa.png
EU crisis response to COVID-19 pandemic	Rada Unii Europejskiej, Sekretariat Generalny	Unia Europejska	Marketing	only the original	Vertical	https://www.consilium.europa.eu/media/43595/eu_response_covid-19-infographic_pl.jpg
Remote working in pandemic mode	Centralny Dom Technologii	Opracowanie Beata Brzózka i Kamil Śliwowski na podstawie Forbs, Buffer, Wyborcza.pl	Informacyjna	only the original	Vertical	https://prowly-uploads.s3.eu-west-1.amazonaws.com/uploads/8650/assets/205767/large-70e4d3d4125c7864dc62f304f6e052e0.png
Impact of COVID-19 pandemic on communications of major Polish companies and institutions	Alert Media Communi-cations	Alert Media Communications, badanie Kryzysometr 2020	Informational	5+ oryginał	Square	https://biznes.newseria.pl/files/_uploaded/glownekonf_547316809,w_1000,r_png,_small.png
Professional situation of Polish women during the pandemic	Promedica24	Badanie IQS dla Promedica24	Informational	6+ oryginał	Square	https://www.promedicaplus.de/wp-content/uploads/2020/06/infografika_praca-na-dzis-i-na-jutro1.png
Where to after the pandemic	Eco Travel	brak danych	Marketing	only the original	Vertical	https://www.ecotravel.pl/getFile.php?type=imageFile&id=4082
E-learning vs pandemic	Learnetic	brak danych	Marketing	only the original	Vertical	https://www.learnetic.pl/wp-content/uploads/2020/06/learnetic_infografika_pandemia_06-2020_ver8.png
We are safe	Polski Związek Przemysłu Kosmetycz-nego	Polski Związek Przemysłu Kosmetycz-nego	Marketing	396+ oryginał	Level	https://biznes.wprost.pl/_thumb/8a/44/d2b066e771c5f33a85e0d6403983.png

(Continued)

Table VII.3.2 Continued

Infographic title	*Publisher*	*Data source*	*Function*	*Potentialviral*	*Format graphics*	*Link*
Expected impact of the pandemic (after it ends)	infoWire.pl	GFK Polonia	Informational	only the original	Level	https://d2xhqqdaxyaju6.cloudfront.net/file/attachment-s/1628946/aa/s-640-x.jpg
Our work during the epidemic	Środowiskowe Centrum Zdrowia Psychicznego dla Dzieci i Młodzieży	Środowiskowe Centrum Zdrowia Psychicznego dla Dzieci i Młodzieży	Marketing	only the original	Vertical	https://sczp.med.pl/wp-content/uploads/2020/07/%C5%9ACZPdim-praca-podczas-lockdown-3.png
How has the epidemic affected the viewing of videos on YouTube?	telepolis.pl	GetHero	Informational	only the original	Vertical	https://www.telepolis.pl/images/2020/03/koronawirus-a-youtube-infografika.jpg
The outlook for banking – what has the pandemic changed?	prnews.pl	Incat	Informational	only the original	Level	https://prnews.pl/wp-content/uploads/2020/08/infografika1.png
Coping with stress during the pandemic	ONZ	WHO, Gisanddata.maps, The World Economic Forum, Centers for Disease Control and Prevention	Educational	7+ oryginał	Vertical	https://unic.un.org.pl/files/522/radzenie%20sobie%20ze%20stresem.jpg
Situation of the Polish financial system during the pandemic	NBP	NBP	Informational	only the original	Level	https://www.nbp.pl/aktualnosci/wiadomosci_2020/20200617_stabilnosc_pl_b.jpg

Quarantine - what you should know	PAP	Ministerstwo Zdrowia, zdrowie.pap.pl	Educational	6+ oryginał	Vertical	https://zdrowie.pap.pl/sites/default/files/inline-images/Kwarantanna.co_warto_wiedzie%C4%87.png
A safer place to work	pcc-exol.pl	brak danych	Educational	Usunięta	X	https://www.pcc-exol.eu/bazy/exol.nsf/images/News_2015/$file/news-safety.jpg
Stress levels related to the coronavirus pandemic	onet.pl	Badanie CAWI na panelu Ariadna	Informational	only the original	Vertical	https://ocdn.eu/pulscms-transforms/1/0J3ktkpTURBXy83NmIzYTI3ZDExYzc4ZmMyNjE1NDhkOGNkMmNlYjZjNC5qcGeRkwLNAxQA
Communication in times of pandemic	alertmedia.pl	Badanie „Kryzysometr - komunikacja w czasach pandemii" Alert Media	Informational	only the original	Level	https://alertmedia.pl/wp-content/uploads/2020/04/Komunikacja-w-czasach-zarazy-infografika-640x480.png

Source: Own compilation based on results of searching Polish-language webpages in Google on 17 August 2020. The analysis includes the first 30 indications of the search engine. The category "viral potential and format" was marked for infographics found under the indicated links on 3 August 2021.

Table VII.3.3 Analysis of search results for the phrase "coronavirus infographic"

Infographic title	*Publisher*	*Data source*	*Function*	*Potential viral*	*Format graphics*	*Link*
Ways to reduce the risk of coronavirus infection	PZH Narodowy Instytut Zdrowia Publicznego	WHO	Educational	95 + oryginał	Square	https://www.pzh.gov.pl/wp-content/uploads/2020/02/Koronawirus-infografiki-1.jpg
Protect others from getting the disease (1)	PZH Narodowy Instytut Zdrowia Publicznego	WHO	Educational	57 + oryginał	Square	https://www.pzh.gov.pl/wp-content/uploads/2020/02/Koronawirus-infografiki-4.jpg
Wash your hands	PZH Narodowy Instytut Zdrowia Publicznego	WHO	Educational	7 + oryginał	Square	https://www.pzh.gov.pl/wp-content/uploads/2020/02/Koronawirus-infografiki-3.jpg
Protect others from getting sick (2)	PZH Narodowy Instytut Zdrowia Publicznego	WHO	Educational	42 + oryginał	Square	https://www.pzh.gov.pl/wp-content/uploads/2020/02/Koronawirus-infografiki-5.jpg
Follow food safety rules	PZH Narodowy Instytut Zdrowia Publicznego	WHO	Educational	49 + oryginał	Square	https://www.pzh.gov.pl/wp-content/uploads/2020/02/Koronawirus-infografiki-13.jpg
Protect yourself and others from getting sick. Wash your hands.	PZH Narodowy Instytut Zdrowia Publicznego	WHO	Educational	37 + oryginał	Square	https://www.pzh.gov.pl/wp-content/uploads/2020/02/Koronawirus-infografiki-2.jpg
Basic protective measures against the new coronavirus	Ministerstwo Zdrowia	Ministerstwo Zdrowia	Educational	8 + oryginał	Level	https://prudnik.pl/download//51146/infografika01.jpeg

Coronavirus	Onet.pl	Telegraph.co.uk	Educational	only the original	Vertical	https://ocdn.eu/pulscms-transforms/1/A9Kk9kpTURBXy84NWNmNWQ1ZGM2OTBlYjNhMzA4YWQzYWMzNTI2MjY5OC5qcGeRlQLNAtAAwsOBoTAF
Stay healthy while travelling (1)	PZH Narodowy Instytut Zdrowia Publicznego	WHO	Educational	56 + oryginał	Square	https://www.pzh.gov.pl/wp-content/uploads/2020/02/Koronawirus-infografiki-7.jpg
Stay healthy while travelling	Ministerstwo Zdrowia	Ministerstwo Zdrowia	Educational	only the original	Level	https://prudnik.pl/download//51147/infografika1.jpeg
Keep	PZH Narodowy Instytut Zdrowia Publicznego	WHO	Educational	56 + oryginał	Square	https://www.pzh.gov.pl/wp-content/uploads/2020/02/Koronawirus-infografiki-8.jpg
stay healthy while travelling	PZH Narodowy Instytut Zdrowia Publicznego	WHO	Educational	31 + oryginał	Square	https://www.pzh.gov.pl/wp-content/uploads/2020/02/Koronawirus-infografiki-6.jpg
Stay healthy while travelling (3)	Ministerstwo Zdrowia	Ministerstwo Zdrowia	Educational	only the original	Vertical	https://prudnik.pl/download//51144/infografika91.jpeg
Ways to reduce the risk of coronavirus infection	GoodAIR	Opracowanie własne	Educational	only the original	Vertical	https://goodair.pl/img/uploads/blog/KORONAWIRUS_infografika_pomniejszona.jpg
Coronavirus 2019-nCoV	Ministerstwo Zdrowia, PIS, NFZ	Opracowanie własne	Educational	88 + oryginał	Vertical	https://rzeszow.uw.gov.pl/wp-content/uploads/2020/02/KV_plakat_A3_DRUK-scaled-e1582975333320.jpg
Coronavirus	GIS	GIS	Educational	76 + oryginał	Square	https://www.powiatwodzislawski.pl/pliki/2020/01/mycie-r%C4%85k-infografika.png

(Continued)

Table VII.3.3 Continued

Infographic title	*Publisher*	*Data source*	*Function*	*Potential viral*	*Format graphics*	*Link*
How to wash your hands effectively?	Enelzdrowie	brak danych	Educational	32 + oryginał	Level	https://enel.pl/zdrowie/Infografiki/koronawirus_infografika.jpg
oronavirus 2019-nCoV	Ministerstwo Zdrowia	Ministerstwo Zdrowia	Educational	5 + oryginał		https://prudnik.pl/download//51149/infografika3.jpeg
Wash your hands	Jastrzębie-Zdrój Urząd Miasta	Brak damych	Informational	only the original	Vertical	https://www.jastrzebie.pl/fileadmin/_processed_/6/3/csm_97993636_2514427175486980_7447203210835525632_o_81c54402d7.png
Coronavirus. Daily report 19.05.2020	TÜV SÜD Polska	Brak damych	Educational	Usunięta	X	https://www.tuv-sud.pl/uploads/images/158393388199962 2550429/tuvsud-10-steps-to-prevent-coronavirus-infographic_294x900.png
How to protect yourself from coronavirus?	Narodowy Instytut Zdrowia Publicznego-PZH	Wytyczne WHO	Educational	32 + oryginał	Vertical	http://www.ud-wlochy.waw.pl/page/file.php?id=1646
Ways to reduce the risk of infection with coronavirus	Onet.pl	WHO	Popular Science	only the original	Vertical	https://ocdn.eu/pulscms-transforms/1/co8k9kpTURBXy8wOWQ2MmUzZGJhZDkwNGMwYWNmMWNhNzM2YjczMmM2Yy5qcGeRlQLNAtAAwsOBoTAF
Coronavirus myths 2019-nCoV	Urząd Miasta Gliwice	Urząd Miasta Gliwice	Informational	Usunięta	X	https://gliwice.eu/sites/default/files/news/images/nowa_koronawirus_www_07_07_2020.jpg

Coronavirus. Gliwice as of July 6	SGB Banki Spółdzielcze	SGB Banki Spółdzielcze	Marketing	6 + oryginał	Vertical	http://www.bs.slesin.sgb.pl/images/stories/news/infografika_koronawirus_20200324.jpg
Neighbour, take care of yourself and others!	Ministerstwo Zdrowia	Ministerstwo Zdrowia	Educational	Usunięta	X	http://psse.slupsk.pl/strona_gis/epidemiologia/2020/koronawirus/algorytm.png
Treatment algorithm	Onet.pl	NFZ, GIS	Educational	only the original	Vertical	https://ocdn.eu/pulscms-transforms/1/fbnk9kpTURBXy80OGJmNjcyNTIxZTUwNTE5MGQzYWU3ODAwY2E5YmMwZS5qcGeRlQLNAfQAwsOBoTAB
CORONAWIRUS. Step by step procedure	PAP	WHO, zdrowie.pap.pl	Popular Science	18 + oryginał	Vertical	https://www.pap.pl/sites/default/files/inline-images/igrafika_20200312_02_0.png
Coronavirus or flu?	Wyborcza.pl	Nature	Popular Science	only the original	Vertical	https://wyborcza.pl/7,75400,25945867,tak-naukowcy-walcza-o-szczepionke-przeciwko-koronawirusowi-infografiki.html
This is how scientists fight for a vaccine against coronavirus	biqdata.pl, wyborcza.pl	Ministerstwo Zdrowia, GIS	Informational	only the original	Vertical	https://static.im-g.pl/im/8/25939/m25939838,SLASK-ZAKAZENIA-2.png
How did Silesia become a coronavirus basin?	Medonet.pl	WHO, GIS, zdrowie.pap.pl	Popular Science	6 + oryginał	Vertical	

Source: Own compilation based on results of searching Polish-language webpages in Google on 17 August 2020. The analysis includes the first 30 indications of the search engine. The category „viral potential" and „format" were marked for infographics found under the indicated links on 3 August 2021.

There are also messages presenting current data on the number of cases, recoveries and deaths, and infographics promoting more detailed knowledge about the epidemic – explaining myths about it in the public space or describing how vaccines are developed.

The differences in the dominant themes of infographics in both research groups can be linked to the type of their sources. In the case of the keyword "pandemic infographics", research institutions, scientific centres and NGOs dominate, often carrying out research commissioned by private entities. The search results for the phrase "infographics coronavirus" are dominated as sources mainly by public entities: WHO, Ministry of Health, National Sanitary Inspectorate or PZH National Institute of Public Health.

3.5 Functions of infographics

The analysis of the 60 search engine indications allows us to assign diverse functions to the individual infographics. An attempt to name them is shown in column 4 in both tables. In characterising these functions, examples of different uses of infographics in a pandemic situation can also be used from outside this dataset.

A. *Educational function*

The basic type of infographics commonly used in connection with a pandemic are instructional infographics, which convey in an accessible way basic knowledge about the rules of staying safe during a pandemic, ways to protect oneself from infection, algorithms for dealing with infection, etc.

(Examples: *How to put on and take off a mask correctly*. Ministry of Health and State Sanitary Inspectorate. https://www.zdzieszowice.pl/download//54570/maseczka.png.

How to wash your hands effectively? Chief Sanitary Inspectorate https://www.gis.gov.pl/wp-content/uploads/2018/04/mycie-r%C4%85k-kwadrat.png.)

B. *Informational function*

The second group of infographics are visualisations of data showing the course of the pandemic. They can show a broad picture observed at the scale of a country, continent or the world, or on the contrary – focus on a detailed analysis of a fragment of reality – the situation of a particular group, industry, customs, etc. They provide a broader knowledge of the scope and intensity of the phenomenon by presenting the current picture of the situation. (Examples:

We must play for time. In this way we will save thousands of people. Gazeta Wyborcza. https://www.static.im-g.pl/im/1/25784/m25784811,SCHEMAT-PANDEMIA.png.

Trajectories of the increase in the number of cases of covid-19. Wyborcza.pl. https://www.bi.im-g.pl/im/c3/9e/18/z25815491FBW,Wzrost-liczby-zachorowan-na-koronawirusa.jpg.

Exceptional Sweden tests for coronavirus three times less frequently than Norway. Biqdata.co.uk. https://www.static.im-g.pl/im/6/25877/m25877346,SKANDYNAWIA-KORONA.png.)

C. *Popular science function*

Popular science infographics explain in an accessible way complex issues, such as the process of infection, the course of the disease, the results of scientific research related to the epidemic, etc. They are aimed at people seeking broader knowledge about epidemics (Examples: Moskal W. and Święcicki W. 2020 *See how coronavirus attacks our body. What we already know*. Gazeta Wyborcza. https://www.wyborcza.pl/7,75400,25822268,jak-koronawirus-atakuje-nasz-organizm-infografika.html.

Moskal. W. and Święcicki W. 2020. *This is how scientists fight for a vaccine against coronavirus*. Gazeta Wyborcza. https://www.wyborcza.pl/7,75400,25945867,tak-naukowcy-walcza-o-szczepionke-przeciwko-koronawirusowi-infografiki.html.)

D. *Marketing function*

A separate subgroup of informational infographics are marketing infographics. They use the high-interest topic of a pandemic to promote a brand, an industry, or certain attitudes among customers (Examples: *W-learning vs pandemic. Learnetic.* https://www.learnetic.pl/wp-content/uploads/2020/06/learnetic_infografika_pandemia_06-2020_ver8.png.

Neighbour, take care of yourself and others! Cooperative Banks. http://www.bs.slesin.sgb.pl/images/stories/news/infografika_koronawirus_20200324.jpg.)

The separation of functions of infographics published during the pandemic and thematically related to it, presented in this chapter, may constitute an initial stage of broader work on a complete catalogue of them. Agreeing on such a catalogue of features seems beneficial for more effective interaction between commissioners and designers of infographics. It may also be helpful in solving – complicated in the light of the jurisprudence – problems of copyright protection of infographics as works.[12]

When analysing the sample of infographics in terms of the functions they perform, the quantitative predominance of educational and informational infographics is clearly noticeable. Together, they account for 75% of all indications. This may indicate that these types of information are in greatest demand and therefore enjoy the greatest popularity. This result also confirms that, due to the characteristics, infographics work very well as an educational tool.

Table VII.3.4 Analysis of search results for the phrases "infographics pandemic" and "infographics coronavirus" in terms of the functions of the indicated infographics

Function	*Informational*	*Educational*	*PopularScience*	*Marketing*
Number of infographics	**19**	**26**	**6**	**9**
Percentage share	**31.7%**	**43.3%**	**10%**	**15%**

Source: Own elaboration based on the results of searching Polish-language sites in the Google browser on 17 August 2020.

12 Ibid., 5–23.

3.6 Internet dissemination

As part of the quantitative analysis, an attempt was made to determine the viral potential of the studied infographics. For this purpose, the image search function available in the Google Chrome browser was used. This allowed us to determine the approximate number of shares of a given infographic.

3.7 Image proportions

The last parameter examined was the aspect ratio of the image. It was decided to check if and how the shape of the infographic influences its popularity, and thus its effectiveness as an information carrier. Three formats were distinguished: vertical, horizontal and square. Among the 56 infographics studied (four on the day of the study, 3 August 2021, were not available at the indicated links), 50% were vertical infographics, 28.6% were horizontal infographics and 21.4% were square infographics. Thus, the predominance of the vertical format is clear.

The situation changes when we correlate the above results with the number of shares. When considering the average number of shares of infographics in each format, square infographics take the lead (44.1 shares), followed by horizontal infographics (31.9 shares), and finally vertical infographics (6.8 shares).

The above results can be interpreted as follows.

Most authors of infographics prefer the vertical format, which is probably related to the typical format of a sheet of paper used in printing. This may be a conscious action, if it is assumed that infographics can be printed by users, or unconscious resulting from the author's habit.

However, on the Internet, which, as already mentioned, has become the dominant sphere of information exchange, graphics in square and horizontal formats are much more popular. This is undoubtedly related to the fact that such formats perform better in social media and therefore are shared more often. As you can see, the viral potential of infographics is determined not only by the attractive content and visual form but also the aspect ratio.

Table VII.3.5 Analysis of search results for the phrases "infographics pandemic" and "infographics coronavirus" in terms of viral potential

Function	*Informational*	*Educational*	*Popular Science*	*Marketing*
Number of infographics	**19**	**26**	**6**	**9**
Number of infographics with at least one share	**5**	**18**	**2**	**4**
Percentage share of infographics with at least one share within a category	**26.3%**	**69.2%**	**33.3%**	**44.4%**

Source: Own elaboration based on the results of a search of Polish-language websites in the Google browser on 17 August 2020 and 3 August 2021.

Analysing the studied sample of infographics in terms of the number of shares showed again the dominance of infographics on educational topics. Not only do they constitute the most numerous collections, but also the largest number of them (69.2%) are willingly shared online.

Finally, it should be noted that most of the materials shared more often came from public domains, while infographics available only under one link were usually found on the websites of private entities. It can be assumed that the popularity of shared materials is influenced by the greater credibility of public institutions and the lack of danger of copyright infringement.

3.8 Use of infographics by public actors in a pandemic situation

In EU law, the term infographics appears only in three decisions of the Council of the EU in four communications of the Commission, among others containing guidelines for the use of infographics in connection with a pandemic. In Polish law, the term appears only in one order and one resolution of a body of an association of municipalities, which do not concern the pandemic. In the legal literature, infographics is considered based on copyright law, cited in works on civil, commercial and criminal law. In publications on administrative law there are positive evaluations of the use of infographics in official documents: strategies of local government units.[13] A view is also expressed about the admissibility of making infographics available on the Internet by the executive body of the local government implementing a resolution of the constituting body, also without explicit authorisation from this resolution.[14] Commentaries on ensuring access to public information do not mention infographics.

To verify the thesis about the usefulness of infographics as an effective way for public institutions to communicate with society in a pandemic situation, the public domain gov.pl was searched for publications marked with the phrase "infographics."

From the 661 results obtained, those which referred to the COVID-19 pandemic were singled out. 45 items were obtained in this way. More than half of them (23), in fact, turned out to be banners presenting a single piece of information (slogan) and, according to the definition quoted above, they cannot be considered infographics, which indicates the deficit of knowledge of public entities about this detailed form of providing access to public information. The remaining 22 infographics were systematised according to their function and the target group to which the message was addressed.

In the sample studied, 68.2% of the infographics were informational in nature, while the rest were educational (31.8%). There were no infographics of a popular science or marketing nature.

The groups to which the infographics were addressed:

- 45.5% all citizens;
- 31.8% firefighters, in particular Voluntary Fire Brigades;

13 M. Obrębska, J. Podgórska-Rykała "Analiza treści strategii pod względem umiejscowienia jednostek pomocniczych" in B. Dolnicki (ed.) "*Pozycja ustrojowa organów jednostek samorządu terytorialnego*" (WolKluw. Polska 2019).

14 A. Misiejko "Budżet obywatelski w praktyce samorządów" (WolKluw. 2020).

- 9.1% local government officials;
- 9.1% senior citizens;
- 4.5% farmers.

The survey shows that infographics are used by public entities, also in connection with the pandemic, but their number is small and knowledge about this specific form of providing access to public information is incomplete.

3.9 Conclusions

In this article, an attempt was made to describe the specific features of infographics, which are conducive to its use as an effective carrier of information in a special situation such as a pandemic. It was found that there is a strong social need for access to reliable and comprehensive data on the epidemic situation and the threats associated with it, with a simultaneous widespread tendency to minimise one's own cognitive load associated with searching for and analysing them. An additional important determinant of effective communication that must be considered is the impatience of media users and their orientation towards a quick reward in the form of a comprehensive and understandable answer.

In this complicated situation, infographics seem to be an ideal solution. It uses mainly images – which makes it visually attractive and universally understandable. It communicates selected and ordered information, chosen in a way that optimally describes the problem. It contains concise messages that are ready portions of information easy to understand and remember. The short form of the message increases the likelihood that more people will read it in its entirety.

Quantitative analysis of searches using the keywords "infographics" and – interchangeably – "pandemic," "coronavirus" and "COVID-19" showed a high representation of infographics related to the coronavirus pandemic on the Internet, which is currently the dominant information and media space. It was possible to identify four main functions that infographics perform: warning (messages), educational (safety rules), informative (data visualisation) and popularising-scientific (extending knowledge). When using the phrases "coronavirus infographics" or "COVID-19 infographics," the results were dominated by infographics presenting basic information related to security from governmental institutions and based primarily on data and indications from international institutions (WHO). On the other hand, in the phrase "pandemic infographics" there was a predominance of visualisations of data from studies carried out by various independent research institutions.

Infographics, thanks to the above-mentioned characteristics, show high so-called viral potential (they are willingly shared on the Internet), which means that they actively reach a wide range of recipients. As an information carrier, they seem to be an optimal solution for communicating with the society in a crisis, such as a pandemic.

Works cited

Babik, W., *Słownik encyklopedyczny informacji, języków i systemów informacyjno-wyszukiwawczych* (Association of Polish Librarians, Warsaw 2020), 305, series: Nauka, Dydaktyka, Praktyka.

Berger, J., *Contagious: Why Things Catch On* (Simon & Schuster, New York, London, Toronto, Sydney, and New Delhi 2016).

European Commision, *Communication from the Commission EU Guidelines for the Gradual Resumption of Services to Tourists and Health Protocols in Hospitality Establishments - COVID-19* (OJ EU. C. 2020), No. 169, 1.

European Commision, *Communication from the Commission - COVID-19 - Guidance on the Implementation of Temporary Restrictions on Non-Essential Travel to the EU, Simplification of Transit Rules for Repatriation of Union Citizens and Consequences for the Common Visa Policy* (OJ EU. C. 2020), 102 as amended.

Misiejko, A., *Budżet obywatelski w praktyce samorządów* (WolKluw., Warsaw 2020).

Monarcha-Matlak, A., *States of Emergency and Cyberpandemics, w:Internet Cyberpandemic Cyberpandemic*, eds. G. Szpor and A. Gryszczyńska (C.H. Beck, Warsaw 2020).

Nazarko-Ludwiczak, E., *Information Materials for Patients as PR Tools - The Latest Trends, ABC.*

Nowak-Gruca, A., *Infographics as an Object of Copyright Protection* (Zeszyty Naukowe Uniwersytetu Jagiellońskiego, Kraków 2017), 5–23.

Obrębska, M., and Podgórska-Rykała, J., *Analiza treści strategii pod względem umiejscowienia jednostek pomocniczych* [in:] *Pozycja ustrojowa organów jednostek samorządu terytorialnego*, ed. B. Dolnicki (WolKluw., Warsaw 2019).

European Economic and Social Committee, *Opinion of the European Economic and Social Committee on "Responsible Use of Social Networks and the Prevention of Related Problems"* (own-initiative opinion) (OJ EU. C. 2012), No. 351, 31.

Schwartz, B., *The Paradox of Choice. Why More Means Less?* (Naukowe PWN, Warsaw 2020).

Święcicki, W., *Infographics: A Mini Guide* (Szkoła Promocji Nauki UJ, Kraków 2015).

Szpor, G., *Openness and its Limitations t.1 Ideas and Concepts* (C. H. Beck, Warsaw 2016).

Szpor, G., and Czaplicki, K. (eds.), *Law on Digital Accessibility of Websites and Mobile Applications. Commentary* (WolKluw., Warsaw 2019).

Final Remarks

Irena Lipowicz and Aleksandra Syryt

I

1. In Poland, similar as in many other European countries, the response to the COVID-19 pandemic was taken by the executive authorities. Through regulations, they regulated essential elements of social and economic life, including the principles of prevention and control of the virus, restrictions on freedoms and human rights concerning the right to privacy, information autonomy, freedom of religion, freedom of movement, freedom of economic activity.[1] In Italy, as indicated by Galetta and Carullo, the most legal solutions were described in regulations but with the proper use of states of emergency.
2. In Poland, the situation has become very complex: on the one hand, it is constitutionally legitimate that the activity in a crisis is to the executive. Under Art. 146(4) point. 7 of the Constitution, the Council of Ministers ensures the internal security of the state and public order. Undoubtedly, threats to the life and health of individuals undermine security. The activity of public entities is required. However, the executive does not act arbitrarily. As a public authority, it must act on the basis and within the limits of the law (Art. 7 of the Constitution). Art. 146(4) indicates that ensuring the security and public order by the Council of Ministers must be done within the scope and on the principles set out in the Constitution and laws. It should be in accordance with the principle of separation and balance of powers and the principle of proportionality.
3. The Polish Constitution provides three extraordinary measures defined in Chapter XI. The COVID-19 pandemic relates to conditions of a state of emergency and a state of natural disaster. Despite it, the public authorities did not introduce any of these institutions. Based on the Act on Prevention and Control of Infections and Infectious Diseases in Humans (A.I.D.), the MoH introduced a state of epidemics by way of regulation. During epidemics,

1 K. Dobrzenicki and B. Przywora (eds.), Ograniczenia praw i wolności w okresie pandemii COVID-19 na tle porównawczym. Pierwsze doświadczenia (Wydawnictwo Instytutu Wymiaru Sprawiedliwości 2021).

human freedoms and rights were limited, and it was usually done using executive acts. This behaviour of public authorities raised doubts in public opinion, literature, judicial decisions as to the legality of such acts and their compliance with the principle of proportionality (Art. 31(3) Constitution).

The state of epidemics is not an extraordinary constitutional measure, and however, it serves as a public law instrument for public authorities to act during the pandemic. It includes the opportunity to introduce restrictions on constitutional freedoms and rights.

The situation of pandemics showed that probably the shape of extraordinary constitutional measures in Poland are not adequate to modern threats. Therefore, it should be considered if revising the measures mentioned above is necessary. It is probably a matter for the legislature to reflect on introducing to the Constitution measures that would better fit the context of the threats related to civilisational changes, digital development or contemporary threats to the life and health of citizens and the environment.

The introduction of such solutions only at the statutory level (as in the state of epidemics) raises doubts about compliance with constitutional standards concerning the balance and cooperation of powers or ensuring an adequate level of guarantees for the protection of human rights.

4. The legislation of the pandemic period raises reservations; analysis of the texts of normative acts indicates that the acts adopted at the statutory and sub-statutory level are defective in terms of the principles of correct legislation and the principles of legislative technique.

   Although the legislature amended A.I.D., based on which the state of an epidemic was introduced, this was done primarily through an incidental law (Polish: *specustawa*). The practice of responding to threats through an incidental statute cannot be considered reasonable. Using this kind of source of the law reveals that public authorities cannot solve problems, and the reasons for it could be different.

   Maybe authorities were unable to use the available normative acts regulating the activity of state authorities in the case of danger (in particular, the provisions of laws on states of emergency or the provisions of the Crisis Management Act). Maybe the existing legal solutions were insufficient and inadequate for the situation. It leads to the reflection that perhaps these rules do not function properly, and the issue should be approached systemically. The second reason is an argument for reviewing the normative acts concerning responses to threats and verifying them in terms of practicality, usefulness and consistency.

   The research also revealed reservations about delegated legislation. Apart from doubts about whether some issues could be shaped through regulations, attention should be drawn to the imperfection of the enabling legislation. The empowering provisions usually did not meet the constitutional requirement of specificity (Art. 92(1) of the Constitution). Moreover, especially in health care, the shaping of social relations through internal acts, e.g., orders, can be seen to have gone beyond Art. 93 of the Constitution (they were directed to entities outside the organisational structure subordinate to the body issuing the Act). In addition, announcements began to play an essential role as an instrument of action of public authorities (especially announcements of the MoH). Although they are not normative acts and not sources of universally binding law, they determine society's rules of behaviour. For example, the introduction of new restrictions related to the pandemic was communicated in the form of announcements, i.e., non-managerial information activities. Although the limits were defined in a regulation that came into force a few days after the announcement of the communiqué, it was the communiqué that was the common source of knowledge about the law. It created uncertainty about what restrictions were in effect and when (sometimes contrary to Art. 2 of the Constitution). Citizens – not always familiar with the rules of the law – relied on announcements, while the restrictions came into effect only after the regulation came into force.

5. A review of legal solutions concerning the use of digital technologies during the pandemic shows that the changes were introduced in haste in most cases. They were often intended to be temporary. No attempt was made to conduct a deeper reflection on whether the proposed solutions – forced, as it were, by the pandemic – can become a permanent element in the activities of public authorities, and if so, to what extent and on what principles.
6. The pandemic experience in regulating public law instruments using digital technologies can shape permanent legal solutions in this area, even if there are doubts both from the realisation of constitutional principles, the principle of proportionality, the quality of legislation and their functionality.

   Good practices should become a point of reference when designing and developing systemic regulations. On the other hand, the conclusions drawn from the experience with flawed solutions, including those raising doubts about their compliance with the Constitution and international standards, should prevent public authorities from making inevitable mistakes in the future, both in terms of creating and applying the law.

II

7. What are the overall conclusions from experience in using public law instruments in pandemic conditions? These are instruments of action based on system norms, tasks and competencies. The problem in Poland in the so-called fourth wave of the pandemic from October 2021 turns out to be the helplessness of citizens in the face of the omission of action by the legislature and the executive, despite the consensus positions of science, also determined by the subsidiary bodies of the Prime Minister and the Minister responsible for health. In the case of knowledge-based administration, rejection of the recommendation of "own" scientific auxiliary body should require substantive justification and an effective control procedure.

In the active, sovereign action from the beginning of the pandemic in 2020, introducing numerous restrictions in this lockdown, the problem turned out to be not so much – also occurring in other countries: Germany, Italy, Croatia, in the conditions of the pandemic – appreciation of the executive, but the violation of the principle of statutory matter in the regulation of rights and obligations of citizens by regulations in place of the necessary in light of the provisions of the Constitution and the body of case law and doctrine.[2] As the author stresses, if the Council of Ministers consciously resigned from the state of emergency at its disposal in the conditions of the epidemic, recognising that it would control the epidemic by ordinary legal means, it cannot invoke extraordinary circumstances and unique legal solutions after making such a choice of the legal route – restrictions on human rights made in the form of regulations cannot be justified in this way. As pointed out,[3]

> the lack of a state of emergency prevents, in the light of the Polish Constitution, extraordinary limitations of individual rights and freedoms. However, the introduction of such limitations prejudges their unconstitutionality because they are subject to assessment in light of the principles in force during the normal functioning of the state.

As the author stresses, the need to limit the rights and freedoms of the individual in an extraordinary situation, such as the epidemic, does not justify the violation of the Constitution by public authorities. In particular, the literature argues the need to respect the principle of proportionality and the prohibition of violating the essence of limited rights and freedoms. The situation is not changed by the amendment of the COVID-19 Act, and the amendment of the A.I.D. The amendment of this Act consisted only in providing the Council of Ministers with the competence to introduce restrictions on freedom or individual rights; the Act did not contain the necessary substantive legal regulations.

8. As the experience of the COVID-19 epidemic has shown, in Poland, the citizen has no effective legal recourse against the inaction of public authorities in the context of the health crisis – legislative inaction as well as administrative inaction – unless they are a party to the proceedings or have access to public information. Participatory entities, e.g., NGOs, present opinions, reports and positions in the digital space, but they cannot effectively influence the action's decision and content. During the pandemic, it became clear how important it is to have a universally accessible online platform with constantly updated information, including infographics. Commonly accepted facts are possible, although not sufficient, basis for agreement. In Polish conditions, this was

2 S. Trociuk, Prawa i wolności w stanie epidemii (WolKluw. 2021) 12–13.

3 M. Florczak-Wątor, 'Niekonstytucyjność ograniczeń praw i wolności jednostki wprowadzonych w związku z epidemią COVID-19 jako przesłanka odpowiedzialności odszkodowawczej państwa' (2020) 898(12) Państwo i Prawo 20.

reconstructed in the digital space in the civic activity of an active private person creating, free of charge, a portal with data on diseases, which was then used both by scientists and ultimately by the public authorities.

9. It is essential to distinguish between the silence of power and inaction. The government's silence is regarded as consent in specific decision-making processes, inaction, contradictory to the principle of the administration's duty to act actively, which is, after all, part of its essence. The inaction of administration - unlike the legislature requires justification – because competence is also a duty, not only a right. In the case of the legislature, accounting for the inaction of public authorities proves more difficult. The democratic mandate from elections also means choosing the legislative policy and ways of action. However, it is possible to establish the lack of implementation of constitutional tasks of Parliament in the conditions of threats to fundamental values, including life and health of citizens.

It is exciting to contribute to the German science of administrative law to the above debate.[4] Concerning the articles, it should be noted that despite the highly different, according to the hierarchy of sources of law, actions of the public administration, there is no lack of criticism and similar conclusions about the growing role of the executive and the crisis of legitimacy of the Parliament; we read about the "hour of the executive," which erupted with the pandemic, unconstitutional excessive restraint of the Bundestag in determining the interference in fundamental rights and about their social consequences; it is not only about the law that is made but also about the role of Parliament as a kind of forum for discussion. This can affect trust in public authority. Christoph Gusy concludes that the pandemic crisis should therefore be "the time of the parliament," which, however, also experiences a loss of control functions that should not be affected by legislation defining the state of emergency. Gusy describes the pandemic as a stress test for democracy faced with the dilemma of choice: a veritable "cascade of statutory changes" or restriction to framework regulations with enormous delegated executive power. Thus, the steering function of Parliament suffers, should be compensated by increased powers of control. In Germany, handling the pandemic crisis has been done using existing legal possibilities and extra-legal tools, including digital forms of action by the rule of law.

Also, in Italy, the doctrine said that an inevitable centralisation of the control powers of the public authority is necessary, for example, in the resolution of quarantine and lockdown. The enormous progress of digitalisation makes it possible to compensate for the loss of partial freedom of movement or to continue education with new tools (Galetta, Carullo).

It seems that it is possible to formulate a postulate of "digital substitution." The loss of a particular entitlement realised in the real world should generate

4 V. Boehme-Neßler, 'Oldenburg, Das Parlament in der Pandemie – Zum Demokratiegrundsatz am Beispiel von § 28a InfSchG' (2021) 6 DÖV 243 et seq.

the possibility and necessity of substitution with digital instruments. For example, the loss of the option to visit a hospital or a nursing home should cause a legal obligation to enable the patient to contact via electronic means and alternative electronic communication. Part of the "mock-ups" of future crisis legislation prepared, as it were, should therefore be the ideas of digital substitution of proportionally limited civil rights and freedoms.

German and Italian experiences clearly show that the public administration and the Parliament can be effective in the conditions of a pandemic (Fraenkel-Haeberle). A difficult situation of a pandemic does not justify a violation of the rule of law and changing the position of the Parliament. It is possible to carry out the necessary obligations without violating the basic principles of the division of powers and the democratic state ruled by law and the participation of local government in the exercise of power. The necessary, limited centralisation of specific activities in the pandemic should be temporary and not violate the principle of decentralisation.

10. The transition to digital instruments of public administration proved to be rapid and widespread. Still, it was instead an isolated, crisis activity of individual ministries and types of public administration – including education and health. The general administration intervened legislatively by drafting normative acts and establishing norms on its own. However, as indicated in this work, it did not develop a qualitatively new approach to digitisation policy in any examined countries about using forms. The case of the Immuni application and its missed opportunities discussed in the volume is an apt example.

    The primary dysfunction in Poland was the use of executive normative acts with the rank of regulations instead of the necessary laws. Often, as in the case of the periodic prohibition of participation in religious rites, this was done in defiance of the explicit constitutional provisions like a guarantee of religious freedom, although statutory regulation was entirely possible here. The legislature, however, concentrated primarily on episodic laws of an economic nature. In contrast to Germany and Italy, these also lacked the coherent character of crisis intervention in Poland. In many cases, this also meant in all four countries, but especially in Poland, a change in system and competence regulations, not always strictly related to the state of the epidemic. However, several dysfunctions in the operation of the public administration during this period were due to the failure in Poland to enact a constitutional state of emergency of an appropriate nature. It would have facilitated the law-abiding operation of the public administration.

11. E-government in Poland during the period in question still had the character of isolated, episodic activities but was often – even very creatively – a reaction to the inability to act in a traditional way, rather than a fragment of broader concepts of digitisation prepared in advance for the crisis. It is not so much the structure as the functioning of the Government Security Center that should be critically assessed considering the texts. We do not know, of course, the classified part of these tasks. The government application

"ProteGo- Safe," due to its inconsistent nature and lack of a sense of consistent state action, failed to fulfil its tasks. Infographics were used too rarely; as indicated above, there was almost no easy-to-read language (EtR) in communication with public authorities. The government information campaign was limited to traditionalist media – outdoor advertising and TV. However, government applications should be evaluated positively: "mCitizen," which includes the EU covidium passport, and the Internet Patient Account, which allows the implementation of e-prescriptions and access to competent medical information.

12. The legal regulation of the sanitary and epidemiological administration in Poland needs urgent revision; its recentralisation on the eve of a pandemic was an inappropriate solution. Furthermore, staff shortages and the backwardness of information technology have had a negative impact on its activities. In addition, the "systemic loneliness" of the government administration proved to be significant at the local level. However, it occurred by choice: the stress test of the COVID-19 epidemic showed fundamental maladjustment of the resources of district sanitary-epidemiological stations, lack of regionalisation, low mobility of resources and their preparation for rapid response; there also arose difficulties in synchronisation of tasks between the state sanitary essentialistic health care state emergency medical services, infectious diseases hospitals deficit was the low efficiency and poor organisation of testing for the presence of the SARS-Cov-2 virus, as well as the transport of patients and their deployment exceptional temporary and specialised hospitals (Sikorski).

The selected administrative policy regulations and modus operandi did not provide for synergy with local government, despite the efforts of the Joint Commission of Government and Local Government and local government organisations. Local self-government has smoothly shifted to using digital instruments to serve the public within existing competencies. Still, external posts for the digitally excluded have also been provided. Telemedicine advice increased by leaps and bounds before the pandemic promoting telemedicine. The public authority strongly restricted the possibility of using it in 2021 for selected groups, e.g., children, seniors.

During the crisis phase in Poland, the potential of the developed private medical sector could have been better considered. Although it was possible to impose additional obligations on these entities in the epidemic conditions, it would have been more advisable to use a new dimension of public-private partnership. Furthermore, these entities had much more experience in telemedicine and e-health, which should have been used in hospitals.

The local government sought greater participation from the central administration in managing the crisis. Still, its involvement and eventual success were seen – it seems – in terms of competition for the democratic legitimacy of the actions of public authorities. The local government in Poland is struggling with recentralisation, the Center's taking away tasks and competencies, and the reduction of revenues. Despite this, it has been actively working to help local businesses, e.g., reduce fees and rents and digitise their services. However, the great potential of NGO participation for optimal strategies and tactics for dealing with the health crisis was not fully utilised. The administration oscillated from extreme power interference in the first and second waves to passivity and general appeals at the beginning of the fourth wave. Such inconsistency promotes the erosion of acceptance. It was avoided in Germany, where the main disputes were over federal powers, the extent of possible coordination of activities (cf. The remarkably coherent and exciting vision in the field of action to the new reconstruction after the pandemic[5]).

13. Civil society in all discussed countries worked well from the beginning: solidarity actions, mutual help, reports and recommendations of science made full use of digital instruments.

    In Poland, the interdisciplinary team for COVID, of the Polish Academy of Sciences, should be singled out – experts representing various fields of science provided in advance the results of the latest research, made comparative analyses of activities in other countries, publishing further expert reports. Characteristic action was the formulation of possible scenarios, anticipatory proposals for action before the peak of incidence, very precisely predicted the growth of infections. Specific recommendations for action in the case of schools, included not only vaccination disinfection and masks but also the demand to remove unvaccinated school personnel from direct contact with pupils. Also, in the case of hybrid and mixed traditional/remote teaching, it was proposed that unvaccinated pupils be kept at home.

    Above all, it was demanded that the laws of the findings and protocols of the Prime Minister's Medical Council should be made public. As a significant dysfunction, the COVID team pointed to the lack of establishment in Poland of institutions for monitoring and communicating imminent health threats to the public, following the example of independent research centres of national health institutes (Robert Koch Institute in Germany or Public Health England in Great Britain). Permanent institutions and groups of advisors, functioning not only in crisis conditions and would be able to maintain institutional knowledge and experienced experts – but such examples also include the Joint Research Center, a group of chief scientific advisors, and the European Centre for Disease Prevention and Control (ECDC). The panel concludes that independence from public authorities must be permanently embedded in the institutional order, advocated for consideration of mandatory vaccination of medical workers (position paper of 29 July 2021). In 2021, the team also advocated for a "culture" of making data more widely available to build trust in government, data should be open to the media, businesses and the general public. The idea is to maintain a sustainable digital platform that allows for the visualisation of data and to download current data in applicable forms. It

5 Hermann Hill, 'Die Kunst, in der Krise neu aufzubauen – Lehren aus Corona' (2021) 14 DÖV 472 et seq.

is also postulated to open administrative datasets for secondary research on COVID-19.

Structurally, it is postulated by the Polish Academy of Sciences that a specialised and independent unit should be established to maintain a repository of research data, particularly from population-based social surveys relating to attitudes and behaviour during a pandemic. The Polish Academy of Sciences COVID team has already developed 23 posts, but only a tiny fraction has been implemented. It indicates the existence of a barrier to good administration as a knowledge-based administration, but also an attempt to work with science and compensate for administration deficits constructively. The lack of partnership with the government brought gradual apathy and elements of social anomie in the fourth wave. Anti-vaccinationists are now effectively organising – and the government administration is modifying plans under the influence of this pressure and openly declaring it. The Polish doctrine of administrative law actively monitors the situation in terms of the legal forms of action used, making their critical analysis, proposals for making the used forms more flexible and greater use of the legal forms of action of local government, but also the use of the necessary authoritative actions.

14. The legal infrastructure – complete – in the transition to a digital state should be ready and "waiting for" the next crisis. When using digital instruments (e.g., in education), it seems to be a condition for success to leave much more freedom and administrative discretion to administrators (e.g., school principals and teachers) – especially in remote education. Teachers must have more freedom to use more online sources and interactive methods.

    The crisis is often of regional or local character in the conditions of digital administration, and it is then possible to digitally support the highly burdened local administration in crisis conditions by even a remote unit. The legal infrastructure for such solutions should already be waiting. The lesson of the crisis is also that it is worthwhile to work within the framework of the Council of Europe on ready-made framework regulations, drawing on experience, which can prove themselves under the conditions of the next crisis. This may be important, especially for smaller countries, and the framework character of regulations does not have the shade of imposing specific solutions.

15. As far as the EU is concerned, it was characteristic that the Commission, Parliament and the European Council were very active. Public activity in the crisis of agencies dealing with fundamental rights and, indirectly, with public health issues did not appear very clear in the public space of the member states.

    The institutions of the EU, the Commission, and the Council, in their core competencies, mainly economic, despite the initial delay, acted actively and creatively not only with a recovery plan but with diverse, primarily due to the need to rebuild economies after the "pandemic shock" instruments. The European Parliament was also very active in the debate. The President of the EC established the Coronavirus Rapid Response Team. This team coordinates the response to the pandemic at the political level in terms of a typical

European reaction. It took those actions that are within the competence of the EU to strengthen the public health sector and mitigate the socio-economic impact of the coronavirus in the EU; it coordinated the actions of the member states, sharing objective information about the pandemic and effective containment measures; it focused on COVID-19 digital certificates – by 18 October 2021, 591 million certificates had been issued, which became a significant success in overcoming travel barriers during the summer pandemic weakening period. On the digital front, the EU has focused on preventing pandemic-specific cybercrime, promoting online activities in remote education, and countering misinformation, especially in the latter area, which are only initial activities that have been strengthened since June 2021. The European Council and the Council of the EU have focused on reducing vaccine scepticism, strengthening the EU system of prevention and pandemic preparedness, and accelerating negotiations on the health union.

Among the EU's digital solutions, essential or want to note that public-private instruments were used to monitor the spread of the virus, improve e-government and e-health, provide Europeans with uninterrupted Internet access and online security. Among the public law tools, soft tools should be distinguished. There is a gradual increase in the speed of action: rapid response team, the creation of an EU code of conduct on combating disinformation, also preventing network congestion during periods of isolation through the body of European regulators of electronic communications; launched a unique reporting mechanism and monitoring of the situation of Internet traffic in each country, created a program to monitor the activities of platforms to reduce disinformation related to COVID-19 which allows assessing the activity of platforms towards future EU regulation. To enhance online safety, Europol has, for example, developed guidance for parents and guardians on online security and the prevention of online fraud. The wealth of activities of the EU, ranging from the work on the development of new drugs and vaccines and their financing to the issues of digital education, digital literacy or the promotion with special subsidies of train travel of young people in Europe during the expected expiry of the pandemic to the gigantic post-pandemic reconstruction plan, does not change the fact that there is a profound gap between the multilingual and competently edited website and the daily action of the national media usually ignoring these constructive initiatives. The EU can only act within the scope of its specific limited competencies and by using such public-private instruments, which are doctrinally referred to as nonviolent forms of action; their richness, diversity and flexibility of application can be noted. However, there is a distinct lack of "ambassadors of communication" or "verifiers of information" of school and European student clubs or "Erasmus – Alumni for Europe," who would translate useful EU activities into a narrative accessible to broad social groups and counteract hidden and overt disinformation. It is especially needed in countries like Poland, where the official media are increasingly distanced from the EU activities and public policies and often ignore its activities. A specific part of financial resources and instruments should be devoted to a different, simplified, attractive narrative about the EU's activities, financed independently from governments.

In some cases, the need to broaden the tasks and competencies of the Union and the corresponding forms of action – not only the future health union – is becoming increasingly apparent. We should positively assess introducing a new category of resilience, something more than immunity – immunity combined with proactive action. However, focusing on "extended resilience" and minimising harmful elements, prevention in the digital space still needs to be translated into public law instruments with respect to the rule of law.

Compared to the activities of other EU institutions, the EU agencies did not propose any new digital solutions. Despite the existence of the Euronews television network, there was no large-scale anti-COVID-19 professional educational campaign on a European scale. The potential for synergies between the activities of ombudsmen, who in their own countries worked intensively for the observance of human rights even under conditions of the pandemic, was also not used. Even though the ombudsmen have a coordination platform (European Ombudsman Institute) and standard coordination networks within the EU, they have not remained in the process of intensive EU-initiated consultation. It should be noted and was advocated by the Fundamental Rights Agency in Vienna (FRA) that the digital instruments and capacities of the agency are underutilised. In the FRA's opinion (No. 7/21), we find that member states could ask national human rights institutions to make recommendations on the impact of draft legislation and policies on fundamental rights to improve respect for them, including during the state of emergency in the context of the COVID-19 pandemic. The FRA recommends maintaining formalised relations of the Parliament with national human rights institutions and ensuring that reports of these institutions to the Parliament are correctly presented and discussed. In the case of Poland, it is difficult to speak of a proper application of Opinion No. 7. The Ombudsman systematically identified and issued his initiative recommendations on the impact of draft legislation and public policies on fundamental rights to improve the observance of these rights despite the failure to declare a state of emergency in the context of the COVID-19 pandemic. However, this was not done at the request of the authorities of a Member State, namely Poland. Polish law, for example, enforces a formalised relationship between Parliament and national human rights institutions. However, political polarisation in Parliament has made it challenging to consider the recent heated debate around the ROP report as a "proper presentation and discussion." There is a need for mandatory discussion of the ROP report in almost every parliamentary committee and to examine which recommendations are still under consideration and have been explicitly rejected or left unanswered by the relevant national authorities.

Turn next to the opinion of the Fundamental Rights Agency. With remarkable diplomacy, it advocates "more regular exchanges with national human rights institutions in, for example, the Council of the European Union its working groups." The very phrasing of the opinion as "could establish" indicates perhaps excessive caution or weakness on the part of the body. Equally diplomatic is the suggestion in Opinion 4 to have exchanges with the EC in areas such as monitoring the CFREU and ensuring the rule of law. Attention should also be drawn to FRA's opinion from a recent EU report entitled "Strong and effective national human rights institutions: challenges, promising practices, and opportunities." In this document, we find the tentative criticism that the EU "could make more coherent use" of national human rights institutions as key actors in the implementation of fundamental rights, including by ensuring independent and effective monitoring of fundamental rights in member states, Such a reliance should be fostered through intensive relations with the European Network of National Human Rights Institutions (ENNHRI). FRA uses the concept of "qualified interaction," which could be – and one could argue should be – reserved for national human rights institutions and ENNHRI in line with the Paris Principles, without, of course, compromising the independence of national human rights institutions. This postulate was already formulated by the European Ombudsman Institute in 2014, and the digitally available reports are a valuable comparative legal inspiration.

Looking for new forms of activities of the Fundamental Rights Agency to counter COVID-19, we find a list of good practices of Finland, Poland, Luxembourg, in particular consisting in the creation of a website and better public communication. The Polish initiative, i.e., creating a targeted website presenting all activities related to the pandemic and monitoring the government's response was singled out. An open letter in Luxembourg expressing "satisfaction with the daily efforts of the government and a reminder of the proportionality of the restrictions on fundamental rights and freedoms" was also included among the actions worthy of promotion. It can hardly be considered a firm instrument on the part of the powerful EU Fundamental Rights Agency. Instead, in the context of the announcement of the creation of new agencies after the pandemic, the question should be asked whether an evaluation of the activities should not precede it to date and the possible expansion and strengthening of the forms of action the Fundamental Rights Agency. A positive message about Poland can be drawn from the survey concerning the awareness of the existence of individual national human rights institutions, from which we can read that 93% of the Polish population is aware of the existence of the Human Rights Defender in Poland, which is high compared to other bodies. The European Ombudsman was also almost "invisible" in this challenging crisis period.

It should also be noted that the "Citizens' Debate on the Future and Institutional Shape of the European Union" (an undoubtedly valuable and well-funded debate) was conducted with great effort and resources, in 2021, when the main concern was to counteract the pandemic. There was a lack of quick reaction and the creation of a new digital platform where the citizens of the EU could share their experiences, criticism and vision of optimal actions of the EU in the conditions of such a health crisis. Such a debate should precede the institutional discussion of the EU. It would have given its citizens – especially in the conditions of technologically advanced processing of received surveys and voice in the Internet discussion – the feeling of actual participation without the polarisation enforced, as we know today, by the algorithms of social networks. This gap is only beginning to be closed, in actions for young European leaders and the "Next Generation politics. The struggle for a European democratic narrative continues."

It seems that an inherent consequence of the current experience, as pointed out in the study (S. Sikorski), will be the demand to strengthen the competence of the EU in matters of prevention and crisis health intervention. However, it should also be noted that creating other agencies and enhancing cooperation in the Union for Health is noticeable.

References

Boehme-Neßler, V., 'Oldenburg, Das Parlament in der Pandemie – Zum Demokratiegrundsatz am Beispiel von § 28a InfSchG' (2021) 6 DÖV 243.

Dobrzenicki, K., and Przywora, B. (eds.), *Ograniczenia praw i wolności w okresie pandemii COVID-19 na tle porównawczym. Pierwsze doświadczenia* (Wydawnictwo Instytutu Wymiaru Sprawiedliwości, Warsaw 2021).

Florczak-Wątor, M., 'Niekonstytucyjność ograniczeń praw i wolności jednostki wprowadzonych w związku z epidemią COVID-19 jako przesłanka odpowiedzialności odszkodowawczej państwa' (2020) 898(12) Państwo i Prawo 5–22.

Hill, H., 'Die Kunst, in der Krise neu aufzubauen – Lehren aus Corona' (2021) 14 DÖV 465–474.

Trociuk, S., *Prawa i wolności w stanie epidemii* (WolKluw., Warsaw 2021).

Index

For Product Safety Concerns and Information please contact our EU
representative GPSR@taylorandfrancis.com
Taylor & Francis Verlag GmbH, Kaufingerstraße 24, 80331 München, Germany

www.ingramcontent.com/pod-product-compliance
Ingram Content Group UK Ltd.
Pitfield, Milton Keynes, MK11 3LW, UK
UKHW020155200926
475702UK00016B/2716

* 9 7 8 1 0 3 2 2 0 5 1 6 8 *